Divine Name Verification

Divine Name Verification

An Essay on Anti-Darwinism, Intelligent Design, and the Computational Nature of Reality

Noah Horwitz

punctum books ✶ brooklyn, ny

 DIVINE NAME VERIFICATION: AN ESSAY ON ANTI-DARWINISM, INTELLIGENT DESIGN, AND THE COMPUTATIONAL NATURE OF REALITY
© Noah Horwitz, 2013.

http://creativecommons.org/licenses/by-nc-nd/3.0

This work is Open Access, which means that you are free to copy, distribute, display, and perform the work as long as you clearly attribute the work to the authors, that you do not use this work for commercial gain in any form whatsoever, and that you in no way alter, transform, or build upon the work outside of its normal use in academic scholarship without express permission of the author and the publisher of this volume. For any reuse or distribution, you must make clear to others the license terms of this work.

First published in 2013 by
punctum books
Brooklyn, New York
http://punctumbooks.com

ISBN-13: 978-0615839080
ISBN-10: 0615839088

Cover Image: detail from Rembrandt, *Belshazaar's Feast* (c. 1635), The National Gallery, London, UK.

Facing-page drawing by Heather Masciandaro.

Table of Contents

Introduction

§1. Introduction: From Hardware to Software ... 1

Part One: Anti-Darwinism

§2. Irreducible Complexity ... 23
§3. The Edge of Evolution ... 27
§4. Not By Chance ... 41
§5. The Developmentalist Critique of Computationalism ... 49
§6. Further Criticisms of Biological Darwinism ... 61
§7. Convergence ... 71
§8. Lynn Margulis and Parts, Wholes, and Code ... 81
§9. Philosophical Excursus: A Critique of 'Object-Oriented Ontology' ... 85
§10. Symbiogenesis ... 109
§11. Maximo Sandin: Nosotros Somos Bacteria y Virus ... 121
§12. Critique of 'Self-Organization' ... 129
§13. The Irony of Darwinist Computer Simulation ... 163
§14. CSI: Dembski—A Critique ... 175

Part Two: The Computational Nature of Reality

§15. The Computational Nature of Reality ... 199
§16. Darwinian Metaphysics ... 237
§17. Darwin's Apotheosis: Quentin Meillassoux's Atheism of Radical Contingency ... 255

Part Two: The Computational Nature of Reality (continued)

§18. Infinite Collapse: The Possible is Not the Actual	267
§19. Parallel Processing	305
§20. Entropy	315
§21. Divine Name Verification: Chaitin's Omega and the Compressibility of Being	333
§22. The Kabbalah of Biology: The Programming of Life	363
§23. The Other, the Omega Point, and the Garden of Eden	383

Bibliography

409

Abbreviations

AG	Margulis and Sagan: *Acquiring Genomes: A Theory of the Origins of Species*
EE	Behe: *The Edge of Evolution*
ID	Dembski: *Intelligent Design*
LS	Morris: *Life's Solution*
NBC	Spetner: *Not By Chance*
NFL	Dembski: *No Free Lunch*
NKS	Wolfram: *A New Kind of Science*
PC	Egan: *Permutation City*
QM	Harman: *Quentin Meillassoux*
RU	Poundstone: *The Recursive Universe*
TH	Lewontin: *The Triple Helix: Gene, Organism, and Environment*
WDGW	Fodor and Piatelli-Palmarini: *What Darwin Got Wrong*

§1
INTRODUCTION:
FROM HARDWARE TO SOFTWARE

The age of Darwin is ending. And with its end, its legacy of eugenics, the 'master race,' social Darwinism, the 'selfish gene,' 'survival of the fittest,' 'natural selection and mutation,' memes, and the interpretation of all biological and social phenomenon, in terms of their alleged teleological use value for reproduction, will pass into historical curiosities discussed only by future historians of science rummaging around in the archives of the past. And when those future historians document that history, they will describe it in classic Kuhnian terms—for it consisted of the erection and establishment of a classic paradigm, one that fought off and denounced as heresy all criticisms aimed at demonstrating the failure of Darwinism as a theory of life and its development.

While the series of criticisms that have been articulated (many of which we will later document) were dismissed as mere religious fantasy that could not conquer the reigning secular dogma, in the future the words of Lynn Margulis will continue to echo: "'Neo-Darwinism,' she said in a 1990 piece in *American Zoologist*, should be seen as 'a minor twentieth-century religious sect within the sprawling religious persuasion of Anglo-Saxon biology.'"[1] In fact, one

---

[1] Lynn Margulis, quoted in Daniel Dennett, "The Hoax of Intelli-

will in retrospect say that it was the inherent failures of Darwinian theory itself that made it so that the criticisms continued to mount until the proverbial dam broke. That event of breakage itself will be signaled ultimately and prominently by at least two names—the aforementioned Margulis (with her notion of 'symbiogenesis') and Maximo Sandin (and his work on the role of the virus in evolution). In the near future, we will all be 'Sandinistas.'

However, of course, not every aspect of Darwinism will be rejected. Often Darwinism and evolution are only defined in the most generic of terms. It is sometimes even taken as being identical with the notion of change over time. In this way, evolution is taken as simply being synonymous with the idea of 'descent with modification' and is thereby contrasted with only the most dogmatic forms of Creationism and Aristotelianism. However, even creationists accept that the world changes. Most creationists are willing to say that the world, since its inception, develops according to its own pattern. The Bible itself states that "the earth brought forth life" (Genesis 1:11). A 'primordial soup' is thus an image in keeping with this passage. Each and every being is not then necessarily created by God out of nothing, and clearly each human being is formed by the joining of a sperm and egg. No one doubts one can rewind the tape of an individual's existence and arrive back at that moment. If an individual human develops in this way, then why should all of life be any different? At Genesis 1:20, the Bible speaks of life swarming out from the waters ('the water teemed with creatures'). It is only after there is aquatic life that life on earth develops in full.

Evolution is seen as having introduced the idea that life arose from past ancestors rather than species being empirical instances of substantial eternal forms. But such a view for creationism only made sense insofar as one accepted a

---

gent Design and How It Was Perpetrated," in *Intelligent Thought: Science versus the Intelligent Design Movement*, ed. John Brockman (New York: Vintage, 2006), 33–49, 46.

Platonic or Aristotelian notion of essence (*eidos*). It was, of course, the overturning of this ancient Greek heritage that made John Dewey revel in the new Darwinian paradigm in his seminal *The Influence of Darwinism on Philosophy* from 1909. There, Dewey noted that philosophy of nature had been dominated for 2000 years by the idea that the concepts of the mind existed as reified entities in some eternal realm. All that existed in nature was but instantiations of these essences. In advocating essences, philosophy preferred the eternal and unchanging over the developing and impermanent. It looked at the final form of the thing as the truth of its nature. Anything that was variable was considered lesser. But Darwinism, Dewey explained, debunked the idea of permanent species that existed for all time or covered all individuals of a certain type. Essences were no longer fixed for all time, and there was no perfection in this world or another. Darwin had given birth to a form of thinking that affected all aspects of thought by showing that no species is eternal and that species have a particular history and date. Species themselves were now things that come into and go out of existence. Nature no longer was ordered by final causes. It was subjected to contingency and chance. Change was to be the dominant principle of science and philosophy. Flux would take priority over ends or purposes. One no longer searched for the final essence that things would realize to understand them, but rather traced their history and treated each as singularities. There is no finished and perfect state because all things are evolving into something new and unexpected.

Dewey also emphasized that nature could no longer be seen as efficient and thereby designed. Nature seems to be excessive. It allows things to arise that are only later destroyed. It works seemingly in vain and without ultimate goal. There is no obvious pre-designed goal according to this view. One type of bird will only lead to another. While human breeders can direct how a particular animal will develop, nature apparently subjected such creatures to the mere whims of chance and its consequences up to and including extinction. It is not just individuals who are mortal. All species are mortal and will pass away. Concepts could then not be seen as anything more than useful fictions. As for discussion of metaphysical issues, they would seem to obscure more than illuminate:

> Such argumentation is a reversion to the logic that explained the extinction of fire by water through the formal essence of acqueousness and the quenching of thirst by water through the final cause of acqueousness. Whether used in the case of the special event or that of life as a whole, such logic only abstracts some aspect of the existing course of events in order to reduplicate it as a petrified eternal principle by which to explain the very changes of which it is the formalization.[2]

Darwinism means more than simply that all life developed from previous life forms and that life forms can come into and out of existence. It means more than that just a rejection of the idea that creatures are exemplifications of eternal forms in the mind of God. It means life in itself is a random and contingent development. And as random and contingent, the development of life can only ever be known via its actual history. While one can formulate general principles for how life develops in its long, purposeless march, one cannot know in advance where it is going. Every species and every life form is merely an accident of natural selection and random mutation. This means that life is governed by chance rather than design. Life could have been different. Humanity need not have arisen. Life only has direction because it keeps reproducing itself. But what continues on is just simply what does (we will return to this tautology).

---

[2] John Dewey, *The Essential Dewey* (Bloomington: Indiana University Press, 1998), 43.

Even in the new, emerging synthesis that incorporates the insights of Margulis (who was initially denounced) and Sandin and thereby rejects random mutation and natural selection as the key motors of life's development, contingency, accident, chance, etc., sill govern life's development—for even if life develops by viruses laterally transferring genes or life forms merging into one another, it is taken for granted that there are no basic laws that are being followed or played out such that one could predict what next step life will take. One can only investigate what actually happened as an archeologist or historian and recount the history of life in its accidental nature. Life could have been otherwise, even on this model. There was no necessity or design. To suggest otherwise would be to suggest that life has a goal and purpose and that humanity might be the pinnacle of creation.

This belief in a lack of inevitability then is one of the legacies of Darwinism that will take more than the work of Sandinistas to overcome. Even if one rejects the idea of species slowly changing step by step via mutation and selection, one still has left intact the idea that the evolution of life is not making improvements or leading to some end. It is this randomness and purposelessness that makes evolution ultimately incompatible with theism. In challenging Darwinism then one must also see the development of life as not merely the result of accident and chance. While, epistemologically, we can, in retrospect, suggest other, possible directions life could have taken in theory, these routes can only have existed in theory if one is to reject Darwinism. The end of Darwinism will not come until we see that life could not have unfolded differently, was not accidental, and was not a product of chance.

Once one accepts this lack of accident, then life's having a goal and purpose will seem more and more reasonable. While any individual life form is mortal, and thus any species can go out of existence, as well as change, it would then not be the case that any life form can appear after the previous ones. This means, as well, that life is advancing and becoming more intelligent. While retrogression may occur, one will need to see future descendants as working out the purpose of life itself rather than just being some new creation. Life therefore creates more complex forms in the sense of life itself becoming more inflected and self-referential. We see this already in the advent of the human mind out of life itself. Self-awareness arose out of life itself. This means humanity, along with all other living things, does not emerge out of blind, natural forces that do not have it in mind. If one advocates intelligent design, one is then advocating that the most important aspects of the history of life are not the result of chance and randomness, but follow some sort of fundamental plan.

Such a view does not have to reject the idea that life came from a single organism (although this idea might itself need to be revised and the acceptance of multiple origins of life might be in order). But it does require that we see all life as emerging from one principle. For this reason, in ending Darwinism, one must go back to the very definition of life and understand what it is. As Stephen Wolfram notes, many definitions have been offered for life, and any such definition both ends up including phenomena normally not considered to be alive and excludes creatures normally thought to be living.[3] For example, life is often defined as that which can re-produce itself, but then mules are not alive, while fire is (*NKS* 1178). In fact, such a definition means that no single being can ever be considered living, since it is only the coupling of a male and female or their equivalents that leads to reproduction.[4] A fertile male and female couple, then, can self-produce as a unit taken together, but many such couples of males and females, of course, do not and cannot. Does that mean they are dead? For this reason, we have to say that the only truly living

---

[3] Stephen Wolfram, *A New Kind of Science* (Illinois: Wolfram Media, 2002), 1178. All subsequent citations indicated as *NKS*.
[4] John Barrow and Frank Tipler, *The Anthropic Cosmological Principle* (New York: Oxford University Press, 1988), 515.

thing is the cell or its equivalent, and other things are living due to being made up of cells.

We also know that crystals will self-replicate when put in a saturated solution, for instance. How do cells differ from crystals and flames? The key difference is that cells have DNA, software. The origin of life lies in the origin of software, for it is not enough to reproduce to be alive, but, also, one needs to contain within oneself the very instructions and code for producing a new version of oneself. Life evolves. And it is the change and alteration done to the code itself, the software of life, which enables this development. But then is not computer software alive? It might be, if it reproduces on its own and also contains and passes on the code for that reproduction. For this reason, we also have to say that what marks a cell is a membrane. No membrane, no life—for what the membrane creates, by incorporating software within itself, is what institutes, for the first time in the universe, the distinction between hardware/software.

Following Wolfram, we can say that any phenomenon is, itself, the product of code. A flame or crystal is itself a computational reality wherein a basic pattern repeats itself. But the flame or crystal does not contain within itself the very coding of that pattern that enables it to reproduce as a material subset. For this reason, software is not alive, because it is only software and not hardware. Life begins with something that reproduces itself and contains in its very being the hardware / software distinction. Again, it's the cell that is alive, and all living things are alive only insofar they are made up of cells. Flames and crystals are thus computational realities that are like electronic devices wherein the hardware and software are one and the same thing. Such devices cannot change or be re-programmed (their reproduction cannot therefore involve evolution):

> The ability to separate in a computer the program from the physical instantiation that performs the computation is an advantage, not a limitation. First

of all, we do have electronic devices with dedicated circuitry in which the 'computer program' are not two, but one. Such devices are not programmable but are hardwired for one specific set of algorithms. Note that I am not just referring to computers with software (called 'firmware') in read-only memory, as may be found in a cell phone or pocket computer. In such a system, the electronics and software may still be considered dualistic even if the program cannot easily be modified.[5]

All phenomena prior to life then can be said to be computational realities wherein the hardware and software are one. But, with life itself, something new arises. There is material software encoded in the cell that can change and be passed on. This software contains the program itself for how to produce the thing. Bill Gates is, of course, well known for having said that DNA is not just a computer program, but "one far more advanced than any software we've ever created."[6] This is not a metaphor or analogy. DNA is chemical software. That it is written in acids rather than electronic circuits is simply another way for it to be embodied. It is a coding. It has, just like a computer program, subroutines (genes and proteins).

Before the split between hardware and software, all phenomena had a code. But no snowflake contained in itself has some materially inscribed place for that code. With life, this split occurs. We can then say that mind itself (consciousness) is a split within the software itself. It is the point at which the software actualizes its ability to compute universally directly. For example, one might find in nature phyllotaxis (the spiraling patterns found in leaves) that follows the Fibonacci sequence of numbers (0, 1, 1, 2, 3, 5, 8 . .

---

[5] Ray Kurzweil, *The Singularity is Near* (New York: Viking, 2005), 444.
[6] Quoted in Donald E. Johnson, *Programming of Life* (Alabama: Big Mac, 2010), 450.

.). But that plant will not also produce leaves or stems via the sequence of prime numbers. It can then compute one sequence, but not all. Even though the plant has a code capable of universal computation, it is, in its actuality, a form of dedicated circuitry. The human mind can not only compute the Fibonacci sequence, but also the sequence of prime numbers and any other computation. Life is then a split within hardware wherein software emerges, but mind is a split within software wherein universal computation is actualized. In the end, we will see that, at the Omega Point, human consciousness, or its equivalent, will enable the universe, itself, to shift from dedicated circuitry to such actualized universal computation.

However, we want to focus on life itself more so for now, since our main critique of evolution is about life rather than mind. Following Margulis on symbiogenesis, we will have to say that, even if one can find isolated strands of RNA or DNA, for instance, and even if those strands reproduce into something with the same coding, one always has life when those strands are incorporated into a nucleus, into a membrane. Then, in reproducing, the code itself is also reproduced, but with it a body, hardware, and an environment. It would be as though one's computer, due to its programming, suddenly instructed itself to make another computer including the keyboard, for a cell membrane will include in itself not just the software but also fluid and materials not related directly to the code. It is then the incorporation of DNA or something equivalent into the membrane that causes the cell to be animated unless one can show that the membrane itself is an outgrowth of the DNA itself, something the chemical sprouts and builds around itself (I will return to these issues).

The mystery of the origin of life is thus not simply the mystery of how DNA formed out of non-living matter, but also how DNA became the software of some hardware. Here the membrane also partitions chemicals interacting. If one imagines some sort of primordial soup with chemicals interacting such as RNA molecules with their lettered sequences and interacting with themselves and other chemicals in the environment, then without a membrane to partition a chemical system, it will eventually be enveloped into the overall environment, and whatever work it does be absorbed and dissipated. Thus, if one imagines a DNA interacting with other chemicals in order to be reproduced by the system or produce amino acids, then without the membrane, this system will be easily broken up by whatever is in the area. It needs the protection of the membrane and the creation of an inside/outside distinction. At the very beginnings of life is the differentiation between inside and outside.

No rock or flame knows such a distinction. Life is about partition and separation in order to form some thing, a first self. Within the membrane, then, all the chemicals working together can produce their products and have a regulated interaction with whatever is on the outside. The membrane determines inputs and outputs. Any system that would include instructions would only be able to survive within a membrane, which is why it is probably the case that membranes were enveloping chemicals (life is thus just a lucky accident that arose from membrane bubbles sucking in chemicals) or simply happened upon such a system or there was first system that was able to in producing products and even reproducing something like DNA was able to also produce a membrane as well. Thus, one needs to find both the system that can reproduce parts of itself, does so by having instructions within itself, and also has an output encircling and partition it from the world.

Now, many think the hardware/software distinction means that the hardware itself becomes less important:

> In life hardware consists of the body, the software, and the genes. The thermodynamic cells and percolating nucleotides we find together today are logically, and historically separable. Just as one can imagine a computer without software . . . so one can picture early thermodynamic life without any genes.

> First came the apparatus, functioning and physiological, and then came the operating systems, user manuals, and codes for making new, improved metabolic machines.[7]

What Dorion Sagan (Margulis's son and often co-author) and Eric Schneider suggest here, not surprisingly, is that the hardware came first. In this way, they would say the cell itself existed in some sense and only later incorporated DNA into it. However, we should not discount the possibility that the cell itself, including its membrane, arose out of DNA as such. They may also have simply been coeval. What this means is that, at its origins, life is the joining of two things together. However, even if the hardware did not emerge from the software itself, the very existence of software reduces the role of hardware, for DNA can be transmitted and extracted. It must exist in some hardware, but is fully detachable from any particular environment. It is a code and language that can be transferred materially and incorporated into another message. Both hardware and software can exist distinctly. One can picture a computer without any software (it makes for a nice paperweight), but the hardware itself can only be plugged into another device in terms of parts and never in terms of elementary elements at the level of letters. By plugging in letters and code into something, the very instructions of the thing change. If we plug some fluid from one cell into another, it does not change at that level. Evolution does occur simply through incorporation of parts and wholes (as Margulis and Sagan have demonstrated). But given that there are basic instructions that can, on their own, lead to a creature, it is probable that it is the code itself which is more fundamental biologically as well as ontologically. For evolution to advance beyond simple forms, there need to be changes to the

---

[7] Eric. D. Schneider and Dorion Sagan, *Into the Cool: Energy Flow, Thermodynamics, and Life* (Chicago: University of Chicago, 2005), 169.

very genomic software itself, rather than just incorporation into a cell of new organelles or the joining of cells together. Just as incorporation can happen in the life of an individual, Sandin has shown us—via viruses, for example—how these changes can occur in the lives of individuals (Darwinism said changes in software only arose due to random mutations). Such information is then inherited by future offspring. The Lamarckianism here is pronounced. Genetic changes occur in the operating system of a thing outside of the process of reproduction. We will see that this means, quite literally, that the bits/letters of the code are flipped, added, duplicated, and transposed.

Now, as Sagan and Schneider note right before the passage quoted above, this distinction between hardware and software was first developed by John von Neumann who must be seen as the non-biologist who truly instituted the new revolution in our thinking about life (as opposed to Schrödinger). Already, in 1948, von Neumann showed how computer cellular automata could reproduce themselves and thus replicate the hardware/software distinction.[8] Today, it comes as no surprise to anyone who uses a computer to know that computer viruses and worms reproduce, as many of us have had to pay money to repair the damage they do. However, nothing shows that a computer virus changes, because it is not clear that any process other than direct human intervention causes its code to change over time. Computer viruses are thus not living in and of themselves. Also, just like a biological virus, a computer virus requires a host program to replicate. Von Neumann is said to have demonstrated how a software program, on its own, gave rise from out of itself to the hardware/software distinction. How did von Neumann do this?

> So Von Neumann adopted an infinite checkerboard as his universe. Each square cell could be in any

---

[8] See Schneider and Sagan, *Into the Cool*.

number of states corresponding roughly to machine components. A 'machine' was a pattern of such cells.[9]

Von Neumann needed "a cellular array with 29 different states for its cells. Twenty-eight of the states are simple machine components; one is the empty state of unoccupied cells" (*RU* 15). Usually, such cells of automata only have two states (filled or blank). In this system, the current state of a cell is directly linked to the states of bordering cells (*RU* 16). Using this checkerboard and multiple states for each cell, von Neumann showed that there exist "patterns that can reproduce themselves" (*RU* 16). Such self-reproducing patterns give rise to the same pattern over and over again: "Start with a self-reproducing pattern, let the rules of the cellular space take either course, and they will eventually be two patterns, and then four, and eight" (*RU* 16). William Poundstone here claims that such repeating patterns are not like a crystal, but rather an elementary form of life. He believes this since each pattern contains "a complete description of its own organization" within itself (*RU* 16). Because the pattern here uses a self-contained set of rules to make new copies of itself, it is more similar to life than a crystal. This experiment by Von Neumann is similar to his one on the universal constructor. Such a universal constructor is a machine that can build any pattern, the rules for which can be inputted into the constructor. The constructor thereby can build another version of itself. It self-reproduces. For Poundstone, what von Neumann's experiment shows is that there is no "life force," but only information itself as a set of rules, an algorithm, that is needed for self-reproduction to take place (*RU* 17). Von Neumann's automata are, therefore, the origin of the idea that for something to be living it must "contain a complete

---

[9] William Poundstone, *The Recursive Universe: Cosmic Complexity and the Limits of Scientific Knowledge* (New York: Contemporary, 1985), 15. All subsequent citations indicated as *RU*.

description of itself and use that information to create new copies" (*RU* 18). For von Neumann, the information contained in his cellular automata could be run on any computer and on any number of different types of hardware. It therefore demonstrated the difference between hardware/software in yet another sense.

It also important to note, already, at this point, that the "cellular space" of von Neumann's constructor machines was "finite" since it took place over a finite amount of time and had a finite number of possible states and rules (*RU* 187). Biological organisms are, of course, always limited in this way and take a limited amount of time to produce offspring. They only produce a defined number of offspring. Life's finitude in this way makes itself possible. If there was an infinite regress, life would not be possible. What would such an infinite regress look like, and why would it make life impossible? We have said that the living contains within itself a complete informational description of how to make that living thing, a set of informational blueprints. But what if the blueprints themselves contained a description of those blueprints, etc.? "A cell's DNA contains a complete description of all essential parts of the cell *except* for the DNA itself (no infinitely regressive blueprints)" (*RU* 189). It is important that, at some level, there be an element that is not itself repeated. There must be some level at which there is no further mirroring. If there was, one needs an infinite amount of time to copy an infinite set of instructions in order for reproduction to take place. Life can only ever be finite. Its coding must ultimately be encoded in something that is not, itself, encoded in some sense.

This is also true even of a computer program. Without some mark of finitude, life will not be possible. The most fundamental unit for DNA as well as for computers is the bit. The bit is the relationship 0/1. It is the possibility of two states (on/off). DNA encodes bits by way of its four chemicals (cytosine, guanine, adenine, and thymine). It is not arbitrary that these four chemicals are represented by four letters (A, C, G, and T), for the letter is another name for the bit. In its fundamentally differential nature, the bit/letter ensures that there is no infinite regress and forms the 'atom' of the final level (although as we will see any type of entity at any scale can function as a bit). In any event, what is important here is that life itself is about the encoding and mapping of the very informational description that makes it up and determines it. The question, then, becomes whether those changes in coding occur by way of random mutation, by way of other processes that are themselves not subject to underlying rules, or are themselves the unfolding of fundamental rules.

What is amazing is that consensus seems to be that, despite seeing Darwinism collapse due to its reliance on purely random mutation in the coding to account for speciation and for natural selection to account for how new creatures arise, all biologists seem to think that, as life develops, the changes in coding that occur in the software are not part of the unfolding of the very initial program of life itself. Take Stephen Wolfram, for example. Wolfram has hinted in a few places that he believes the entire universe is a cellular automaton. That is, Wolfram thinks all that is, is the unfolding of a program with a few basic simple rules. And yet, when it comes to life, Wolfram says that the differences we see in living creatures "are in essence just a reflection of completely random changes in underlying genetic programs, with no systemic effects from natural selection" (*NKS* 396). While Wolfram here discounts the idea that natural selection gives rise to new programs in living things, he still holds on to the idea that such changes are totally random. This is amazing, given that it is Wolfram, himself, who has shown us how perfectly random patterns can be the result of programs with very simple rules. Rather than seeing higher and more developed organisms as resulting from some unfolding of a program, Wolfram insists that, "it is essentially just a consequence of strings of random mutations that happened to add more and more features without introducing fatal flaws" (*NKS* 398).

It is our purpose to challenge this view. If simple programs can give rise to random patterns, and life itself is fundamentally defined by way of its being related to software, then it is not clear why it is not the very playing out of that software itself that gives rise to and enables the variety we see. Complexity emerges, not due to chance, but due to set rules. Wolfram himself showed us that complexity is not a matter of chaos and randomness, but a result of simple rules iterating themselves. That should be shocking, as, in the past, someone like Hegel would say such iteration cannot be anything more than a pure, stupid, mechanical repetition. But we have already attempted to show that such repetition, even if mechanical in character is the very 'life force' itself, as opposed to any dialectic or nebulous 'energy.' Now, we may not be able to see how that it is the case unless we look at evolution and life as a whole. For us, critiquing natural selection in this way is not enough; Darwinism and its legacy will not be finished with until we also put into question this reliance on randomness. We will therefore have to read Wolfram against himself, as it is his views that offer us hope in finding that the seemingly random sequence of changes that the code of life has undergone actually took place due to the unfolding of that code, itself. After all, if the universe is the unfolding of a single computer program, is not life part of that program and its development?

Think here about yourself. In nine months each of us went from a single cell to an infant, mainly due to the playing out of the basic instructions encoded in that original cell. During those nine months, we underwent a great deal of changes and took on many forms. But, more importantly, as theists, it is not acceptable to think that life is simply a random process. To show that life is designed is to show that it, like the universe itself, is not really forming randomly, but rather through the unfolding of some basic program. I call that program the 'Name of God.' In this way, we should not be quick to agree with Margulis, who argues that "the DNA molecule" is like a "computer disk" insofar as it only "stores evolutionary information but does not create it."[10] However, at the same time, insofar as we locate the issue at the level of code itself, we are not locating it at the level of genes that act selfishly and can agree with Margulis and Sagan when they say:

> Selfish genes, since they are not 'selves' in any coherent sense, can be taken as figments of an overactive primarily English-speaking imagination. The living cell is the true self. (*AG* xvi)

A cell is the first living thing, but that is because it is split between hardware and software. A gene is but part of that software—a subroutine. What causes a cell to create more copies of itself is no different than what causes any cellular automata to run. It is simply iterating and executing its rules. One should not look at the level of the cell for an explanation of reproduction rather than the gene and DNA base pairs, even if the cell, as a unit, is more self-like than the gene.

The ability to find a program that explains life and its development would mean that biology itself could become a truly hard science, insofar as it would be capable of real prediction. It would mean, to borrow Stephen Gould's famous phrase, that we could 'replay life's tape' and find that essentially the same things happen over and over again. Gould, of course, thought that every time we would replay this tape we would find that new scenarios played out. In one, humans might emerge. In another, life might not go beyond bacteria. For Gould, life can and would take new paths in any rerun of the process. New animals and plants would arise. Gould felt that life was based on a series of improbable accidents that merely happened. If one such accident does not occur or occurs differently, the entire

---

[10] Lynn Margulis and Dorion Sagan, *Acquiring Genomes: A Theory of the Origins of Species* (New York: Basic Books, 2003), xvi. All subsequent citations indicated by *AG*.

history of life will be different. We want to demonstrate or, at least, cause one to think Gould's view is probably false. We want to show that, in such a replaying of and viewing of life's tape, the same basic thing would occur, if one could construct the right simulation that started with the basic program life had at its beginning (and given the hardware / software distinction such software can in principle be run on inorganic software).

George McGhee argues interestingly that adopting Gould's view is the same as suggesting that "the elemental composition of the universe would be entirely different, that it is highly unlikely that neon or argon would be present in that new universe . . ." and finds such a suggestion absurd.[11] For McGhee, anyone trained in chemistry

> knows, that if you start again with an atom with one proton, hydrogen, that the process of stellar atomic fusion will eventually produce an atom with two protons, helium, and that eventually one atom of argon would evolve.[12]

McGhee is suggesting the evolution of atomic elements is the same in principle as the evolution of life. Now, such evolution is more involved. The key is that, whereas atoms are purely hardware/software as one, life involves the hardware/software split such that the software can, itself, be changed. But that does not, in and of itself, mean that the development of life is unpredictable as such, whereas the evolution of atomic elements is not. If evolution is like the development of atomic types, then one can predict where it is going. Before one knew how elements arise from other ones, one might have thought it was merely a random mess. But, now that we know the patterns and rules for how that

---

[11] George McGhee, "Convergent Evolution: A Periodic Table of Life?" in *The Deep Structure of Biology*, ed. Simon Conway Morris (Pennsylvania: Templeton, 2008), 21.

[12] McGhee, "Convergent Evolution," 21.

evolves, we can make predictions and fully understand the reason why there is the number of atoms there is, their composition, etc.[13]

We will return to these issues in our discussion of 'convergence,' for example. But if life itself is the unfolding of some basic structure in the same way that elements are, then we are pushed down a road leading to intelligent design. For there are, in principle, many different pathways life can take. If it always takes this same one, can one then say it is not designed? We do not intend to prove God exists based on life's designed nature (we think God can only be proved using ontological/modal proofs), but we rather want to show that life itself is not something that flies in the face of arguing that God did create all and that reality is itself the unfolding of a divine program, the divine name.

Many attempts to see order in the world, of course, were mistaken. Kepler, for example, thought that there would be only six planets, because each planet would correspond to one of the Platonic solids. Such a universe would reflect a divine perfection in the world, as God would choose to use such prefect shapes and solids to construct the planets. Kepler was, of course, mistaken, insofar as there are both more planets and those planets do not have the shapes and ratios needed to fit this paradigm. Kepler's mistake here was also to think that God would need to act in the same way Kepler would if Kepler had created the solar system. But divine creation might take on a more surprising form. We need to still observe the world for how it is in fact and find design in that way, rather than taking it as deducible from reason alone. Reason is limited such that we cannot know ahead of time, without experimental results, what shape the creation will take. But that does not mean we cannot find its shape. And a simulation of life, itself, replaying its tape, will one day precisely form such an experiment.

---

[13] McGhee, "Convergent Evolution," 18.

Since the advent of Darwinism, biology has grown in import. Some today like to say that it is biology, rather than physics, which is the fundamental science. They claim that because the universe itself is seen to be subject to the rules of natural selection, as well. However, it is actually, as always, metaphysics that is the fundamental science. As we will show, questions concerning life, its development, and its nature lead necessarily to metaphysical issues and to dealing with the metaphysical assumptions lying behind various views. All roads lead back to metaphysics. And, just as for Dewey, Darwin signaled a new way to think about essences, for instance, what emerges after Darwin forces us as well to conceive of the world in new metaphysical terms.

Part One

Anti-Darwinism

§2
IRREDUCIBLE COMPLEXITY

Let us review, first, some of the reasons why the Darwinian theory (the theory that says all life develops based on natural selection and random mutation) was exposed as a fundamentally flawed theory. Almost invariably, the first name one encounters when discovering such criticism is that of 'renegade' biochemist Michael Behe. Behe has not articulated a theory accounting for how life itself develops. That is, of course, true for almost all critics of Darwinism outside of figures like Margulis and Sandin. His critique is aimed purely at exposing the flaws and limitations in the idea of basing the development of life solely on the gradual change that natural selection, coupled with random mutation, can bring forth. Behe is best known for his notion of 'irreducible complexity.' This notion was first developed in his seminal *Darwin's Black Box: The Biochemical Challenge to Evolution*. For Behe, the complexity of something like wings could not arise due to step-by-step selection and mutation. With its idea of slow and gradual change Darwinism lead us to believe that something like wing develops such that at one point a creature has only a proto-wing that, if flapped, would be of no aid and only at some later point, after one small change after another, did a full set of wings that would enable flight to develop. We therefore have the image of a creature that attempts to fly and is unable with his proto-wing. This creature's descendants cannot, either, until, suddenly, the proto-wings, after the last of many changes, become fully useable wings. But each step along the way had to be only a slight modification to what would eventually become wings.[14]

To take another example: one has to posit that the liquid that a snake produces that is not lethal is only a step of many steps on the way to venom. And no changes are allowed to occur during the lifetime of a creature. One is born with all the changes one will have. In this way, if, for some reason, the change was negative (leading away from wings), it would make the long journey from proto-wing to wings that fly even longer. Not only does this view not match what one sees in the actual fossil records where such things as wings seem to abruptly appear suddenly—and not after proto-versions appear for many stages—but, also, such a view is mistaken about the nature of biological parts. Forty percent of wings are still useless as wings. Only the entire thing will enable flight. There is no advantage to having sixty percent wings. If you have only incomplete wings, you cannot fly away from a predator. In addition, the slow, step-by-step development of something like a spider's ability to spin a web presupposes that all the right steps come one after the other. One needs all the steps to be in the right order. But if each change is only the product of random chance (random mutation), then one needs enough time for all these random events to occur.

Behe often likes to use human inventions as analogies to highlight these issues. His most famous example is a mousetrap. Without all its many parts working together at once, the mousetrap is useless. For a mousetrap to evolve, one has to imagine that by random mutation (chance) each part falls into place one after the other, generation after generation (even though in each generation it is useless until the last). To argue that a mousetrap is not a living creature, as living creatures change as a system when they

---

[14] Michael Behe, *Darwin's Black Box: The Biochemical Challenge to Evolution* (New York: Free Press, 2006), 44.

evolve, is already to speak from a non-Darwinian perspective. Darwinism does not as such have a way of explaining how one change can lead to a cascade of changes, such that one goes from an arm to a wing. Behe's favorite biological example is, of course, the flagellar motor (a tail-like appendage on bacteria that enables propulsion). For a bacteria to develop such a motor on Darwinian accounts, one has to imagine a large number of single point mutations to its DNA code that occur generation after generation until the flagellum emerges as such. This motor depends on a long series of proteins for its development. Without each and every protein encoded in the bacteria's code, the flagellum cannot develop, and the bacteria would be left with no way to move.

Margulis's theory would offer more help here, as it would say that, perhaps, the flagellum is actually an independent microscopic entity that merged with a bacterial one (then, one has to still explain where each independent creature came from), but with Darwinism, one is dependent on a long series of improbable steps. Until the flagellum appears as a whole, the bacterium merely floats without any ability to move about. To my knowledge, no Darwinian has been able to specify all the steps needed to lead to the flagellum and also shown—either using the fossil record or even experimentation on bacteria in the lab—how it can develop thusly.

Irreducible complexity then means, for Behe, that a system needs all its parts to be in place to function. Step-by-step, random mutation is such an inefficient way for complex systems to appear that one should be highly skeptical that they appear in that way. There is no true, empirical evidence that nature works in this manner. For example, the typical Darwinian will here object that, at each stage on the way to the flagellum, there existed something unlike a flagellum but still functional (and that would transform into the needed thing). With the case of wings, there was first an arm. But no Darwinian has been able to show more than one or two stages of this nature (from arm to wing) such that the gap is too large to avoid the issue of irreducible complexity. One would have to show how, for each stage on the way to the flagellum, there was a precursor that functioned in some other way and, step by step, became the flagellum.[15] But there is no empirical evidence of such.

For Behe and many of his cohorts, of course, this failure means that one has to see biological systems as having been designed:

> For discrete physical systems—if there is not a gradual route to their production—design is evident when a number of separate, interacting components are ordered in such a way as to accomplish a function beyond the individual components. The greater the specificity of the interacting components required to produce the function, the greater is our confidence in the conclusion of design.[16]

Obviously, intelligent agents like humans build mousetraps. We will return to this question of "intelligent design." But it is clear that gradual, point-by-point chance will not account for complexity. We will also need to compare Behe's notion of irreducible complexity with that of Gregory Chaitin's, as Chaitin's view of irreducible complexity refers to software itself and, ultimately, something like the flagellum is a product of software instructions.

---

[15] I am here drawing on William Dembski and Jonathan Witt's explanation and defense of Behe's notion of irreducible complexity in their *Intelligent Design Uncensored: An Easy-to-Understand Guide to the Controversy* (Nottingham: InterVarsity Press, 2010), 49–54.

[16] Behe, *Darwin's Black Box*, 194.

§3
THE EDGE OF EVOLUTION

In addition to his notion of irreducible complexity, Behe has also developed the concept of the 'edge of evolution.' This idea criticizes Darwinian evolution by showing what it is, in fact, capable of and what things are beyond the reach of Darwinian mechanisms. This concept is not simply a restatement of what was argued with the idea of irreducible complexity, but, rather, an attempt to show what exactly step-by-step, gradual change is capable of and where, in fact, its limits are. Behe here wants to show that, while Darwinism should be credited with showing that all life has common ancestors, the notion of random mutation, coupled with selection, can work; in particular cases where one only needs one or two steps of changes, random mutation and natural selection cannot explain the most fundamental and important aspects of living organisms, such as the structures that make up life.[17] To account for the many changes that one needs to show life's development, one needs something more than random change; one needs to see that most changes "that built the great structures of life must have been nonrandom" (*EE* 83). Behe here also wants to show that evolution can, essentially, only work within kinds and species, rather than leading itself to speciation.

---

[17] Michael Behe, *The Edge of Evolution: The Search for the Limits of Darwinism* (New York: Free Press, 2008), 83. All subsequent citations indicated as *EE*.

Natural selection is therefore very much like the artificial selection (dog breeding, plant breeding, etc.) Darwin looked to via analogy. Evolution can show us large dogs being bred into smaller dogs, red roses becoming white roses, etc., but it does not show us dogs becoming cats.

What Behe means by the 'edge of evolution' is, then, what many call 'microevolution.' This view says that evolution occurs within types of organisms but does not give rise to metamorphoses into new kinds. Natural selection and random mutation can yield changes within a species or phylum, but not speciation, as such. A white rose remains a rose. The problem here is that random mutation, due to its very randomness, is limited. Ultimately, what Behe wants to show is that natural selection coupled with random mutation (although real phenomena can be documented in particular cases) are marginal phenomena when it comes to looking at the development of life and its diversification into a variety of forms. But it is important to note that, here, natural selection and random mutation occur in precise time frames and are not taken as occurring over long periods of time since they do not together enable what has happened in the history of this planet to have occurred in the time it did.

Behe notes that "a mutation comes along relatively rarely and few of the mutations that do come along are helpful" (*EE* 11). One has to keep in mind that some biological organisms are more susceptible to random mutations than others. This is due often to the overwhelming amount of such organisms, their rate of reproduction, and the amount of genetic material they contain. For example,

> viruses contain much less genetic material [than we do], but it mutates so rapidly, and there are so many copies of it, that HIV alone, in just the past fifty years, has undergone more of at least some kinds of mutations than all cells have experienced since the beginning of the world. (*EE* 13)

Viruses are then organisms in which natural selection and mutation can lead to changes. We see it, ourselves, in our own lifetimes. But these changes are due to the specific qualities of viruses that are not shared by other organisms upon which these mechanisms are also said to work. We will return later to Maximo Sandin's work on viruses and lateral gene transfer, but we can say at this point that if viruses are also responsible for speciation in other creatures, it is not by way of natural selection and random mutation in those creatures but rather by way of how viruses reprogram them.

Behe focuses on human beings and on the acquisition of the sickle cell trait: "The gene that carried the sickle mutation arose in a human population in Africa ten thousand years ago. The mutation is a single, simple genetic change—nothing at all complicated" (*EE* 15). This change in the human genome is simple because it requires a single point mutation to one letter of DNA. This mutation occurred during the creation of the sperm or an egg when a single copying error of DNA occurred. The change of one letter (out of literally billions) led to a new protein being in that infant's hemoglobin (*EE* 24–25). What is interesting is that such a single error may have only occurred once or a few times in human history. Was it, then, a matter of chance? Perhaps. It certainly looks that way if one only looks at things within the context of the point mutation itself. But it may not be. What if this mutation occurs when a male or female is sick already with malaria and, in producing an egg or sperm, the mutation is itself induced? I only speculate here. Such small changes may be random. But it did not lead to a new human—only to an ever so slightly different one.

The problem is that this mutation has a downside, as people with sickle cell disease well know. 'Evolution' has not given rise to any further mutations that overcome that disease while also allowing for immunity from malaria. And that is, probably, mostly an index of the extreme rarity of such chance events. It is also important to note that humanity's suffering at the hands of malaria only produced this mutation. It has caused problems in addition to protecting against malaria. Humanity here was not, as it were, improved or made better. Humanity did not receive a new bodily system, but only impairment by a small change in one already existing code. It did not involve a new weapon as the human was damaged to defend itself. The new protein coded for is not more complicated than the one that previously helped make up hemoglobin.

But what is interesting is that, despite modern medicine not being able to defeat malaria with drug remedies, this single change to the human genome that occurred long ago is able to defeat malaria, a single-celled organism, by giving humans this immunity (*EE* 24–25). In other words, malaria has not been able to 'evolve' to overcome the sickle-cell defense, despite being a protozoon. This contrasts with HIV, a virus, where it constantly builds resistance and changes, due to its being a small amount of RNA code that reproduces at a very fast rate. We then see already the difference between HIV and malaria that shows the edge of evolution at work. Seemingly, malaria is already too animal-like and contains too much code to be able to evolve simply by natural selection and random mutation. One can also see such point mutations at work in bacteria. Even if the random chances of a point mutation enabling a bacterium to be resistant to a drug are one in a billion, then odds are that it will happen, given the vast number of such bacterial cells (*EE* 55–56). The vast number means that more than a billion are very easily being treated with the drug and, thereby, the chances lead to a point mutation needed to cause drug resistance. In this way, point mutations will be more likely amongst bacteria than other organisms in the circumstances in which a drug is destroying them.

But, given that such a point mutation can occur in this way, why is Behe sure the bacteria already have it before encountering the drug? This is a question Behe does not ask, because he is taking mutations to only ever be random. Behe also likes pointing to the E. coli bacteria. This bacterium has been subject to countless experiments over many decades in laboratories throughout the world. It duplicates at a rate of "seven times a day" such that one has seen in the laboratory the equivalent of "a million human-years" of 'evolution' on it, but no speciation has occurred (*EE* 16). One could say that the amount of malaria cells produced in our own lifetimes will be greater than the number of mammals that will ever live (*EE* 146). This means that we can draw lessons about how evolution works for entire types and for the whole history of life by looking at these cases. Indeed, this bacterium has devolved—including losing genetic material—and has thereby lost abilities it once had: "The lesson of E. coli is that it's easier for evolution to break things than make things" (*EE* 146). For this reason, the only true evolution we have easily witnessed on the large scale—other than that what we see with sickle cell—is simply the extinction of that species.

Species with large body size (that live many years, that have few children, etc.) will not see much more than microevolution occur if only random mutation and natural selection are at work. And even then, those changes are often deleterious. The harmfulness of these changes was already recognized by one of the scientists who discovered DNA—Francis Crick:

> Sequences would result in a large number of defective proteins. Nearly any conceivable change to the genetic code would be lethal to the cell. The scientists who suggest that natural selection shaped the genetic code are fully aware of Crick's work. Still they rely on evolution to explain the code's optimal design because of the existence of nonuniversal genetic codes. While the genetic code in nature is generally regarded as universal, some nonuniversal genetic codes exist—codes that employ slightly different codon assignments. Presumably, these nonuniversal codes evolved from the universal genetic

code. Therefore, researchers argue that such evolution is possible.

But, the codon assignments of the nonuniversal genetic codes are nearly identical to those of the universal genetic code with only one or two exceptions. Nonuniversal genetic codes can be thought of as deviants of the universal genetic code. Does the existence of nonuniversal codes imply that wholesale genetic code evolution is possible? Careful study reveals that codon changes in the nonuniversal genetic codes always occur in relatively small genomes, such as those in mitochondria. These changes involve (1) codons that occur at low frequencies in that particular genome or (2) stop codons.

Changes in assignment for these codons could occur without producing a lethal scenario because only a small number of polypeptides in the cell or organelle would experience an altered amino acid sequence. So it seems limited evolution of the genetic code can take place, but only in special circumstances. The existence of nonuniversal genetic codes does not necessarily justify an evolutionary origin of the amazingly optimal genetic code found in nature.[18]

Behe draws some key lessons from these experimental and empirical results: (1) that natural selection and random mutation only work in specific contexts, (2) that the 'red queen hypothesis'—wherein organisms fight for survival—does not lead to improvements but to devolution and breakdown in organisms, (3) that random mutation, due to its very randomness, cannot provide more than one or two of the steps needed to provide new systems, and (4) that

---

[18] Fazale Rana, *The Cell's Design* (Michigan: Baker Books, 2008), 176–177.

extrapolating from the data on an enormous number of familiar pairs allows us to roughly but consistently establish the limits of Darwinian evolution for all of life on earth over the past several billion years. (*EE* 19)

Behe draws the line for evolution at what he calls the "double CCC" for two substitutions of three DNA letters at the same time (*EE* 63). Behe writes:

So let's accept my earlier conservative estimation, and spell out some implications. The immediate, most important implication is that complexes with more than two different binding sites—ones that require three or more different kinds of proteins—are beyond the edge of evolution, past what is biologically reasonable to expect Darwinian evolution to have accomplished in all of life in all of the billion-year history of the world. The reasoning is straightforward. The odds of getting two independent things right are the multiple of the odds of getting each right by itself. So, other things being equal, the likelihood of developing two binding sites in a protein complex would be the square of the probability for getting one: a double CCC, 10^{20} times 10^{20}, which is 10^{40}. There have likely been fewer than 10^{40} cells in the world in the past four billion years, so the odds are against a single event of this variety in the history of life. It is biologically unreasonable. (*EE* 146)

Such a CCC mutation occurs in bacteria developing resistance to chloroquine. Even over the vast expanse of billions of years of life, there is simply not enough time for such an event to occur by pure random mutation: "We would not expect such an event to happen in all of the organisms that have ever lived over the entire history of life on this planet" (*EE* 63). The problem for the Darwinists is that these are precisely the features they want to explain. For Behe, then, any aspects of living things we find that require more than a double CCC change did not emerge due simply to natural selection coupled with random mutation. We can, then, say simply that two simultaneous mutations marks the limits and edge of evolution.

Behe illustrates this again with malaria, for the sickle cell trait is formed by a point mutation but causes problems in addition to creating immunity. What Behe calls the C-Harlem mutation only leads to malarial immunity and no negatives. Behe then asks a simple question: Why does not nature immediately go from the typical hemoglobin type to C-Harlem and avoid the problems of sickle cell disease (*EE* 109)? The reason is that C-Harlem would require two simultaneous mutations to emerge suddenly from a normal human with the typical human hemoglobin structure. Those two simultaneous mutations are not within the realm of probability. It would take much longer than the existence of the entire universe for one to hit upon by chance such a double simultaneous mutation (*EE* 110).

We also see that, while the sickle cell trait required one mutation, producing C-Harlem could build on sickle cell, but only by way of another purely random step. Even with bacteria, with their billions of offspring, the CCC barrier looms. It may be the case that Behe is actually understating the improbability of random mutations, even in bacteria. Even if there is a one in a billion chance that such a mutation will occur, that still may not be enough. After all, if a bacterium has 23 million base pairs, how many possible mutations are there? Behe admits that, with a fly/mosquito deluged with insecticides, "mutation has to work with pre-existing cellular machinery so there is a very limited number of things it can do" such that "even though there are trillions upon trillions of possible simple mutations to an insect's genome, all but a handful are irrelevant" (*EE* 76). It then should cause us pause that out of trillions of possible mutations "the same few mutations pop up in organisms as diverse as mosquito and fly because no others work" (*EE*

77). But is it because no others work? That seems odd, given that, if trillions and trillions are possible, then the odds are trillions and trillions to one that any one mutation will occur. That means, for it to be reasonable for it to occur, one would need trillions and trillions of examples.

Take a rat. Rats developed immunity to the rat poison Warfarin, and that was due to a "change in any one of several amino acids in a certain rat protein" (*EE* 77). But if it is purely random that any one mutation will occur, there are not billions of rats exposed to Warfarin. Why did those mutations show up? Was it mere luck? One has to presume that, in a population, all mutations are being explored. One has to assume that mutations are like numbers that all get read out in some sort of sequence. But it's not clear that nature works that way. Even if there are one billion rats in the world, are all being exposed to the poison? Does each one contain some mutation that aids them? If there are one hundred million rats, does that mean that, necessarily, one has the right mutation, because each has a different mutation? What is fascinating is that not all rats were exposed to this poison—only a select few—and yet this mutation arose multiple times. Was this just a matter of luck? A lucky mutant?

Let's examine this issue of chance itself, as Behe, even in criticizing evolution, may buy too much into the idea that evolution conveniently actualizes all possibilities. This is doubtful, given that life itself does not seem to actualize all its potentiality. That is, we can theoretically lay out all sorts of possible life forms, shapes, etc., but the history of life only explores a fraction. Let's say a genome has 1 trillion possible mutations. Each mutation is then a one in a trillion chance. But if one has a trillion examples, Behe and Darwinism need to say that each entity only will necessarily have at least one mutation of each kind for the genome to produce all the possible mutations (and we will see that Darwinian metaphysics is forced precisely to make this claim). How many times would one have to run a lottery until all the possible combinations were produced in reality? A lottery might go for weeks precisely because not every single sequence is bought.

Behe claims that HIV, for instance, has gone through every possible mutation, and, yet, the virus has remained essentially the same (*EE* 154–155). Perhaps. Behe's main point here is that only something like HIV (that reproduces as it does, given its size, etc.) could explore all such mutations, and that, even in doing so, the virus does not become something new or different in kind (which undermines the idea that life evolved from some string of RNA, like a virus randomly mutating). He also wants to show that organisms with much longer genomes would need billions of years to do what HIV has done, thus indicating to us what even billions of years of evolution would produce.

But randomness may be even more limited than Behe thinks. This is not to say that Behe does not point out the flaws in random mutation. For instance, he notes that, in being dependent on random mutation, every "evolutionary step a population of organisms takes is very likely to be connected to the last step," such that, if one must go step by step, each step will have large odds stacked against it (*EE* 113). Is it reasonable to suggest that complex systems (to return to Behe's first criticism) can arise from step-by-step random mutations? This would only seem to make sense if, somehow, things are pre-organized and pre-arranged. Too many possibilities exist for such blind searches (I will not neglect the issue of how Darwinists see natural selection as being better than purely blind search).

Now, Behe notes that the mutation rate in humans is one in a hundred million nucleotides," such that any baby has 30 such changes in her genome (*EE* 110). To get something like the sickle cell trait, we need a point mutation at a particular point. But that means, at best, "one out of every hundred million babies is born with a new mutation that gives it sickle hemoglobin" (*EE* 110). Had over a hundred million humans lived at the point at which it developed? Had there been "a hundred generations with a population of a million people?" (*EE*).

Think about a twenty-sided die. If it is rolled twenty times, will all twenty numbers have been rolled? How many times will it need to be rolled to do so? 1/20 is an epistemological construction. What if the die, in reality, is weighted on a few sides? With something like DNA, we need to imagine a die with many millions of sides. Seeing things in merely statistical terms means that we disregard possible differential rates of mutation. If things are purely random, they cannot be predicted. But, if their rates of mutations, for instance, are guided, perhaps, even by the code itself or something in the environment, the very development of life would most likely have direction. Finding that some mutations are much more likely than others would undermine the idea that there is no direction to life. For this reason, all likelihoods are seen as equal by Darwinism. Darwinism demands that life have no direction. But, in demanding such a thing, it will, as we will soon see, make its own mechanisms of marginal value in explaining life itself.

Behe himself admits that often chance mutations are lost and not passed on such that for any number of reasons (the person with the mutation dies before passing it on, does not have children, cannot have children, the mutation is changed back in the child during production of sperm or egg, etc.) "we may have to wait for another hundred million carriers of the sickle gene to be born before another new C-Harlem mutation arise?" (*EE* 111). Such considerations lead us to see that the given odds are greater against random mutation. Mutations only truly have a chance when, like the sickle cell trait, they provide an obvious advantage in a particular situation. It is then most likely it will be passed on. But the number of mutations that have that character are rare, themselves, because, like sickle cell, they are only ones out of millions. Again, if all possible mutations are not explored necessarily in a population, then chances are slimmer. And even if a mutation is passed on, one has many other steps to go if one wants more than just a new protein for the hemoglobin group of proteins.

Now, we should not rule out in advance that mutations can be used in some sort of designed process that has some sort of goal built into it, but, in a non-designed and random process, mutations cause problems and are harmful. As Hugh Ross notes, "deleterious mutations outnumber beneficial mutations by at least as much as ten thousand to one, and in some species by as much as ten million to one."[19] Darwinism is dependent on chance alone, for the most part, to move the process along. And, as we saw with sickle cell trait, even beneficial mutations can be partially harmful. The overwhelming nature of harmful mutations should lead to species devolving rather than evolving, and natural selection cannot be expected to remove both the deleterious and near neutral mutations as quickly as they arise.[20] The accumulation of so many harmful mutations every generation that are not and cannot be removed by natural selection leads to genetic decline.

Some people think this is an explanation for why in the Bible people have such long lifetimes compared to the ones we have today. But that means we are seeing regression and devolution rather than evolution. Darwinism is also arguing that, between two closely related species, the small percentage in genetic difference is due mainly to mutations. But then, if there are, for example, only 100 mutations differentiating two species, one has to show how those 100 mutations are enough to account for all the differences in behavior, brain type, physical appearance, etc., between the two. Given the blindness of the forces at work in Darwinism (mutations arise randomly such that it will not know in advance if a mutation is good or bad), one should expect the constant impairment of life.[21] As we saw with bacteria in the laboratory, genetic deterioration arose. If the emer-

---

[19] Hugh Ross, *More Than a Theory: Revealing a Testable Model for Creation* (Michigan: Baker Books, 2009), 164.
[20] Ross, *More Than a Theory*, 164.
[21] Ross, *More Than a Theory*, 164.

gence of new species is based on the cumulative effect of positive mutations, then the odds are stacked against it.

§4
NOT BY CHANCE

The improbability of mutations is, itself, mirrored in the improbability of self-reproducing DNA and life arising at all. Many years ago already, Michael Denton explained that

> The space of all possible amino acid sequences (as with letter sequences) is unimaginably large and consequently sequences which must obey particular restrictions which can defined, like the rules of grammar, are bound to be fantastically rare.[22]

Even a sequence of "just ten amino acids long only occurs by chance in about 10^{13} average proteins."[23] Such considerations led to the conclusion that the probability of life arising on its own by chance is infinitesimal. We should keep in mind that, prior to life arising, the laws of Darwinian evolution cannot be said to have operated. So Darwinism either cannot comment on how life arises or only says that it arises via blind search by nature combining chemicals in all possible sequences. But such random combinations would require much more time than the universe has existed. As Stephen Meyer puts it,

---

[22] Michael Denton, *Evolution: A Theory in Crisis* (New York: Adler & Adler, 1986), 323.
[23] Denton, *Evolution*, 323.

> Given the probabilistic resources of the whole universe, it is extremely unlikely that even one functional protein or DNA molecule—to say nothing of the suite of such molecules necessary to establish natural selection—would arise by chance.[24]

The very probability of blind search in the finite time from the beginning of the universe makes it unreasonable to claim that life arose by pure chance, given the odds.

When we think of DNA or RNA, we need to imagine a string many, many letters (or bits) long. But to have life we need to have just the right string. The odds are simply astronomically against the right bit string arising on its own. Many people faced with such odds immediately either claim that such an event had to be ordained and designed or simply due to our world and universe being suited to life. Both answers indicate non-randomness at the heart of the origin of life itself. To argue that natural processes were right for life itself gives rise to the question of why that was the case and if it was itself a result of chance. Given enough time, of course, life could form by chance. It is not physically impossible. It is simply incredibly improbable. It would take many times longer than the earth itself has existed. All life is based on DNA and on variations on the same code. In many different life forms, for instance, there are differences of only a few percents between their bit-strings. All DNA sequences are related, even if many refer to very different life forms.

Darwinism rules out that the environment can play a role, as it insists that change is random. The environment might lead to the elimination of some life forms, but that is considered contingent and random by Darwinism. By ruling out any force driving or guiding evolution, Darwinism can only lean on random mutation and natural selection to show how things work. It is important to remember that

---

[24] Stephen Meyer, *Signature in the Cell* (New York: Harper One, 2010), 276.

Darwinism only looks at what happened in the past in attempt to retrodict and explain it. But due to its relying on chance, it cannot do so. For this reason, as we will later see, some metaphysicians are left saying that an infinite time exists such that anything can happen in order to overcome these problems. Of course, here many Darwinists point to Stanley Miller's experiment wherein amino acids arose in a laboratory experiment. But Miller was only ever able to produce "nonbiological substances" in addition to amino acids, thereby neutralizing them.[25] In this way, Miller was never able to come anywhere close to producing something like the DNA molecule. It is also not enough to simply create amino acids in labs in this manner. The amino acids also have to be arranged in the right sequence. As we see then, one can win amino acids sequences in the purely chemical sense in the lab, but that does not mean one will win the improbable sequence needed.

Many Darwinists here might also reply that one needs to see chance as cumulative. In this way, as with a nine-digit number, once one has the first number, the odds of what the number will be are reduced (if these processes are cumulative). As more digits come into place, the odds on what digits are possible are reduced. But that presupposes that the problem with things like amino acids by way of this analogy is that the odds of each link are not astronomical. Each stage along the way is astronomical rather than being a one in ten chance of getting one particular digit. It is also not clear that amino acids are linked together step by step in this fashion, rather than needing to come together all at once for things to work. Like with a lock, one does not know when one has the right combination. One cannot just claim one is right with the first number and then start working on the second. One needs to get all three in a row. It is not a matter of taking any old number as the first.

The key to unlocking the origin of life is showing chemicals coming together in the laboratory into larger mole-

---

[25] Meyer, *Signature in the Cell*, 226.

cules that are able to self-reproduce. I am not aware of any chemical experiment showing this. We did see, however, a computer experiment that could do this. But that was not a matter of random mutation.

The one who has most laid out the problems with a biological theory of life's development that puts chance at the forefront has been Lee Spetner in his aptly titled *Not By Chance: Shattering the Modern Theory of Evolution*. In this text, Spetner undermines the idea that the development of life could have occurred simply by random variation, as such randomness cannot give rise to the changes needed if one is to trace a history from the first string of DNA to a human being. As Spetner notes, the main reason Darwinism is seen as the basis of modern atheism is due to its reliance on chance and conclusion—that all that life is but a "cosmic accident."[26]

Spetner, unlike almost all critics of Darwinism, is not satisfied just in showing the implausibility of Darwinism, but also develops his own theory that attempts to show that

> the capacity to adapt to a variety of environments is built into the organism. The environment induces the expression of its capacity. Cues from the environments combine with the information in the genes to develop the form of the organism. (*NBC* xi)

This view, of course, contradicts Darwinism, since it posits nonrandom and directional development. Spetner, like most critics of Darwinism, does not posit a divine creation from nothing to account for life as "life comes only from life" and thus has to have a material origin (*NBC* 2). Like most creationists, we only advocate a creation out of nothing at the origin of being itself. Life has not always been around. It has an origin, but not at the origin of existence

---

[26] Lee Spetner, *Not By Chance: Shattering the Modern Theory of Evolution* (New York: Judaica, 1998), viii. All subsequent citations indicated as *NBC*.

itself.

Spetner attempts to show that, at its origin, life had built into itself capacities that only later arose. For example, one might say populations of organisms have the size and shape they do due to outside factors like "starvation or diseases," but the evidence actually shows that it is something built into animals that controls how many offspring they have or, with plants, "by sensing the density of the planting" (*NBC* 16). The information for doing this is already in the seed of the plant. Spetner repeats the idea that we have articulated here that even positive developments in the development of life would be lost completely or degraded by further deleterious mutations. The odds on positive mutations even being around long enough to be passed on are slim. But Darwinism has to argue that positive mutations not only occur frequently enough to be passed on, but that they must be passed on to whole populations (*NBC* 52). Spetner notes that such positive mutations have a better chance of being spread through the whole population if the population is small, but, if the population is small, then the chances of getting such a mutation increase radically (*NBC* 56–57).

Now, high rates of mutation can occur if an organism is subject to radiation or toxic chemicals, but there is not much evidence this has occurred often in the history of life (*NBC* 58). Darwinism thus needs a high random mutation rate, but, if that rate is too high, there is devolution, as the organism will be overwhelmed by deleterious mutations. Darwinism needs to find a Goldilocks mutation rate. What is interesting is that creatures like flies do not seem to mutate any faster than creatures slightly larger than them or more diversified. Point mutations and other random changes also almost only "juggle existing genes" rather than adding new genetic information (*NBC* 62). Unless one adds the insights of the likes of anti-Darwinists Margulis and Sandin, there is little way for new information to accumulate rather than be shuffled. In this way, it's not surprising that, given the way mutation rates work, something like a horse would need "50 million births" to produce one evolutionary step (*NBC* 97). For this reason, Spetner investigates the possibility that genomes are stacked decks in which genetic functions get turned on when needed, or that one change needs to lead to a cascade at various points for true change to occur (*NBC* 65). Spetner concludes that, per his calculations, one would need 500 individual steps of positive mutation for speciation per purely Darwinian mechanisms (*NBC* 98). But here we are faced with a lock combination where each stage has a low probability and must link to each following stage.

Against Darwinism, Spetner draws upon experimental research to try to show that mutations only occur when they are needed, as mutations generally "do not occur when they are not needed" (*NBC* 159). Here, Spetner points to bacteria that mutated in the lab to be able to digest a new chemical when its normal food supply was no longer available (*NBC* 149–154). These bacteria, when put under environmental stress, exceeded Behe's edge of evolution by developing multiple positive mutations. Such an improbable occurrence, due to environmental stress, suggests non-Darwinian mechanisms at work. Spetner thereby concludes that it is the plasticity of the organism's genetic code in combination with the environment that enables change. Note I do not here distinguish between the genome and genetic code. Doing so leads to the belief that only part of our DNA is significant (the part involved in making proteins), but all of the genome is part of our software, and even what was once considered 'junk' has functions.

But not all genetic information is found in what is referred to in molecular biology as the genetic code. The rest of the DNA is a mosaic of other structures and sequences. This DNA is not only part of the software for sending info to the cellular machinery. While the genetic code might have its operating set of instructions, the rest of the genome as modular units, for instance, inserted by viruses, might have distinct and unrelated algorithmic rules. It will not be rules for generating proteins. Since the genome is the way we can specify species and is composed via Lamarkianism it must all be seen as key to understanding an organism as well the development of life. This is not to say that the genetic code as that which is elated to proteins is not important. It is but subsequence of the genome. Codons specify what amino acids are to be manufactured. However, mitochondria have a different code for proteins, and that code would need to be a part of any attempt to understand the cell itself with its hardware computationally.

At the same time, even if we just speak of the genetic code and not the overall genome, there are a seemingly endless number of possible genetic codes that could arise as well as genome sequences. Nonetheless, the genetic code that is part of the genome we have is used by almost all life forms and thus has an unreality about it. All of life is about making essentially the same proteins in essentially the same way, for instance. At the same time, the rest of the genome is made of a mosaic of subroutines that are themselves modular units repeated throughout the fabric of life. Not only does that imply that all of life is part of the same fabric and history, but that it has a unique origin.

The genetic code—but also the genome itself—refers to a unique origin. But how it formed when so many other possibilities are conceivable is yet to be explained. There would not be enough time in the history of the universe to produce the genetic code or genome at the origin here, and that is universally used via blind, random permutations. This code specifies things in such a way that it appears like software and thus assigns values and functions in particular ways. The overall genome itself does not use a hodgepodge of subsequences, but a very finite set of possibilities. But, of course, we are focusing here more so on how the environment can affect how the genome itself and the information it contains are expressed. For instance, change in embryonic development due to environmental stress in just "the timing of a molecular signal" can lead to physical changes (*NBC* 180). Spetner believes the environment induces such changes. Spetner also points to genetic recombination such as occurs during sexual reproduction and notes this is not random, as it follows rules for combination and thus cannot be strictly classified as Darwinian in nature (*NBC* 186).

Spetner notes ways new information can be added but does not note lateral gene transfer. However, his main point is that the large amount of information in organisms has accumulated, remained, and has a plasticity in its own coding and articulation that allows for change to occur by design rather than via mere chance. Many changes we see in species are due to changes in their physical traits without any change in their DNA code, such as the way birds will have differing beak shapes simply due to eating different types of seeds from birth (and note how Darwin himself focused on such differences) (*NBC* 203). Fish living in cold versus warm water show differences that seem to appear only due to how the fish develop from the egg onwards due to the water's temperature (*NBC* 208). We see such changes in humans, such as Eskimos, where, due to the influence of cold temperature on them from the start, they have shorter arms than people living at the equator (*NBC* 207). We should therefore not be quick to think any change we see is due to some mutation. It might be the same code at work being expressed and articulated differently leading to different results simply due to the environment.

The code itself, in almost all organisms, is so long that it includes many aspects that are unexpressed. One need not change any aspect of the code itself but only to allow for those unexpressed genes to be turned on for significant phenotypical changes to occur. To return to experiments on E. Coli, Spetner cites research showing that, when E. Coli only has lactose to digest, a dormant gene that enables it to do so turns on (*NBC* 190). What Spetner is showing is that, given that random mutation is not enough, one must look to the very interaction of organisms with their environments to show how change occurs. Of course, the changes appearing are only further examples of microevolution.

§5
THE DEVELOPMENTALIST CRITIQUE OF COMPUTATIONALISM

Since Spetner published his work in the late 1990's, evolutionary biology has begun to incorporate Spetner's observations concerning the role of the environment and epigenetic changes. Of course, Spetner's text is not mentioned, since Spetner is an outlier articulating a theory that ultimately attempts to justify intelligent design, but his review of the literature has been confirmed through these later texts. Perhaps most prominent among these new interpretations of the empirical evidence is a text by Eva Jablonka and Mary Lamb entitled *Evolution in Four Dimensions*. In this text, a developmental view is presented in which the nature and composition of an organism is explained, in large part via the influence of environmental factors, rather than via genetics. That is, epigenetic change is put forth as having a fundamental role to play in how creatures appear. Also, epigenetics involves how changes in appearance (the phenotype) can themselves be inherited. Here, we do not simply see changes in cellular hardware inherited, but also changes that appear on a larger scale. The DNA itself cannot explain these change and do not code from them but, rather, changes in other parts of the creature occur during its lifetime and are passed on. Thus, Jablonka and Lamb argue directly for a Lamarckian view.

However, the DNA itself is not changed and only

changes in the cell or some other part of the organism occurs without genetic factors being involved. Jablonka, in particular, focuses on DNA methylation, wherein a methyl group of chemicals is added to the DNA sequence and thus affects how the DNA is able to express itself and articulate its instructions.[27] Thus, while the code remains the same, it is bound and delimited, and, thus, delimitation, as a changer to the cellular hardware, is passed on. Jablonka and Lamb also believe that information and changes can be passed on via, for instance, the milk of a mother. In this way, what a mother experiences is transferred to an offspring still very much in a formative stage. It is the very plasticity of the child that affects things. The authors here also like the example of a mother rat that does not lick its offspring and that this stimulation (or lack thereof) is linked to the methylation of the genome that can then be transferred on. Here, information and variation are transmitted from one generation to the next via non-DNA routes. DNA is only one form in which information is encoded and transmitted. There can also be changes to the cytoplasm of a germ cell and, thus, these changes in hardware can be passed on. The key is that a variation in the phenotype is occurring independent of DNA and its processes. Jablonka believes that, in order to understand how an organism comes to appear phenotypically as it does, one has to look at DNA in addition to the cellular machinery of the organism (whether that be cytoplasm or organelles) as well as the organism's environment (including its earliest context of parental care) and its cultural contexts (in which behaviors can be transmitted). Whatever change can be transmitted would be one that will account for how a particular type of organism arises rather than how one individual does. But this also means it is occurring outside of random mutation, for instance.

---

[27] Eva Jablonka and Mary Lamb, *Evolution In Four Dimensions: Genetic, Epigenetic, Behavioral, and Symbolic Variation in the History of Life* (New York: Bradford, 2006), 128–144.

Also, if a change occurs in mice due to being poisoned, and future generations inherit this change, then there is no natural selection at work, as it was not that one type of mouse died off and another did not, but simply a change via the environment that is passed on if all embryos in such a situation survive. The womb itself can be seen, for instance, as the environment of a very plastic offspring that changes and gets a different phenotype based on the conditions of the womb. These changes are then passed down to the other generations. One might think here that these changes in cellular hardware or via the environment are completely incompatible with a computational view, but the key here is that Jablonka is not giving examples of how the actual genome changes. This means we see the program unfolding, but change occurs on another level, affecting it. But that environment can be included in a computation. If one wanted to simulate the changes on a computer, for instance, one can code for the environ-ment itself and how it will affect the computation. Also, the key here is that information is being transmitted. When we examine organisms, we do not necessarily want to know how they will appear phenotypically in one environment rather than another. We want, rather, to know how their most basic hardware and software takes on its composition.

Changes in hardware can be mapped computationally, as can the changes in any other thing. For instance, one could see the changes in a rock formation from erosion. One would then look to see if the changes follow a pattern or not. If one has a creature with the same DNA code, one always has a creature that can change back to another state due to an inverse set of environmental influences. There are not seemingly irreversible changes here. Ultimately, one has to ask how fundamental epigenetic changes are if the DNA coding is not affected. Is it like, for instance, the difference between identical human twins? Certainly, they are slightly different. But, even if one replays things in different environments, it is not clear that one is not showing that there is an actual invariant core throughout these variations. If we replayed the history of a life form the fist cell and produced the entirety of forms, we might generate changes; but, if they were like the differences between identical twins, it is not clear we see this as an essential difference or ultimately significant. We would still have life starting from the fist cell and would still see the same life forms pass in and out of existence.

Many also see in epigenetic change a reinforcement of the idea that only microevolution is important, since one sees a change within kinds without a change in kind. Epigenetic change shows how something can change without there being fundamental changes at the level of its continuously inherited DNA. Thus, one has the instructions not for producing a thing, but a variation on it, like members of a family or identical twins. The influence of environment is not seen as inherently based on chance. While it may seem contingent, that presupposes that there is not some more all-encompassing view one cannot take with respect to the development of life itself, whereby those change do fit into a neat pattern.

While, in the work of Jablonka and Lamb, there is not a direct critique of a computationalist view, this is not the case in the key work of Richard Lewontin, *The Triple Helix*. Lewontin criticizes Sydney Brenner's alleged claim

> that if [Brenner] had the complete sequence of DNA of an organism and a large enough computer then he could compute the organism.[28]

I do not know if or where Brenner made this claim, but Lewontin, of course, argues that, with DNA alone, one could not know how an organism would appear in all its details. One would also need to know the particular cellular machine reading the DNA and the role of the environment.

---

[28] Richard Lewontin, *The Triple Helix: Gene, Organism, and Environment* (Cambridge: Harvard University Press, 2002), 10. All subsequent citations indicated as *TH*.

But this is presumably what Brenner means when he says he needs a "large enough computer." A computer with enough computational power would run all the possible permutations for how DNA could be read and how it could develop. That is, one computes here not how, for instance, a particular person looks, but all the possible permutations of how that person could look. Thus, one would not need to know the particular environment in which one was raised or the particulars of cellular machinery as all the variations would be tried.

What remains invariant is only the DNA itself, the genome, throughout. This invariance shows that what is essential to any creature is, at least in part, this one routine, this one set of letters, the software known as DNA. Now, of course, one needs all the added cellular machinery to interpret and assemble the DNA, but this can be done by various types—although not all. Lewontin is under the mistaken impression that computationalism is a form of "pre-formationism" insofar as it claims that

> the organism is already formed in the fertilized egg and the view that the complete blueprint of the organism and all the information necessary to specify it is contained there. (*TH* 6)

But DNA is not a blueprint; it is not a complete map that is the very thing itself in miniature. It is only a set of letters. That set of letters can be read and realized in multiple ways. The set of letters has no meaning in itself outside of its being read. A reading enacts it. It is only executed by something reacting to it. This is why it is a set of instructions.

Computationalism is about how an organism unfolds, but one cannot predict what it will be from its initial state and the instructions that form it. It is the differentiation of information that does this. A fully computational view of any specific developed organism would include a compiling of not just an organism's DNA, but also its cellular machinery as well as its environment. The idea that the environment in which an organism develops cannot be included in its computation is part of the classic mistake Lewontin repeats. Lewontin presents an image of multiple of the same plant with the same genome developing different due to growing at different elevations (*TH* 21). In this example, clippings of the same plant have been planted in the varying environment. One sees, via the image Lewontin provides, the permutations one and the same creature with the exact same genome and even the same cellular machinery can go through.

But there is no reason why such a schema cannot be simulated on even the computers we have today—much less a very large and very powerful one. Having the complete DNA and genome, we could, in fact, compute all the various scenarios Lewontin produces because we could vary its development in terms of new environment. We thus see how what is invariant in each, by Lewontin's own admission, is a basic program. This program certainly has subroutines, of which DNA is one. It has a collection of different software of different types, but that does not mean we cannot compute the organism. In fact, we should look at the experiment Lewontin provides as precisely a computation of one and the same organism—its permutation and transformation. Lewontin has this misconception that, for computationalism, a DNA string computes itself on its own—as though simply the chemicals composing DNA alone do this. But no one has ever made such a claim, to my knowledge. DNA is not software and hardware together, but only one type of software in a cell.

Cells do compute, but the fact that anything exists in an environment does not subtract from that. When we want to find the invariant essence of a thing, we only get a string of letters or subroutine. This is an abstraction made flesh. But it is still a program. Also, the environment in which life develops is itself a function of life. This is called Gaia. Thus, any individual organism is caught up with ontogeny in an interaction with the very context life has made. Lewontin is also here focusing on phenotypic differences. But we are not always necessarily interested in phenotypic differences, precisely because the environment could play such a key role in differentiating between how even two identical plants appear. That one can take any of the plants in Lewontin's example, plant them at a different elevation, and obtain the same plant as was planted there is what is essential. If a plant will, if transferred, look only certain ways in certain environments, then this is what we want to know to thereby find out what is invariant in it. The plant does not turn into a butterfly. One environment does not produce the same things.

This is why we need to compile the entire sequence (DNA plus cell plus environment) to see precisely what role each plays. It may be that DNA is, for instance, the source code, while the environment plays the more superficial role of isolated subroutine affecting only specific parameters, or it may be like an oracle function that is externally imposed on what the more basic program outputs. Reading Lewontin, one would guess that biologists of the recent past, present, and, more importantly, future should resign themselves to only ever running experiments via plantings and chemical labs rather than using computers to learn about organisms, their histories, and their ontogeny. But the sheer power of computation has (and will more and more so) disproved the likes of Lewontin. Lewontin would have to argue there is something inherently incomputable about the environment itself.

Lewontin also believes environments are contingent, but that overlooks how, for the history of life, the most important environment is the one made by life itself and thus is itself an unfolding of the organisms themselves. Lewontin's view would make something like cloning into a mystery. But his own examples of plants show that one and the same phenotype can be produced if one makes use of the same environment. Lewontin claims that phenotypical change alters the instructions involved, but he cannot give an example of how the genome is changed in his example of plants growing at different elevations (*TH* 21–25). It is clear, on the other hand, that changes in the programming do cause phenotypic changes. If Lewontin were willing to be more anti-Darwinian than he is and advocate Lamarckianism he could show how changes outside of DNA related processes occur and are inherited. Lewontin is right that if one has a recipe for a cake and burns it, the cake comes out different, but it is also true that if one bakes it at five degrees hotter nothing will occur. Thus, the baking has to be included if one wants to know why the cake came out looking as it does.

Lewontin is also keen on criticizing the idea that DNA 'self-replicates,' but DNA is only ever software and thus is instructions. Instructions are in themselves meaningless. But the fact that replication occurs on the level of the cell itself does not change the fact that the DNA, in itself, is purely letters waiting to be permuted. Lewontin also brings up the issue of 'noise.' He argues there is "*developmental noise*, a consequence of random events within cells at the level of molecular interactions" (*TH* 36). Presumably, Lewontin wants to say that there is variation that is not a product of the genetic code and not a product of the environment and not even the interaction between the two. Rather, there is a third dimension of noise that accounts for changes in an organism and for how it develops. But this overlooks how the cell itself may have all sorts of error-correcting codes to deal with this noise, just as occurs today in transfers of digital information. Also, this noise is taken to be fully random, but in our world there is only ever pseudo-randomness that is itself a product of rules a la Wolfram. Thus, pointing to noise does not itself cause consternation for the computationalist view.

The one example where Lewontin claims directly that a computer cannot do something comes in terms of protein folding (*TH* 73). Here, Lewontin argues we do not have the rule for how proteins fold and that this folding is specified neither by DNA nor by amino acids made by DNA. Thus, the folding pattern of any protein will always be unique to the specific cell in which it occurs. Here, the folding only occurs if all the intervening processes occur one after the other, and those formations occur only if the cell is in the right, general environment. But the fact that no one has succeeded, yet, in emulating or simulating this process on a program does not mean it will not. But it will not occur based on predicting the folding of the protein molecule based on the DNA sequence. Rather, computationalism always puts forth the principle of computational irreducibility. And this principle insists that, while one can compute this process, it cannot be predicted. It can only ever be simulated or emulated.

One cannot predict what a cellular automata will look like, given its rules, so why would one be able to predict protein folding? The point is to simulate and emulate and not to predict having only the software. If the simulation does not take long to run, then one can say what the prediction is, but not until the simulation has run itself out. Here, the program appears to be so long and involved that it would take more efforts to simulate what is at stake here. Computationalism is not arguing that all the information that is needed is contained in DNA, for instance. There is no information in DNA. It does not contain semiotic signs that mean something to someone, but only syntactic information, only letters, only bits. And these bits are senseless in themselves. Lewontin believes that organisms construct their environment and that the environment, in turn, shapes the organism. But the organism can always be subtracted from an environment and placed into a new one.

That means one has to know what is invariant in the organism to be able to say how it will fare in the new environment. Computationalism gives one those tools. That organ-isms shape and change their environment does not mean that the environment itself is so plastic that it can allow any possibility. The environment taken on its own is a program that, via its programming, delimits possibilities and inputs only certain types of information. It is important to remember that we are contending that out of all the possibilities that exist for things, it is programming that delimits what actually occurs. Darwinism contends that natural selection does the work of delimitation, but we will have tried to show that contention is, at best, tautologous and lacks true explanatory power. If we have all possibilities, then we do not truly know anything. We only have knowledge and information when delimitation occurs.

This is, again, why not subtracting Gaia itself from any computational view is important. Lewontin criticizes the idea of "ecological niches" pre-existing in the "absence of organisms so that when the organisms evolved on Mars they would come to occupy those empty niches" (*TH* 51), but, even though life itself constructs Gaia, there are elements of Gaia that are part of programming running independent of Gaia, such as what occurs under the crust of the planet or what arrives from outer space. There is always a programmed context in which living software develops even if the development of life shapes it. That is, even if it is an abstraction to view the organism outside of any environment, it is necessary, since one can put an organism in any environment just as one can run one and the same program on any number of platforms.

While Lewontin thinks computation is just a "trendy metaphor" (*TH* 38), it is, in our view, the only hope for making biology a hard science, for demonstrating many theories, and for making any real predictions or retrodictions. Thankfully, because it is not just a trend, but the future itself, there is not too much to worry about when it comes to Lewontin's criticisms here. DNA as software is not something that is destroyed when it interacts with other things. It is preserved precisely because it is a source code and one that is stored materially. This is what DNA signals—that moment when information is not simply found in an interaction but is formed as a material subset within a thing. It can thus be read over and over again in different environments. It exists, therefore, as a text outside its interpretation. It is not changed by that interaction for the most important, by its reading. Whereas a cloud is ended when it develops rain, DNA is not so destroyed. Even if the same DNA sequence can be read in more than one way and be the first step in chains leading in different directions, this is not different than how four different letters can be combined into 24 different words four letters long. That one and the same DNA can lead to different appearances, but also that different genomes can lead to similar phenotypes, shows us that DNA is only one subset of the overall code. But computation is just as plastic. One and the same basic set of instructions can be varied to produce a large variety of cellular automata.

§6
FURTHER CRITICISMS OF BIOLOGICAL DARWINISM

It is important to continue to highlight the problems with the Darwinian paradigm before being able to articulate a different approach, since only through noting the failures of Darwinism can one see the type of phenomena a true theory of the development of life would need to account for. Some of these problems have to do not only with the origin of life already noted, but also with the origin of sexual reproduction (which makes no sense from a Darwinian perspective, as half of the genetic information is discarded when sex cells are made, and that is too costly and too problematic to be selected for via natural selection). Sex through recombination seems to make diversity more likely, but, at the same time, it has lead to a much lower birth rate. Darwinism would have to argue it arose via random mutation, but it is not clear what mutation would induce it. Margulis can explain multicellularity, potentially, but she can only do so by emphasizing symbiogenesis, not competition. Consciousness for evolution is also a mystery.

In addition to these issues, the fossil record does not show gradual evolution. It shows abrupt and sudden emergence of new kinds. Fossils from an older section of rock are almost the same as the same type of organism fossilized in a more recent layer. Such problems, of course, lead to the famous theory of "punctuated equilibrium." But this theory seems to do no more than describe the issue, rather than explain how it occurred. It does not say how or why as much as restate what the fossil record shows. Darwinism, in its traditional garb, requires gradualism. Darwin himself was honest enough in his *Origin of Species* to admit that gaps in the fossil record were a problem for his theory. One needs a theory that explains why species persist in unchanged form and only suddenly emerge into new ones. This is one of the reasons the notion of irreducible complexity is so important. When species appear, they appear in a way that is not reducible to their predecessors. For a Darwinian, a land animal becoming aquatic (per the current theory) would have to undergo a series of subtle and small changes with very large creatures exemplifying them existing over a long time. But there are simply no bones to be found showing this. Rather, we see whale skeletons stretching back to a particular point and then suddenly ceasing to appear. Darwinism would say that every single individual whale that ever lived was a 'transitional form' insofar as each one had some subtle, if small, difference in its coding. That's fine. But it still does not give us the fossils we need. It still, at most, calls for an explanation of how the code suddenly leads from a creature not at all like a whale to a whale. If subtle micro changes make all the difference, then why is it that only the 100th suddenly breaks the proverbial camel's back rather than the 101st?

One here has to show a reptile giving birth to a bird or something clearly bird-like. That's a fairly radical mutation. One also has to imagine it happening, possibly, multiple times at roughly the same time. Now, perhaps species stasis is due to populations growing larger and larger, such that it is more difficult for mutations to spread, but, at the same time, we see that small, inbred populations often simply refine and emphasize certain quirks of their founders (think of the Hapsburgs or toy poodles) rather than diversifying or leaping suddenly to something radically new. It is precisely Darwinism that nicely shows us microevolution, in which things like an elk's antlers become so large that

Divine Name Verification | 63

they are impractical. But that is change within a type. That is, we find two reptiles (to return to the earlier example) that inbreed, refining the type inbred but not becoming bird-like. And, if inbreeding in such small groups does lead to the jumps, we then need a theory that explains why, at the level of code, such recombination of similar material has this effect, since it is something similar combining. The difference between two separately born human siblings can be as little as 30 base pairs out of billions.

Gould insists that evolution is purely contingent. That means any species can suddenly go extinct as much as suddenly leap to a new form. But if the process causing the leaps is itself regular or a function of the fundamental code governing all life, then it appears nonrandom. Even if meteorites are responsible for all life—if the universe itself is run by a code and life itself is part of the universe—it may not be contingent in the sense of a matter of blind chance. Gould would have us believe that life would not evolve again if, for instance, a meteorite destroyed the specific primordial soup where it arose. But are we truly aware of chemical processes that require such special conditions that they can only happen once in the entire history of the earth? We may have to decide that different genomes are ultimately part of one genome, which forms an operating system that gave rise to the entirety of life itself ('Gaia') and that the system is itself unfolding in a nonrandom way. That Gaia is a part of a universe also unfolding per its own coding means that meteorites striking the earth are no longer contingent in Gould's sense of being blind and onetime random accidents. Interactions between creatures are expressions of an underlying genomic code that brought about the entire living surface of the planet. Organisms would then be specific informational patterns and instantiations of code, themselves interacting but not divested from the code itself. We would have to see individual organisms as subroutines of the overall code. In the same way we would not believe that the interaction of computer programs is simply a matter of blind forces and not somehow itself determined by the code, we should not see something like punctuated equilibrium as some contingent mystery that we can only record.

Microevolution, punctuated equilibrium, etc., would then be no more a product of non-design than a musical composition on a player piano. Darwinism argues that it can account for some of these issues by the idea that a single genetic subroutine has multiple phenotypic effects such that any changes to it will have a cascade of effects. But most common point mutations do not lead to such effects. Leaps from one kind to another in the fossil record that includes long stretches of organisms repeating without change before an abrupt change present the new formation of one life form, but Darwinism needed there to be gradual changes from one type to the next.

Jerry Fodor and Massimo Piatelli-Palmarini have articulated a critique of natural selection itself on epistemological grounds. They agree that the role of random mutation and selection has been entirely exaggerated in terms of the role it plays in the development of life. Fodor and his co-author note that evolution is not about optimization, but about, at best, a creature coming to fit its environmental niche, as creatures remain unchanged when their environment remains the same.[29] Evolution in this way should not be thought about as bringing about the best possible organism, but only what will exist well in an environment. For this reason, many different solutions can arise for the same problems, as the issue is not finding the best solution, but only what will enable survival (*WDGW* 22). The history of life shows that many different types of organisms can come from only very subtle changes to the same set of genetic code and by the activation of previously dormant code (*WDGW* 31). Fodor and his co-author are highly skeptical of the idea of constant mutation rates and argue

---

[29] Jerry Fodor and Massimo Piatelli-Palmarini, *What Darwin Got Wrong* (New York: Picador, 2011), 10. All subsequent citations indicated as *WDGW*.

the empirical research does not show that there is a fixed rate of mutation for all possible cases (*WDGW* 33). The authors also emphasize that, before a mutation would ever be able to articulate itself phenotypically, for example, it has to undergo several processes that occur only at the genetic level such that a mutation occurring at the genotype level at one point does not guarantee anything at any later stage (*WDGW* 39).

Fodor and his co-author are again, on the basis of empirical research, forced, like Spetner, to suggest that environmental situations produce changes. They point to the Dutch famine from 1944-1945 that led to women giving birth to smaller and lower-weight babies (*WDGW* 66–67). What is interesting is that not only did these women have such babies, but their granddaughters also did, even though they did not live in famine-like conditions (*WDGW* 66). The research seems to indicate that it was actually something that occurred in sperm formation itself during the famine as well as issues in the formation of the eggs in the grandmothers that led to the issue (*WDGW* 67). However, there is no known genetic change in these people. That is, the change is inherited without any genetic change to be inherited. My guess is that the code was altered at some level in both sperm and egg and during their recombination. But it was due to environmental stress. Or the hardware itself was altered and damaged, and this change in the hardware itself is recorded non-genetically and passed on with every cell duplication (*WDGW* 67). We therefore have to consider that changes in hardware itself might be able to influence the development of life itself and not just changes in software.

Such changes probably have to occur at the cellular level or smaller. But such a view is decisively Lamarckian in character. It is not just Lamarckian at the level of code, but also at the level of hardware. The cytoplasm, chromosomes, and bacteria in a creature can be passed on to offspring insofar as they inhabit the interiors of any cell or, at least, the reproductive sex cells. If one has symbiotic entities in the sperm and/or egg, then it is passed on without being included in the coding as such. It is a hardware feature that was acquired. It is part of a system at the scales of interacting parts and structures. Such nesting of parts and structures in the hardware itself is different from how things work at the level of the code letters, and one needs an analysis of both to understand life and its workings. One can have symbionts inside symbionts here—and those passed on in a way that bypasses the code itself insofar as it is part of the hardware—but that does to mean that one need forget about code and its differential and relational structure.

The authors of *What Darwin Got Wrong* probably articulate their most unique contribution to anti-Darwinism when they argue that to rely on natural selection as an explanatory principle is to rely on a tautology and that natural selection cannot overcome the free-rider problem. Natural selection seems to be a purely circular point. It says that what survived survived because it did survive. What survived was fit to its environment and thereby survived, but something is fit only because it survives. An example of a free rider is the noises made by the heart. One can never tell if, for example, a particular heart configuration was selected for the noise made by the heart or the configuration, since one never comes without the other (WDGW 100–101). A heart makes noise. And the noise cannot be separated from the heart. But one can never know if it was the noise that was selected or some other aspect of the heart. Of course, common sense says that heart noise is just a free rider and is inconsequential. The noise is only selected because something else about the heart is. But there is no epistemological way for Darwinism to show that, given its principles. It can only say that something with such a heart survived because it did, in fact, survive. One cannot say here that if one trait of the heart had not been selected, neither would have the noise, because the two always are joined.

Given the problems with Darwinism, Fodor and his coauthor ultimately argue for a non-theoretical perspective.

That is, they believe that biology will have to just become a form of natural history where one researches the "invariably post hoc" way life did in fact develop, in the same way as human history charts how one damn thing happened after another without any necessary underlying rule (*WDGW* 149). No system will be in the offering—only a sequential tale of what the archeological evidence suggests one can infer. There will then be many causal chains, but no over-arching pattern (*WDGW* 160). In other words, biology has no hopes of being a hard science like physics. I think this is mostly a cop out and an appeal to ignorance.

This is not to say that Darwinism does not highlight biological phenomena that it seems best able to explain. Darwinism wants to say it can best explain through natural selection why more offspring occur for one type of individual than for others. But it only truly states this tautologically. Darwinists like to point to 'vestigial organs' as a point in their favor. But, most often, allegedly vestigial organs turn out to have a function. Tonsils were once thought to be useless. They also, at best, show that there is modification with descent, but that only eliminates the idea that creatures appear ready, made out of nothing. That is, it merely notes change itself. Darwinists believe they only need to show that life has changed over time. They then think any explanation for that change is a point in their favor. But Darwinism is a specific theory with a specific viewpoint. If it fails, there still might be descent with modification, but an entirely different theory might explain it with differing results (such as this change being nonrandom). A theory that can accept any explanation for descent with modification is a poorer theory than one that argues for particular mechanisms and can explain why those mechanisms are the right ones. And not all theories will advocate gradual change.

Natural selection can lead to genetic drift via reproductive isolation. Such isolation concentrates a population, which then inbreeds. But that means, more so, that it is the act of inbreeding and recombination that drives evolution rather than natural selection itself. For instance, a population of birds might be separated. But they might be isolated simply due to a change in how they sing rather than any geographical isolation. And this isolation might occur due to environmental stress. When one part of a population is separated from another, a new variety occurs. The separated population may have only part of the genetic information that the entire population had. But what this shows is that natural selection is actually playing a marginal role, since natural selection chooses the same thing over and over again. It is not only when like merges with like due to inbreeding that genetic variety arises.

Natural selection is, then, anti-diversity. If anything, it works *against* evolution. Darwinists also claim there is non-functional or 'junk DNA,' but again, this is usually due to our not knowing how this extra genetic material plays a role or contains future possible uses in a dormant state. Darwinists believe these sections of DNA contain only code that was useful to some ancestors. But how does random mutation or natural selection show why such genes could be rendered inert? Can Darwinism explain how so much DNA accumulated without positing several gradual steps that could lead to so much duplicate DNA for instance? This so-called 'junk DNA' might guide any number of processes at the genetic level.

One of the favorite examples of Darwinists is human childbirth. They claim it is disastrous, given the infant mortality rate for most of human history. If one claims, per this view, it is a product of design, then one has to posit a flawed designer. Human children have large brains, but they must be closely attended to for years, as opposed to other creatures, making them vulnerable. Humans cannot give birth to as many offspring as other creatures. But it is then Darwinism that actually has the problem, because, unless it can directly be shown how human childbirth occurred due to random chance, it does not appear to be something that would ever be selected for (I will return to the issue of such things being alleged disproof of design later). Darwinists look to the giraffe that has a laryngeal nerve taking a circuitous path rather than taking the shortest possible path between two points. But it could simply be that that path was needed so that not too much blood flowed at once to the giraffe's head. At this point, we can simply say that design need not be what we assume to be is the most logical or efficient design. Design need only be the product of something programmed.

§7
Convergence

There are more important phenomena that Darwinism needs to account for that speak against its orientation. Cambridge paleontologist Simon Conway Morris, the very paleontologist who presented and analyzed the Burgess Shale fossils, is responsible for the concept of 'convergence' which he mainly outlined and defended in his book *Life's Solution: Inevitable Humans in a Lonely Universe*. Convergence names how biological organisms that are only distantly related develop the same or analogous systems.[30]

The most famous example of such a common development is, of course, the eye. Eyes have developed several times by several different creatures that only are remotely connected and have, as far as things go, very different genomes and phenotypes. Morris suggests that convergence occurs because there are only a "finite set of natural forms that will recur and over again anywhere in the cosmos where there is carbon-based life" (*LS* 11). Convergence is an indisputable aspect of life itself and something confirmed by several empirical examples. From distinct and different pathways, life ends up coming to the same endpoint over and over again.

Morris suggests that this repetition of similar life sys-

---

[30] Simon Conway Morris, *Life's Solution: Inevitable Humans in a Lonely Universe* (New York: Cambridge University Press, 2003), 11. All subsequent references indicated as *LS*.

tems suddenly developing in varying contexts might simply be due to life sharing "one code" (*LS* 21). Morris is not willing to argue that the genetic code characterizing life on Earth is "the best possible code," but admits that this code has been astonishingly effective at producing a diversity of life forms (*LS* 18). Morris is skeptical that such a code can be the "product of selection," but it is not clear how selection could not be again anything more than a tautology such that this code survived because it survived (*LS* 18). It also presupposes that there were multiple other self-reproducing codes that somehow did not survive or that, from a chemical viewpoint, several different permutations were being attempted in some primordial soup. Just generating one code seems amazing. There are millions possible. To suggest that others were competing seems to simply project back onto a hypothetical primordial soup mechanisms that only work on life itself and may not have any true explanatory power.

Morris persuasively argues that if chance truly governed the development of life forms, then we would expect life to go in endless different directions and not keep returning to the same solutions over and over again (*LS* 121). Morris believes one has to relegate chance to the sidelines when explaining how, for instance, E. Coli "learns to get to grips with maltose," although he still seems to think that it is selection of the most adaptable things that leads to convergence at this point (*LS* 121–122). But adaption via selection works only in ever changing environments. Certainly on this planet, there are only so many environmental types, and they repeat themselves. But this view would say that life will converge on the same things in the same environments such that the seeming randomness of the sequence of local environments (if it is truly random, given Gaia's systematicity) would overlap with the finite capacities of life itself. One should, then, only see functional convergence but not the use of the same chemical apparatus and the same systems. If environmental changes were truly random along with life's internal development, then one should not expect to see convergence. One would see totally indiscriminate results.

Keep in mind that these environments are mainly made up of life itself. And environments are not determinative. Creatures in varying biospheric niches also demonstrate convergence. Convergence is not about the same stressors and environmental issues leading to the same solutions as such. Hugh Ross notes how chameleons and some fish have similar eyes, skin, and tongues and yet live in totally different conditions.[31] Totally random development and evolution would also have to include a lot of devolution in it, but we do not see it and, rather, see multiple examples where—from one creature to another—clear systems develop without setback. Robert Wright in his *Non-Zero: The Logic of Human Destiny*, for instance, notes how, from early humanoids to humanity, one sees brain sizes growing at a rapid pace without any interruptions.[32]

One of the main Darwinist responses to convergence is to insist that evolutionary events are singular and irreversible. One does not see lizards turning back into fish. First, humans do turn into fish when they create sperm, etc. But the idea of singular events only means that the development of life has directionality. It actually counts against Darwinism—with its mechanisms of blind natural selection and random mutation—that life does not backtrack, as that would show it is much more contingent and random. However, selection can only select something. In this way, it would have to be something more profound, like code itself, that offers up things to be selected. It is the code that is then pushing things in one direction more so than selection. Homeotic genes, for instance, may tell us how embryos should develop or may be the first set of directions leading to all biological structures.

Morris believes convergence minimizes the role of

---

[31] Ross, *More Than a Theory*, 168.
[32] Robert Wright, *Non-Zero: The Logic of Human Destiny* (New York: Vintage, 2001), 272.

chance to such a degree that he wonders at what point ("ape, mammal, fish, worm, or even single cell") something "humanoid" in character becomes "inevitable" (*LS* 234). For example, the fossil and biological evidence shows us "vertebrates converge in various ways on the mammal" and that legs are "highly probable" (Morris even sees parallel trajectories towards limbs in "Devonian fish") (*LS* 234). As we already saw, McGhee wants to say that convergence itself will be part of a biological picture that allows for the same kind of predictability we have in other scientific fields. Morris only allows for retrodiction. But that is mostly because he does not highlight the role of the genomic code. Morris's own findings show that evolution is not as open-ended as Darwinists would like. Morris suggests that—if there is only a finite set of biological forms possible, and life keeps arriving at them repeatedly—there might be an "eternal return" of the same forms the longer life develops and survives (*LS* 297). History will then become a matter of déjà vu more so than it already has as it goes on (only the current and ongoing mass extinction of species might prevent that or the development of a new code and new life such as robotic life). Given that Darwinism states that natural section works on unpredictable and singular events, there should not be such convergence. Morris suggests two main mechanisms for understanding convergence: attractors and physical constraints (*LS*). Convergence shows us how we are "in a constrained world, where all may not be possible" (*LS* 298). Morris contends that there might simply be certain physical laws of matter and chemistry that make only some types of carbon-based life possible. It would then not be a matter of a code playing itself out as much as the pressures and forces of the material world itself that play the fundamental causal role. This view certainly argues a view of life that sees it as non-contingent and non-random. But things like gravity probably only put a ceiling on things (how tall animals will grow, for instance) rather than actually shaping life itself in its particularity. It is programming that delimits possibilities.

As for 'attractors,' this seems to be a metaphor gone awry. With magnets, there is clearly an attracting force, but what would be the material attracting force here? Gravity attracts things to the earth, given its size, but it remains unrevealed how there is something pulling out eyes over and over again from biological flesh. The fact that convergence shows that the "replaying of the evolutionary tape" will have the same "predictable results" seems to be best explained by looking for the underlying rules in the genetic code itself and in the system it articulates in its iteration, rather than by positing 'attractors' that can only be detected in their effects (and for whom there is no material force detectable). Attractors simply become another name for an Aristotelian final cause. If a particular algorithm leads to the same numbers emerging as a result from it, are the numbers then attractors or the final causes of the algorithm? I do not think so.

The idea of an attractor returns us to Aristotle's acorn, which is attracted and directed by the final end and cause of the oak tree. It is a view that precisely ignores our new knowledge of how in the acorn itself we have a code that explains how the acorn unfolds in time into an oak. If one has rules iterating themselves, one does not have a need for attractors here. The development, then, is connected to the rules themselves and is intrinsic to them. But rules do not arise out of non-rules or out of the elements rules are made of. At some level, rules themselves are programmed in. Thus, we do not have to imagine some substantial form of oak-ness existing somewhere that haunts and dominates the process. The counter to seeing biological phenomena as contingent is not Aristotelianism.

The idea of convergence in and of itself undermines the idea that any contingencies that do occur in the history of life can ultimately prevent the same life forms from emerging by some other pathway: "contingencies of biological history will make no long-term difference to the outcome" (*LS* 328). This means we should stop seeing improbabilities (like the origin of life) as improbabilities and rather as outcomes of some process that is being played out in the history of life itself. Morris does not dismiss that life itself may have been created and programmed precisely with a code that enables convergence and explains it. He notes the dependence of life "on a handful of building blocks," how life takes functional pathways despite the overwhelming number of other physical possibilities, the manner in which pathways not taken would be deleterious for the life form, the emergence of complexity through the permutation of the same, basic underlying code, the existence of both amazing and beautiful diversity along with convergence, and that consciousness would, itself, be an inevitable result along with all the others (*LS* 329). Of course, Morris (unlike me) is completely agnostic: "For some it will remain as the pointless activity of the Blind Watchmaker, but others may prefer to remove their dark glasses. The choice, of course, is yours" (*LS* 330). While we agree that convergence would not prove the existence of God (only ontological/modal proofs do that), it does add weight to seeing life as programmed.

Now, some might say here that not all life has the same code as each genome is different. But look at cellular automata. One can have different sets of rules such that one has several variations. But, in each variation, one sees similar patt-erns emerge despite being based on different rules. For example, in John Conway's *Game of Life* artificial life simulator, one sees 'guns' and 'space ships' despite two different automata having different sets of rules. They are all parts of the same programming. We then see how two different sets of rules for how to play this cellular automata game come up with convergent forms. This is analogous to two creatures having different genomes and having similar forms, such as the eye. The difference in the genomes should not lead us to say the programming is not involved in the same way that we would not say the difference between Game of Life cellular automata 23 and 36 means something other than the program rules lead to the phenomena. 23 and 36 are simple variations on the same pos-

Divine Name Verification | 77

sibility space, given that they take place in the same grid and have the same general language for articulating their directions.

This would, then, be an explanation for homology. Homology simply names the structural affinities between systems in different creatures. One does not need the same exact code to get the same structure, in the same way that one does not need the same exact code in two 'Game of Life' automata for both to produce the 'glider' pattern. Here, from 0/1 and rules for operating on 0/1, we see the transformations of things—their evolution. These entities are always a relation between squares that are filled and those that are not. Structural homology thereby does not force one to refer even to a common ancestor—only to the same programming language. Many like to point out how, in frogs and humans limbs, digits grow in two different ways and yet look similar. This view does not rule out another level wherein there is symbiogenesis in which wholes merge with wholes. Such units are then plugged one into the other, but that might mean we have to look for the code for how such elements and patterns emerge at a different level than at the level of the genome alone.

Viewing code as crucial also reduces the issue of natural selection, as natural selection is not of primary importance: given the code, we will get similar results and convergence. In fact, if homologous structures were due just to the Darwinian mechanisms of natural selection and random mutation, homologous structures should be only controlled by the exact same coding, since such random occurrence should not occur twice.

There is also no persuasive reason that environmental forces will lead to two distinct creatures coming up with similar structures, much less many, in common. Creatures would simply each come up with unique and unheard of solutions. But we see that in Australia there are all sorts of marsupials, when we do not find them elsewhere. For this reason, just because two creatures do not need identical coding to come up with homologous features, it does not mean that it is precisely the code that is at work. I do not deny that creatures might have common ancestors. Chimps have many genes in the exact same order as we do, in the same places in the genome, with the same mutations recorded in it (*EE* 71). When we see such similar highly improbable sequences in two creatures that have such close similarity at the level of coding, it is likely that it is due to inheritance from a common source. But common ancestry, given a common programming language, need not be the only or even main explanation for structural affinities. As Jonathan Wells notes, we need a different way to explain homology, since the way Darwinism does is merely tautologous: Homology is said to come from common ancestry, but homology proves common ancestry.[33] Wells also argues that if we put automobiles (Corvettes from different years) alongside each other, we would see obvious homology, but, as Wells notes, that is due to intelligent agents designing them.[34] However, as many have noted, we are talking about machines that make other machines, just as Von Neumann's universal constructor did. Notice the difference between explaining such features using code (which is ultimately numbers, letters, differential relations, rules, etc.) and explaining things using a Platonic essence or Aristotelian substantial form that determines things by way of a final cause. In this way, there is no conflict between saying things are the result of code and that code is inherited and passed along from common sources.

At the same time, we will need to explain how the same code can lead to two different results in two different life forms. The same gene can play a key role in producing different structures. There need not be full correspondence between structure and gene. A gene, as we have said, is a subroutine. But, as we will see, such subroutines may only operate on rules that lead to other rules operating at a later

---

[33] Jonathan Wells, *Icons of Evolution: Science or Myth?* (Washington, DC: Regenery, 2002), 77–79.
[34] Wells, *Icons of Evolution*, 68–70.

point (I will return to this issue when discussing parallel processing). Having the same subroutine at the beginning may not, then, have to lead to the same result. One needs to look at the overall digital framework. But just having random point mutations, for instance, is unlikely to lead to the same or even similar structures. Additionally, a number of chemical processes do originate independently in various life forms. This means that the code itself is being assembled into place at the molecular level the same way by different pathways. There is convergence at the level code as much as at the level of phenotypes. The permutation of the letters at the level of the code as life itself develops leads to the same instructions appearing. Many would say this seems simply to be a result of random shuffling, given that this code only has four basic elements. But its sequential convergence should be surprising, given that that number of base pairs in humans is in the billions, and one here is talking about entire regions of genetics and strings of proteins with the same amino acid or nucleotide arrangement.

§8
LYNN MARGULIS AND PARTS, WHOLES, AND CODE

The work of Lynn Margulis does not focus on the level of the code (although she does not exclude it from her account), but rather at the level of parts and wholes. Margulis wants to show that life developed not through competition between organisms but by organisms uniting together to form networks: "Life did not take over the globe by combat, but by networking. Life forms multiplied and complexified by co-opting, not just by killing them."[35] Her most famous discovery and example (the one that perhaps should have marked her as the new Darwin) is, of course, that of mitochondria. Margulis demonstrated (although she met with fierce resistance from the Church of Darwinism) that the mitochondria had once been independent entities as much as any other cell. At some point, the mitochondria were engulfed by larger, single-celled organisms and became integrated into them. In this way, the mitochondrion is a part of a greater whole. It is a part that is detachable and independent. That is, the mitochondrion itself is a whole. Organisms are, then, at one level, assemblages made up of parts that can be wholes and wholes that are made up of parts. Margulis' first crucial discovery is thus that the de-

---

[35] Lynn Margulis and Dorion Sagan, *Microcosmos: Four Billion Years of Microbial Evolution* (New York: Touchstone, 1986), 17.

velopment of life is a mereological process.

But Margulis, interestingly, sees this symbiogenesis (the joining of two wholes such that one becomes part of the other whole) as irreversible. That is, Margulis does not describe processes where the mitochondrion exits a cell and becomes independent again. The mitochondrion becomes fully integrated into the cell and becomes a key organelle in its body. Margulis also likes the examples of slugs eating—but not digesting—algae, which then become part of the tissue of these animals and are passed on with reproduction (*AG* 13). While, today, we extract kidneys, for example, from our bodies and place them in others, this sort of phenomena does not seem to happen at the microbial level. A kidney is a system and structure. Margulis says that, once we reach eukaryotic cells, we have a structure that includes multiple structures within itself.

If such organelles only move in one direction, genetic information does not: "prokaryotes routinely and rapidly transfer different bits of genetic material to other individuals" (*AG* 17). Parts that are wholes are not transferred elements of the code. Bacteria, for instance, all can transfer sequences of their DNA between each other such that it does not make sense to say there are individual bacterial species. Bacteria, as it were, are constantly in sexual contact with each other, no matter where they are from, and such "bacterial sex" leads to the complication of all life and its code (*AG* 82). Such transfer does not just take place during the mating season, but at any point. It is all one interacting unit.

However, sequences of DNA are not parts in the same way that mitochondria are. These sequences are detachable. They are, therefore, parts that become whole. DNA is also part of the set of instructions and code. There is an aspect, then, of DNA and its letters that only makes sense as letters. That is, these entities are elements that are, at one level, purely relational in character, even though they can be captured and treated as unities and transferred. One should think of this along the lines of language itself. Mitochondria would be like a sentence. Mitochondria do not contain, however, the code for the organism. It only contains its own code. It is not a cell, like a kidney cell, in this way. A kidney, when taken out, still has our code in it. Since mitochondria do not have our code, it is not enough, again, to speak of parts and wholes. As a sentence, it could exist in any text. It can be a part of a whole or a whole with parts. DNA letters are like letters themselves. They make up words. They are phonemes that in one aspect only exist as differential relations (b/p in one language, or f/p in another).

As we have noted, there are other possible DNA based codes. There is very little that is not detachable and that cannot exist as a unit itself. To understand how this is so, think of Edmund Husserl's distinction between moments and pieces. Moments are something that cannot exist outside of a unity. They cannot become parts of another whole or independent wholes. Pitch (and here we have a good example of a material qualia as well) in the musical sense cannot exist except as united to sound. However, there are very few examples of this type. For example, we earlier used Fodor's example of heart sounds as free-riders. These sounds can exist separately from the heart. One could easily record them. It is possible that another phenomenon in nature could exactly reproduce their sound, but pitch cannot exist without a tone. One can find the sound of a heartbeat without a heart, but one cannot find a pitch without some sort of tone. Words cannot exist without letters or some sort of lettering (even if spoken, there is lettering as phonemes), but this is not an example of a moment. Words are rather emergent phenomena. Words in this context would be genes wherein DNA letters take on a directed meaning and function.

It is important to note that, when DNA sequences are transferred or when we think of organelles as distinct from the cell, we are then treating them as non-living things, for living things always contain their own software inside of themselves. A small sequence of DNA cannot reproduce and is not a living thing. However, chemicals do not have to be living to be.

Margulis's theory, then, shows us why we cannot be satisfied with just parts and wholes or even parts, wholes, and elements. The idea of elements gives us the idea that something is not detachable. But almost everything is. Elements have to be conceived of as elements of code, since it is code that especially expresses an organism and allows for it to reproduce and give rise to a new one. It is not clear that, in DNA transfers, anything smaller than a gene itself is transferred. That reinforces the idea that we have here an element that purely works as an element of code and that, for the most part, can only be understood in its differential character rather than its status as a non-empty set containing something.

§9
PHILOSOPHICAL EXCURSUS
A Critique of 'Object-Oriented Ontology'

These observations about parts, wholes, and code are particularly apropos given the popularity of a new movement in Continental Philosophy calling itself 'Object-Oriented Ontology' (OOO). Those interested in ontology owe this movement a debt if only for the manner in which it has caused a shift in the discourse surrounding ontology. It has, at least rhetorically, heralded a shift from a focus on the way entities are accessed and known to an attempt to understand how they are constituted in themselves, from the idealism of the constituting mind (or equivalents) to a realism that seeks reality as it is in-itself. It therefore heralds a move from repeating and interpreting the theories of the great thinkers of the last centuries to an attempt to argue for and articulate new approaches. It signals, also, a desire to situate the human being within a larger field of all entities.

However, OOO's own ontological positions, in their specificity, are not persuasive. OOO argues that beings are inherently withdrawn and bases this claim on a misreading of the infinity marking objects, contends that the mereology characterizing objects as parts and wholes is unavoidably involved in infinite regress, and believes that it has a key for rendering how entities interact with each other based on how they perceive each other when it is secretly making all things analogous with human perception without offering an explanation as to why that is legitimate.

But rather than engage in a direct critique of OOO, let us begin first by seeing how OOO would criticize the digital philosophy we are and will be proposing. In an essay entitled "Realism Without Materialism" Graham Harman, the father and main spokesman of the OOO movement, attempts to characterize all previous ontological positions relative to OOO positions and thereby show why those previous positions come up short.[36] For Harman, all ontologies other than OOO and those conforming to its view of objects as primary can be accused of what he calls 'undermining' and/or 'overmining' objects. An undermining ontology says that objects such as "tables and armies" are not primary as they can be decomposed into more primary components such as atoms.[37] Undermining is thus a form of "reductionism" that does not accept, as OOO does, that, at all scales, there are objects and entities just as real as the things we see at the human scale or larger. For Harman, such atomistic, naturalist, and materialist ontologies also commit the sin of not treating objects as independent substances, but rather, due to their atomism, believe that an object is nothing more than a list of qualities.[38] The objects we confront in daily experience that OOO wants to show are irreducible and primary such as tables, baseball teams, and oranges are thus taken to be epiphenomenal effects of some more real and deeper set of components.

On the other hand, an overmining ontology argues that the common unities and objects we experience on a day to day basis are but illusions obscuring a greater all encompassing reality.[39] Here, monism is a good example, as it argues that all things are ultimately one (Harman says

---

[36] Graham Harman, "Realism without Materialism," *Substance* 40.2 (2011): 52–72.

[37] Harman, "Realism without Materialism," 56.

[38] Harman, "Realism without Materialism," 50.

[39] Harman, "Realism without Materialism," 60.

monism is an example of undermining, but I think, based on his own typology, it works as overmining). All particular objects or unities are thus an illusion, as differentiation itself is illusory, given the unity of all things. In other words, all the individual objects truly give way to some fundamental object or unity of which they are parts. Is it the fallacy of composition here to say that if all objects are made of objects, and objects are withdrawn, then those objects are made up of voids? Or is this again how set theory imposes itself? For Harman, monism does not really know how to deal with difference and diversity and can only treat it as external, illusory, and secondary. Harman notes that for many theories such as Anaximander's, the real is just a single blob of oneness that only mind comes about, externally, to cut and up divide into the differentiated and diverse reality we know.[40] Anaxagoras invented mind to end a state of primordial disorder, but it is not clear where mind comes from and how it relates to things if it is only ever external to them.

Another example of overmining would, of course, be Plato's theory of the forms. Here, the dog one pets is but an illusory double of a more real, eternal object that encompasses all examples—which only ever imperfectly approximate it. The Platonic forms are, of course, eternal and unchanging. Thus, it is not clear how change occurs. Harman also takes 'undermining' to be synonymous with theories that say that objects exist "through relations, qualities, or givenness to a human observer."[41] Platonic forms are perfectly actual, since they are nothing but qualities. Harman notes that such theories always end in a dualistic metaphysics in which one sphere is deemed to be truly real and the other only an epiphenomenal effect of the most real level:

> For on the one side, we have a rumbling unformat-

---

[40] Harman, "Realism without Materialism," 60.
[41] Harman, "Realism without Materialism," 65.

> ted blob, free of all articulation, and other side we have specified individual entities appearing in the midst of human life. The only truly important gaps for such philosophers are the one that lies between these two layers.[42]

Harman has interestingly characterized positions allegedly different from his own. However, characterization is not the same as critique. Undermining theories certainly do say that unities we encounter are made up of other components, but they do not have to, by any means, say that that means the unities we experience are less real or not entities in their own right. Presumably, Harman would accuse an informational ontology of bits of undermining objects. However, we will have shown that stars and light bulbs themselves can function as bits. OOO cannot admit the notion of the bit. The bit is not simply an object, even if it is a state of electricity at some point. It's characterized first by a pure relation, 0/1. It's a relation that involves the void itself, 0 –> 1. That's not an object, pure and simple. An object is some sort of unity. A bit is only a positive entity and unity in its guise as empty set. Harman focuses on objects. We used to just call them phenomena. Yet, the bit is prior to unity, as such. For example, phonemes in language are not yet signifiers. An OOO object is not even a signifier. It is, at best, the signified. It should really be called eidos-oriented ontology. That is, OOO is stuck in the Imaginary (so was the Phenomenology on which it is based). This is what structuralists were saying about Husserlianism all along (notice how, today, they can already take our image of an apple in the brain, have a computer read it, and produce an image of it on a screen every time one thinks of it, if one is hooked up with electrodes).

To think computation, one has to think the letter. Lacan says letters are of the Real and not the symbolic. Signifiers

---

[42] Harman, "Realism without Materialism," 62.

are of the symbolic. With modern science, the letter is what literally replaces reality and marks the real itself. AIT (Algorithmic Information Theory), for example, is a way of understanding how the real works insofar as it is about how bits compute (that is, how the letters conjugate themselves). To speak of being is, then, to speak of the letter and how it never ceases being written. OOO is saying that the apple withdraws in its unity in its being. I only have apple profiles. But if the apple is a set and computation of that set, then there is no withdrawal. The apple is incomplete (we do not yet know how it will develop), but it is not withdraw in any sense. Being open is not the same as being withdrawn. It is just the name of a unity. But that unity itself is marked by the set containing the relations rather than being withdrawn. An acorn will become an oak. However, we already have the code for the development inscribed in the acorn.

Speaking about withdrawal is a model based on empirical perception at bottom. Think about it this way: take a flame, an amoeba, and a super duper computer that can compute much more than a human. Does a flame have any sense of object-hood? It does not experience a piece of paper as a thing independent of itself and as a unity. It burns 'whatever' is in its path. There is no reason to say whatever perceives perceives a reality divided up into unities (although, since reality is, in itself, differentiated literally, it always engages in a differentiated reality). An amoeba probably does distinguish inside from outside and a signal to enter and exit for example. But that is far from what OOO needs. Now take a super-duper computer. I would contend such a computer only sees numbers, letters, sets, bits, etc. This is why it was so incredibly difficult to get optical sensors to distinguish distinct things at the beginning. They were just seeing bits and numbers. They had to be forced to sectionalize them into particular sets. And here even we see it is a matter of sets/letters rather than the signified. Bits are not mental units. They are phonemes and letters. There is no need for mind to determine bits. In fact, I argued in my first book that mind itself is not reducible to bits whereas thoughts are obviously articulated as computation.

Objects cannot be sets of irreducible, complex bit strings in the OOO sense. I do not think OOO can even admit the notion of the bit, since it would only confuse it with the atoms it sees in undermining ontologies (a bit is both a positive entity as empty set and a pure relation of states, 0/1). OOO is transposing Husserlian intentional objects onto being itself in an act of reification (with the caveat that they 'withdraw'—which just means that their unity is not perceivable and is only intended ultimately—and perceive each other, although there is no phenomenological analysis of the analogy from human perception that could flesh out such a claim in the way Husserl gives such an analysis in Cartesian Meditations relative to intersubjectivity). If an OOO object was a set of non-compressible bits, then the object itself would be the computation of those bits. That means one has a formula that captures the object itself as such. The thing and the conception of the thing would be the same. It's then just a matter a la Wolfram to see how that computation plays out. The bit, I will argue, involves the existence of the void, numbers, pure differentiality, etc. Admitting that things are bit strings means admitting that, at bottom, there is an 'atom,' and that atom is relationality in itself and a positive entity at the same time.

It's not surprising that OOO has nothing, to my knowledge, to say about numbers as objects or the nothing/void as non-object. Recursive procedures are, themselves, a series of relations and dependent on bits. This is why, at bottom, it is on/off in computers. A theory proposing atoms can simply argue that there is emergence at each scale, such that atoms give rise to new entities with their properties. This is not to say that there are not some purely reductionist versions of materialism or atomism, but, today, with theories of emergence prominent, they are rare. Harman is also right to criticize Platonic and monistic theories for both making unities and individual substances illusory and failing to explain differentiation, as well as for dividing up the world into two spheres. But these are familiar criticisms in philosophy both ancient and modern. Hegel, for example, is the first thinker to argue that difference cannot be thought externally to things. Nietzsche demonstrated for us the problems inherent in dualistic metaphysics. In this way, all of post-Hegelian philosophy is engaged in attempting to avoid the issues Harman outlines. All of post-Hegelian theory is thus premised, in part, on beginning with the idea that difference and differentiation are inherently part of reality, rather than it being some static unity and oneness.

Harman has nicely shifted our attention to ask about "interactions between things" and to asking how different scales are made up of objects from other scales (stars and galaxies), but OOO is far from being the only way to engage with such issues, and such issues do not require, necessarily, a view of objects as totally withdrawn unities.[43] For example, we have and will argue that, beyond parts and wholes and wholes being parts, there is a level of code that is at work. Take stars and galaxies as an example. Here, wholes (stars) become parts of the galaxy. But to understand how stars, for instance, rotate around an axis, one needs to see those stars as computing some program itself. And if we take things as but wholes and wholes that can be parts and part that can be wholes, we will never reach this dimension. In fact, for Harman, given the phenomenological and Whiteheadian background of his theory, we should seemingly ask how stars 'perceive' each other to know how they rotate as though each star perceived all the others. For us, there is differentiation at the heart of things, but it is due to the bit being fundamentally differential in relation. Heterogeneity is thus introduce into the core of being without having to be about, first and foremost, withdrawn substances that only ever interact with each other by perceiving each other and touching by way of intermediaries (for one of the consequences of seeing all things as irreduc-

---

[43] Harman, "Realism without Materialism," 63.

ible, individual substances is that things never directly interact with each other).

Harman believes that the only way to avoid the problems of a vulgar monism is to accept that there are "individual entities" and that such unities are primary and irreducible to "anything pre-individual,"[44] but we would then never be able to understand individual words and how they mean anything. Words are certainly individual entities and unities, but they are not, as such, totally irreducible or primary, since, otherwise, we would not be able to understand how they function. They are differential in their nature, as are the phonemes out of which they are built.

At one point, Harman's own undermining/overmining distinction begins to deconstruct itself. In attempting to characterize pre-Socratic philosophers, Harman says that Thales' water theory is not actually an act of undermining, wherein individual things are but surface effects of more basic and more profound components, but, rather, an overmining, insofar as, at bottom, we find "properties," "certain of palpable properties belonging to the ultimate elements, without addressing the *being* of these things that withdraws behind."[45] In other words, any position can thus be characterized as overmining and/or undermining if it does not accept Harman's position that reality is fundamentally made up of irreducible unities that withdraw and yet can be parts of wholes, and those wholes parts of some other whole. And that means what Harman does is essentially characterize all positions not his own as failing. A position overmines, undermines, or does both (materialism, for instance, is said to do both at once). It all comes down to the same thing—if a position does not argue that reality is made up of individual things that are totally withdrawn from relations with each other, then that theory allegedly fails. The only theories that neither undermine nor overmine are the ones that Harman sees as precursors (Ar-

---

[44] Harman, "Realism without Materialism," 64.
[45] Harman, "Realism without Materialism," 65.

istotelianism and Husserl/Heidegger). This characterization as critique ultimately backfires on Harman's own position, since he ends up turning his own theory into an overmining one. Harman argues that there are real objects "withdrawn behind any of the specific qualities through which they are manifest," but that leads him to argue that there is a difference between the real and sensual objects.[46] And this distinction ends up thrusting Harman's OOO back into the overmining of Platonic forms, *eidos*. Here, instead of a form, we have a totally withdrawn and ineffable object that we only ever have imperfect approximations of in empirical, sensual perception. The withdrawn thing therefore, in its pure self-identity and presence to self, yields, not surprisingly, to sensual manifestations that only poorly mirror the thing. In arguing that real objects are not their qualities and have some sort of identity above and beyond any properties they have, Harman ends up having to reproduce one of the key distinctions of undermining/overmining theories he was keen to transcend. And that is because Harman does not get at the key issue here surrounding the problem of the one and the many. The issue is what makes something identical to itself. Harman takes it for granted that, if one posits a withdrawn object, then it is fully identical and present to itself. But such identity is always itself undermined, as Hegel showed merely by its recognition as such. This is why Harman cannot avoid the issue of vulgar Platonism, as he does not think through what makes self-identity itself possible—it is taken as a primitive categorical intuition (which only a human has) or necessary postulate.

Granted, for OOO, objects are not eternal, but one does not need to posit eternity for this problem to arise. The lack of eternity make it so that issues of the void make themselves felt, but OOO has not reached yet the point where it also posits the fundamental ontological question concerning the fact that there is something rather than nothing. Harman wants to view individual objects as being totally

---

[46] Harman, "Realism without Materialism," 59.

isolated substances, but, while he should be commended for focusing philosophy's attention on engagement with entities of all types, at the same time, what makes a unity a unity and what makes unity possible is not thought through and is taken for granted. Simply arguing that things are not their qualities and that something must exist that is not reducible to them does not in itself answer the question for how that is possible. Part of the problem is that Harman is simply arguing from authority and plugs in views of past thinkers willy nilly into new views. Here, Husserl's eidetic intuition is simply projected onto the world such that one need not ask about the self-identify of things. Saying things are not their qualities is classical Aristotelianism, but Aristotle himself could not isolate what substance truly is (beyond isolating it as form or some sort of form/matter combination). Harman simply turns substantiality into an ineffable as though that evades the inherent problems in identifying such a pure identity. Such a pure identity makes change and contact between things mysterious. Change is not explained here, but only taken as a primitive. However, not explaining change was earlier taken as a devastating blow against other theories by Harman himself. In fact, for an atomist theory to avoid the charge of undermining, it merely has to agree that atoms are not the fundamental objects but that objects pertain at all scales. An overmining theory need only admit that human consciousness does not constitute all objects as such, but that objects exist independent of mind.

Harman's key insight is mereological in nature—that objects exist as irreducible unities at all levels and scales and that such objects can be parts of wholes or wholes with unities as parts. However, Harman's failure to engage with set theory, the ultimate discourse on mereology, means that the very nature of unity and part-whole relations is not thought through. It also means that relations that are just as fundamental are left out of the picture or made out to be purely external between isolated things. Harman has offered us a key critique of reductionist moves in philosophy, but he takes for granted that such mereology enables an infinite regress. However, such an infinite regress renders part-whole relations nonsensical, and an engagement with set theory would show this. If there is an infinite regress, then one has a pure, actual infinity of unities and, thereby, it is not clear why or how there is any one, any unity (recall here Badiou's key thesis concerning the one). Admitting that both atoms and trees are really real objects is only a first step—one that cannot be thought through without the aid of engaging explicitly in set theory and the implications of the actual infinite.

Now, one of the main points in favor of substance ontology is that when we have relations, there is always seemingly a presumption that two things are related (there are two relata). One cannot seemingly say how such distinct relata arise via relations, since any relations will bring up the same need for relata. But this argument was itself premised on an avoidance of infinite regress, especially in its Aristotelian form. The monad was only needed to avoid infinite regress. But if an infinite regress is allowable for individual things and parts and wholes for Harman, then there is no reason why such infinite regress cannot be allowed for relations. Again, transfinite set theory is the theory that can decide such issues. As we have already tried to show, one must posit something like the bit, which is both empty set and inherent relation, in order to avoid these problems and the antinomy of the two positions. Aristotle thought that no primary substances are relational, and Harman proves himself to be a good Aristotelian. But to return to Aristotle is to return to the Dark Ages indeed. The true cause of the Dark Ages was Aristotelianism, not Christianity or religion. And this is why one needs to be much more Hegelian and find relationality already in the primary substance itself.

The problems for Harman's theory do not end here, for, even though Harman claims to be offering a flat ontology in which the human is but one of many entities, human perception is itself secretly privileged throughout, as already argued. Speaking about withdrawal is a model based on empirical perception at bottom. Given the spectrum of perceptions we have laid out, it is numbers/letters/sets that prove themselves to be most comprehensive and fundamental, as all the possibilities on the spectrum can be comprehended in those terms. Most things do not simply see objects in any sense. To say reality is made up of unities, then, is already to privilege human consciousness (or, at best, a specific set of living organisms) as having the most fundamental look at reality as it is in itself. Humans then just happen to discover reality as it is in itself in a way a mountain simply will not. Part of the problem here is that everything a la Whitehead is being based on perception for Harman. But why is a thing essentially the set of perceptions something has of it? Is a tree really all the ways it is perceived, or is it a particular fractal program that is iterated and gives rise to a particular phenomenon? Harman also believes that the set of perceptions of anything is actually infinite. And it is by way of this alleged infinity that he believes he can ground the fact that no act of conceptualization can grasp things and thereby proves their withdrawal. But there is no secular, negative theology of the potato. Potatoes are not infinite things that exist beyond all things and are isolated in a realm of their own—unless one posits a Platonic potato. The number of perceptions of a potato, for instance, is only ever finite. The only way the set of perceptions of a potato is transfinite is in the sense of its being incomplete and thereby open (not withdrawn) and/or inconsistent (any perception can be added to the set of any kind). There is no withdrawal of the potato, but rather a total openness characterizing it. It is incomplete. A potato is not a closed off thing. There is no ontological closure here.

The potato is not simply a set of perceptions of it, but is a program, or mathematized expression of it. A potato is formed via the repetition of a specific code. That means again that it is open. Potatoes might, in fact, be a matter of a very simple bit string. In that way, if we do speak of what the potato is, one can mark that bit string as its set and identity. If it is just a matter of showing its mathematical character in a very complicated way, that is due to our lack of computational abilities rather than because the object is itself some inherently hidden thing. What is not there is like a number not yet counted.

Now, Harman's model is based on taking the Husserlian model of how phenomenological, intentional consciousness constitutes unities and transposing that model onto reality itself. But the problem is that, without consciousness to constitute the unity of things, it is not clear how it occurs, other than taking unities as primitive givens. Here again, set theory makes its need apparent. For, without consciousness itself to constitute the unity of thing, one needs to argue that a thing, in itself, is void. This point makes itself felt perhaps most forcefully when Harman considers the real implications of treating objects as withdrawn. If all real objects are totally withdrawn, then they are all rendered as the same—as pure voids. They are all the same as real objects. All is swallowed up into the great dark night of the real. Pure presence to self and self-identity are identical with the void, which is why they can only be comprehended by the empty set. The substance of a thing is never perceived and never experienced. We only ever deal with properties and qualities. For Harman, this means the object is hidden away, but Husserl was more honest insofar as he saw that consciousness itself was constituting and projecting the set that contains all these qualities. Also, substance here is emptied of all qualities and is above and beyond them. That leaves it as a literal nothing, but the only way nothing has substance is in the empty set and its equivalents. This is why we need set theory to think of bare substratums.

Harman himself never deals with the implications of saying that all objects are the same in his theory, given their withdrawal, but set theory is willing to accept such an identity between all sets insofar as it accepts the undeniable role played by the empty set. Only the empty set as name can mark the difference between the thing and its inscription, between the thing and what it is. This point is made in set theory via the axiom of separation (although the empty set is not referred to by it). This is why anything has to be related to as a signifier. The thing always contains absence within itself. It is not withdrawn into absence or afloat in a void. It has absence as part of it internally (and thus it is necessarily relational as well as being a positive entity). No list of properties captures a thing, since its identity is a framework, like the name and the set. But this is a Lacanian insight—an insight that leads him to say that all things of all types are signifiers. It is not that reality is discursively constituted or is the effect of human speech or language (it is the effect of divine speech). It is a way of capturing the inherently differential nature of reality. Things are unities and collections, always. Because of the way reality is marked by the transfinite, we also play a role then in isolating collectives. We are the determiner when we encounter a mountain rather than a range, for a mountain is part of the range, and the range part of the land, and the land part of the planet, and the planet part of the solar system, etc. OOO is railing against this aspect of Lacanianism when it should be reifying it rather than Husserlianism or returning to Aristotelianism. Husserl spoke of intended objects, what Derrida and Lacan showed is that what makes such objects possible is the subject's alienation in the signifier, in a differential network of signifiers. And that is, again, why merely transposing Husserlianism onto mind-independent reality hides what was revealed in the (post-)Structuralist critique.

The empty set is, of course, included in any set. In that way, the empty set functions as the name/thing. It is the brackets around which all is included. Each thing must have a name. That name is the embodiment of the empty set and the framework of the thing. The thing itself is thus void, and this void is included in the set as the set's name. In this way, we are saying that Harman's notion of withdrawal is thinkable as the empty set itself, the name of each individual thing. The name by which each thing is called is another way of inscribing it as marked by the empty set. A name is itself a rigid designator, as Saul Kripke laid out many years ago. In this way, to speak of a thing that is totally withdrawn is to transpose the rigid designator onto the real. We are not referring simply to the name as a thing spoken or written. That is something always dependent on the thing's real, hidden name. We are speaking here of the void as the identity in itself of the thing. The two are linked and make themselves felt in their impact via the name. This way any name is a name of a thing, a name and a thing.

Harman himself rejects the substance/aggregate distinction, and the implication of that is that any unity is a thing. Ontologies traditionally argued for a distinction between substances and aggregates to ensure a grounded realism. It was with modern philosophy culminating in Husserl that consciousness intends the unity of things such that a swarm of bees can be a unity and thing as much as a bee itself is, in traditional realism. The bee is the only truly mind independent thing per the latter view. Today for us, it is a matter of following the realism of set theory. Insofar as OOO continues to see numbers as abstract things, it continues to implicitly rely on the substance/aggregate distinction, even though it claims to have toppled it.

One might ask what difference there is between saying 'this door' is a name and, thereby, a set that is transfinite and thus incomplete and inconsistent, rather than something withdrawn. The point is that what Harman mistakes as withdrawn and vacuum-packed is just that, the set itself, as empty set, as mark of the void. The difference between our views is important. A set contains things. It can include anything. This door can, then, be all its perceptions as well as its mathematicization. Harman's' rendering of things as withdrawn, real substances is about designating a transcendental signified. All the different manifestations of the door always referred to 'this door,' but if 'this door' is an embodiment of the empty set as name, then one is connecting it to the circuit of numbers and letters rather than to the ineffable world of the withdrawn. This is important, since, in Harman's view, something is always beyond me, and, per our view, created things are always renderable and specifiable—only God and the void are truly transcendent. Why do we connect a particular image of the door to the door? Harman has no better answer than because we refer it to the transcendental signified 'this door.' But that is already to treat the door as a set.

What we see today in Continental Philosophy is an attempt to take the insights of the last 100 years or so and apply them to reality itself. That is to say, the structures once said to be inherent in consciousness are not just on the side of subject but also on the side of substance. In this way, the problem with Harman is not that he reifies Husserl, but that he reifies a pre-Derridean Husserl. The problem is not that what Husserl thought was inherent to the immanent space of the mind that is, in turn, inherent in mind-independent reality itself, but that the model here of phenomenology does not take into account what the Derridean and Lacanian critiques revealed about this Husserlian model. We thus need to find mind in things, but in a strict Lacanian sense. An objectified Lacan is needed rather than an objectified Husserl, and that means making things renderable in relation to the signifier, letter, and set.

OOO takes it as a given that objects are made of objects, so they see no need to offer an explanation of how one object comes to be itself an object. But that is the mystery. Husserl could offer such an explanation, but only by constantly having recourse to intentional consciousness. Aristotle could, as well, but only by having recourse to grammar and predication (some things are said of others, but substance is not said of anything else). A snowflake is an object, but it was not always there, such that we need to understand how it arose and why it looks as it does. Simply looking at things as parts and wholes will not do that. One needs the bit and letter to explain its emergence. It did not arise out of nothing and did not arise due to some agent or final cause imposing itself on inert mater. If energy is just matter and is constantly giving rise to new things, then OOO must be aware of that and be able to account for how objects arise. But OOO can only say there is always a composition of objects. But, even if that were true, it cannot tell us why it takes this shape and in this way. Why are those objects the ones that make up a phenomenon?

Harman says other ontologies are wrong because they see reality as an apeiron chopped up by an external mind, but OOO's reliance on perception ends up doing the same, since it cannot tell us how a reality differentiated into objects yields to change and the formation of specific new objects. One needs numbers, letters, sets, and bits to do that, since an apple is always one thing and, therefore, has a number inherent to it. That needs accounting for; perception only counts what is always there. If these things were withdrawn and vacuum-packed, no one would ever be able to write computer programs and exchange the code. I just do not see how computational irreducibility can be talked about in terms of withdrawal. At all stages of the computation, one knows that it is a computation of that particular program. Here is the problem: OOO is saying that the real itself is differentiated into real unities that are withdrawn. But those unities presuppose that numbers are not constructions but are real, since one thing is one thing and not two. If any object is just an aggregate, the only way to unlock the logic of its unity and mere-ology is by doing set theory, as set theory is the very ontology of mereology as such. This is why one should side with Badiou over Aristotle.

Take a cube. Husserl merely says we never see all sides of a cube at once. But consciousness always posits a cube unit as a thing over and beyond the profiles and sides we see of it. OOO now says that unity is a real, withdrawn thing. But this leaves as a mystery why a cube has the shape it does, why it looks the way it does, etc. We do not explain the inherent symmetry that is invariant in it and why that symmetry does not change, no matter how we look at it. Even if we turn it around, the cube maintains certain properties. It has six identical faces. We can see each one. There is no face that is withdrawn and only hidden. And this is why we need to understand it as a mathematized thing, as set of letters, to understand this invariance. Only then will we make sense of how each face and edge are identical. A number is all there and present with no withdrawal and no profiles. When I think the number one, it is there as one. It is not hiding. This is really why OOO theories are completely mute about numbers. They are ignoring the mark of unity itself and the notion of the mark as such.

OOO argues there is no total object. But that is the same as arguing there is no set of all sets—no universal universal, no whole or totality of totality. Again, the only way to establish such a thesis is by using set theory. But that means there must be something not contained and not an object. The empty set marks that non-containment. OOO does not say explicitly that withdrawal must be related to the void to do the same. OOO might here respond that if everything is sets of letters and bits, then we can speak of man and woman as universals rather than as individuals. But that is because there is also the signifier. OOO can only treat man and woman as Aristotelian, secondary substances, which, again, gives rise to the problem allegedly left behind with overmining and undermining theories by making one thing depend on something more fundamental (a hierarchy). But, for us, man and woman are signifiers such that to think them is to continue thinking sets and collections.

Rather than Aristotle's substance ontology it, would have been better to adopt here Aristotle's theory of the soul. There, Aristotle argues the soul is the form of the activity of the body. That might have lead OOO to see that a living organism, for instance, has its soul in a particular program that is iterating itself. It would then have found a need to think through programming. OOO would have been better off learning from Object-Oriented Programming about how sets and subsets work in conjunction with code. We must think compositions and collections based on letters and syllables. This is not an arbitrary metaphor, but one that imposes itself on us and exposes the inherent structure of things. The structure of things is always mathematizable. All wholes have structural natures that show how they are always already mathematized—if only in the sense of having relations as part of them. Things are woven together. It is only in this way we can understand emergence. OOO itself is made up of three Os, such that each O alone does not speak of it. If we were to take three marks and put them together, it is clear we always get a new thing. The issue is, then, whether the new thing is compressible or irreducibly complex. I can take the things on my desk, but it is only a collection and one reducible to those three things, unlike how the letters c, a, and t come together to make 'cat.'

Let's finish this excursus into contemporary Philosophy (although we were always engaging in it and always will be) and return more explicitly to biology. But, to be fair to OOO, let's look at its second articulation in the work of Levi Bryant.[47] Bryant adds to Harman's notion of withdrawal and objects being made up of objects the idea that objects are always systems and that, in addition to parts and wholes, such systems have elements. Parts are unities within objects, whereas elements for Bryant are parts that cannot exist independently of the system. However, as we saw in the moment/pieces distinction, such non-independent elements are very rare. Bryant needs here to think of elements as elements of code and in terms of their differential nature, rather than as parts that cannot be separated. One would then have a way of thinking through how a system itself operates in the manner it does.

Bryant sees reality as differentiated into allopoetic and autopoetic entities. Autopoetic entities constitute their parts and elements, but one cannot understand how they do that without understanding how they are computational

---

[47] Levi R. Bryant, *The Democracy of Objects* (Ann Arbor: Open Humanities Press, 2011): http://openhumanitiespress.org/democracy-of-objects.html.

in nature. A cell, for instance, reproduces, but that is only because it has a code to do so. Flames also reproduce, but they do not explicitly in doing so contain a code for doing so. That element of code here is missing. Bryant also takes allopoetic entities to be ones created by another entity and that do not do anything to maintain themselves from disintegrating via entropy. For example, a factory produces a tennis shoe, but if that tennis shoe is torn, it does not, on its own, fix itself. A human being is made of trillion of cells, but if one has an arm removed it does not grow back. Are human beings then not autopoetic? It would appear that the explanation has to do with code rather than autopoesis (some creatures are coded to repair this damage). Humans do not grow back arms, but do grow back hair. The code explains why. The factory, however, as dynamic system, will replace a worker with another one if that worker gets sick. But the problem here is that this distinction does not work, since any and all entities are produced by other entities. A human being is made by its parents, for example, so all are allopoetic. Autopoetic entities then become special cases of allopoetic entities. But the only way one can get an allopoetic entity is from autopoetic ones. One then has here a vicious circle without explanation. Where did the first autopoetic entity come from? And if it came from nowhere, then how did it create itself?

All such entities are negentropic. That means they cannot be eternal. They could all disappear. It is, then, not clear how one allows an infinite regress to take place. Also, knowing an entity was produced by another and does nothing to repeat itself tells us nothing about how an entity is in itself constituted and why in that way. The issue here is really the one between the living and the inorganic (that was the distinction the autopoetic/allopoetic was designed by its founders to replace). The living, as we have argued, requires code. Even if Bryant is willing to admit that a flame or a crystal is alive, one still is unable to explain the difference between a crystal and a cell. Bryant attempts to explain such things with reference to a virtual dimension and regimes of attractions.[48] But this only seems to defer the problem by inventing another dimension of being (we will address the issue of the virtual later via a critique of Deluezianism). In essence, I do not think such a virtual dimension can be anything more than an epistemological projection. Regimes of attractions can only be made concrete if mathematized and run through a mathematical model that sees reality itself as inherently mathematized. Even Deleuze's virtual ontology was modeled for instance on the insights of differential equations, the notion of infinitesimals, and Riemannian geometry.

Part of the problem here is that Bryant is taking it for granted that reality being differentiated means it is differentiated into objects and objects as systems (no recourse to the work of Roy Bhaskar and the practical workings of scientists can show this, either, ontologically speaking). But this is precisely what needs explanation. Why is any unity a system? If all unities are not, then where do those systematic unities come from if the non-systematic ones only ever come from the systematic? It seems, then, that Bryant is not explaining or accounting for the empirical ontologically but merely doubling it (hence, the centrality of a virtual domain in the ontology here). He is adopting the empirical nature of things as given and then restating them without explaining or accounting for how things have the properties they do in the empirical descriptions used. This makes the entire analysis dependent on having the right empirical description to start with. For instance, Bryant would argue that asking how the first cell achieved a membrane is a purely empirical question. But it is one that he has to ontologically double, insofar as one has to account for how unities arise and exist. Accounting for the cell then gives one an occasion for making the ontological point. Instead, Bryant looks into the world and sees cells and now wants to describe them as examples of the autopoetic. The allegedly true nature of things (we are told that the account given

---

[48] Bryant, *The Democracy of Objects*, §3.3.

reveals the true nature of reality) is then presupposed rather than explained.

The problem is that even that description leaves one wanting (although Bryant is very good at reproducing the empirical research he has read and presenting it as a form of phenomenological analysis in lieu of traditional Husserlian analysis of lived experience). OOO is suggesting reality is made up of black-boxed and withdrawn substances, but it does not show us how to deduce that black-boxing. We want an objectified philosophy that shows how thing are marked by undecidability and incompletion and not to see it imported from the outside. Bryant argues that autopoetic systems are operationally closed and self-referential such that they are related to their own internal operations and not an outside. But how is that possible? Without explaining how such a thing is possible one has not given an ontological account. Bryant does not give a full account of how such things work (what makes it so that things are operationally closed, other than by taking it as a given), but that just bears witness to the extent to which his view does not go beyond a restatement of the empirical descriptions he borrows from the scientific studies he has read.

In Bryant's system, an element of the system refers to other elements of the same type. But there is no element of code here such that those elements take on differential qualities and act as purely differential relations. Information is then taken only semiotically as something that represents something for something else. Shannon information as purely syntactical information is missed here. This is why Bryant sees all systems as closed off and only jostled by things external to them. However, no system is so closed, because they are always comprehended by codes and relations that exceed them and relate them to other things. Even if we simply look at the atomic level, a system is always receiving its parts from outside since these elements are part of its structuration at that level. The very idea of information in Shannon's sense allows for the same thing to be transferred between two things without problem. There, substitution occurs, just as one atomic element can substitute for another. If things were closed off, the technology we now have—where I think of an apple and an apple image appears on a screen—would not be possible. It is possible because the bit allows for a universal translation system. For Bryant, my mental representations only link to other mental representations or neurons to other neurons without any hope of anything on the outside receiving more than a confused noise relating to this internal process. Bryant might be able to render out of his system a sense of elements as structurally related to each other, but this needs to be articulated as a code itself, and this code as comprehending the thing, to truly understand and explain how systems work.

But, in that way, Bryant's OOO would be violating a principle of OOO by isolating something which is not simply an object, strictly speaking. Such elements would be differential elements within a system. Again, Bryant needs to offer us an ontological account for why what he calls 'operational closure' occurs and how is it ontologically possible. This means an explanation of how a system forms and how it becomes closed off. It means an explanation for why what he calls the elements in the system only communicate with each other and not with the outside. Here, for instance, it might be due to the very nature of the elements, or it might be due to the nature of relationality. We would, of course, argue that it is due to such elements being both positive entities and relational as part of their nature that makes it possible. Operational closure might be due to all entities always being related to one another, such as how the first replicated DNA was necessarily related to a cell membrane and other cellular machinery.

For Bryant, autopoesis, as with Humberto Maturana and Francisco Varela, the two scientists who invented this distinction, is mainly about negentropy and maintenance of existence. But even pillows and buildings do that, as they do not immediately crumble. A question left unanswered here is: What is it about being, as such, that makes it entropic and about all beings, such that they seem to evade it, if it is so fundamental? But if OOO is willing to admit differential elements and, thus, how differentiality is inherent in things, then it is no longer clear why objects are independent and what makes such independence possible. Bryant also needs to differentiate between parts as systems, subsets of a whole, and seeing elements as themselves parts (lack of detachability will not do the trick). Code is not made up of non-detachable parts. Things lose their statuses as simple unities when functioning in codes. Bryant may mean here that things only have a meaning effect when in relation to other things, but that should not allow us to overlook how they are detachable and how that relationality is built into them When we speak of how, for instance, DNA chemicals can exist on their own outside of the DNA code, we miss how they function in a code. This is why we should not focus on if an element can exist independently, but on how it functions differentially.

If Bryant wants to think of substance as processes and activities, then we need the rules and code that they are computing. Once we have that code, we can then explain how a thing is not reducible to it material parts insofar as it can compute its structure and nature using any parts, such as atomic elements that are plugged in. And the separability of elements is due to a thing's relation, minimally, to the void rather than to its being always in excess of itself.

§10
Symbiogenesis

As Margulis notes, single-celled organisms can mutate and develop at a very quick rate precisely because they are able to easily take into themselves new elements of code. If we do not include code itself in our consideration of parts and wholes, then we cannot understand truly how life develops. Mitochondria themselves have their own DNA and, thereby, their own genes and own genetic elements.[49] Our own genetic code is made up of distinct elements of bacterial DNA, and we need to see that the majority of our code is due to the conjugation of bacteria and the combination of DNA lettering that took place in bacterial interaction.[50] The same sequences that were transferred long ago between two bacteria exist as sequences still in our DNA and operate as such. While Margulis does not detail, to my knowledge, any underlying order or rules for symbiogenesis, she does insist that the transfer of DNA cannot occur by any means as "chemicals do not combine randomly, but in ordered, patterned ways."[51] Margulis thereby gives one the impression, at the very least, that actual events of incorporation of wholes into other wholes and the transfer of information are not purely contingent and unpredictable and adhere to no fundamental rules, even if we try to look at the system

---

[49] Margulis and Sagan, *Microcosmos*, 19.
[50] Margulis and Sagan, *Microcosmos*, 22.
[51] Margulis and Sagan, *Microcosmos*, 51.

from the context of Gaia itself, for instance. But symbiogenetic theory is only willing to allow explicitly such order at the level of chemistry itself, when basic molecules join together and form into the code itself (I will return to these issues when engaging in a critique of the notion of 'self-organization').[52] It is not clear why molecules, when joining together, do follow rules and occur only in certain conditions, but mitochondria, bacteria, etc., are not also subject to such an analysis.

Margulis herself does not engage in analysis of how "small organic chemicals, such as amino acids and nucleotides" can join and lead to emergent phenomena like "RNA and proteins" as the gaps between one level and another is "enormous."[53] But, despite expressing clear confidence that some sort of systematic set of rules can be delineated for it, no such confidence or interest is shown when it comes to symbiogenesis or gene transfer. In any event, the code we see operating in life forms is itself a longer version of what was a shorter and more condensed version of the same language. This is because the code is a "living language" and "still carries evidence of its etymological roots."[54] We see here how point mutations are not the only way that the code changes. Point mutations could only shuffle the code itself (substituting one letter for another). Here, one has the addition of entire strings of letters at once. By way of such a mechanism, it becomes more reasonable to accept that life has developed over a long period of time, as single point mutations were not enough to produce the development we see in the fossil record (even with the long expanses described by modern science).

However, Margulis is not saying that gene transfer is the only way in which the code develops. One can still speak of point mutations, copying errors, the environment via radiation and other influences causing chemicals to break

---

[52] Margulis and Sagan, *Microcosmos*, 52.
[53] Margulis and Sagan, *Microcosmos*, 55.
[54] Margulis and Sagan, *Microcosmos*, 62.

and reform, etc. But the most consistent processes from this perspective are certainly symbiogenesis and the lateral transfer of information. At the same time, we cannot say that life forms are themselves immediately changed simply by the transfer of information: "Bacteria are not altered by an automatic addition of 50 percent new genes."[55] Such an observation calls for an analysis of the code itself and its articulation to understand why this material does not affect it. Of course, at one level, it may simply be due to the code itself being inert right after transfer. But it may be inert even after that and the creation of offspring. Bacteria, of course, produce such offspring by dividing into two, thus leading to two distinct creatures with the same DNA code. Bacteria can also lay eggs, as it were, by releasing a tiny version of themselves with a complete DNA code that then grows outside the mother cell. This is called budding. Either way, one has the same DNA code reproduced as will now exist in the parent.

Margulis notes that this retaining of DNA has led some to suggest that "a kind of cellular predestination: future evolution, they say, is already encoded in the DNA, which will become useful with the passage of time."[56] However, Margulis does not endorse such a view, since she seems mainly interested in documenting how certain processes repeat themselves and where they have led without attempting to descend into the level of the code itself to see how this living language may contain in itself the rules for these phenomena. That is, if life is evolving from a common source using the same living code, it is strange indeed to suggest that processes it leads to are not themselves somehow coded for and part of its own internal development. Why should we not shift to seeing all life as a single body (Gaia)? If we did, should we be any more surprised by lateral gene transfer than we are that the human body has circulating elements in it? The consensus seems to be that

---

[55] Margulis and Sagan, *Microcosmos*, 88.
[56] Margulis and Sagan, *Microcosmos*, 118.

the human body itself is already coded for in its DNA. Margulis is perfectly aware of such a Gaia perceptive, but does not take up this perspective in this sense (to my knowledge), since, for her, the entire history of symbiogenesis and gene transfer seems to be a contingent mess. But we know that many other phenomena that initially appeared to have such a character were themselves, despite their complex and actual randomness, compressible into a finite set of rules. Even if one were to argue that the entire history of life is itself irreducibly complex, it is then one such irreducibly complex object in the universe and has to be thereby thought in relationship to the planet as larger formation, the solar system, etc.

At any rate, Margulis is presenting us with a thoroughly anti-Darwinist viewpoint. For her, speciation does not primarily take place via natural selection and random mutation, but, rather, species are formed as products of symbiogenesis itself: "That is, because A and B share the same number of the same different kinds of integrated genomes they are assigned to the same species" (*AG* 6). Here, speciation is not a gradual process that occurs over long expanses due to pure chance, but a sudden and abrupt effect of the merging of two entities. Margulis's theory is, of course, subject to verification in a much simpler fashion than Darwinism, as one can, with the mitochondria, show how what exists still contains its past and the assemblage out of which it is made. One does not need to look for missing transitional forms, as those forms themselves exist still within one. This can also be seen at the level of the code, as one can sequence a genome and determine how it is a mosaic and tapestry of integrated sequences.

This view also changes our understanding of species. To return to an earlier point, we cannot say that bacteria have species, as species do not arise from two cells joining (the bacteria is already a cell), but from gene transfer amongst any other bacteria (*AG*). Margulis thereby relegates random mutation to its true status as a marginal phenomenon. Another shocking (shocking to the Darwinian hegemony) consequence of this theory is that "no visible organism or group of organisms is descended 'from a single common ancestor'" (*AG* 7). One here has to possibly posit at the origin of life some sort of entity with a membrane integrating a self-replicating molecule. One then has always at least two common ancestors. Once one reaches the level of bacteria, one has multiple ancestors, given informational transfer. Life then involves always at least two at its origin. This may be another key way in which life differentiates itself from matter. There need to be at least two different entities for life to occur. All living things have common ancestors. The history of life is not a tree as much as it is a slime mold. It is a web or network and not simply a seed becoming a tree. Here, the tree branches fuse back together (*AG* 202). Animals arise out of the web, but the web remains and persists as the background context and platform of life. A tree is often a pattern that is repeating itself. But here the pattern might be more complex than that and not have any discernible order, like a Wolfram Rule 30 cellular automaton.[57]

We then see new patterns emerge and cells emerge out of the web without divorcing themselves from it. The ancestor here is also not a thing, strictly speaking, but a complex molecule or a set of relations and a code. If we see the origin as being simply a nucleated cell, we overlook the complexity of things—not only would it be possibly the joining of a molecule with a membrane, but a matter of

---

[57] "Rule 30 is a one-dimensional binary cellular automaton rule introduced by Stephen Wolfram in 1983. Using Wolfram's classification scheme, Rule 30 is a Class III rule, displaying aperiodic, chaotic behaviour. This rule is of particular interest because it produces complex, seemingly random patterns from simple, well-defined rules. Because of this, Wolfram believes that Rule 30, and cellular automata in general, are the key to understanding how simple rules produce complex structures and behaviour in nature": "Rule 30," *Wikipedia*: http://en.wikipedia.org/wiki/Rule_30 [retrieved July 31, 2013].

conjugating a set of letters. Here, one might want to turn the tree of life on its head in an act of inversion. It is not that one thing lead to multiple paths, but that multiple paths and things lead to one entity. It would also be wrong to see sex as simply a later effect of life insofar as there were two at life's very inception. Sexual reproduction would be a reintroduction of the split found at the origin.

And what of natural selection? Margulis agrees that natural selection, if it is not to be tautological, can at most state that most things do not reproduce or do not reproduce in an optimal fashion: "'Differential survival' is all it really is" (*AG* 9). Many things do die. They do not survive. Not all possibilities are pursued by life, and organisms do not produce as many offspring as is physically possible. Margulis's perspective is much closer to Lamarck's in stating that as what occurs to an organism during its lifetime is passed on. Algae eaten but not digested becoame part of the tissue and are passed on to creatures. Symbiogenetic theory also has an answer to Behe's criticism of irreducible complexity as it arises due to the incorporation of new genetic material and entire entities into an organism (*AG* 96-97). Each organism that exists, especially those above the first organisms, "protrude[s] from the microbial underworld" and is not simply an individual beings insofar as they it is an assemblages of multiple beings (*AG* 97). However, that does not mean that an individual human is not an individual thing as opposed to a mouse. One can still sequence each individual's DNA and coding. That coding is now a variegated composite of multiple previous acts of symbiogenesis. And two individual humans appear as such (as two members of the same species) insofar as one can compare the sequencings of their DNA and find an almost identical overlap in their mosaics.

However, given that each thing is a mosaic, one will have to see each thing as just that—an individual thing that is itself a permutation and conjugation of the coding itself. This is, again, why one cannot be satisfied with wholes and parts, since one has to look at each sequence to think through the individuality of such amalgams. That means looking at a string of—in the case of humans—billions of base pairs. A human is a set of billions of letters that have been joined and spliced together by the code itself and its development. All individual things that have coding are connected in this fashion. One can, of course, categorize things based on how they overlap. And this overlap has been taken as a sign of common descent. If things were not descended from the same thing or things, one would expect them to be radically different. For Margulis, two humans are part of the same species because they have identical sets of symbionts in them, even if they do not have the exact DNA sequence of base pairs as within subsets of symbionts sequenced (the letters might have been permuted). All things are composites, even at the level of DNA base pairs themselves. One can see the billions of pairs in a human as segmented into sets and subsets.

At some point, one needs to accept that it is at the level of the letters themselves that individuality appears. Each individual is a particular set of letters. Each human is a text condensed from the great permutation and assembling of life's elements. Two cells might have all the same modular units (mitochondria, ribosomes, etc.), but one cannot know what type of creature it is without knowing the code. However, the use of modular units shows that in the history of life there is a repetition of the same units and the ability to switch out small units without breaking down the entire system involved. That does not mean that modular units that were incorporated do not have any influence. In fact, Margulis argues one cannot speak of speciation until one has "the nucleated cell" (*AG* 145). But there are different scales, and at different scales different rules pertain. At the level of the letters there is one set of rules playing out. Here, new information is incorporated, the flipping of bits occurs, subroutines are formed, etc. At the level of organelles one has the incorporation of whole systems. The history and development of life and individual life forms is a computation of all these scales.

Margulis and Sagan focus on Neil Todd's research on karyotypes. Darwinism says that highly related species should have the same karyotypes (*AG* 192). While karyotypes are not something that was incorporated, they are related to the symbiogenetic inclusion of the "centromere-kinetochore of the chromosome" (*AG* 193). Because of this past symbiotic joining, the karyotypes fission at the same time and double themselves. Because chromosomes once were independent of cells, it is not surprising that they double themselves and do so in a way that does not follow from the code. Because these karyotypes break themselves, one has double the number of chromosomes. One thus has more places where genetic info is coded, even if the code itself is not thereby changed. But in having more places of inscription, further effects can occur. This doubling of sites occurs at a different scalar level than the code itself. Even if all animal cells have such chromosomes and their features due to the same event of incorporation, at later points, fissioning can occur at different intervals and rates due to interaction with different cell environments or cues produced by different codes, such that humans will have 46 chromosomes and another creature 24. In this way, we have processes in the cell, for instance, that are not following from the code itself, but occurring at the level of unities and their division.

Humans and mice actually have many genes that occur in both and even appear in the same order in the genome sequence. But such genetic information is itself distributed over the chromosomes in many different ways. This is itself a function of this fissioning. Biological functions are thus spread out over many chromosomes: genetic functions and coding spread out amongst these fashioned entities. One has to ask here if it is purely contingent that these karyotypes fission. A crystal, when put in a saturated solution starts to reproduce, but no one says that occurs purely by chance. Wholes turn into parts that are themselves wholes and parts of wholes. One can then see how entities created with code have emergent abilities and powers that occur at a different scalar level. The logic of modular units is then not necessarily the same logic as that of the code, even if it is a later development of it and dependent on it, as is all life.

Sagan and Schneider say that "organisms are not put together atom by atom, or molecule by molecule, but modularly, a genome at a time,"[58] but that does not mean one could not do so with genetic engineering. The method by which something arose does not determine its essence and nature that completely. In a manner similar to Spetner, Margulis ack-nowledges the plasticity of bacteria and the manner in which they can change based on outside influences:

> Practicing bacteriologists are aware of this definition's arbitrariness, since bacteria change traits so rapidly. By this rule, bacteria change all the time. Placement in a refrigerator or warm incubator can cause bacteria to change 'species' in a few days." (*AG* 142)

Margulis does not explain such phenomena, but only marks them to show all bacteria are essentially the same. Margulis also has no particular answer to the origin of information itself and the first replicated molecule. This theory explains how sudden and large-scale change occurs at once, but it is always a question of taking ready-made things and combining them. There is no explanation of the first membrane and its unity with DNA, which is the most important event it needs to detail. There is no explanation of the first nucleated cell. Margulis's theory, then, is truly a theory that starts from the point of the nucleated cell and explains how life developed from that point of departure. It thereby does not have a theory of the origin of complex systems in and of themselves. But this may be largely due to its being a biological rather than biochemical theory. With-

---

[58] Sagan and Schneider, *Into the Cool*, 320.

out such a theory, one might have to suggest that life occurred multiple times.

If the formation of life is something that necessarily happens, it may have happened multiple times. It is highly probable, but, if things are programmed for its occurrence, then it happening multiple times would be less astonishing. We have seen that life itself might presuppose at least two things. But it might presuppose multiple common ancestors beyond that. However, whereas Darwinism cannot truly be observed in fact, symbiogenesis is something that can. Bacteria also here do not remain the same after countless generations of reproduction, since, given their past formation via transfer, they can easily undergo metamorphosis. It is probably the case that one does not witness bacteria changing in the laboratory because scientists are always attempting to prove Darwinism and thereby just reproduce the same thing over and over again without allowing it to interact with other bacteria. It also may not occur due to a limit of gene transfer that bacteria may have reached long ago. In this way, all possible transfers have already played out. No future transfers will enable bacteria to achieve any more than what it already has. If that is true, it means the evolution of bacteria has witnessed development through the constant transfer of material to its limit point. The actual sequence of the transfers is not so important, since it has been exhausted. Such exhaustion means one cannot see it as random, since its end product is what one gets no matter what pathway one takes.

Stephen Gould liked to insist that life need not give rise to larger and larger forms. Gould loved to point out that most of life was bacterial and similarly sized creatures and that these creatures were very successful. Gould wanted to dissuade people from seeing in the history of life any progress or teleological movement. But if life is about symbiogenesis, then it is constantly including parts into wholes. It therefore does have a trajectory. A bacterium, in a sense we will look at later, might not be more complex than a human, but the history of life might be about the inclusion of more and more genomes in it and, in that way, later entities have a larger number of genomes in them.

There are obviously more bacteria than humans in the world, but humans include within themselves a large percentage of that bacterial world. Bacteria may simply represent the barrier of what such inclusion can affect at their level. It is only when organisms become more and more multicellular and use sexual reproduction that more incorporation can occur. Gould insisted on the Darwinian view of random mutation and chance playing key roles. But Margulis has marginalized those mechanisms.

§11

Maximo Sandin
Nosotros Somos Bacteria y Virus

Spanish biologist Maximo Sandin has built very directly on Margulis's work and explicitly argues that Darwinism must be abandoned. Sandin has graciously made a large part of his work available to the public at his website (www.somosbacteriasyvirus.com). My attempt to render his views is based on what he has detailed on that site. Sandin's most original work is on the virus. The virus makes changes in life forms' very codes at various scales. Sandin is therefore looking at changes at the level of code and not at the incorporation of modular units, as did Margulis. With the virus, Sandin is offering a radically new way to understand how the living language of life changes. Sexual recombination does merge two parental genomes. Random mutations do rarely occur. Bacteria have shared information. But viruses affect creatures at all levels and affect them at the code's level. Margulis was aware of this but does not highlight it in her work. Margulis mostly saw viruses as destructive. She saw it as taking over the cell and "wreaking havoc," as opposed to bacteria, which form copacetic unions with us.[59] Sandin brings us back to the living language that is the true universal ancestor of all living things. This living language is a process, not in and of itself an organism. One, thereby,

---

[59] Sagan and Margulis, *Microcosmos*, 93.

at the level of texts, needs to look at the exchange of the letters—genetic material—rather than looking at the incorporation of modular units—parts and wholes. Viruses do take control of cells, but, in doing so, they do not simply manage to reproduce themselves. They also affect the cells they exploit.

Fred Hoyle recognized this long ago, as, for him, "diseases" were "failed evolutionary leaps."[60] Hoyle clearly saw things in terms of programming, as a virus's essential task is to stop a cell from running its typical programming.[61] The virus thereby is about introducing new code. It does just that by injecting new code into the genome of the host. If a creature survives the virus, then it retains the new programming language. Hoyle conceived the issue as a "clash" between the virus and the cell in terms of different instructions, but one can be incorporated into the other at the level of code—as it is only when the virus forces a cell to reproduce it that problems occur and not the adoption of new code, as such.[62] Hoyle also speculated this might only be of importance if it happens in "sex cells."[63] The sex cells receive the new genetic material, which is then passed onto offspring. Viral infections are evolutionary events.

Hoyle also speculated that viruses and chemical material for life originally came from outer space. This view is, of course, a mirroring of the viral theory at a strictly inorganic level. This theory, called 'Panspermia,' argues that life—or at least its chemical building blocks—is prevalent throughout the universe.[64] Given the vast expanses of the universe, the number of possible suns and planets like Earth is very large. Also, life depends on a select few elements (carbon, hydrogen, oxygen, and nitrogen) that exist at various places

---

[60] Fred Hoyle, *The Intelligent Universe* (New York: Holt, Rinehart, and Wilson, 1988), 128.
[61] Hoyle, *The Intelligent Universe*, 125.
[62] Hoyle, *The Intelligent Universe*, 127.
[63] Hoyle, *The Intelligent Universe*, 117.
[64] Hoyle, *The Intelligent Universe*, 110.

in the universe. Life depends on a proportional relation of these four elements—and comets have these four elements in the right proportion—no matter how it expresses itself in a particular form.[65] Only comets can be said to contain these four elements in the right manner (even the surface of the Earth does not have it, including the oceans and rocks).[66] When planets collide, the debris disseminates comets carrying these seeds of life. Comets are thus spores or large-scale viruses. They carry life from one point to another and change the nature of the entity impacted. A comet coming from a planet with life allows that planet to reproduce itself. Some say Gaia itself will one day reproduce itself by using humans as a transfer device rather than a comet.

Viruses are the comets of the living world. They enter living cells and deposit genetic material. Comets deposit chemical material, at least (if not viruses and bacteria themselves). We then should see comets as a secondary phenomenon following from the formation of planetary bodies. Viruses are the same sort of secondary phenomenon following from the development of life. Both act as emissaries and agents of change. Now, most would say planetary formation is something that follows specific rules, such that it is not itself contingent—especially the larger the system we look at. It would then follow that we see, if not a smaller scale version of the same structure at work with viruses and life, then a structure itself that follows. There are rules at work in planetary formation. One would say that, just as in a cellular automaton, one has a gun formation (where a particular particle is shot out from a iterating structure); here we have comets acting in the same way at the level of planet formation (we have already seen McGhee compare life to the formation of elements which occurs via nucleosynthesis).

Viruses convey bits/letters from one network to another

---

[65] Hoyle, *The Intelligent Universe*, 73.
[66] Hoyle, *The Intelligent Universe*, 73.

network. That may be their primary role in life. It is like a fundamental program: DNA giving rise to a sub-function that enables code to be passed along. Viruses pass genetic information between species. A virus might consist of pig DNA as well as bird DNA since it has infected both. It is thereby not simply depositing DNA but also extracting information and passing it between creatures that would, of course, not breed. What we see here is that elements of code function in relational manner with each other and have meaning in that way, but due to their material inscription can also be segmented and turned into a thing, a set of elements. Code is detachable in one of its aspects, even though in another it is simply relational. We can see this in letters. In English b/p is a relation that allows one to distinguish 'ball' from 'Paul.' But in Hebrew, it is p/f such that one contrasts words like 'falafel' and 'pilpel.' In fact, p and f are written with the same letter (they can be differentiated, if one wants, by a dot). Such differential relations make for accents, for example. But one states the letter as if it was a word and writes it out in isolation. It is thereby treated as if it were a unit. Viruses extract letters as units to transfer. The letter is thereby not simply a relation, but has an ontological autonomy and unity as a fragment, a set. In fact, one might have an entire sequence, such that it is more like grafting a signifier itself or word to another place. The word can then be extracted from its code relation to enter into a new code relation.

Things are not fixed in place. Pig DNA is not fixed by the context of being part of the pig genome and can take on new meaning or simply function relationally within a new genome. However, the letter as such makes no sense outside of this relation. It is thereby internally constituted as a new element. The 'p' of English is simply a different entity than that of the Hebrew 'peh.' The letter, ontologically, is always minimally related to itself and its place of inscription. It can never be subtracted from that relation. It is also like anything else related to itself and its absence. If one takes a DNA letter and looks at it as just a chemical existing by itself in a laboratory, it is then just an isolated thing—just as the sound made by 'p' in isolation is just a vibration of air. A letter on its own is meaningless. It can only exist as meaningful when related to the other letters. Then, one letter is always copied by its corresponding letter, but that a letter can be so abstracted does not mean, even as a thing, it is not relational. However, when the letter is part of the living language, then it is its differential relation with other elements that truly constitutes it.

Sandin suggests the true majority of our genome is made up of viral and bacterial DNA that are now permanently part of us. They are not there as some alien sequence that always marks itself as such, but are now constitutive parts of our genomes. Sandin emphasizes the existence in genetic sequences of mobile elements, repeated sequences, and homeotic genes in addition to viral elements. He believes that embryological development itself is due largely to viral sequences that are now operating and functioning in a new context. As we already noted, viruses are themselves much more prone to Darwinian mechanisms in this way, while larger creatures with more involved sequences are not. It is clear that they receive their genes from creatures that are more prone to random mutation given their high reproduction rates. One would then look to see the significance of Darwinian mechanisms on viruses themselves to see how they form and obtain their composition.

But Darwinism never accounted for how viruses contain various genomes themselves. With his model, Sandin can account for punctuated equilibrium with an actual mechanism, as the sudden leaps in evolution would arise due to viruses inputting enough information into organisms to cause new forms. Since viruses can affect any cell, these changes can be seen throughout an entire biosphere. Bacteria are, then, like wholes—cells, that contain within them all the fundamental things needed for life and its future development into creatures at larger scales. But viruses infect things and thereby function as carriers for the development of life. They are messengers distributing messages and disseminating ideas. The message reaches many organisms, given precisely their infectious character. That does not mean viruses are positive. They can lead to death of an organism—even mass death or extinction of a species. Such events interrupt the flow of life and send it into a new direction.

Viruses are like spores beings sent out by the living language of life itself in order to disperse instructions. These instructions then become part of the living tissue of organisms and help direct their development. When Sandin refers to mobile elements, he means that some viral sequences can still detach themselves and move about within the code. They can transpose themselves to other parts of the genome, for instance. In looking at a genome, one should see oneself, in part, as an archeologist or etymologist uncovering fossils there that reveal a long history of amalgamation. Without the instructions viral DNA provides, Sandin does not think embryonic development would be possible. It is not thinkable in terms of random mutation. Only the accumulation of key instruction elements would allow for something like a single cell to become a creature containing trillions of cells.

Viruses remodulate genomes and also give them regulatory instructions for how to perform new tasks. Viruses are software patches sent by the code itself to update the operating system. These changes can come simply by the way the genome reacts to the virus' presence and attempts at infiltration. Viral DNA backs up and also can remain dormant, awaiting a time when it will be switched on to perform its role. The amazing fact that viral DNA has mobility and can change place means that internal changes occur that have nothing to do with copying errors. Retroviruses, in particular, developed the ability to produce DNA from the RNA it contains. The tools viruses offer genomes also include the ability to repair copying errors. In this way, not only do viruses show that evolution is not proceeding by Darwinian mechanisms, but also they are a mechanism that would neutralize these mechanisms directly. Due to the actions of viruses, one can also understand how parts of the genome reproduce themselves, since viruses can affect such duplication. The genome itself is an inscription point, like one on a hard drive that can be updated and changed. In one's CPU there is an operating system that runs a machine language, but here the machine language is updated and patched at key points at its core.

Sandin militates against chance and randomness, but he makes it appear as though the function of viruses is itself contingent. However, if we are right that viruses are themselves a function that the living code produces to disperse messages, then there should be a way to see viral functioning as a function of the programming language. That programming language can be billions of bits long, which makes it very involved. Much more so than any computer language we have now. But that might also be why we needed human operators to send out patches to help correct problems, whereas the living code does not. It repairs itself in a way analogous to how a human body repairs itself when cut. It sends out new messages in the same way a programmer will in changing how a program is set up to run. Sandin, along with Margulis, still highlights the role of pure chance and contingency in life's unfolding. It will take a way of conceptualizing the functioning of bacteria and viruses as parts of the living code of life to no longer see life as not a contingent accident depending on things the happenstance of what actually occurs. Otherwise, we can only be etymologists and archeologists and describe how something like the human happened to arise.

§12
Critique of 'Self-Organization'

How life emerged out of matter is, of course, a great mystery. Even creationists do not argue that life emerges out of nothing (they only claim such an event for the creation of being itself). Life somehow arose on the basis of what already was. Despite not having a detailed model for how this did in fact occur, there is a clear consensus that life emerged spontaneously from chemical matter. The leading proponent and articulator of this view is, of course, Stuart Kauffman: "Life is an expected, collectively self-organized property of catalytic polymers."[67] Kauffman here uses the concept of 'self-organization;' however, that term is highly misleading. There is no self here already existing that then actively organizes itself. An entity is itself constituted here. For this reason, the term 'emergence' is less misleading. A hurricane does not organize itself from water vapor, etc. It is a phenomenon that emerges out of the interaction of various processes.

The term 'self-organization' is, of course, used to attempt to make it seem as though there were no transcendent hand directing the process. But recall again cellular

---

[67] Stuart Kauffman, *The Origins of Order: Self-Organization and Selection in Evolution* (New York: Oxford University Press, 1993), 289.

automata. In Conway's 'Game of Life,' there are specific rules programmed that iterate themselves. Out of this computation emerge all sorts of phenomena, such as 'spaceship' patterns. It would not be fair to say these spaceships 'self-organize.' In any event, even if we substitute conjugations of the verb 'to emerge' for 'self-organization,' we have still have the problem of understanding how it works. If life is an "expected property" as Kauffman puts forth, then life should have emerged multiple times on this planet. To say that is the same as saying a 'spaceship' or gun pattern is expected when a specific program is run. The gun itself suddenly emerges and is not considered mysterious, since we can repeat the cellular automaton program repeatedly and see that it occurs over and over. No laboratory experiment using chemicals has yet produced a self-replicating DNA or RNA molecular, much less a nucleated cell, spontaneously out of processes left to run on their own. For this reason, if life is expected, it may be expected only when a comet per Hoyle strikes the earth. It would then be reasonable to see life as having one single origin, given that it came from the impact of a single comet. If life is expected on earth, then one would have to see it happening multiple times, rather than in one singular primordial soup, given the prevalence of the chemicals.

As already noted, amino acids have been made in the lab. But such building blocks have not assembled themselves into a structure, much less one that self-replicates. One needs to see the emergence of replicated molecules to have the first point of departure of life. But that replication requires cellular machinery to occur. One of the reasons this process seems to be difficult to reproduce is that amino acids assembling together to form peptides (and thereby proteins) requires a clear violation of the second law of thermodynamics. One hereby needs a clear energy source. In our own bodies, this process occurs as proteins and peptides forming inside of us, but we can clearly see how it occurs as well as the role energy plays. Ultimately when we say a phenomenon is emergent, we mean it is not clearly deducible from what came before. In logic, we can have two propositions that clearly contain all one needs to spell out a deduced conclusion, but in a cellular automaton it is not clear how the program itself, when read, indicates that it will lead to a spaceship pattern as opposed to a glider. This is due to the phenomenon itself being a computation of rules and instructions. One generates the phenomenon, but it can only be known by the generation itself. This is why such phenomena depend on simulation and emulation to be tested and understood. If life is an emergent phenomenon, we will only be able to say we understand it once we can simulate or emulate its emergence.

Such emergent patterns are nonrandom. They also require information and instructions. Cellular automata are clearly programmed to provide the emergent patterns they do. When looking at emergent phenomena, we then need to see how they are programmed and how they are running a set of instructions. This is true as much of a hurricane as of a snowflake. If one focuses simply on the improbability of phenomena, it will be incomprehensible. However, if one sees all phenomena as relating to information and instructions, then one no longer needs to see emergence as some sort of spontaneous 'self-organization. Self-organization is therefore similar to the theory of spontaneous generation, where life was seen as suddenly emerging out of things—maggots spontaneously emerging out of a corpse.

Emergence is also seen as being the emergence of order out of chaos. However, often, chaos is simply itself ordered or the product of simple rules (pi yields a seemingly random series of numbers after its decimal point, but we know the simple rule for generating them one by one). Order does not come from chaos; chaos comes from order. This is, of course, the revolution in thought being led by Stephen Wolfram. Design is found in the programming of all things, such that even random phenomena are the products of series of finite rules. One should therefore also not look at the constraints inherent in matter or chemical processes to understand emergence. Many want to focus on the 'singular' (maximum or minimum) point or 'critical point' at which a phenomenon emerges. For example, water being heated reaches a boiling point. One here focuses on the conditions, the pressures, forces, etc., that give rise to the boiling, but that requires one to see everything from an external point of view. Emergence is meant to be an immanent phenomenon that follows from the unfolding of a system itself. All of the components (forces, pressures, atoms, molecules, etc.) have to be seen as a part of the system; but then the system is a computation and susceptible to explanation via programs and instructions in the same way as a cellular automaton.

One of the motives for not looking at things from the perspective we are suggesting is that emergence is seen as a purely anti-theistic phenomena. But this thrust leads to anthropomorphization and personalization of forces. One speaks of sodium chloride itself minimizing bonding energy in order to 'organize itself' into a cube. Darwinism, of course, seems to have no problem with such language (insofar as the sort of Darwinism practiced today in many humanities departments speaks about how something exists only in order to do something else, as though natural selection had some intentionality). This language occurs since natural selection itself is seen as the main motor of life's development. One wants to see everything as coming together externally in order to make emergence seem like some spontaneous phenomenon that refuses any explanation that might make it appear designed. The discourse of emergence is saying new unities appear that are simply selections of already formed potentialities, but there is no reason to even see potentialities or tendencies here. Many want to project, back into some other ontological realm, tendencies that allegedly activated themselves, but, unless one can point to something like dormant DNA code, this is no more than a psychological projection.

This projection of tendencies is, again, to ensure that the phenomenon of emergence came not from something programmed like rules, but only from a nebulous space.

However, to say that one cannot know what results and emerges prior to the iteration of known rules does not mean that one has to posit tendencies or implicit possibilities that themselves cannot explain the phenomenon. If emergent phenomena are not the result of pre-formed possibilities or archetypical forms, then one should see them as purely actual. The programming of cellular automata is purely actual itself. It is not a form that is then instantiated and embodied. The cellular automaton is its rules just as pi is the relationship of the circumference of a circle to its diameter. Pi is this relation and an expression of it. Given that it is that relation, it is an infinity that is based on the circle itself, and that is finitely inscribed.

A good example of how a self-organizational view has played out in the discussion of evolutionary biology is in the work of Brian Goodwin. In his *How the Leopard Changed its Spots,* Goodwin attempts to show how chaos theory is at work in the development of organisms and their history of changes. Chaos theories believe that one cannot truly determine initial conditions, that whatever develops from initial conditions is unpredictable precisely because of this imprecision (thus, a butterfly can lead to a storm because this small aspect of initial conditions is magnified when things are repeated), that all systems revolve around attractors that shape them or lead them, that changes as crucial points (like the point at which a pot of hot water boils) or bifurcations occur at far-from-equilibrium states, and that order appears to arise for no reason out of disordered states. It is this last point that is most crucial. Chaos theory sees reality as made of disordered stats that then, suddenly and without reason, issue in ordered states. Goodwin writes the following in what is the most important passage of his book:

> This is the emphasis on self-organization, the capacity of these fields to generate patterns spontaneously without any specific instructions telling them what to do, as in a genetic program. These systems pro-

duce something out of nothing. Now, we can see precisely what is meant by 'nothing' in this context. There is no plan, no blueprint, no instructions, about the pattern that emerges.[68]

Here, we have stated that no order or instructions are involved. That is, Goodwin's view is directly opposed to a computational view, where the patterns emerge from the iteration of rules themselves seen in cellular automata. Goodwin believes because there is no generic code to be found in the phenomena, he notes, then there can be no instructions. But if we can run a simulation of this phenomenon on a computer, for instance, then that itself shows the pattern emerges from instructions. Instructions do not need to be in something like DNA for them to be immanent in a phenomenon.

While part of Goodwin's point here is that genes do not unilaterally control what an organism looks like, that in and of itself does not tell us that there is a not a larger computation that occurs.[69] Things are not in disorder. True disorder would be a state of full entropy, but to say order arises out of that implies one has more time than the universe has existed to wait around. Now, Goodwin thinks that Darwinism has been reductionist, as it does not see "organisms are as real, as fundamental, and as irreducible as the molecules out of which they are made," but to see there being emergent scales in biology and within the history of life does not rule out order itself.[70] The failing here is to think that irreducible levels can arise only if there are no plans or instructions involved. But it is rather that such emerge if there are such rules at work explicitly or implicitly. Goodwin seems to think that computation is opposed to

---

[68] Brian Goodwin, *How the Leopard Changed Its Spots: The Evolution of Complexity* (Princeton: Princeton University Press, 1994), 51.
[69] Goodwin, *How the Leopard Changed Its Spots*, 142.
[70] Goodwin, *How the Leopard Changed Its Spots*, x.

"dynamic behavior," but computation is itself the explanation of how that dynamism works as it does rather than in another way. Goodwin might be right that "molecular reductionism" has predominated in biology, but that does not mean that computationalism cannot also see organisms as irreducible entities that exist in their own right. Dynamic order and organization are not explained when one simply describes its occurrence. Chaos theory does not really explain how order arises, whereas computational theories do. It is computationalism itself that can best explain how something can emerge from a lower level without simply noting it or describing the process, but rather detailing the rules themselves involved.

To explain things means to offer an account for why they occur. To say things occur spontaneously is the very opposite of that. If biology is to be more than a set of historical accounts in which one damn thing appears after another and actually explain those things, it needs more than a reference to spontaneous leaps and an assertion that there is a lack of instructions involved. Even Goodwin seems to understand this: "Explanations in terms of history and natural selection are not very helpful since they merely redescribe what is observed in terms of functions and costs, but one is no wiser for the 'explanation.'"[71] Goodwin thinks positing paths of least resistance and attractors does the work, but this theory of morphogenesis only ever posits external forces to explain how things arise. It sees the distinct forms produced by the history of life as externally imposed by outside forces, but that would itself be overturned if it could be shown that an emulation of this emergence can be done on a computer. That emulation could then tell us what the plant will look in another environment precisely because the plant on its own has code and instructions. Biology will only be done more and more on computers and not less. Thus, it would be shown that morphogenesis is not about being pulled, as if by some

---

[71] Goodwin, *How the Leopard Changed Its Spots*, 88.

force like 'gravity' by so-called attractors, but by the unfolding of a program—whether at the level of DNA or the cell itself with its hardware as well involved.

For example, Goodwin sees phyllotactic patterns as the result of "relative probabilities of the morphogenetic trajectories of the various forms" and not having to do with "natural selection."[72] However, while we agree with Goodwin that natural selection does not play a key role, these phyllotactic patterns reveal profound sequences reflecting the computational nature of pants. It is not that just any form can occur in different environments; because the plant is computing a specific set of rules, we can predict what it will look in different settings. Is it really just a matter of probability that a phyllotactic pattern will reveal the Fibonacci sequence? Part of Goodwin's point here is that "all the phyllotactic patterns may serve well enough for light-gathering by leaves,"[73] but that such patterns reveal complex computational patterns suggests it is not a matter of simply trying many different patterns so that various ones appear. The plants are themselves computational in nature all the way down, and, thus, it is clear which patterns will arise and which will not out of the vast domain space of conceivable possibilities. Goodwin gives the impression that there is just such a large "generative space" that we will see various patterns, but we seem to only find patterns that reflect specific rules.[74] It is Goodwin himself who is overlooking a theory that can truly explain how and why the phyllotactic pattern has the specific sequence and form it does, because Goodwin insists on a theory that emphasizes an alleged disorder in things and randomness.

While Goodwin has criticized natural selection, the other key aspect of Darwinism remains firmly entrenched. Once Goodwin admits that phenotypical patterns of, for instance, plants can be simulated well by computers, he has

---

[72] Goodwin, *How the Leopard Changed Its Spots*, 132.

[73] Goodwin, *How the Leopard Changed Its Spots*, 132.

[74] Goodwin, *How the Leopard Changed Its Spots*, 132.

already admitted that the 'real word' patterns of the plants must themselves also be computational in nature. To see things as shaped by external factors like sunlight, water, air quality, etc., is to forget that these factors can be made themselves part of any computation and that the same plant in a different environment—while having a different shape—will have the same code. If a process has computational properties, then it is a computational process, even if one must include environmental factors in the overall computation. This computation explains things that water and air cannot because pointing to water and air involves not an explanation, but a description. Or, at most, water and air are material causes, but not formal or even truly efficient causes here (as it is only how the plant itself reads the water information and input that allows for the changes—thus again, computation). It takes for granted how and why the plant is growing and, only then, says how external factors shape it, but it is precisely that growth that is not a sum process of spontaneous generation, but the iteration of clear rules.

Emergent phenomena are also phenomena that relate to traits not found in their precursors. The properties of water are not found in hydrogen and oxygen when taken alone. The properties of water are irreducible to hydrogen and water and could not have been predicted from them. At the same time, emergence speaks to the way in which the new phenomena at a new scale can in turn act upon the phenomena at the previous scale. This would be like water acting on and influencing hydrogen and oxygen atoms. But no one can speak of tendencies in hydrogen and oxygen precisely due to the lack of reducibility. Any discussion of such tendencies or capacities would be a retroactive psychological projection. Now, those who follow Gilles Deleuze in their thinking speak of the 'virtual' rather than of possibilities, potentialities, tendencies, capacities, etc. But the virtual can only ever be what we are calling programming if it is to avoid being nothing but a retroactive, psychological projection. If one were just to look at a spaceship cellular automaton pattern, one would not see or know, as such, its program rules. Those rules are then virtually contained in it—just as when seeing an expansion of pi to 20 decimal places one does not see a circumference or diameter. They are virtually there. The virtual cannot have any other meaning without requiring the creation of an entirely new ontological domain and world that split the world into two and cause the problem of explaining how it is so split and how the two split sides meet each other. The number pi is not an actualization of a relationship within a circle. It is that relationship. A cellular automaton is not an actualization of a program; it is its iteration. One explains the development only via the iteration of rules.

One can see in the work of Deleuze scholar John Protevi precisely an attempt to argue that a virtual ontology best explains the history of life and, in particular, works best to explain the biological insights of a developmental view. Protevi sees in this new work a move from a viewpoint that sees "'one string of DNA = one gene = one protein = one function' to 'one string of DNA (structural / hereditary gene) = many (functional) genes (many mature mRNA transcripts) = many proteins = many functions.'"[75] But this insight does not indicate a need for a virtual ontology. Rather, it shows us that DNA is not a machine language. Machine langue is not ambiguous. The biochemicals composing a cell would form that code. DNA is rather a higher-order software language, and thus can its computation, by the cellular machinery, allow for more than a one-to-one relation between DNA and genes, for instance.

The problem with a Deleuzian view is that it does not truly account for how the actual organism—with its actual biochemistry—is already fully differentiated and that it unfolds through the iteration of the rules informing that differentiation rather than through the actualization of something that exists only in a virtual nether world. With

---

[75] John Protevi, *Life, War, Earth: Deleuze and the Sciences* (Minneapolis: University of Minnesota Press, 2013), 200–201.

computation, one does not need to posit any potential, only the ability of something to unfold via the iteration of rules. The virtual view thinks that structures are themselves not simply the name for how things are in actuality, but the name for the invariant structure of things and patterns that are only ever actualized in things. But with life, in particular, we have a code itself in the creature always already there as DNA. Thus, we have information and instructions. Life is about how information is passed on and how chemicals interact. There is no actualization of a pattern that exists eternally or in another dimension of being.

Ultimately, a virtual ontology thinks that there exists a realm of possibilities that we can epistemologically project, but, to understand how a creature unfolds, we do not need to know about possibilities, only its actual composition and the immanent rules it is unfolding. Even a crystal that is unfolding, for instance, does not actualize some specific possibility but computes a pattern. This is why we can simulate it on a computer. The computer does not select from a realm of possibilities but rather allows an actual set of instructions to play out. With life, the code does exist, even before it is played. It is actually there all the time as DNA and not in some other dimension of being. Just because that set of instructions leads to different results does not mean one needs to have recourse to a virtual field of possibilities but only to the fully compiled code the computation is playing out.

Recall cellular automatons. There are permutations on particular cellular automata, but each permutation is a different code and thus unfolds into different cellular automata. However, one can make cellular automata appear as different colors. One simply adds code rather than it actualizing some nebulous possibility. Protevi wants to avoid seeing the Deleuzian virtual as a Platonic realm of essences, but the only way to avoid such a Platonic realm, in its vulgar sense of preformed things, is to see how in the differentiation of the actuality of the actual one can account for how things develop via the computation of that actuality.

Protevi caricatures a computational view by saying that "the potentiality of the hereditary DNA is not preformationism: there's no present/actual/homuncular/already-determined 'unit' or 'program' in the DNA that determines the actualization of the potential."[76] But this shows a misunderstanding of the nature of code. The code does not compute itself here but rather is computed by cellular hardware. However, there is no potential, only what is emergent from the computation of the code. Code is not some semiotic set of signs with meaning, but a series of letters. The conjugation of the letters themselves can lead to emergent phenomena. It is not a question of preformation, but of the emergent power of the letter. But these letters are themselves present as chemicals, whether in the DNA or in the cell as a whole. The program is not some set of blue prints that already forms a shadowy complete version of the thing, but a program is here both as an actuality and one that, in its unfolding, does determine the process.

Thus, genes are not virtual but rather emergent, like words out of letters. Letters can be permuted into many different words, but that does not mean the words are virtual. They are actual as much as the letters are. Genes are actualized by the permutation of the code itself. Protevi thinks there is, following Mary West-Eberhard, unexpressed genetic variation, but that is like saying there are unexpressed words in English. However, all one needs is the 26 letters of the alphabet and a rule for their combination to express those words. It is not clear what saying these unexpressed words exist as potentialities gives, since they do not arise in the world by being taken and the elements composing do exist actually. If potentiality is not pre-existent, then it can only be a mental projection. However, what we are interested in scientifically is why a particular pattern emerges and how a particular set of letters came to form specific words and why that happened via specific rules. Retroactively positing potentialities does not help us

---

[76] Protevi, *Life, War, Earth*, 211.

to understand how that can occur, as it is obvious that with 26 letters we have a vast space of possible English words to speak.

Also, we should not forget here Wolfram's notion of computational irreducibility. Even if one has rules, one cannot know in advance how a computation will play out. So after the fact, we can see how and why it produced what it did. But that does not mean it was only selecting out possibilities. If the genotype is not itself being affected, that is like saying the alphabet is not being affected. One then only has immanent rules for how to permute the letters themselves. The code does not operate itself here, and thus it is not a matter of drawing upon a realm of potentiality that is unexpressed, but of the code being actuated via specific rules and instructions that leads to variation and permutations in its expression. This is why with developmental accounts of biology the environmental is but one more operator on the code, just as the cellular machinery is. Since the code is only a series of letters, one needs interpreters. But this is all arising on the basis of something actual and not via something non-actual coming into being. It is all actual. It is all a part of the order of existence. Anything non-actual here is only accessible by mind with its eidetic intuition and ability to project beyond what is seen. This is again why we can and will do more and more biology using computers.

Imagine if one had to truly work with some dimension of unexpressed variation first. One would use sorcery rather than computers. Thus, it is deceptive to say one is moving away here from a view dominated by genetic programming. One needs to understand that computation is not so restricted. There are differences between machine code, assemblers, compilers, interpreters, higher-levels of software, etc. The cell plays one role in that. But one will not be able to truly capture what one is going to if one forgets that it is on the basis of the differentiation of the actual rather than the realization of potentials. This is why we cannot ever get rid of the act of producing mRNA. mRNA itself transcribes a series of genetic lettering. But in doing so, it is precisely permuting the letters rather than realizing some potential. When we see it is as a realization of potential, we miss precisely how specific actual rules are being operated on existing elements.

While it is true that DNA is only one of many components in this process, that is no different than saying that, in a computer, an operating system is not the same as a machine code and not the same as a specific word processing program. If one cannot show how the DNA is not genetic information fundamental to the composition of the organism and passed on, then one cannot say there is not any pre-existing genetic information. One simply needs to remember that information is purely syntactic and differential in nature. DNA is not semiotic information representing something for someone like smoke representing a fire to a person. The problem with a Deleuzian account is also that it thinks there are virtual patterns, but we see here that there are only elements and rules for transformations of those elements.

Virtual patterns are still close to Platonic essences that exist independently of things. But those patterns could only at best be sets of letters, bit strings. Deleuzians speak as though the actual is only differentiated by its relation to the virtual. But it is much more so the opposite. We only see what the virtual field could be, insofar as there is one, by permuting the actual. It is thus the actual that shows us what the virtual could be. We have 26 letters of the alphabet, and it is based on the rules for their combination and transformation that we see patterns. But those permutations do not change the alphabet. We do not have 27 letters are a result. There is no counter-effectuation of the virtual on the actual. Rather than the relation between the virtual and the actual, the real issue is how the actual itself is segmented into sets and collections. That is why if letters can be permuted in so many ways, we only see a particular word or sentence and only a particular text.

But with life, we see that is because there are interpreters and assemblers that know how to take the syntactic information as bits and transform them. There are chemicals that perform Boolean operations on each other in their catalysis and interactions. What one chemical or chemical system outputs becomes the input for another chemical or chemical system. One can see "and," "or," and "not" processes at work such that the chemicals act as logic gates. If two differing chemicals are needed in order for a further step to occur, then we have, for instance, an "and" operation.[77] But if what one chemical produces becomes input for another chemical system and two different types are needed, but either will yield the future step, then one has an 'or' operation.

At the same time, any chemical or chemical system can be seen as a transistors or switches where informational input is transformed into a new output. If we do not see things computationally, we will miss this dimension, as we will be thinking that all the reactions are a matter of cause and effect or the result of some sort of spontaneous self-organization or random drift. But if we see inputs transformed into outputs, then we know that it is programmed, as the programming itself delimits what can be and cannot be. Since chemicals essentially function by sending information to each other in order to activate, Boolean logic can comprehend them. We have chemical computers at work. However, these chemical computers are difficult to program and create and keep stable such that simulating these processes on a computer is needed. No virtual patterns are changed—only the actual coding of the DNA or the hardware of cells.

It is the lack of change to the genotype as noted by West-Eberhard and the developmental theorists that shows that there is at least one subset of the overall code for an organism, for instance, that is unaffected and that forms a

---

[77] I am drawing on Dennis Bray's *Wetware: A Computer in Every Living Cell* (New Haven: Yale, 2011), 75–85, for my account of how Boolean logic works with chemicals.

key program for the rest and is always running. But that key subset is not in some potential field. Even if one looks at cell conditions and the environment, they are simply additional subroutines here and part of a larger program for even individual organisms. The essence of the thing, the invariant in it, is then some particular subroutine that is part of an overall program. The essence of things is then a subset rather than the whole. The whole would be the program for how it exists and why it exists as it does. Subroutines are not virtual patterns but code. If they are changed (such as changes that occur in the cytoplasm) it is not the actual affecting the virtual but a change within the actual itself. It is the actual itself that is split, for instance, between hardware and software when it comes to the living. Finally, while developmental biologists love to talk about how one cannot predict from the genome alone what particular organism will arise, that just itself proves the principle of computational irreducibility. Saying potentialities are actualized cannot even show us how we can re-run what occurred and see how it happened or how it can be simulated for future experimentation.

Take water again as an example. Hydrogen and oxygen do not organize themselves into water. The atoms bond together. It is a pattern that emerges from that bonding. One should not speak as though there were just some dead particles lying around and that something external shocks them with energy or something else, joining them and suddenly giving them shape. Nothing in this world is simply static. The entire universe has been unfolding since the Big Bang. Such particles also are not simply swimming around in some chaotic dance. Even the seeming chaos of fluid dynamics has been shown by Wolfram to be the result of a program with relatively simple rules. Often theorists of self-organization subtract something like a hurricane from the larger set of atmospheric phenomena of which it is part in order to make it appear as though it is not itself the result of computational phenomena. They do not want to think the rule is programmed, because emergence was allegedly going to show us how all is contingent, random, spontaneous, and outside the purview of any transcendent hand.

To return phenomena to the purview of finite sets of rules is to return them to the purview of intelligence and agents. There are no fully closed systems. Any system that seems closed (like a cell) is itself inside of some larger system. The only possibly closed system is the universe itself. Energy and matter flow into and out of all possibly enumerated and determinable systems. For this reason, as we will see, all phenomena are computational and concern input and output states. Computers are thus a way of permuting letters/bits. A computer takes one sequence of letters and knows how to produce a second sequence. If it receives as input one sequence of bits, then it has a program telling it what the next sequence should be. Computers thus take sequences of bits and, based on them, produce a second sequence as per their programming. In nature one sees the coordinated motions of mater induced to bring about new scalar phenomena, but this emergence is seen as being incompatible with intelligent design. However, that can only be true if there is no programming.

Energy here is often anthropomorphized and given personal qualities as though it knew what to do or chooses to produce a particular result. Now with energy input it is often said that a system will break down and dissipate into the background out of which it emerged. Hurricanes require moist air as part of their engine and to form their spirals. The interaction with land undercuts this engine, and the hurricane dies out. But here one of the issues is from what context we examine the hurricane. If we look at the hurricane itself as an isolated phenomenon we will see this occur. But we can always scale back and see it as part of a global weather system. Hurricanes would then be local occurrences. To do metaphysics, one has to push such questions to their ultimate point and take each conditioned phenomenon to its unconditioned condition, whether that is its origin or endpoint. We then have already started to engage in metaphysics but have not engaged in it at every point.

At this point, we are simply attempting a critique of this specific notion of self-organization. Any complex system will itself arise from a large number of local phenomena, such as when bees swarm together and interact with each other directly or via a honeycomb, chemicals left on flowers, etc. In fact, swarms are taken often as a paradigmatic example of 'self-organization.' Such systems thus need many moving parts that are themselves wholes. Any bee can exist independently of the swarm, but as we saw already with life itself, there has to be some element of code at work in order to make sense of how things develop. This is also true of hurricanes, which are not living insofar as they have no independent software but are material phenomena (hardware/software being joined together). Interaction between components at a local level leads to global results.

Such phenomena have serial scales; in regards to a hurricane, one can speak of air and water molecules but also of winds. A hurricane appears one way when seen from space and another when from land. But if one just looks at each stage in terms of how the vapor condenses into rain, how the low pressure fronts meet high pressure ones, how heat causes air to rise and fuels it, etc., one misses the phenomenon as such. It would be like describing a space ship automaton by how it fills in grids, how it would look to an ant crawling across the screen, etc. Because complex system theories do not look at programming, they speak about positive feedback loops. However, such concepts only repeat phenomenological descriptions of what is going on and thereby do not truly explain how the phenomena arise. Positive feedback loops supposedly regulate how such phenomena function, but a loop is itself a phenomenon to be explained. It would be like saying that a particular cellular automaton constantly repeats itself and thereby is regulated by that repetition loop rather than looking at how the programming itself plays a role. This is again because complexity theory in its usual atheism wants to see phenomena as self-made ('autocatalysis') to the point where each is responsible for itself and not due to some ground outside of itself. Phenomena need to be seen as simply unfolding on their own. That's fine, as long as one does not exclude the fact that there is a program or rule at work.

Any energy said to be inputted from outside can, by scaling back, be seen as an internal part of the phenomenon itself. Any phenomenon of chance, especially those in nature, can be seen as the function of rules. Part of the reason here for emphasizing self-organization is to emphasize arbitrariness. But science, decade after decade, has indicated the non-arbitrary nature of what appears. One can conceive of the physical world as a series of levels, but, as we saw already via von Neumann, there needs to be a level at which there is a differential relation itself, the bit, to explain how things function. Given that all natural phenomena are finite, these levels have a lowest common denominator. We will also later attempt to conceive of where their end point is. That is, we will ask as to what the Omega Point of all being is insofar as things do not simply run on forever or dissipate into near nothing. We can then find different levels and scales of being with different logics at work in them. But ultimately, all are susceptible to the same programming and to the same rules.

To return to our discussion of life, a chemical can be a DNA letter in the code, but it can also function as a whole and part of a code. Mitochondria can itself be a whole and then function as a part. It is not simply that at each level there are new phenomenological properties to describe, but one has to see how at each level entities that functioned as parts now become wholes or elements of a code. To do metaphysics is then to ask what level is fundamental (if there is one). But we have already said that, due to the finite nature of phenomena, it is always the bit that forms the ultimate level even if, at further levels up the scales, phenomena that functioned as wholes at one level can function as bits at the new level. Each level is a new viewpoint on reality itself. But there are not infinite levels—at least not when one speaks of material and living phenomena.

This is far from the first critique of emergence and self-organization. William Dembski articulated one in his most important book *No Free Lunch*. There, Dembski argues emergence is an "empty word" unless the nature of the emergence can be specified.[78] For Dembski, the whole idea of emergence is often a name for ignorance, where we merely point to how things arise out of other things without detailing how that occurs. We need explanations to do the work, and catch-all phrases should not substitute for that. To explain means to provide a specific account and detail those things that together form sufficient conditions for the phenomenon to follow from them. Dembski believes that the discourse of emergence is today's version of "alchemy" (*NFL* 243). However, that only means we do not have the specific sequence for how life did emerge.

Dembski does not rule out emergence as such. He notes simply that when we say "X emerges from Y" both variables need detail (*NFL* 244). Until the specific steps life took to emerge can be detailed, Dembski believes that a commitment to life emerging in this manner is a symptom of a specific metaphysical orientation (metaphysical naturalism) that requires life to emerge this way as no other way is possible given that metaphysical commitment (*NFL* 245). A different metaphysical commitment would offer a different account for life's beginning. Naturalism can only accept life as an emergent property. All very true. And we are, in this, amidst offering just such a pan-ontic computationalism to account for how this occurs.

Let us return to the origin of life. One often hears it said that life emerged from a set of chemicals under the right conditions. But we have already recounted the sheer improbability of such an event occurring by chance. One can then say it follows from the laws of this universe. If it is not by chance, but expected, that is to already say some non-random processes are a work. The main theory popular

---

[78] William Dembski, *No Free Lunch* (New York: Rowman and Littlefield, 2007), 240. All subsequent citations included as *NFL*.

nowadays, to my knowledge, is that at some very early stage the precursors of life were simple RNA sequences that suddenly began self-replicating. RNA here needs to be read by a ribosome such that one has to posit not just a RNA sequence, but a ribosome to read it. In other words, it is not enough to have a tape; one needs something to read the tape to form the rudiments of a Turing machine. The mRNA is a "tape" that "records information" that is sent through the ribosome to be read and translated (*NBC* 36). This tape has the base pairs as its letters/bits. One thereby needs RNA acting in a divided way to copy itself. The ribosomes read the incoming RNA and outputs proteins as a result. We may need here to posit the joining together of two separate RNA sequences that come together to form this function.

One also sees here that translation of information is decisive. One set of letters must be transformed into another set. One thus has a self-replicating molecular structure. In chemicals themselves, one has information. All living things essentially have this same basic genetic code and are based on the same proteins that occur through the translation and interpretation of the instructions contained in the recorded bits. Genes can themselves be seen as blueprints and instructions telling other chemical and organic processes what to do. They include a mapping of how things should develop. That does not mean that there might not be parallel processing wherein other programs are unfolding at the same time. For that reason it would not be necessarily the genes themselves that alone can contain everything in seed form. But we should not see things as having their own morphogenic structure outside of some code and some computational process. The key is that with life we have a small detailed replica at the level of the code itself even though it does not resemble the thing to be made in any analogical sense.

DNA may simply be "the best of all possible codes" and optimal in its very coding in terms of bringing about the very diversity of life we have.[79] Despite its obvious complexity, our own biochemistry and that of every living creature can still exhibit the most elegant forms possible for the kind of life that can exist here: "Take, for example, sugars, the main energy source of life. These are built up from the two commonest molecules in the universe, the molecules of hydrogen and carbon monoxide."[80] There may not be, in fact, another system conceivable that works as effectively, given that ours is based on the most basic of molecules and common elements found all over creation. What is fascinating about DNA is that the letters are not in "some regular pattern like TGCATGCATGCA" but in a seemingly random and "non-repetitive order."[81] The key is to decide whether such an order can itself be the product of chance or is programmed to be so and the result of computational order. As we will see, we will need to evaluate the work of William Dembski, who will argue that information cannot be in random order to function as information. If DNA did not just come in random order, it would be simply compressible into a simple program (TGCA for instance). It would thereby potentially have very little to say. On the other hand, we may find it is so compressible that its seeming randomness emerges from a simple program or one just like it. As Dembski and Witt note, if a book were written using just "recurring patterns of letters" it would not have much to say:

> It would be like trying to write a friend where B always had to follow A, and the Cs had to come in threes. If every letter you set down was governed by a rule like 'repeat the letter and then skip ahead two letters in the alphabet,' you'd never get anything

---

[79] Johnson, *Programming of Life*, 28.
[80] Hoyle, *The Intelligent Universe*, 18.
[81] Dembski and Witt, *Intelligent Design Uncensored*, 16.

meaningful written.[82]

There should be some way to distinguish between a meaningful DNA sequence and one that is nonsense in the same way that we can tell the difference between a letter written that makes sense and one that is incomprehensible. DNA should not be thought of as *like* a computer program, but *as* one. There are identical aspects at work in both. Such considerations would lead us to a future science in which we discuss the notion of design since only intelligent agents are known to be able to produce such highly detailed codes.

At the same time, Wolfram has shown us that the iteration of simple rules need not simply result in fractal and nested patterns. In this way, the DNA code has to be seemingly random in order to do its work. Is each DNA sequence for each individual irreducibly complex? Perhaps. But it is still a definite program made of the same code. It still needs to be in some ordered sequence in order to function. Presumably, if the letters of a DNA sequence were ordered just by flipping a four-sided code, one would not produce any sort of living creature. If not, then even the seemingly random sequence of DNA lettering must itself be the product of simple rules. Some random flipping of DNA letters is possible, but even a small number of point mutations have deleterious effects. DNA is a recipe. If one put some parts of a recipe in random order, it may not result in the baking of a cake.

One must also recall how we keep getting similar results over and over again both at the level of phenotype and at the molecular level via convergence. And we have already ruled that out as being due to chance. To think the DNA code, we need to think it as four irreducible letters and permutations that can be written in binary code (00, 11, 01, 10). There are about 3 billion such letters in the human DNA sequence. These billions of bits of data are rolled up

---

[82] Dembski and Witt, *Intelligent Design Uncensored*, 16.

like a scroll in each cell. Via permutations there is conjugation into, for example, the 30,000 genes of the human which form subsets/subroutines. The flexibility of DNA is such that there are multiple DNA sequences that can code for such genes as amino acids which, in turn, can be built up from different DNA sequences (that lead, in turn, to proteins). DNA is thus getting to the same point by many different paths. The code is not a one-to-one correspondence between letters or a set of letters and a meaning. It is not a semiotic code where each word only means one thing. The elements are mobile and can take on meaning based on context. They are relational in nature first. Such relationality also allows for different organisms to have different programs and coding and yet end up in the same place. But such convergence, as we have tried to show is not necessarily a sign of each being descended from the same thing. It is the code itself that is enabling such convergence.

This is not to say one coding is as good as another. Some coding will not be able to achieve anything and others might be redundant to the point of causing problems. Our own English alphabet has 26 letters (the Hebrew 22). These letters can be combined in an extremely large number of possible ways. If we allow that a word has no finite limit to it (that is, a word can be of any possible length), then the set of permutations is transfinite. However, it is very rare to find words of even 30 letters in length. A protein can be thousands of such DNA letters because it is already made up of words (amino acids). The determinacy of the code here should not lead one to think that proteins do not have some specificity and actual coding rules that must be met. Like with anything else, ultimately only certain sequences can count and work. There is a finite list. But we cannot necessarily go backwards to relate an amino acid, protein, gene, etc., to the underlying code:

> The code could not be deduced form the chemical properties of amino acids and nucleotide bases. It had to be cracked. Just as a specific letter of the Eng-

lish language can be represented by any combination of binary digits, so too could a given amino acid correspond to any combination of nucleotide bases. The assignments are, in both cases, arbitrary. For this reason, the progressive elimination of the many chemically possible types of codes would eventually prove a laborious task. Yet precisely this feature of chemical underdetermination would also later prove the key to understanding DNA's information-carrying capacity.[83]

This is why, rather than accepting things as given, one needs to search for the code of the code. One needs to search for the manner in which such a code is itself unfolding and according to what is perhaps a complex but finite program. This code would indicate how the four letters of DNA become the subset of subroutines known as proteins, for example. And that means, in addition to the DNA software, one needs to compile the hardware (cellular machinery) and environment into one's ultimate computation.

Of course, one of the steps here is DNA becoming RNA through a translation that consists of flipping all its bits. One then needs to find how that operation itself is encoded and how such a computation itself results. While DNA is based on four letters, amino acids are themselves twenty characters in length and therefore have more or less the same sophistication as human languages (even more given the length of sequences they can form as opposed to the way we limit words to just a few letters). What is interesting here is that the machine for reading DNA appears to be another molecule similar to DNA. As we already suggested, to have the first replication, one needed a ribosome in addition to a RNA strip. Thus, no single molecule is ever enough to have life. DNA or RNA without help will simply not be replicated. And yet still we get strings of letters

---

[83] Meyer, *Signature in the Cell*, 118.

transformed into other strings, letters combined into words, words combined into sentences, paragraphs, and texts. All things are ultimately made one from the other and then later operated on their own.

While amino acids might be made of letters as words, they later function as letters, if one likes. There is no life without proteins, which means no life without amino acids and DNA. But notice, even if there is a doubling at each level and an element in which one and the same unit functions differently, ultimately one needs a base level of the letter to prevent infinite regress. With DNA, the letter is also sorted and inscribed in a specific location. DNA is then putting together words from letters, but these words can go into sentences that have different words but the same over all meaning and function. The amount of DNA is also not crucial to undemanding why something is complex. As Hoyle notes, "the lungfish, for example has ten times as much DNA in each of its cells as a human, whereas an amoeba may have as much as five . . . times our amount."[84] The key to a code is not its length. One longer is not necessarily going to lead to more complexity or a more interesting end product. This is why beyond the DNA code is the code that includes the cellular machinery itself in compiled form along with Gaia (the environment).

Hoyle here suggests that 95 percent of DNA is inactive. That may be true, but it may also be that it has different functions. It may be that at the level of the amoeba enough coding was already accumulated such that only a small percentage is needed, as the rest lies dormant as backup, patches, etc. For example, the way to code genetically the color of a butterfly's wings is in the human genome, but not activated.[85] The key to a code is not simply what exists in it, but how it is read, when, and by what. The data must itself be processed. As some have already suggested, the environment itself might influence how this data is processed in

---

[84] Hoyle, *The Intelligent Universe*, 119.
[85] Hoyle, *The Intelligent Universe*, 120.

contrast to Darwinism. Why does each human cell contain the genetic information for a butterfly wing or some other form? This question is related to why some parts of the DNA are processed and others not. The metaphysical question of whether one can show or must argue for a programmer for such code cannot and will not be avoided here.

Robert Wright suggests that the environment might play a role insofar as E. coli DNA absorbs "information from its environment (which, in the case of humans is often other cells)" that controls "its cell's behavior," a "child's skin hue" is adjusted to sunlight, "cell surfaces have sensed which direction holds more light and heat," "when grass grows up instead of downward," etc.[86] In this way, the data processing might itself be influenced and induced. Given the fact that the code functions in a relational manner, there is a fundamental way in which a product of a code is itself the result of the same iteration. But if the code is changed or sections can be activated and deactivated, then one cannot say for sure what results in full the code will lead to. This leads us to wonder why the code has the specific sequence it does. It appears that it is not a matter simply of chemical reactions leading to one code, but rather the production of a code that was itself arranged. DNA contains information and instructions, but if all of reality is computational, then its sequencing is itself the function of another type of code. That code includes the entire cellular machinery and also, if need be, environmental factors. That code might be more deterministic when it is truly understood (despite appearing to give rise to multiple forms). One of the differences between life and matter might be in this very indeterminacy itself, given that life contains within itself its coded replica for the purposes of replication.

We should not think about the origin of life in terms of laws that show how a particular sequence arose. Laws are too wide and baggy to fit the phenomena here. They are too

---

[86] Wright, *Non-Zero*, 248.

external and abstract. One will need computational rules already at work for such informational sequences to arise. To echo Deleuze, laws are conditions of possible experience, but computational rules are conditions of real experience. Laws speak of what is needed as a prerequisite for any phenomenon. But computational rules speak to what one needs for specific phenomenon to arise and take form. The law of gravitation on chemicals is itself not going to explain how the first replicated molecule arose. If life unfolds in a deterministic story despite some of the indeterminacy of the code, it is not due to the force of laws of nature like gravity, but due to all of nature (anything in existence is computational hardware/software) being already computational in its functioning. One needs specific rules and processes to talk about the specific transformation of, for instance, one arrangement of elementary particles into another arrangement.

At this point, of course, many point to a vicious circle at the heart of the possible origin of life, proteins require DNA to be made, but DNA also needs proteins. For this reason, one must look to RNA itself. Out of chemicals comes information. One thus needs networking to achieve life:

> No DNA molecules replicate nude in free-living organisms. DNA replicates only as a part of a complex, collectively autocatalytic network of reactions and enzymes in cells. No RNA molecules replicate themselves. The cell is a whole, mysterious in its origins perhaps, but not mystical.[87]

Kauffman here speaks of how things work in the cell now. But to speak about the origin of life one does need to find a way for RNA to be replicated. One needs to find catalysis of

---

[87] Stuart Kauffman, *At Home in the Universe: The Search for the Laws of Self-Organization and Complexity* (New York: Oxford University Press, 1996), 50.

reactions outside or before the cell that then either builds itself a membrane or gets incorporated into one. At the origin one already has to have base pairings in the replicating machinery, otherwise one will not be able to produce software.

It is wrong to see things as a matter of chemicals simply coming together willy-nilly. There are many chemical systems that are closed off as systems on their own. But without the division between hardware and software—without a Turing machine—one will not get life. One then has to find, via the chemicals that make up RNA or DNA, how such a machine is built. If such a machine is a natural and expected occurrence then one needs to find the hardware already programmed for enacting it—a web of reactions crystallizing together. Kauffman says as much when he says it is "almost inevitable," but that means it is not random or by chance.[88]

Kauffman notes having done computer simulations where chemical reactions swarm together to form a living organism.[89] This is certainly not Darwinian. Life here emerges whole and not piecemeal. But when Kauffman talks about catalysis between molecules, he is essentially saying that each one computes the other. Often catalysis is thought about along the mode of a lock fitting into a key and by turning the key, creating a change. But what we see here is that the issue is more so one of reading instructions. One molecule catalyzes the other because the molecule is already a bit that tells the other one what to do—turn on or off. Catalytic chemicals are thereby already instructions. When they swarm together, they are running a relational software sequence. One thus needs a split between hardware and software to get a working, living thing.

Kauffman believes the swarms of catalyzing molecules illustrate Kantian holism, but the issue here is not wholes

---

[88] Kauffman, *At Home in the Universe*, 61.
[89] Kauffman, *At Home in the Universe*, 64.

or parts.[90] It is not even parts interacting as part of a whole. It is about code and information wherein a molecule acts as instructions for another. It is about the formation of an elementary computer by first forming the software from within the hardware. It is not an issue of a whole that arises out of its parts and perhaps synergistically has properties exceeding the sum of its parts. It is about elements of code arising out of the formation of chemicals. It is the formation of bits out of chemicals. There are any number of enclosed wholes in the world, but enclosed wholes, closure, limits, etc., do not explain life itself. There are emergent properties in several nonliving phenomena, and holism is not specific to life.

Kauffman sees catalysis as a causal action, but it needs to be seen as a translation and interpretation of instructions. One molecule is not forcing another to act like billiard balls bouncing off each other. To turn on another molecule is to issue instructions to it on what to do. The one turned on receives the message. Kauffman admits there are "control rules" at work, such as the Boolean functions 'and' and 'or,' but thinks that some rules lead to chaos.[91] The iteration of rules can lead to chaotic patterns, but that is not the same as a lack of rules. To speak of Boolean functions is already to speak of 0s and 1s at work. Here we are clearly stating that, at its most basic level, being is characterized by Boolean logic. Boolean logic is not just a product of mind or something we input into processes, but already at work in being itself since the Big Bang. However, it is not an issue of order arising out of chaos. The molecules were not some mess of static entities beforehand. They were themselves functioning per rules. It is just that here they are forming themselves explicitly into a software and hardware split (rather than just being hardware / software as one—computation).

---

[90] Kauffman, *At Home in the Universe*, 70.
[91] Kauffman, *At Home in the Universe*, 81.

It is also important to note that it is a not a matter of each molecule randomly interacting with each other. One needs, as noted before, the rudiments of a Turing machine, where a tape is run through. Kauffman offers more so a model where each molecule is interacting with the others to give rise to some overall synergistic effect. But that will not elicit life any more than a hurricane will (there is no reason to say a hurricane is alive). Kauffman also speaks about attractors, which, we have seen, should be avoided since, if one is speaking about 0s and 1s and Boolean functions, one has entered the realm of iterating rules and not magnetic or gravitational forces pulling chemicals in a particular direction. A cell repeats itself because the rules themselves do not have a direction to stop being read. To stop iteration, one needs an instruction built into the code itself that says to stop. Because Kauffman is speaking about attractors, he cannot come to this conclusion. Also, Kaufman thinks that a system has to go through every possible state, but if that is true, then the system he is talking about by his own admission never ends, as it would need more time than the whole universe has existed to iterate.[92] Again, one has to see how software iterates its own rules and how that iteration is built into its coding.

The coding itself determines what states will occur, and not all possible states occur. That is why it is not an issue of each molecule interacting each with the other, but of two sequences translating one into the other. If one just has 200 chemicals with on and off states and all states must be activated, then one will never have a repeating pattern. But to have life, one needs a finite number of repeating patterns. That is achieved since, by being sequenced in a way that changes either suddenly or very little, one can, via the interaction of a reading strip and tape, produce the same proteins over and over again (recall our early discussion of the ribosome). We should not rule out that even material phenomenon like planets in their formation, stars, nucleosyn-

---

[92] Kauffman, *At Home in the Universe*, 83.

thesis, etc., already involved Boolean algebra insofar as these phenomena are computational. In that way, it is not a matter of chemicals spontaneously becoming computational but of forming an inflection point wherein they form a system split between a software formation and hardware (both materially being chemicals).

At the same time, these chemical Turing machines are not actively universal computers since these organisms only compute the same thing over and over again. They have a set of explicit instructions enclosed in them. But those instructions state to do the same thing over and over again. As life evolves, the instructions will change themselves if we look at an individual organism's code, but we also need to see that individual organism as an output state of the system, which brings us back to a single code for all life, the initial point of formation. Stephen Meyer's critique of Kauffman is here apropos:

> To the extent that Kauffman's systems do succeed in producing interesting nonrandom patterns, they do so only because of an unexplained intervention of information. For example, Kauffman notes that if his system of flashing lights is properly "tuned," then it will shift from a chaotic regime to an orderly regime that will produce the outcomes or patterns he regards as analogous to processes or structures within living systems. By "tuning," Kauffman means the careful setting of a particular "bias parameter" to make his system shift from a chaotic regime into one in which order is produced. In other words, the tuning of this parameter ensures that certain kinds of outcomes are actualized and others precluded. Such an act constitutes nothing less than an infusion of information. When someone tunes a radio dial or a musical instrument, he or she selects a certain frequency and excludes many others. Yet Shannon de-

fined an informative intervention as precisely electing one option and excluding others.[93]

Given Meyer's critique, one must see information as always already present at every level of phenomena, since otherwise one needs precisely the outside intervention that Kauffman claims has no place here as he claims an interventionist God has no place. God might intervene, but we would never know it because we would only see what we already do see—chemical letters conjugating. Kauffman also presupposes that chemicals operate chaotically before coming to form the living, but they are synthesizing and catalyzing before this per clear rules. Some results are precluded due to the programming itself and its rules and how the instructions are read out rather than due to external conditions.

Kauffman's problems arise because he wants to insert information from the outside when information is something that must always already be at work and presupposed—that is its very nature. Information was there in the formation of planets, but now, with life, we have digital characters and a full alphabet (even if only 4 letter long) in the form of chemicals. One could have light bulbs as bits as Kauffman himself shows, but he is not willing to go the next step and show that if light bulbs can form bits, then bits are at work already in all phenomena. The problem of life is related to the origin of information. It is the origin of information in chemical form, but it is not the origin of information as such ontologically. Kauffman can suggest (he does not have a way of showing how it actually occurred) how chemicals take on a specific sequential form and thereby act as information, but information ontologically was always there insofar as all phenomena are computational in nature. And it is due to ontology being informational at its core that explains how chemical mate-

---

[93] Meyer, *Signature in the Cell*, 266–267.

riality can form itself into software. Otherwise, one would have to explain how information occurs without rules in a random way. That is not simply unlikely, but almost physically impossible.

It is thus not a matter of information arising for the first time, but of already informationally formed material entities taking on new forms due to the very rule based nature of their being. Because one needs a specific arrangement and sequence of chemicals, one needs there already to be rule-following, since otherwise one is dependent on chance. This is why it has been important for us to critique the concept of self-organization, since otherwise it appears as though systems merely arise spontaneously for no reason out of others, as though they are rabbits pulled out of hats. Things may emerge for no apparent reason, but it will not be outside the iteration of rules and instructions. And all existence itself can arise out of nothing for free only via the divine.

§13

THE IRONY OF DARWINIST COMPUTER SIMULATION

Of course, I am only building on the work of others and countless observations when I point out that DNA is a computer language. It may be the machine code, while other parts of the celluar machinery might be the machine code. Or the cellular machinery, taken as a whole, might be the machine, and DNA might be some more specific programming language like 'C.' This observation has already led to a few attempts to simulate evolution in computer environments. The problem is that such attempts at simulation have been led by Darwinian presuppositions, and, due to that, they have failed to much more then exhibit the ability of pre-designed programs to generate and select a preset pattern. What is interesting is that in all these attempts to simulate evolution the designers insist they are showing that evolution is based on chance, randomness, and a lack of design, despite the fact they are intelligently designing these programs. That is, these attempts to simulate evolution do not think evolution is bound by programmable rules and, because they think evolution is based on natural selection, only end up producing a single preselected product. They prove despite themselves that only the information pre-existing in the program (their selected algorithm's search pattern) will appear. While the history of life in its actuality will ultimately be demonstrated via computer simulations and emulations (just as any of the views we are arguing for here will be), the ones so far offered offer no hope of demonstrating 'Darwinism'.

These programs focus on how some sub-programs meet a preset selection pattern, while others do not. Those that do not meet the preset selection pattern are eliminated and do not continue on. In the end then, the program always gets exactly what it was looking for in an obvious, self-fulfilling prophecy. But the process then stops. It does not continue on. There is no endless evolution. Rather than seeing that as a contestation of Darwinism—insofar as it appears replaying the same program over and over again will end in the same way—the programmers believe it somehow vindicates Darwinism. However, Darwinism would have to say that the selection criteria would have to itself be randomly varied. Why do these simulations not do that? Because they know if they did so where to begin would be arbitrary and the process would probably almost always go nowhere. At best, what these programs show is what was already shown by artificial selection and in labs, that microevolution does occur. However, that should not be surprising, given that these programs are a form of artificial selection themselves.

Take Richard Dawkins's biomorphs as an example. As Spetner points out, this simulation does not allow "lethal mutations" or deleterious ones as "every figure can survive and reproduce" and the processes allows for so much mutation at once that it overlooks that random mutation simply cannot occur that quickly (*NBC* 172). Not only does such a system not mirror how Darwinian evolution would have to work in nature, but it ensures that one will always get the form one wants as the "program decides if an organism is to reproduce" (*NBC* 172). It is not clear why such a staunch advocate of Darwinism would think it could be demonstrated in this manner. Perhaps it is an admittance that in Darwinism 'natural selection' has truly been not only anthropomorphized, but also deified. Now perhaps, if Dawkins and a viral theory of mutation, one could get closer to the mutation rate he needs here, but one thus has the anti-Darwinian and, more so, Lamarckian view of Sandin being tested.

Also note that such computer simulations do not explain where the initial rules come from. They merely state that starting with a situation of such and such nature, we then observe what will be produced given a certain way of permuting programs and selection patterns. In other words, there is no explanation of how life replicates, how it came to have a code, etc., it is already presupposed. One then does not see any simulation of life itself. One takes life as already programmed in and self-replicating. While Michael Behe argues (and he is wrong) that the mistake here is to believe "that simple rules that can generate patterns on a computer screen are the rules that generate patterns in biology," the mistake is actually in that the simulation itself is wrong due to being wedded to Darwinism rather than thinking simple rules can generate evolution (*EE* 189).

Dawkins offered another possible simulation to try to prove Darwinism by suggesting that through random variation of letters one can go from a string of gibberish letters to the sentence 'Methinks it is a weasel.'[94] Dawkins believes that such a simulation will show that natural selection coupled with random mutation is better than pure chance and not so improbable as to not be a reasonable mechanism for evolution. One first produces a random list of letters the same length as the desired last sentence. Nothing is said about how such a sentence is produced other than that it appears and is random. The random string is then repeated at each sentence except that one letter of the string is randomly switched. I believe Dawkins claims that the desired sentence is produced in 43 steps. But what Dawkins does not emphasize is that each string is being compared with

---

[94] I am relying here on the Wikipedia entry on this topic entitled "Weasel program," since it offers a refreshingly condensed and simple version of it: http://en.wikipedia.org/wiki/Weasel_program [retrieved January 20, 2012].

the targeted desired result. In other words, there is a pattern guiding the whole thing using external criteria. No wonder it takes only 43 steps. At each stage, the fitness of the string is checked. Only 28 letter strings area allowed. If evolution is Darwinian, it's not supposed to have any target goal.

In most examples of this simulation, Dawkins has any character letter matching the desired end goal maintained. I am not sure why anyone thinks that is not stacking the deck. What happened to the blind watchmaker? Did he go to the eye doctor? Such a simulation could at most relate to the chemical evolution of a first RNA sequence, for instance, of a particular specificity, but it is not clear why, in such an evolution, there would be any target sequence to compare each result to. Even if Dawkins wants to show that Darwinian mechanisms are better than pure chance, he still has to show they are efficient enough to produce the needed components without imposing external search patterns in this fashion. For this simulation to truly be like Darwinian mechanisms there would have to be no external final product to test each stage. Each stage would have to have some random selection criteria (for instance, that the fifth letter be a B). That would be the only clear way to have an actual selector here. If one selects for the whole 28 letter sequence, then it is clearly not good to ever select almost anything short of it as not even the basic message will get out until one has almost all the letters. And Dawkins appears to believe that ultimately selection is working on the total 28 letter sequence. Messages can be understood when some of the letters are wrong (one needs for words, for example, sometimes just the first and last letter). In that way, having a couple of generations that were off would most likely end the whole simulation right then and there. Michael Behe explains:

> . . . if your life depended on . . . the combination METHINKSITISAWEASEL, and you tried MDTUIFKQINIOAFERSCI [that has half the letters right],

you would be pushing up daisies. If your reproductive success depends on opening locks, you would have no offspring.[95]

For Behe, of course, such a 28-letter sequence is an irreducibly complex system that cannot emerge step by step. If one thinks that natural selection is selecting more than 1/28 traits in each generation, one could have more than one such selection pattern. Given how evolution works (punctuated equilibrium), one would probably also have to schedule it so that the same sequence is selected over and over again without almost no change for many steps.

Many supporters of Dawkins here argue that Dawkins' model does not have to simulate actual evolution, but only show that random variation coupled with a law for selecting such variations is better than pure chance and can lead to the production of a particular end product. But no one ever disputed that such an external search pattern coupled with random sequencing was worse than pure chance. This is why microevolution can work at the level of viruses, for instance. If one has something constantly searching for the desired final goal, one does not have Darwinism, as then the selection itself would be effectively random. But here it is clearly not. It is also not clear that in nature any such selection would be random or contingent, and part of the way to test that is to allow a code to unfold. Dawkins has ironically proven that intelligence design via an inputted, intelligently imposed selection pattern works, whereas Darwinism does not.

Another such simulation is Tierra, as designed by Thomas Ray.[96] Tierra is about programs in a computational space being selected or not after they reproduce to see if a

---

[95] Behe, *Darwin's Black Box*, 221.
[96] Again, Wikipedia is better here than any other source I researched at giving the basics of this program. See "Tierra (computer simulation)," *Wikipedia*: http://en.wikipedia.org/wiki/Tierra_(computer_ simulation) [retrieved January 20, 2012].

final type of program (the fittest one) will emerge. Here, unless one specifically sets up the program in advance to select for larger program size (many bits) the program tends towards simplicity (*NFL* 211). In Tierra, all programs reproduce, no matter what. Tierra does not see any mutation as deleterious and allows for an extreme mutation rate. Tierra has an interesting feature in which a destroyed program is not eliminated, but left to exist in its parts in the computer space. Other programs can then appropriate these parts. But this function seems to have no relation to evolution other than perhaps being related to symbiogenesis (a decidedly anti-Darwinian and Lamarckian process). It is not clear that symbiogenesis happens so randomly, and it is not a Darwinian phenomenon. Also symbiogenesis is about two programs merging into one rather than selecting specific parts of another's code. This might then come close to viruses, but viruses can also destroy a program.

In Tierra, programs are given CPU time and memory resources. Tierra claims there are no built in fitness functions, as programs either are destroyed or continue on. Tierra does not allow endless evolution but always reaches a point at which there are no more new programs to be made. At that point, the program simply repeats itself over and over again. At best, then, Tierra might show how things work in the viral world, but not in the bacterial world—much less beyond (or how larger entities arise).

Tierra simulates random mutation by flipping bits randomly. It also incorporates some of the insights of Sandin and Margulis by allowing parts of code to be exchanged between programs. However, it is still selecting for the longest code despite its claim to have no external selection criteria. Given that Tierra allows for code exchange, it is not surprising that there is a rise in the length of programs, but this shows non-Darwinian process driving the issue. A creature might also need very little energy to survive. If it was truly a matter of competing for energy and resources, then the simplest creature that can survive on the least amount would evolve per Darwinian mechanisms. Tierra only overcomes this because it allows for non-Darwinian evolution.

Lastly, let us look at Avida, which, although less successful than Tierra, has been much more celebrated (I know that Gregory Chaitin has also developed a model, but it is also Darwinian and fails for other reasons—given that we will be engaging with his main computational theory at a later point, we will save any comments on it for that time). Philosopher Robert T. Pennock has been deeply involved in the development of this Darwinian simulator. Avida is another attempt to simulate random mutation coupled with natural selection. Programs replicate and, in replicating, pass on whatever changes to the code were acquired. If no changes occurred in bit strings, then the offspring of the parent programs are identical. Just like in Tierra, random mutations occur by means of randomly flipping elements of the bit string. The Avida team tweaked the system to find what mutation rate works best to achieve the maximum results. Programs not meeting fitness criteria are filtered out. Offspring are also created randomly rather than by just combining half the material of parents, for example.

In the Avida universe, even if you have just randomly selected bit strings, you can move on and survive. It is not clear how that is supposed to mirror anything in nature. Any program is functional because all programs simply compute as 1s and 0s. But Tierra is not open-ended evolution. It is limited by the very structuration of the model it uses, because there are only a preset number of genes that can only function in a preset number of ways. It is also important to note that the programs here are not even simulations of organisms, as they do not contain within themselves their own instructions. The programs are always replicated by an external mechanism. The selection criteria ultimately always ends up in the same place with the same end, precisely because it is never allowed to be truly random. Thus, for example, programs are rewarded based on a set selection criteria that is repeated.[97] Computers are, for instance, rewarded for their ability to perform a logical function and only the more involved program is selected for.[98] Given the repeated selection feature, it is not surprising that many paths are found to reach the same exact end product in Avida over and over again.

This is similar to other experiments done by Pennock and his team, where, essentially, a program is incentivized to go down one path or another.[99] The program turns left or right but always ends up in the same place due to the incentives given. This shows that it is also about cues and selection. If one gives something reason not to go one direction, then one will not. This is simulating a rat in a maze rather than Darwinian evolution. There is nothing random about this process as well. In another paper, Pennock and his team discuss getting a walking pattern to emerge, but learning how evolution works is not about learning how to walk.[100] If one needs to walk, it needs to be there to escape—otherwise it is not useful. This paper perhaps illustrates machine learning but not evolution, as evolution cannot make use of partially usable walking procedures.

Often these simulations do brute randomization, as if the environment were constantly being bombarded with cosmic rays or in a situation after a massive nuclear disaster. What is fascinating is that the fact that these simulations end with this same result every time one runs them leads to no reflection on the part of the teams creating them. They also violate their own Darwinian principles,

---

[97] Richard E. Lenski et al., "The Evolutionary Origin of Complex Features" *Nature* 43 (May 2003): 142 [139–144].
[98] Lenski et al., "Evolutionary Origin," 143.
[99] Laura M. Grabowski et al., " Early Evolution of Memory Usage in Digital Organisms," *Proceedings of the Artificial Life XII Conference* (2010): 225–231.
[100] Jeff Clune et al., "On the Performance of Indirect Encoding Across the Continuum of Regularity," *IEE Transactions on Evolutionary Computation* 15 (June 2011): 346–367.

since fitness should simply mean an ability to reproduce and nothing more in that context. But here either only a very select type of organism is given the right to reproduce or all reproduce. Is it any wonder than that a pre-selected criterion finds what it is looking for even with random bit flipping?

Such simulations show that Darwinian mechanisms are as good as artificial selection. Here, if one knows what type of creature one wants, one can let the computer design it for you rather than combining known plant types, as a breeder would. However, it's always a question of imposed intelligent design. Insofar as we will be arguing for design here, it will not be on the side of selection but on the side of the code itself and computation. This differentiates us from even intelligent design theorists like Dembski and Behe, much less Darwinists. What these simulations show is that Darwinian selection was always an anthropomorphized intelligent process that was not acting randomly. Just because a program does logic functions more so, gets more energy, and thereby produces more does not mean it is showing how things work in nature. Behe has also criticized Avida on this score:

> In Avida, airing new abilities is only one way for an organism to get computer food. Another way is by simply acquiring surplus instructions, *whether or not they do anything.* In fact, instructions that aren't ever executed—making them utterly useless for performing tasks—are beneficial in Avida cause they provide additional food. . . . It's survival of the fattest!" (*EE* 276)

It is not clear why this activity should be rewarded. Non-functional instructions would be lost or simply rendered inactive. Without programming this in as a predesigned selection criteria, one ends up with the simplest programs possible. This shows the way intelligent design is working here. If the program was left to itself, one would simply get devolution to the simples possible set of instructions. Only by stacking the deck with selection criteria can this be avoided. However, that means it is externally forced on the situation. Everything is predestined and predetermined, and yet it is said to demonstrate Darwinism, which Gould himself said will not result in the same thing over and over again.

Here, we have very clever programmers who know how to ensure the right result will come about, but natural selection was not supposed to function in that way. There is a goal here, and all is directed at it. These simulations are good evidence to lead a reasonable person to think that if Darwinism does describe things then there truly must be a designer who imposes from the outside the right selection criteria always to get a certain desired result. The irony is palpable. Oftentimes in nature there is an abundance of resources, and oftentimes the simplest of creatures reproduces the most. Such simulations force complexity on the programs by constantly selecting for it. But it is not clear that a human being is any more complex from the perspective of code than an amoeba. The more one reads the articles by Pennock and his team (they are available at: www.msu.edu/~pennock5/), the more one realizes that they constantly state that what is being shown is evolution as such, when what is being demonstrated is intelligent design. If it were real evolution, the selection criteria would randomly change.

It is also important to note that in Avida a program can be rewarded for lowering the number of instructions it has.[101] But then we are talking about reversing evolution and producing simpler things. This is not something we see

---

[101] Jeff Clune, Charles Ofria, and Robert T. Pennock, "Investigating the Emergence of Phenotype Plasticity in Evolving Digital Organisms," in F. Almeida e Costa, *Advances in Artificial Life*, eds. Luis Mateo Rocha, Ernesto Costa, Inman Harvey, and Antonio Coutinho (Berlin: Springer, 2007), 74–83.

in nature. This result, however, brings home the point that one constantly selects for something and gets it if the model is sufficiently set up, despite any bit flipping and recombination allowed at the level of the program. Darwinian evolution thus works best as a principle for intelligent design when one wants to engineer something new fitting known general criteria. Given that one knows what one wants to produce in general, one can constantly select for that feature and thereby arrive at it given the parameters inputted into one's system. All of this scientific effort to prove again the intelligent design of artificial selection! The dog breeders of the world long for these budgets. If one plays out the simulation again and again, one will constantly arrive at the same result.

It is also interesting the way competition is seen as the key to life evolving. This shows that the insights Margulis imitated have not been incorporated by the establishment. Margulis shows how evolution occurs via cooperation and incorporation rather than competition and survival. The symbiogenetic revolution is yet to take place. Pennock and his team focus on competition. In fact, it is the organism that produces first and fastest that wins in the competition. But it is not clear why that should be so. If it was, how would a human that gestates for nine months ever arise?

§14
CSI
Dembski—A Critique

If computer simulations demonstrate the human ability to intelligently design a system to produce a desired outcome, what about what we observe amongst biological, living things? Here, we need to turn to the trailblazing work of William Dembski, in whose shadow we walk. Democritus is famously quoted as having said that, "everything in the universe is the fruit of chance and necessity." Dembski's work is an attempt to suggest that we need to add design to that list. He wants to specify the conditions under which a contingent event can be attributed to design rather than chance. The key is contingency here. Dembski cites Maimonides looking at the "irregular distribution of stars in the heavens" and stating that it did not have to look that way (*NFL* 1–2). Of course, for Maimonides the distribution of the stars was a matter of design by the creator, but one can say the universe itself did not have to happen or look the way it does which leads one to ask if that contingency is a matter of chance or design. To say it is designed is to see it as not purposeless, even if we do not know the ultimate reason for the thing's being designed in precisely the way it is.

Dembski has attempted to offer a precise definition of design with his notion of 'specified complexity' or 'complex specified information (CSI).' Dembski argues interestingly that the products of human efforts (for which there is no debate as to their being designed) exhibit CSI. By complex, Dembski means not much more than that there is a very low probability that such a thing would form on its own spontaneously.[102] An important point here is that Dembski is using this notion to suggest that the "greater the complexity the smaller the probability" (*NFL* 9). The key is that the probability is so low as to make it seem unreasonable a phenomenon occurred by way of blind natural causes. There is a probability, for instance, that tree branches lying around in a forest will arrange themselves into a log cabin, but it is almost zero. By specified, Dembski simply means that the thing is not random in its ordering. It betrays some sort of structure. Any old random string of base pairs will not make for a good DNA code; it needs to be specified in a limited number of sequences. The need for this specified complexity is obvious insofar as, for instance, a protein can become dysfunctional by its coding having one element changed. If one puts chromosomes in a differ order, genes also will not work. Jumbling information leads to problems in communicating the desired message. Information itself needs such specification in order to function. It counts as much for a sentence in English as for DNA.

For Dembski any natural set of causes that would account for how a DNA sequence took on its specified complexity presupposes that those natural causes themselves are an example of specified complexity, because such causes would have to be capable of the same amount of permutational possibilities as DNA (*NFL* 151). In the same way that one cannot detail the origin of human language—as one must presuppose humans being linguistic for language to arise—the origin of CSI cannot be detailed using natural causes. After all, if humans grunting to each other already understand each other, then they must have some innate

---

[102] William Dembski, *Intelligent Design: The Bridge Between Science and Theology* (Nottingham: InterVarsity Press, 1999), 170. Hereafter referred to in the text parenthetically as *ID*.

language in them. Dembski likes the example of "a pencil-making machine" being "more complex than the pencils it makes" (*ID* 171). This is what, in many places, Dembski calls his principle of the 'Conservation of Information.' One already has to have CSI in operation for information to emerge and change. One cannot give a natural account of its emergence from non-CSI. One has good reason to say something is defined if that thing is both complex and specified at the same time, but only if one finds both at the same time.

Dembski believes it is only reasonable to ascribe to some intelligent source causality when we find specified complexity. This is of course what humans do all the time. When we pick up a book, we do not think that the book spontaneously formed out of pre-existing matter, but that the text contains meaningful information due to its having been written. Chance alone is then said not to be a reasonable explanation for specified complexity (*ID* 151). Chance processes can only take already existing CSI and jumble it up for Dembski (*ID* 175). Behe's notion of irreducible complexity is also a good example of what Dembski means by CSI. Dembski argues that CSI is not just taking a series of non-informational parts or elements and adding them together, as the CSI effect is synergistic insofar as, just like in a sentence, the letters used give rise to an effect not found in the letters or words (*ID* 173-174). Thus, Dembski is willing to admit that "chance can generate complex unspecified information," but not willing to admit that "chance can generate complex specified information" in the most improbable of cases, such as with the proverbial group of monkeys typing away for infinity (*ID* 165). That means Dembski is only willing to allow false positives, given his criteria in the most improbable of circumstances. These circumstances are such that it is physically impossible for them to occur, given the age of the universe (*ID* 166).

However, we do seemingly have examples of false positives. For instance, Dembski believes that ink spontaneously, via natural causes or chance alone, coming to form the words on this page "is reducible to the physics and chemistry of paper and ink" (*NFL* 8). The problem is that one can imagine spilling a bottle of ink and it forming a word. The chances are probably infinitesimal, but that the mere possibility exists means that one cannot ever have certainty that a phenomenon was in fact designed.

One can also have false negatives here. An environmental artist might arrange something in nature randomly for the purposes of art. One would then think it is not designed, as it does not seem at first blush to show any specificity, but, in fact, it was designed by an intelligent agent: "One difficulty is that intelligent causes can mimic necessity and chance" (*ID* 140). Human beings can even consciously conceal their having designed something, as Dembski is willing to admit, by covering and erasing the signs of their design (*ID* 140-141). Dembski's criteria here are, then, not foolproof. Dembski would probably respond that there are no such foolproof criteria possible. In the case of false negatives, the criteria will not work, and it will not be exceedingly rare that it does not work. That means Dembski cannot say that his criteria always detects design. For Dembski, that does not mean one stops looking for design, as a detective who mistakes a crime scene for a natural accident still needs to use CSI to find the criminal, eventually (*NFL* 24).

I will return to the problem of false positives and negatives and its implications, but, first, let's look at what critics of Dembski have said. One of the key criticisms is that Darwinian mechanisms operate more efficiently than pure chance or blind search. Mark Perakh highlights this criticism in his essay "There is a Free Lunch After All: William Dembski's Wrong Answers to Irrelevant Questions."[103] The

---

[103] Mark Perakh, "There is a Free Lunch After All: William Dembski's Wrong Answers to Irrelevant Questions," in *Why Intelligent Design Fails*, eds. Matt Young and Taner Edis (New Brunswick: Rutgers University Press, 2006), 153–171.

problem is that one of Perakh's main examples is Dawkins' simulations, which we have already criticized.[104] The problem here is that even if these search algorithms are better than blind search, they are probably not efficient enough—if actually simulated per how Darwinian mechanisms can work in nature—to output the needed phenomena in the amount of time allotted. Perakh argues that "because of the enormous variety of possible evolutionary algorithms and fitness functions, the probability of some fraction of algorithms being naturally fine-tuned to the existing landscapes is close to certainty."[105] But it is actually quite the opposite. Because there are such an exceedingly large number of possibilities for what can be selected in any environment, if one truly allows it to vary per how things in work nature, one cannot come up with the same results. Only if one has a stacked deck, like with Dawkins' weasel, where at each step one checks to see if one has the desired result, can one avoid these algorithms being too close to blind search to function.[106] In other words, only intelligent design (checking each stage for a desired end) can work if one wants Darwinism.

Because intelligent design is involved, one need not constantly search the endless possibilities available. Dembski notes himself that one of main criticisms of his view is that natural selection and Darwinian mechanisms can cause phenomena to emerge that have specific complexity (*NFL* xiii). Perakh also notes this criticism. Again referring to Dawkins' weasel program, he notes that even if we allow random variation, such a program can go from a purely scrambled 28-letter sequence to an intelligible message.[107] Here, Perakh is on much firmer ground, as even Dembski has to acknowledge that such CSI can emerge from the random shifting of letters. Dembski simply argues such

---

[104] Perakh, "There is a Free Lunch After All," 165.
[105] Perakh, "There is a Free Lunch After All," 168.
[106] Perakh, "There is a Free Lunch After All," 170.
[107] Perakh, "There is a Free Lunch After All," 170.

false positives are so improbable that they are not relevant, and that it is not reasonable to see them as playing a role in biological phenomena (or probably any phenomena in the observable universe). Darwinism is not impossible. It is simply not likely. CSI can emerge from randomly changing base letters, and one cannot deny that CSI emerges in this manner.

Dembski here needs to argue of course that base pairs are already an example of CSI such that one is here simply showing that once one has such letters it is not surprising that even randomly one can get CSI. The analogy with language here is obvious. Language is already obviously CSI such that with it already firmly in place and presupposed one can get CSI in a random manner. Notice that with Dawkins' weasel the number of probabilities has to be reduced at each stage by comparison with a final product. It is therefore not surprising that it is better than pure chance. The key is reducing probability as such. Intelligent design clearly can do that. If one only has one 28-letter sentence in mind to compare things, one will get to a final goal much quicker than allowing things to vary randomly. The probability here increases toward one with each step and each check. For this reason, Dembski argues such "evolutionary algorithms are therefore incapable of generating true complexity" (*NFL* 180). They actually depend on low complexity in the sense of low varying possibilities. It is only a semblance of CSI for Dembski.

However, if randomness can produce even some type of CSI, imagine what non-Darwinian mechanisms like symbiogenesis and lateral DNA transfer can do. They can clearly do so and occur much more frequently in nature. If these phenomena are simply contingent in nature and follow from natural causes, then Dembski has a problem that, to my knowledge, he does not engage with. If nature works mindlessly and blindly to affect such combinations of DNA on a regular basis, then it is producing new CSI not on the basis seemingly of intelligent design. Dembski here might reply that that is fine, as in both cases one is combing CSI rather than generating it from chaos or nonsense. When two beings join together, it is like joining together two sentences. Gene transfer is like inserting new words in a sentence. CSI is created on the basis of already existing CSI. Dembski needs to show that these processes are designed and not done by necessity. Perhaps symbiogenesis is a purely natural phenomenon that happens by necessity.

Dembski himself states that a rock falling by the force of gravity is not designed to do so in the sense of CSI, as there is no low probability it will go up rather than down. One is then in a situation of specified simplicity. Dembski's work only applies to things where there is no physical force forcing things to join together or take on the form they do. If symbiogenesis happens like rocks falling, should we then not see it as a designed? That is a metaphysical question (all of these questions always were). One thus needs a metaphysics that would show why such a necessity is itself designed. With necessity, it is actually violations of the law (rocks floating upwards) that are taken as designed (in the sense of miracles, for example).

Let us return to what is happening when chance does produce CSI. Chance seems to only very rarely do so. Chance will only rarely take a 28-letter, scrambled, nonsense sequence and turn it into something that makes sense (and probably only after so many tries that the universe will have ended). But it is possible. Chance will almost always give us nonsense. One can start with a sentence and randomize its letters in a limited way and have that lead to other sentences. On would then say that the first sentence is the ancestor of other sentences. This is what is happening with the DNA code. One started with a specified code and, through iterations, elaborations, additions, mutations, etc., produced all the living codes we now see. But prior to having this sentence, one needed the letters themselves. That is why it is more important to see how the letters themselves came to be formed and how they are already the result of a computational process. Necessity, on the other hand, is always giving us sense. In this way, what we see is that genetic mutations do re-arrange things such that they become non-functional and lack sense or take on a new sense on the basis of the code already there. But code transfer increases the information content of the genome. If the code transfers something already there, one has duplication. The question is if such transfers follow rules such that, for instance, genes are coded as subroutines and repeated between each other by coding that indicates only that space is indicated. If new code information is then inserted, it would have to follow this sort of process. The key here is that the code is not arrangeable in any old way.

This is why Victor Stengers' critique of Dembski misses the mark.[108] Stengers thinks Dembski's view consists of saying: "the number of bits of information cannot change in any natural process such as chance or be the creation of some physical law."[109] However, no one could defend such a thesis. I do not know if anyone even tries to. A mutation that would duplicate some code would add more bits. Dembski's point is not about the amount of bits, but about those bits having to be in a non-random order to function. Random mutation could add bits, but it only ever is on the basis of already existing bits. Dembski is not speaking about bits as Shannon does. He is speaking of information in a more defined sense, as specified. Unless Stengers thinks that any bit sequence produced by flipping a coin would work in DNA, his point is not as relevant as he thinks.

Stengers uses the example of flipping five coins and flipping the bits (as in presumably some random mutation), but then one has the same number of bits even, in the sense of Shannon information.[110] The bits are the same, but

---

[108] Victor Stengers, "Physics, Cosmology, and the New Creationism," in *Scientists Confront Creationism: Intelligent Design and Beyond* (New York: W.W. Norton, 2007), 131–149.
[109] Stengers, "Physics, Cosmology, and the New Creationism," 135.
[110] Stengers, "Physics, Cosmology, and the New Creationism," 135–136.

the message may be different, or it may be nonsense. If a life form flipped all of its bits, it would probably die before developing beyond a very earlier point (if that, even). The amount of information is not the key. One can have an RNA molecule, but not just any old sequence is going to allow for future replication. The issue is not simply a matter of enlarging information here. Stengers is right that life forms and DNA codes are not hermetically sealed and closed off systems, but the issue is not if informational quantity can be increased but rather if that increase is going to have any effect.[111] One can add information to a computer program randomly, but it won't aid its functioning.

With symbiogenesis, clearly, information is being added. But it is not clear this process is random. Stengers focuses on an increase in entropy, but entropy is essentially scrambling information.[112] That means it most likely leads to nonsense. Stengers is wrong that Dembski contradicts himself by saying information can degrade, as Dembski just wants to show that chance is not going to produce CSI rather than indiscriminate bit strings.[113] Stengers offers an interesting example of magnets stacked on top of each other:

> When one magnet sits atop the other, information about the two possible configurations can be combined in one bit of information. But if a random event, such as a strong breeze, comes along and separates the two magnets, then the minimum number of bits necessary to describe the situation is in-

---

[111] Stengers, "Physics, Cosmology, and the New Creationism," 136.
[112] Stengers, "Physics, Cosmology, and the New Creationism," 137.
[113] Stengers, "Physics, Cosmology, and the New Creationism," 138.

creased.[114]

But, first, notice that in Stengers example there is already information. Stengers does not explain where the bits come from. Of course, Stengers, as an atheist, thinks bits can appear on their own out of nothing (we will return to this view and why the bit cannot appear so). Stengers' example is not good for nature, because there we see regularities and not just random bit sequences. We see not just random bit strings but compressible ones—ones that produce repeating patterns. It is not clear random strings of DNA do that. One can, for instance, have all the chemicals one wants in a test tube but not see them start replicating just because one has a lot of information in the test tube.

In Stengers's example, one already has a binary operation, and now that operation is elaborated and iterated. It is then not clear that one is not simply iterating randomly already existing bits here. This is why Dembski does not use Shannon information. Any information, ultimately, can be reduced to Shannon information, since all information can be compiled into bits, but that does not mean any old bit sequence and amount of bits will do. Stengers also has faith in Darwinian mechanisms: "While chance probability might be less than the probability bound, the probability for chance plus other natural processes, such as natural selection, will always be greater."[115] True, it will be greater, but, again, it is not all clear it will be great enough to generate the needed phenomena in the time allotted.

Now, with symbiogenesis and viral transfer as natural processes, one's probability is greatly increased, but that is because we are no longer talking about chance and Darwinism. Perakh argues that:

---

[114] Stengers, "Physics, Cosmology, and the New Creationism," 138.
[115] Stengers, "Physics, Cosmology, and the New Creationism," 141.

> ... the very concept of [specified complexity] is contradictory. In fact ... a meaningful phrase and a string of gibberish are "specified," if the concept of specification is given back its commonsense meaning by clearing it of the embellishments and unnecessary complications ...[116]

But that means that any string of letters is specified. That may be true at one level, but it is mostly irrelevant when dealing with biology. Simply being different than other sequences is not enough specification here. There are, with 28 letter sequences, a very large number of such specific strings. The issue is not if the string is gibberish or not but with Perakh that that specific 28-letter sequence is constantly being checked.

It is the same for Stengers. Generating a bit string is not the problem here; the problem is that not just any bit string will do. This is why it appears things are not random even once the bit string is established. The bit string's transformations have to follow rules and processes so that one does not have that process run aground immediately. It is the prefixed sequencing of base letters that leads to the agreement of amino acids and then proteins, etc. The bit string thus needs to ensure that its transformations forming each step follow some sort of rule. We need to look for that program as well as looking at the program produced. This is part and parcel of what it means to say DNA is software. It means there are only specific arrangements that can be functional. That does not mean that, at first blush, a bit string of code, when examined simply as bits, will not seem random and irreducibly complex. As long as there is a process that leads to that bit string and is itself made up of rules, one is not in a Darwinian world. That is, the big string, for a particular organism, might lack symmetry and repetition in its pattern such that that arrangement seems

---

[116] Perakh, "There is a Free Lunch After All," 156.

to lack any kind of order, but that does not mean it is not there or that it is not the result of some other set of rules for procuring such a sequence.

Let us return to our ink blot. Dembski cannot rule out this false positive. If ink spilled on a sheet suddenly produces a word, we as humans will immediately see it as meaningful. It will be taken as a sign. It is not physically impossible. It can occur on its own. What this shows us is that it is our own human presuppositions that are at work when it comes to design. This is essentially the view that Wolfram takes when it comes to design. For Wolfram we cannot find intelligence or intelligent design by looking at "meaningful communication" as a model, since everyday experience shows that we attribute design to those things we believe or know to be done by humans and do not when it is not (*NKS* 828). Most artifacts we come across on a day to day basis look like other things human have made (*NKS* 828). We are aware of the history of design such things are part of and therefore never think that such things arose by natural processes or chance. For that reason, in doing archeology the presumption is that if we find a certain artifact, it is made by humans, since we know that the same geometric patterns have been used over and over again (*NKS* 828). Seeing design is therefore based on a presupposition we make, since all sorts of natural phenomena exhibit simple patterns and regular forms. They can be just as complex as something designed by human hands. What this shows is that we say there is design when we claim to know there was an actual human agent and do not claim design when we believe no human or intelligent agent is responsible. We claim to know how crystals, snowflakes, galaxies are formed and see them as solely natural processes. However, if the universe itself is created by an intelligence, then we would see all such phenomena as designed. In other words, seeing design is based on a metaphysical framework. This is why the issue of methodological atheism—that arises so often in the intelligent design literature and criticisms of it—is important. If one metaphysically is

Divine Name Verification | 187

committed to existence being created, then all things will appear as designed. The question then becomes what difference such a metaphysical framework makes to the operation of science. Clearly Darwinism would not have gotten off the ground, given a theistic metaphysical framework. But science can easily be done within a theistic framework, as shown by Newton and Kepler. Seeing all things as designed actually encourages science, since then one knows that there are underlying rules for how things occurred to find in the first place.

Look at Fodor: his critique of Darwinism can only lead to seeing biology as natural history and recounting of what just happened to occur in the history of life. In this way, to truly advance intelligent design means to advance a metaphysical framework that makes it possible. Just arguing for God is not enough, as one needs, in addition, a theology and ontology that explain how that design works. Such a metaphysics cannot overlook the very nature of phenomena. Wolfram has shown that the common sense assumption that the more complex something is the more complex of an origin it has is not true—it can come from simple rules (*NKS* 828). That counts for human created phenomena as well as snowflakes. That means that every phenomenon is the product of rules and will appear just as much designed as any other, potentially. We take Stonehenge to be designed by humans because it exhibits CSI, but natural phenomena can also exhibit CSI once in a while, and very commonly do, once we adopt the computational approach that Wolfram has most prominently outlined.

Now, those who do not advocate God can always say that if the evidence points reasonably only to design, aliens did it. That would be intelligence like ours but well short of God's. Some believe life was planted on Earth by aliens, and others believe that we exist in a computer simulation designed by superior beings. So be it. That view will also see all things as designed. God then, as always, still exists as a metaphysical issue. That physical processes consist of computational processes means that they will be as complex as anything humans do (*NKS* 834). For Wolfram, this view is an advance over previous views that would attribute any computational reality to a divine intelligence given its regularity. However, we will not hesitate still to argue that such regularity only truly makes sense if it ultimately has a divine source. The issue is then not if random chance can do things, but if something other than a divine source can be responsible for the actual computational reality with its regularities and patterns that we observe everywhere.

This computational approach clearly changes the game. Darwinism is left aside, and a new challenge is at stake. This one asks if our fundamentally computational reality can itself not be divinely created. Wolfram thinks that his having shown that physical processes are computational phenomena and are the norm does not necessitate a reference to the divine (*NKS* 837). That would only have been the case in the past for him, when any regularity was attributed to divine creation. But it is not clear that Wolfram has shown metaphysically that the computational nature of reality shows it is not programmed. He would have to show us how programming can arise by necessary laws and how necessary laws themselves do not depend on divine invention. We do not need super intelligent aliens necessarily to make these points. Wolfram believes that because all systems essentially are engaged in clear-cut computations means that there is no intelligence involved. But that position seems odd, since computation itself seems to be a form of intelligence in and of itself. What is computation if not thinking in action? What is thinking itself other than moving from one state to another following explicit or implicit rules? The fact that natural phenomena are indistinguishable at a certain level form suggests that human generated ones should lead us to the opposite conclusions from the ones Wolfram suggests. It should suggest that finding such detail similar to human thought in nature reinforces again the reasonableness of seeing creation as designed.

Wolfram points to a few different phenomena in this context. First, he notes that bird songs might seem like the product of bird intelligence, but that such patterns of sounds can be produced by phenomena we would normally classify as non-living (*NKS* 827). But such an observation leads us more so to say that all of creation is alive in some sense rather than that the bird is unintelligent. Most Darwinists say that Darwinism sees all organism as being equal and that no organism can be 'better' than another. A rat is not less perfect than a human being, but has only found one particular way of surviving. Evolution does not improve things over time, but merely elaborates more and more ways to survive. Things are then equally complex. But such a view disregards the arrow of time and how life has moved forward and never backwards. Let's look at what Wolfram says about SETI. SETI is the array of satellites searching the universe for signs of intelligence. The idea behind SETI presumably, as Dembski likes to point out, is that one searches through all the sounds and other data being projected by the universe for CSI. If one finds such CSI the theory goes, then one has probably found an intelligent alien society that is trying to contact us. Wolfram's point then is that, since all phenomena are computational in nature, it is totally undecidable whether any CSI detected by SETI actually comes from an intelligent source or not. It might simply be generated by a quasar. A quasar exhibits a regular pattern of radio waves that is very involved and rhythmic such that it was at first confused with a signal from aliens.[117] Recall the earlier example of a plant computing the Fibonacci sequence in its phyllotaxis. If a plant can do that, there is no reason a stellar phenomena cannot compute the prime number sequence. And, of course, famously, according to Carl Sagan's novel *Contact* that is precisely the sequence that will alert us to the presence of extra-terrestrials. SETI was based on the idea that, given the number of stars and planets, there should be a very large number of advanced civilizations existing in the universe. But the heavens are not filled with communications from

---

[117] Dembski, *Intelligent Design*, 90.

aliens. Some have taken that as an indication that we are alone in the universe, despite its size and age. Simply finding CSI will not indicate little green men exist, since the computational nature of phenomena means there is no clear distinction between human or intelligently made artifacts and naturally occurring phenomena. That means unless we see something like a spaceship, etc., SETI is probably not going to provide us with the goods.

Of course, one might say here that that means we need simply to increase the complexity aspect there. One needs to look for phenomena that are so incredibly rare or improbable that they will never occur by physical processes. However if SETI fails to provide the key, it is our metaphysical framework that will allow us to see the universe itself as designed precisely due to its computational nature. In this way we may lose out on an easy way to detect little green men but gain, metaphysically, a new approach to reality. The object is thus to show intelligent design by way of showing the fundamentally computational nature of reality. One can then, on the basis of such a computational metaphysics, show why intelligent design is the only solution to why phenomena appear as they do. From a computational perspective, a snowflake that alights on our tongue is only one of a very large number of possible snowflake patterns. That means that each snowflake is as computationally complex as most other phenomena. A snowflake then does exhibit CSI. The snowflakes form from water crystallizing into hexagonal patterns or other geometric shapes. But it is not a matter of pure chance. Each snowflake is a particular program unfolding, following simple rules. Even if one thinks that one has to look at the context at work here, one then can take the broadest context as itself a computational process and a set of simple rules unfolding. Each snowflake has its own program and thereby is unique. That shows in itself its own specific complexity. Just like crystals, snowflakes are iterations. If we bombarded crystals with a large amount of gravity, that might shape its development, but still, against that force, a program is unfolding.

Wolfram's insights also show us that complexity itself is something that all phenomena exhibit. In this way, it will always be undecidable whether a signal SETI picked up is a one coming from aliens or from a naturally occurring phenomenon. Our technology cannot be more computationally complex than what nature already can achieve on its own per Wolfram's theory. Wolfram, with his principle of computational equivalence, shows that even seemingly very basic natural phenomena are just as capable of universal computation as a human being for, example. The difference is that a human being actually engages in such computation.

The overall amount of DNA in an organism does not show us if it is more complex. A one-celled organism might have a lot more DNA than a human. In other words, it might be a much longer program. Complexity, then, is not a key in and of itself to seeing design, as most phenomena have reached the maximal level of complexity. The undecidability here is like the undecidability related to the false negatives that cropped up for Dembski. Humans can cover their traces in what they produce. But if all things are computational such that all is programmed, then anything can exhibit this feature. That means we have to argue with Descartes that the designer is not a deceiver, even if certain aspects of creation remain epistemologically opaque to us.

Recall the metaphor of replaying the tape of evolution. If we replay it many times and get the same result, most will say that shows necessity rather than design. Again, design can only be shown given a metaphysical framework that shows such seeming necessity is the product of direction. Design is always an inference that is more or less probable and always dependent ultimately on a methodological framework set up by other means. For us, God can only be truly proven using ontological/modal proofs. Once God is established, the true design of things can come into focus. The signifier and its existence or necessity must first be established before any phenomena can be grasped as designed. The designer always must come before the design.

In this way, one will truly not make judgments that there is a designer independent of knowledge of that designer. The inference, then, is always from designer to designed rather than the opposite. We first will need to encounter little green men before we can see that their space ships and signals are designed, given the undecidability that a computational reality contains in it.

It is the same with things as they are here and now. The wooden bench I sit on I know to be designed because I infer from the designers already known to me and how they work that they constructed the bench rather than the bench arising out of blind processes. This is Wolfram's point—seeing some-thing as designed involves a reference to a known history of designers and how they designed things. We think we know this about all the things we use in our everyday life, so we do not question that they are designed. Thus, if I know God, via ontological reasoning, caused the world and programmed it, I will see all of reality as designed. Seeing it as programmed thus follows from the designer rather than the other way around. Information is thus a fundamental aspect of existence as such. Information is how we understand the structuring and ordering of all that is. We can then understand even basic phenomena like entropy, matter, and energy in its terms. Natural causes might seem to repeat things, but that repetition would be an iteration of rules.

Information being a basic structure of the universe means it is not random at its beginning. It is created in an ordered state as informational. Science cannot reach God. So what we are showing is that science itself needs a metaphysical supplement to interpret its results. Here, metaphysics guides science to see itself as a form of reverse engineering. Dembski offers a list of new questions that a design perspective raises (*NFL* 313). It guides us to see all phenomena as transmitting new meaning and to find how meaning in information is constructed. It also allows for a deeply historical account of things at all times, since a design can undergo variations. One can speak of the first design and its variations. To find design in necessity again depends on one of Dembski's insights—the insight that information always must be presupposed and in the end cannot arise on its own. Information, at its heart, must be created out of nothing even if later things made from it are not. Ethically, if humans are designed, we should not be surprised if some "psychosocial constraints" are actually "hardwired into us" such that if we work against those constraints, we will meet resistance.[118] One is led here to ask if the designed aspect of creation is beautiful and what the basic idea that is being realized in it is. We also have to ask about the designer.

Beside the points we have asked, if thing are designed, we can also ask if the design is optimal. This is, of course, a point on which Darwinists believe they find further evidence for their view. Darwinians love to point out how things do not appear to be optimally designed. But this is an observation that has been made throughout recorded time. People have noticed that disasters occur, people die, disease spreads, etc. One did not need Darwin to see that creation appears to be imperfect. When we say a design is imperfect, we are implying that we know what the perfect and optimal design looks like. We also assume we know the ultimate reasons for why the design looks the way it does. It may be the case that, while something looks imperfect, such imperfection is part of a scheme that maximizes complexity or diversity. Darwinians note that their view explains imperfection, since evolution is always co-opting already existing structures and modifying them such that one should not be surprised at less than optimal design. On the other hand, intelligent design, allegedly, should always show the best possible design. The problem for Darwinians is that often what they take to be non-optimally designed shows clear aspects of efficiency, for example. What are being created here are also machines that reproduce and produce other machines. This unfolding process has not itself end-

---

[118] Dembski, *Intelligent Design*, 151.

ed, so we do not what it will produce such that it might still look optimal in the end.

This viewpoint assumes that God will optimize creation, but God has clearly created an imperfect and finite world such that it is not clear why it should be optimal. The perfection of the world might lie precisely in its being imperfect and finite and yet created by the perfect one. Clearly, many natural phenomena such as the human heart exceed the design capacities of current humans. Ultimately, the argument from non-optimization is a variation on the argument from evil. Because the world is imperfect (the story goes), God did not create it. Just as the argument from evil finally cannot say anything more than that there is (in the view of this argument's proponents) an excess of evil in the world despite the need for freedom, human development, etc., the argument from non-optimization will only ever be able to say they think there is an excess of imperfection.

David Hume famously criticized the argument for God's existence from design. We are not employing it in that sense. Hume, in his critique, noted that such an argument is an argument from analogy, but, like any analogy, one can find disanalogies between two things, since an analogy is never saying two things are completely identical. Thus, if the argument is like William Paley's and claims that just as we infer a designer of a watch we should infer a designer of living things, we can always point out that watches do not reproduce as living things do. This is where, again, the computational view is different, since it sees things as programmed. Given programming, the issue of reproduction is eliminated as von Neumann already showed how computer programs can reproduce in this way. Even though we have argued that we do not seek to prove God by way of the argument from design (after all, if we look at life, it can never be ruled out that superior aliens did not create it), we can still see how God did design life and programmed it once we adopt the right metaphysical view.

Many like a new version of the argument from design called 'fine-tuning.' This argument claims that the universe has of all the many possible conditions, the right conditions for life. But such a perspective takes these conditions as external to life itself. It sees the universe as a series of disconnected parameters and measurements that are all at the right levels to allow for life to emerge when each of them individually could be any number of other values. But this is to take the universe itself as a series of disconnected values. It is therefore an abstract and disconnected view in itself. We need rather to provide a metaphysical account showing God did specify biology and determine its structure. God would then explain why biology looks the way it is, given its programming. But we can say initially that God would not choose Darwinian mechanisms, since such mechanisms are about pure chance. That suggests that the process is out of God's hands. But God might produce things with redundancy and backup systems in place. However, even if God does not use Darwinian mechanisms as the main motor of life's development, clearly there are still copying errors and other breakages that occur in the development of life, but, again, such occurrences are just as problematic as natural disasters and disease. That is why one has to argue that such issues ultimately prove to be for the best in the end. What appears to be just copying errors is a mechanism for creativity. What appears to be breakage is a way to enable life to continue on its course.

Even the eye, which was once seen as a poor design, is being wondered at today, given its assemblage. Some people believe, for example, that order can occur without information, but all order, whether as a message or otherwise, needs to have information. Any order itself is the result of informational processes via computation. Energy is itself explicable in terms of information. Information must be what allows for order, since none of these other phenomena can create information by themselves. Information comes ultimately from nothing, then, and thus needs a creator. Information implies a creator and order does as well. Crystals are information as much as any computer program due to their computational nature.

Some people claim that only intelligence can choose to be unpredictable and thus can produce anything of any type. Thus, we will never know that anything was ever made by a divine intelligence. That is why God must not be a deceiver, even if God is epistemologically otherwise opaque to us.

Part Two

The Computational Nature of Reality

§15
THE COMPUTATIONAL NATURE OF REALITY

Throughout, I have claimed explicitly that existence is computational in nature. This view has been given a few names—pan-ontic computationalism, Digital Philosophy, Digital Metaphysics, Neo-Pythagoreanism, etc. Any of these names will suffice. Key thinkers have been involved in the articulation of this view such as Stephen Wolfram, Gregory Chaitin, Frank Tipler, Edward Fredkin, Tommaso Toffoli, Jürgen Schmidhuber, Gerard 't Hooft, Konrad Zuse, Seth Lloyd, etc. Interestingly, such thinkers do not have any formal philosophical training and yet have blazed new trails. Part of the reason for this is that as physicists, mathematicians, computer scientists, etc., they have been forced to conceptualize new ways of viewing things based on the issues they have encountered in their research. Despite the obvious importance of the digital revolution in all spheres of our lives and the inherent interest of the work these men are doing, there has been shockingly little real intellectual research done on them.

It is in particular Fredkin who has tried to systematize this viewpoint. Fredkin has only published his work on his web page: www.digitalphilosophy.org. There, Fredkin notes the key elements of his model:

The development of a DM [Digital Metaphysics] model:
1. Finite nature—the assumption that all is discrete and finite
2. Computational Universality
3. Reversibility and Conservation of Information
4. CPT symmetry
5. Discrete
6. Allowing for particles and their properties[119]

Let's highlight the key aspects of this view. First, let's look at what Fredkin can mean by the conservation of information. Presumably he uses this phrase to recall the notion of the conservation of energy. This idea states that the quantity of energy in the world is always preserved. Energy can be trans-formed into new forms, it can be randomized, it can become pure radiation, and radiation might itself possibly, if given enough time, turn into mass, but there is always the same amount of energy in the final tally. The total amount of energy itself never changes. With information, I think things work differently. It is not that we do not gain new information; it is that all that occurs in the world is itself a playing out of the initial programming of the universe. It is an information sequence that is at work there. The world is itself compressible into this information. That does not mean it will not be possible to see parts of the universe that are being elaborated as themselves irreducibly complex and non-compressible, but that is no different than an iteration of the rule for producing positive integers leading to primes. The repetition of the same, in its difference, can produce new and complex things without them not being only repetitions of the same.

---

[119] Edward Fredkin, "Introduction to Digital Philosophy, Chapter 20," *Digital Philosophy* [weblog]: http://www.digitalphilosophy.org/Home/Papers/TOC/Chapter20UnitsBLTPDRAI/tabid/84/Default.aspx [retrieved January 20, 2012].

Fredkin is arguing that the universe is finite in nature. To argue that all is discrete requires that, because there is no infinite regress of levels and scales. All is not continuous such that it could go on forever. That means any phenomenon we see in nature is itself at most a finite state machine. Barrow and Tipler argue that such a machine is still finite "even if it exists forever and processes an infinite amount of data."[120] That is true because continuity itself in this view is a function of all being discrete. As Fredkin puts it, "there are no infinitesimals. If finite nature is true, then there are certain consequences that hold independent of scale."[121] That means the system will always work on the same elements even if it goes on indefinitely. It also means that there is an ultimate scale that one can speak of, and that ultimate scale operates at every scale. For that reason, we can then find the same operations at work at the level of snowflakes and galaxies. And this is because algorithms are perfectly indifferent in their computations as to what they are computing. The algorithm just involves the specific steps and rules to be performed on any set of bits, data, entities, etc.

People laugh at Kabbalah or Pythagoreanism when it says that the numerical values of two different things cause them to be related. Pythagoreans believed that if two phenomena exhibit that each is an expression of the essence of seven, then those phenomena were somehow related. But this is precisely what computationalism allows us to see. It allows us to see that electrons circling around nuclei and stars circling around black holes might be related because they are the same structured sets of integers. Computation thus ensures that we do not just have numbers as letters, as meaningless literal marks, but also numbers as structured

---

[120] Barrow and Tipler, *The Anthropic Cosmological Principle*, 661.
[121] Edward Fredkin, (1992) "Finite Nature," *Digital Philosophy* [weblog]: http://www.digitalphilosophy.org/Home/Papers/Finite Nature/tabid/106/Default.aspx [retrieved January 20, 2012].

sets of integers, as esoteric keys for linking disparate and seemingly unrelated phenomena.

Here, most people do not believe that the sheer richness of the world they see can itself be grasped by the letter. The richness of the world is always changing and different, but when we see that the world is always already literalized, we are not idealizing the empirical, but rather rendering it in its true materiality. The richness of the world is literalized in its materiality and in its diversity. This is why one needs the dimension of the letter and not just as numbers. People laugh at Kabbalah or Pythagoreanism because they take it as treating numbers in only a semiotic sense, as signs representing something for someone. But numbers do not function like signs in this way without reference to their configuration as letters.

The new kind of science thus being inaugurated by Wolfram, amongst others, involves the mathematization of all, of seeing all as already always mathematized. But in reducing all to the letter, the dimension of the number as connecting things together is not lost. To be mathematized is to be made algorithmic. In this new kind of science, the letter grasps and substitutes for the richness of nature not in order simply to articulate a general law like 'F = ma,' but in order to capture the program a planet is computing through its orbit. Reality is already cut up in this way by way of the letter, because reality is already discrete.

However, reality is marked by the impossible, that is, by God. God leaves no sign of his existence other than his Name. Creation is not missing this sign. It is missing God, who withdraws from it. The creator self-effaces:

> And the LORD said, "I will cause all my goodness to pass in front of you, and I will proclaim my name, the LORD, in your presence. I will have mercy on whom I will have mercy, and I will have compassion on whom I will have compassion. But," he said, "you cannot see my face, for no one may see me and live." Then the LORD said, "There is a place near me

> where you may stand on a rock. When my glory passes by, I will put you in a cleft in the rock and cover you with my hand until I have passed by. Then I will remove my hand and you will see my back; but my face must not be seen. (Exodus 33:19-23)

In this way, reality is bound to the impossible. And this has consequences, insofar as it marks reality as incomplete. The real, for Lacan, is not the idea that all is possible but that not all is, and that is because it is linked essentially to an impossibility. The real is always grounded in the impossible. God is named by the name of the void, indicating the lack of knowledge we have of the nameless one. God is the cause of that name. And thus God is not a positive entity in this world. We will not find him as long as we search for something other than a name and effects. This is why the paradoxes we have associated with logic are actually paradoxes and lacunae in the Real itself.

And how does God see the world? He sees reality as it is in itself, as letters, numbers, sets, etc. If we want to see ourselves how as are seen, we would need to look at ourselves in this manner. No one should expect reality to look to the divine as it does to us. This is why we were given the Torah, a sequence of letters, as the divine gift. It is a way for us to see the world in its divinity. This is also why science itself is possible via the letter and literalization of being, because it is only in that way that we can gain true knowledge of it.

Of course, for Fredkin, here nature itself is being conceived as a digital computer, and all phenomena as computational in nature. At its most basic, this means that we can think of things as being in one state and then transitioning into a new state and so on.[122] The transition itself is not random, but a function of specific rules and instructions. We can look at any scale and find the same thing happen-

---

[122] Fredkin, "Finite Nature."

ing—one state transitioning into another. That is why Wolfram has tried to exemplify these processes using cellular automata, as the computer itself in its computation is such an automaton. Here one sees a finite state machine directly at work and thereby finite nature itself. Finite nature is therefore not motionless as computation is a constant process. Information is undergoing constant permutation and transformation. Before the computational revolution in thought, scientists, for example, looked for laws and equations to express how the world worked, but these laws could not themselves express how the world unfolded and changed. They could only express the rate at which something happened. They thus could only present a frozen picture of the world and a reflection of it. But with computation, rules unfold and express themselves in the unfolding of the universe itself. The model and what it models collapse into the same thing.

Not only is nature finite, but computations are made up of a finite set of rules that can be listed in principle. All systems have such rules and follow them. A computation is ultimately a process that consists of a finite set of rules that can be represented. Computation is thinking itself in the flesh. It is an embodied form of thinking. Computation is not about Platonic forms. The world itself is thinking. Computation is the materiality of the world and its flesh. It's like that old computer commercial said: "Shh, it's thinking." What this means is it is not only conscious thought or even unconscious primary processes that are computing and thinking; the entirety of existence is. Freud revealed to us how our unconscious minds are computing and thinking without our being aware of it. But now we see that being in itself is doing so. It's not a question of mental presentations, of course. It's a question of the letter and its permutation. The system is itself the iteration and repetition of the rules.

Any set of finite rules, any computation, can itself unfold in the universe. This is why the universe is itself a digital computer. That should not be surprising, since, for instance, the human brain and the computers we use are themselves parts of the universe itself. Their existence in themselves would be enough to show that the universe can allow itself to emulate any behavior. But before we had these two things, it could have been known that the universe is computationally universal. Universal here indicates that the universe can compute any computation. It is not limited to the multiplication of a limited number of things as, for instance, some primitive calculating machines were. A universal computer can do anything any other computer can do. What really differentiates any two computers is the speed at which they compute and the amount of memory they have. Nature itself must be computationally universal, if only because otherwise I would not be able to use the computer I am using now. But the universe itself, outside of my own mind and the computer I type on, is also capable of and is computing many other computations. What is interesting is that this computational universality is completely compatible with the finite nature of all systems. What then also differentiates such systems, once they demonstrate their own computational universality, is the specific program they happen to run and mostly seem to only ever run. Any aspect of being can itself be seen as a finite state machine programmed to be whatever that particular section is. Of course, some programs will be simpler than others. But any thing can be understood as a computation. In this way, a tree might be a very simple and elegant computation. But one can take an entire forest—even one with people in it—if that set of rules will be a highly detailed one. There is a mathematical expression for any possible set one selects of being. That might seem trivial, but it is not. One might think that not everything can be mathematized, but, even if that mathematization shows no elegance or reducibility, it can be found. It is still a decisive metaphysical point that such mathematization can, in effect, take place. Scientists are only interested in elegant equations and programs, but metaphysicians are interested in the very idea that anything can be mathematized, because that implies something basic about the very nature of all things. That one can always find an equation to express things is not interesting to the scientist who wants simple expressions, but that it can be done has decisive metaphysical implications.[123] The mathematization of all means that there is an algorithm that can produce each thing as an output based on previous input. This should not be surprising, since it should be seen as part of the universality of a universal computer, like the universe itself. It can express every well-defined sequence of mathematical rules it is given to carry out.

Here, the alphabet or language that is manipulated is matter itself as bits and numbers, sets and letters. Universal computers can compute any possible algorithm. That means it can run any program. Now some programs might go on forever in a loop, and some might run without end. Everything indicates that nature does not allow such programs. In other words, the universe, at its most basic level, seems to be about elegant programs. Darwinians might suggest that the useless or non-halting programs have been selected out. But it appears more so that the universe is running some program that, in and of itself, disallows such halting problems. Nature thus contains intricate and sophisticated programs that guide all other phenomena. In this way, when we encounter a system that is itself non-elegant, it is probably the case that we will need to ultimately look at it from the perspective of the entire universe to understand how it follows from an elegant program. Darwinians think that nature's being a universal computer means it can run every computer and is somehow trying to articulate every single one. That mean one needs some sort of selection mechanism to weed out programs, but we will try to show that it is more so that the program running this universal computer itself self-delimits and eliminates pos-

---

[123] Chaitin speaks, himself, of how all can be mathematized, but does not give it too much importance: Gregory Chaitin, *Meta Math!: The Quest for Omega* (New York: Vintage, 2006), 64.

sibilities without any need of such 'natural selection.' The source of order is then not selection, but rather the coding itself that causes development and its patterns.

Darwinians cannot believe that elegant programs can follow from the fact that the universe itself is elegant, but that is because they see randomness and chance as the operative principles in the world. The universe as a digital computer can emulate any and all physical processes and, in doing so, demonstrates universal computations. There are almost endless examples, so a few will suffice. It is well known that the life cycle of a cicada exhibits the computation of the series of prime numbers. Other physical processes generate extremely complex patterns. Snowflakes have already been mentioned as examples of simple programs that exhibit contingency, insofar as any number of snowflake patterns is, in principle, possible. Given the large number of patterns, finding any single one on your tongue is highly improbable. If one looks closely at galaxies, they appear to follow similar patterns. I have mentioned a couple of times the phyllotaxis of things like pine cones and flowers, where their spirals show computation of the Fibonacci series. In this way, the leaves unfold from the center, alternating in patterns in the same series as a very elegant mathematical equation.

However, if we just have the equation, we do not have its unfolding. Only by inputting data and calculating does that happen. With pine cones it happens automatically and dynamically:

> Consider phyllotaxis, conveniently seen in pine cones and sun flowers. The scales, as is well known, form in double spirals which radiate from a center, one clockwise, the other counterclockwise. The surprising feature is that the number of spirals in one direction is related to the number in the other direc-

tion as two adjacent numbers in the Fibonacci series 1, 1, 2, 3, 5, 8, 13, 21, 34.[124]

What would probably have previously looked like sheer randomness now exhibits its existence as a program. The leaves are programmed to generate this sequence. It is not reasonable to suggest it is a function of chance. What looked like chance turned out to be a function of rules. This computational complexity suggests that the evolution of life itself, with its specific history, was also a program unfolding by way of genetic sequencing. In a species, for example, one finds the same sequence of genomes that determine that each organism will undergo the same changes at the same time. The information here coded in the genes thus is not simply about copying itself, but also of unfolding a program that computes specific patterns.

Not surprisingly, Wolfram has used computers to produce exactly the same sort of patterns as plants and snowflakes exhibit. This should not have been shocking given that nature is a digital computer and a computer can emulate all the physical processes that the universe itself can compute. The complexity here is not an issue. The computers we have are also universal, so they can simulate any system in itself. They are not built in the same way as all in the universe is, but they do compute in the same fashion. We can only simulate rather than emulate planets at this point. But given the principles involved, there is no reason to think that we will only have to be satisfied with simulation. Any system can be simulated. Most argue we cannot simulate the entire universe, but that is more so because one would need a computer the size of the universe itself to do it.

Given the computational nature of things, it may be possible to reverse any computation in the computers we use, just as nature seems to prevent irreversible systems

---

[124] Kauffman, *The Origins of Order*, 15.

through entropy. But we will have to return to this issue and clarify it from a computational perspective. As Paul Davies, one of the first to explain and engage in these issues, expounds, the

> computer is in essence simply a procedure for converting one set of symbols into another according to some rule. Usually we think of the symbols as numbers; more specifically as strings of ones and zeroes, these being the most appropriate formulation for machines to use.[125]

But what are ones and zeros when it comes to things outside of the computer I am typing on? That being itself is discreet means that it is made up of numbers and bits in its very essence, for if reality is fundamentally discrete, as Fredkin argues, then seeing it as ones and zeros is to see it how it is in itself. Any number is itself a string of zeros and ones.

Computationalism as a realist ontology demands a realist theory of numbers, but it demands that realism only insofar as numbers are themselves bits. Computationalism is saying that, in one state, one has a bit string of zeros and ones and then, via a set of finite rules, another bit string emerges. A computer program is itself a bit string that is a set of instructions for converting bit strings into other bit strings. Laws of nature are algorithms, as Wolfram has said repeatedly. Davies here uses the example of a "planet going around the sun" such that every phase transition of the planet is itself a transition from one bit string to another.[126] But for computationalism to be a realist ontology, it cannot just be a question of translating or compiling phenomena into 0s and 1s, but for these phenomena in their very dis-

---

[125] Paul Davies, *The Mind of God: The Scientific Basis for a Rational World* (New York: Simon and Schuster, 1993), 118.
[126] Davies, *The Mind of God*, 118.

crete nature to be made of bits. The bit must be the new atom of ontology.

It is clear that information can be translated into bits and that binary form can comprehend it. To most, that will seem simply like a representation or an analogy with what computers do. To say the universe it is a string of 0s and 1s and the permutation of those bits means formulating a concept of the bit that allows it to function as the atom of all things. Part of the need for such an atom is to avoid infinite regress. If one has an infinite regress of scales and levels, then one will never be able to see how things compute. An infinite computation never ends and outputs its result. Bits are also translated as such, due to their discrete nature, into a blueprint, but, if that blueprint is itself always contained in another blueprint, one will never be able to constitute any phenomenon. Digital metaphysics requires such a blueprint:

> "There can be no information without a means of its representation." This means that if a particle is moving with a particular velocity, it must be true that there is an interpretation of conglomeration of bits of information in the system that represent the information that describes the particle's velocity.[127]

All things are already information in themselves such that they are their representation. That is why a fundamental element must be involved: to avoid an endless number of representations inside representations. To have such a regress would mean that no system would ever get started in its computation. The bit is the relation between 0 and 1—an on state and an off state, but also a positive entity in the sense of the empty set. One is in either one of those states, but each state is necessarily related to its other. To be

---

[127] Edward Fredkin, "Introduction to Digital Philosophy, Chapter 14," http://64.78.31.152/wp-content/uploads/2012/08/intro-to-DP.pdf [retrieved January 20, 2012].

in the on state is to not be in the off one. The bit is thereby relational at its core. That is also what allows it to be the true atom.

Atoms, in the sense of particles, are simply like billiard balls—solid points. They are thereby static. However, today we know that bits can be encoded on atoms. Atoms, when taken together, should be seen as being like cells in a cellular automaton. As the first atomists understood, the atom as particle is always related to the void. It can only move if there is the void. The positing of the void here is not arbitrary, because the bit as particle is simply the 'on' state, the 1. The 1 is always related to its place and to its point of instantiation, the void, or its absence and absenting.

Computation is dynamical. It allows for transition precisely as the 0 can become 1 and again 0. The bit can thus transform itself into its absence. This was something the traditional atom could not do. It could only move within the void as an empty space. But if particles are themselves information, then it contains the void within it as part of it. Atoms themselves are almost entirely empty space. The nucleus of the atom is but a small point inside a vast emptiness. It thereby embodies this relation between something and its absence at the heart of matter itself. If the bit were not fundamentally relational, it would not be clear why one could not keep dividing. It would be purely arbitrary to designate a final particle. As we have seen, the atom was split open and revealed subatomic particles, showing it was not the ultimate point it was imagined to be. However, a relation itself is indivisible as such.

Given the fundamental nature of the bit, it is clear that one is not representing things when one models them as much as reproducing the very being of the thing as information moving from one state to another. An empty space is then itself the 0 state. Empty space is therefore not alien to the bit in the way that the void was alien to the atom. Atoms themselves were also static in the void. They need the swerve, clinamen, to move. But the bit itself is its own iteration. It is a repetition by its very nature. It is repeating itself—0 and then 1. This repetition is what allows for the repetitive patterns we see filling space and time at all levels and scales. When life begins, we see how a code that is itself a bit string can function as instructions, whereas matter is hardware/software joined together in dedicated algorithms. We do not need, however to suggest there is a set of instructions inscribed elsewhere that is run to produce the phenomena we see in the night sky any more than we do with a machine that runs on its own. The circuitry here is the very matter and energy that makes up the phenomena.

The classical bit is a system with only two states. But with only two states of any information, what one wants to express is formulated. Qualities can be formatted. And with that, one has defined the very processes of the world itself. If this were not true, one would not be able to display the same patterns as one sees in galaxy spirals on a screen. Fredkin prefers the notation 1 and -1 rather than 0 and 1 for bits, since this notion shows that the void as such is never truly existent in nature.[128] The void always sublates itself into something. We have, at best, in this world, false vacuums. Such false vacuums need energy to persist, and that is because, ultimately, it is a positive entity, something in the world. But the fact that 1 is related to -1 means it is related to its negation. Negation itself depends on voiding, which means that non-being is already a part of being. With negatives one indicates that, from the beginning, there is absence marking being itself. For this reason, the negative one might, in this world, be something, but it is still related to the nothing else than the void, since otherwise there would be no voiding. Fredkin here might want to simply insist on the fact that -1 should not be thought of as not a bit or as pure nothing. The vacuum, for him, as well as matter and energy, are made up of bits, but even writing

---

[128] Edward Fredkin, "Introduction to Digital Philosophy, Chapter 21": http://64.78.31.152/wp-content/uploads/2012/08/intro-to-DP.pdf [retrieved January 20, 2012].

-1 rather than 0 does not erase the way in which bit itself is related to absence itself.

For Fredkin, the false vacuums we encounter in nature are just a place where all the bits are in the 0 or -1 state.[129] Everything there is turned off without being pure nothingness itself:

> This implies that, in a 2 state DM model, empty space must be some kind of pattern that is symmetrical with respect to matter and antimatter. This particular problem is considerably simpler in the case of a 2 statement, where the terms could be 1, 0, and -1.[130]

Fredkin here probably refers to quantum computation and the qubit. The qubit can be in a 0 state or 1 state or 01 at the same time via superposition. This presents the possibility then of two seemingly mutually exclusive stats existing at once, but also of computations of real numbers—here, any number between 0 and 1.

What is interesting here is that the bit allows us to see how phenomena at all scales compute. One can show how a series of light bulbs turning on and off compute as much as a series of buckets filled and drained of water per Kauffman's examples. Anything that can pixilated as in an on and off state then can function as a bit and compute. Computation is nothing but the operations on and transitions of these bits—their turning on and off. The important point is the dynamic behavior they demonstrate. From the point of view of computation, all bits are identical. All things in the on state are identical; all things in the off state are the same.[131] This is why, no matter what set we use, we can

---

[129] Fredkin, "Introduction to Digital Philosophy, Chapter 21."

[130] Fredkin, "Introduction to Digital Philosophy, Chapter 21."

[131] Edward Fredkin, "Introduction to Digital Philosophy, Chapter 10": http://64.78.31.152/wp-content/uploads/2012/08/intro-to-DP.pdf [retrieved January 20, 2012].

come to the same results using computation. This means also that the manner in which digital processes operate in the memory systems of computers demonstrates the fundamental traits of how things unfold and change in the world outside that memory chip.[132] This is why showing how a galactic spiral forms on a computer screen is not a model in the sense of an analogy, but an exact model, since both phenomena are digital.

These observations should not lead us to believe all is a fractal in nature. As Wolfram has shown, nested patterns are the most common type of program, but there are programs, like the one he calls 'Rule 30,' that give rise to non-repeating patterns. This is also why cellular automata nicely express the fundamental nature of digital processes. These automata are made up of cells that are either filled or not. In other words, these cells are bits in either a 0 or 1 state. Each cell has a value. Simultaneously, the cells are immanently instructed to achieve their state, and this happens at whatever interval is selected. The filling of states or emptying of them is not random; it is always a matter of a rule that determines what value each cell has. Often, such rules do so in relation to what the previous value of the cell was. The cells themselves can acquire value simply by their relationships to neighboring cells.

What is stunning here is the sheer complexity of behaviors even one-dimensional automata display simply using these elements. It shows us directly and overtly how the continuous emerges from the discrete. How is that possible? We can say, following Poundstone and also Seth Lloyd, that recursion is the reason:

> Recursion is a process in which two things are put together to produce third. For example, taking "I" together with "see" yields "I see." "I" is a concept ("myself") and 'see' is an action; putting them to-

---

[132] Fredkin, "Introduction to Digital Philosophy, Chapter 10."

gether yields a sentence that combines aspects of "I" and "see." Here two important features of recursion: First, the two original things that are put together remain intact; second, the things produced by recursion can themselves be put together to produce new things. "You see" and "I see" can be put together to yield "You see I see." (Followed by "I see you see I see," and so on.) Recursion is the basis not only of human language but also of computer languages. Computer languages instruct computers to perform tasks (word processing, number crunching, game playing) that are built up recursively, out of simple underlying logic operations (AND, OR, NOT COPY, and so on). Recursion is a simple process that is potentially very powerful.[133]

Recursion shows how putting together smaller elements (at least two of them) leads to new, emergent properties and objects. But that new, emergent phenomenon can itself function as a part or element in a new whole or in a new code. Iteration is precisely this process. Intricate patterns emerge through, for instance, letters becoming words becoming sentences becoming paragraphs becoming texts.

The conjugation of bits is just such a recursive product. 0 and 1 come together to form a new thing, 01. This process can go on indefinitely, but if it does not end, the program itself will not halt and output a result. Part of nature being finite means that, ultimately, the program ends this process. Cellular automata are not doing much more than this, insofar as they empty and fill cells over and over again and thus bring about new patterns and phenomena. The binary nature of bits does not end with just on and off, as the conjunction of bits can then become instructions as complicated as 'copy.' Interestingly enough, Lloyd brings up these

---

[133] Seth Lloyd, "How Smart is the Universe?" in *Intelligent Thought: Science Versus the Intelligent Design Movement* (New York: Vintage, 2006), 179–191, 183.

points in the context of life. However, life is not adding new bits necessarily in a random way and not by Darwinian processes.

As finite state machines, living organisms might also have a finite number of possible combinations, even if it is open as to how those combinations will be rendered. We have seen that amoebas can have more bits than a human being such that it is not the number of bits that leads to larger organisms. Lloyd discusses two species producing a third, but that is symbiogenesis and not Darwinian random mutation and selection.[134] We cannot close off the possibility that symbiogenesis itself is operating by way of a clear and simple program. Lloyd in this essay suggests with his "free lunch theorems" that universal computation means that systems such as the universe that are universally computational will necessarily bring about subsystems that include all possible structures.[135] That view assumes that a computer, simply because it is universal, necessarily is going to run all programs. However, the computer itself might be running a particular program. It is not clear why that program has to lead to all possible programs arising. This program might itself be self-delimiting such that only ever a select number can be realized.

Lloyd also suggests here that a universal computer necessarily has to give rise to living things.[136] That statement again presupposes that universal computation means all possibilities are actualized. We will argue it means exactly the reverse. Lloyd's point here is that recursion is such a part of computing that it will give rise to open-endedness, but that will not be true, as we are speaking of bit strings, and a bit string can include within itself instructions to cease operating. It is more likely that the universe as digital includes in its computation an instruction to cease at some point rather than to go on forever, even if that means re-

---

[134] Lloyd, "How Smart is the Universe?" 184.
[135] Lloyd, "How Smart is the Universe?" 188.
[136] Lloyd, "How Smart is the Universe?"

versing itself.

Lloyd interestingly suggests that entropy itself produces chaos and randomly shuffles bits. Entropy would scramble bits, but not necessarily add new ones. To add new ones, one needs anti-entropic occurrences like symbiogenesis, for example. For Lloyd, entropy explains all the variation we see in all things, as entropy is constantly shuffling the bits strings making up things. However, entropy itself might not be random, as it might be a program constantly running at a quantum level that produces Rule 30 randomness. I will return to entropy in the next section and also to Darwinian metaphysics that always sees nature as exploring all possible ways of doing something and having various ways selected in order to move along to the next stage. What is amazing is that someone like Lloyd adopts this position, when he himself, as a digital philosopher, should know that programs do not explore all possibilities. A program as a set of rules necessarily excludes many things by its very finite set of rules. Lloyd himself admits even Darwinian selection cannot occur until life emerges but still projects such procedures all the way back to the atomic level.

Fredkin's view of the fundamental finitude of nature means that all is made up of digital information, but he wants us to hear in digital also digits. That is, to say all is made up of bits is to say all is made up of integers and the relations between them. That is, all is number. The world is made up of digits. Saying all is bits is the same as saying all is digits. Numbers, as we use them, are, of course, relational, but the reason they work to express the world is because the digital and discrete nature of phenomena is always already represented: "If we had the right kind of magic microscope, we should always be able to see the digits that present whatever information is present. Information is never 'just there.'"[137] Included in the idea that all phenomena can be programmed and are computational is the idea that all phenomena are made up of numbers. The finite

---

[137] Fredkin, "Finite Nature."

nature of things means, also, that it is finite integers that are at the basis of things.

Now such finite integers can be put into relations with each other, but, ultimately, a digital philosophy argues that it is finite positive integers that form the basis of all operations. Since any finite integer can be generated from the base ten, that means all things are made of the base ten of integers and their relations. All things can be measured by the base ten. This is a purely realist science of mathematics. The base ten are not something we construct. They are there as a part of being itself. Now a bit is simpler than any single number other than the zero itself. It is the empty set itself. Just as all numbers can be generated by the empty set being included in each set, so the numbers can be generated by string bits together. The problem then concerns how we count the empty set and zero. Do they count as 1? It probably means that we have to say that 0 itself is not a positive integer. It is the source of the positive integers. Only when 0 is itself counted do we get 1, but 0 is not pure nothingness, pure absence, pure negation. This is why it is the bit. It is the void in its being marked. This is why the bit is always fundamentally relational at its core—it is the relation between something in itself and its absence.

Bit strings then are "structured sets of integers" as Fredkin puts it.[138] Each bit string is a number or a list of numbers. These numbers are part of reality itself. When I think of a length, my thought does not have length; when I think of a color it does not have hue, but any thought must minimally be at least one thought and thus be denumerable and numerical in nature. What the transformation of bit strings into each other involves is counting itself. We see series like the Fibonacci series unfolding. Just like the Fibonacci series or the series of integers coming after the decimal point for pi, there is a rule that expresses each series.

---

[138] Edward Fredkin, "Digital Mechanics," *Digital Philosophy* [weblog]: http://www.digitalphilosophy.org/Home/Papers/tabid/61/Default.aspx [retrieved January 20, 2012].

This mathematical realism is arguing that, at the very least, such positive integers exist independent of human thought. The very fact that any thou-ght is numerical in nature works in conjunction with that fact that anything outside of thought has the same nature. If one holds an apple, it is one apple. Humans did not invent mathematics. They discovered it. If we invented it, then other creatures would not be capable of counting. However, various animals seem to be aware of basic numbers and are able to tell the difference between two going into a forest and only one coming out.

This view is not saying that numbers are Platonic forms. To see numbers are real is to say that all things are necessarily numerical. If we have one atom of hydrogen, it is one atom. That oneness is there as part of the atom itself. Our definitions and constructs are made of the numerical, of sets and scales, but so are the things of the world itself, including such thoughts. Physical bodies are classes. We do not count a thought and then it becomes one. It is already one, as it is a set, and bits are directly related to sets. Not only is the empty set the primordial bit, but bit strings are themselves structured sets of integers.

Of course, I do not think anyone will dispute that the digital objects we see displayed on computer screens do exhibit these aspects. All such objects are fully describable in mathematical terms precisely because they are themselves sets of bits. Any shape or pattern one sees displayed is also that code. Such images are clearly programmable and appear by way of algorithmic computation. I also think that most will not dispute that today we are able to convert almost any image or sound into such a digitized form by mathematizing it. What that compilation into bits of sounds shows from this ontological perspective is but one more example of the transformation of the discrete nature of things into another discrete form. Many wish to see this as a digitization of the analog, as the continuous becoming discrete, but it is, in fact, the exposure of the always already existent differential nature of the phenomena.

The view that the bit is differentiality in itself is, of

course, a view in concert with Hegelianism, for which what cannot be further differentiated is differentiation itself. This is why for Hegel, non-identity is inscribed in any existing thing. That non-identity is the void itself. The bit is always related to the void, to its place of inscription. If the bit did not have this relationship, computation would not be able to be dynamic in nature. The bit thus would be, for instance, split between its mark as empty set and the nothing it includes. There is then a split between 0/1 in the empty set itself. Pan-ontic computationalism requires 0/1 (the mark and its absence) and ways of repeating and operating this relation. The empty set, any time we recognize it, is already 0 as 1. 0 and 1 come together. They are always a pair. This is an irreducible factum of being itself. It is part and parcel of its creation and its creativity. The bit in being 0/1 at once means that the absence included in it is always a missing half. Once we have 0/1 we see that reality itself is already thinking, already computational. We can easily translate this again into Hegelese by saying that the split in reality, in substance, is why it is also always subject. Here, subject means computation, but let's not fall into the trap of the thinking that the only algorithm is the dialectic of universal and particular or subject and object. Even though the heart of being is marked by the bit/letter, there are many more algorithms available and many more steps. In the human mind, we have subject as consciousness. The bit then names and conditions this division between substance and subject and the reason why they are always related.

I believe I am doing more than rehearsing the Lacanian Hegelianism that Žižek and his Slovenian cohorts have been detailing for the last 20 years or so, for what I am arguing here is that the bit, the key concept of pan-ontic computationalism, embodies this structure. And in doing that, we are opening up ourselves to a Lacanian realism of the letter (the very ontology signaled by the first text of Lacan's *Ecrits*), to an ontology that speaks about more than the impasses of thought. The Slovenians are, and were, interested in reading Lacan as a German idealist, which meant the real was always the impossible that consciousness could not grasp. Our Lacanian realism begins with the observation that, for Lacan, letters are of the Real rather than the Symbolic. We passively see that that such sets hold independently of us, counting them up as such in the same way that we passively perceive a tree or coffee cup. To say we create 0, the empty set, is like saying we created the universe itself. Numbers subsist as much as trees and coffee cups, because such things themselves are numerical. Numbers therefore subsist in them.

If there were no individual things there still would at least be the empty set, which is itself a thing. If there were no empty set, then there would be nothing. This is why set theory captures the nature of numbers. Numbers are things. Two apples is the set of two things. This way, even a child can see how the world is fundamentally numerical. Bits name all things precisely because one piece of paper is the set of one paper. There is the one. If there were no things, there would be nothingness so no numbers. If there was nothing but the vacuum, then the empty set that is itself already one, insofar as it includes nothing, subsists. But, as we have argued, nothing comes from nothing, such that only God could count the void and include it as empty set. The void has no self to 'self-organize.' God, the impossible Other, does this counting by way of God's own self-withdrawal, *tzimtzum*.

This thesis, like others presented here, I first developed in my first book *Reality in the Name of God*. There, I presented what I think is a new way to do philosophical theology. As opposed to Kantian and, more importantly, Husserlian influenced phenomenological theology, we no longer remained entrapped within the immanent realm of an intentional consciousness that must bracket all transcendence including, most importantly, God himself, but rather come to understand God as having self-bracketed himself (withdrawn) in order to create nothing and, through it, the world itself. Plato believes that oneness exists as an eternal form, but his forms are ultimately only tautologies (beauty itself is that which is most beautiful). They cannot be anything other than tautologies, since they are totally empty of content. That means ultimately they themselves do not escape the logic of the empty set and thereby the void (which they presuppose and cannot create). For example, Beauty itself is the set of that thing which is most beautiful. But any set already presupposes the empty set as the frame out of which it is made. Self-identity is nothing more than to be marked as a set. Instead of positing numbers as Platonic forms, we see them as things that are created by way of the empty set. That means there is no problem with an apple being made of oneness, insofar as it a set of one thing. The one does not exist in heaven. It is part of this world and its substantiality and subsistence. Numbers are not withdrawn and do not hide. They are there always before us in all we think and see.

One avoids the problems inherent in the Platonic model of participation by adopting the Pythagorean model of being, wherein being is numbers. As for an infinite set of numbers, this is itself a mark and an example of the self-referential power of the signifier as set. The point is that a piece of paper is one, but so is any mark of 'one' on that paper. This is similar to Frege's notion that we do not have objects without concepts and classes. Without concepts and classes, there are no things (so nothing) to count. The concepts and classes are the sets. They are the brackets of a set. That's why we write the brackets ([. . .]). We have to understand that the brackets of any set are the empty set; they embody how the empty set is included in any possible set. This is why all sets of objects are finally numbers, as they exist in the same basic form and form the raw material for all things. The empty set is the first thing and the most fundamental. The empty set is itself a thing. That should never be forgotten. It is both a positive entity in the world and a relation with the void and its place of inscription. It is thereby another name for the bit. Because it is always marking itself and the void, it is always itself and its relation to the void that it includes. It is relational. It is also the unit and unity as empty set, a thing that includes nothing. The empty set is the atom. All sets and things have it. For that reason, one should not say there is a master particle. There is only a master relation, the bit.

However, anything can be bits, whether it is pixels on a screen or atomic elements in nature. Atoms can be bits, but so can many other marks. It makes no more sense to treat atoms as bits than the squares in the Conway's Game of Life. All things are in relation and in relation to each other. That is how we can explain why stars encircling a black hole and an electrons revolving around an atomic nucleus have similar structures. The bit is the basic thing.

Many people like to point to the quark as being the fundamental particle. But the quark already has spin, which means there is the spin up/spin down relation. Quarks are also colored. The empty set is included in everything, and that is what makes it most basic. It is their frame. It is their name. It is that which embodies the self-identity of things through time. Now, implicitly, we have already been contesting Kant's view of concepts as formulated during his critique of the ontological proof of God's existence. There, Kant famously argued 'being is not a real predicate.' By this thesis, Kant means that while our concept of a coin includes all sorts of predicates (silvery, two-sided, etc.), the very existence of the coin is not included as one of those predicates. We only know the coin we conceive exists if we observe it. But Kant is misleading here. The coin still exists as concept. It exists as we conceive it. And as we conceive it, what is included is that it is one concept. That is, oneness is included in it and existence, since to conceive is to observe it intellectually. It cannot be conceived without being observed. It is one and the same thing.

Kant is speaking as though the imaginary silver dollars he has in his mind are not inscribed anywhere, but they are, and on a screen, if only a mental one. He is pretending, as though a concept is not something that exists. Even images in the brain have a minimal materiality to them, and that is a problem for Kant. Kant simply lived in a time when the brain was not understood in the way it is now, so he thought pure thought thinking and imagination were purely non-material acts (in the same way, breath and sound were once thought to be purely non-material). Every thought in its very conception is incarnated in a space, even if in an imaginary one. What Kant is saying is the silver dollars he conceives cannot be exchanged with anyone. But one can exchange bits, and we do so regularly today. Otherwise, there would be no e-commerce. But the fact that that e-commerce takes place via microprocessors, etc., does not mean what takes place due to neurons is less real. It is simply less functional. So numbers show that existence is included as a real predicate in numbers themselves, because nothing can be seen or perceived without them. We do not need to go beyond any conception to see that. This is why a neo-Pythagorean view is intimately linked to the ontological/modal proof for God's existence. It requires that existence be a real predicate. The difference between God and all else is that God necessarily obtains outside of the mind, and that is what the ontological proofs following Anselm show. It is a question of necessity in relation to possibility that is at issue, first and foremost, rather than being and existence. Numbers might not exist. It is possible. There might be nothing. By if anything other than God exists, then it is informed by number. God cannot but obtain outside of the mind. That is to say, we can conceive numbers and see existence as a predicate included in them and yet know them as created and contingent. All is contingent other than God.

But if there is existence, and in order for there to be existence, numbers must exist. In other words, if there is something, it is irrevocably marked by number. One of Alain Badiou's main contributions to Philosophy (a contribution that will echo into the future) is that being qua being is number. This is why reality is fundamentally computational and describes existence at its core. The two, number and computation, are interlinked as being and existence. But perhaps surprisingly, despite arguing that number

Divine Name Verification | 225

plays this fundamental role, it does not mean that all that is possible is actual. We will see this (all that is possible is actual) is one of the principles of Darwinian metaphysics. Kant was right that observation plays a role. It tells us what of the computational universe that we uncover epistemologically actually obtains in this reality. What exists can be opposed to what we can epistemologically model and conceive. We will try to demonstrate that existence, in its necessary self-delimitation, its having been created, is marked by a radical incompletion.

Kant wants to say numbers are just a function and product of our own minds, that they are the function of a pure intuition specific to humans or human-like minds. This is an intuitionist position that acts as if numbers only are there if we count them up, but numbers are no more dependent on intuition than the things that are made of them, like apples and paper. One should no more accept intuitionism when it comes to numbers than idealism when it comes to 'empirical objects.' This neo-Pythagorean view also puts forth set theory itself as the fundamental theory for comprehending mathematics. Some have suggested Category Theory is the key rival for doing so, but Category Theory describes the world purely in terms of relations between already constituted and distinct things. The empty set itself is already a relation between itself and the void it includes. For this reason, the notion of the bit does not require us to oppose relations to distinct things as they arise out of the process. Category theory needs to be seen as fundamentally linked to set theory, and computation does that, since computation shows how one set is transformed by specific rules and operations and turns into another set. This is this same as in Category Theory, where an operation like multiplication takes one thing and turns it into a second thing. The emphasis thereby is on how another empty set is included in the set of 1 to make 2, and how that, in and of itself, acts as an operation. One should not emphasize identity (2 as identical to and just another name for 1 plus 1) as much as computation as the manner in which the transformations between two sets occur. Two distinct things are thus two sets. This process is dynamic insofar as the first thing gives rise to the second. Distinct relata are then no more than distinct sets here.

This is also whey the empty set is important again to avoid infinite regress (which is another name for incoherence). The empty set enables for there to be distinct relata that cannot otherwise be noted. The empty set as bit is itself a monad that is also a relation in and of itself, a relation of pure differentiality. The only irreducible monadic property or entity is this differentiality itself, and all relational properties require this atom/monad to be in operation. But the bit can be any number of things at any scale. At one scale, it can be light bulbs and at another atoms and at another cells in an automaton. At each scale, the bit can operate as a monad, since it is in itself a pure differentiation between itself and its place of inscription. It is not surprising that, in cellular automata, no cell is purely distinct and always enacts relations to others, since otherwise there would only be one square. We also see in cellular automata that distinct entities like 'spaceships' arise precisely out of these actions due to the nature of the bit. If the bit did not have these properties, we would have infinite regress.

The new informational ontology, wherein bits are monads/atoms and yet relationality, means we no longer need to see the world as made up of hard particles floating in a void. That does not mean that the discovery of the atom was not already a step towards understanding the world as discrete, but it was not a full step, because it was understood as isolating disconnected points. If a bit were not relational, then an automaton cell would never be capable of more than one state, but it can take at least two states and change from one state to another. That is because the empty square (read: empty set) is always operational as the place in which it is inscribed. The cell then, as empty or filled, is always related to its place of inscription.

One of the crucial views being asserted here is that set theory, as a seemingly purely formal rendering of numbers and how they emerge, does not only detail numbers and their properties. It is not simply about numerical structure, since the properties of numbers cannot be unique to numbers themselves and not touch on other objects. Other objects also have numerical properties, the same exact properties as numbers. There is not thus a universe of numbers that is in some Platonic heaven along with a set of empirical or material things that mirror them or operate differently. Being is one. However, epistemologically we can see that not only are numerical relations observed outside of models and our own minds and computational devices, but that such devices and our minds are part of being as well, of course. Numerical relations are also the relations between things commonly thought to not be numbers. Things are included in a system, which means that they are structured. That means there is no way to separate them from number, even if one tries. It is thus a mistake to think numbers are static immaterialities that do not relate to things. They are relations and thereby relations to things and within things and between things. One should not reify numbers any more than anything else.

Many will here ask about transfinite sets of numbers. If all things are structured sets of integers, then why is it not that some are sets of an infinite number of integers? No one has ever, of course, counted such an infinite set. No one has ever been able to write one. One has only said that, in principle, it exists, since we do not invent numbers, we discover them. That means that any number we write down is always already presupposed as obtaining outside the conception. But what that really means is that the set is radically incomplete. We can always write another number. However, that does not mean in any given set encountered we will not find a finite number of things there. And we always have.

Another sense of infinite is that the set of positive integers, when taken as a whole, seems to have subsets that are just as large. The set of even or odd numbers is just as large as the set of positive integers and can be shown to be so by one-to-one correspondence. But any set of numbers we write out is incomplete as infinite. The transfinite marks the set of numbers we would write as always incomplete—finite and yet unbounded. For Cantor, that means the existence of these numbers is always presupposed. When we write a number, we are not inventing it. For Cantor, there is a domain where there is the complete set of positive integers, etc. God is the name of that place for Cantor, but this mistakes God for absolute infinitude and existent outside of time. Cantor's view implied that all that is possible is actualized. God can choose to limit creation. And we have, I will argue, a world that is marked by a radical self-delimitation. Saying that because God can think all positive integers simultaneously, that all are created, is a Platonic view in which numbering is a mimesis of another, divine domain. We need to resist saying God is the set of all sets. Cantor was wrong on his ontological proof of God as the necessary domain given the transfinite. Instead, we need a modal version of the classical ontological proof.

One need only presuppose the empty set itself. One does not need to presuppose that there is a domain in which all the numbers exist actually and that our own world is only a portion of it. To get the numbers, we need only the creation of the nothingness and its mark. Cantor's version of the ontological proof is not as strong as Anselm's here for this reason. It is still too Platonic, insofar as it makes it appear as though God constitutes that heaven where all numbers exist such that the numerical structure we have here is but a shadow of that realm. God is not the set of all sets, but God can have omniscient knowledge of numerical structures. To know them is not the same as stating they pre-exist in a domain, because God does not pre-exist in this temporal sense, as God's eternity resists any such temporal determinations. God is Other, and that Other has thoughts unlike our thoughts. On this topic, we can only say that God is the Other presupposed by finite nature.

What is unique to a transfinite set is that it contains a subset that has the same cardinality as it does. It thereby has a part that is as great and as complex as it is. Life also has this property, in a sense. DNA is a part of a cell and thus a subset containing the very thing itself. And yet organisms are finite. Ultimately, transfinite means that the infinite becomes finite, as it marks the radical incompletion of what is. It does not mean we will come across a thing with an infinity of parts. Any infinite set that one can point to in our world will be finite but unbounded. Think of a minute. A minute can seemingly be divided into seconds, microseconds, nanoseconds, etc. The minute is then like a line between two points, like a number line between 0 and 1. And yet that minute passes into the next, and we count from one 0 to 1.

The danger here comes from the fallacy of division and not the fallacy of composition. Many will say we have committed the latter, insofar as we are claiming that even transfinite sets are finite, insofar as they are composed of the empty set and integers, but that charge does not hold, insofar as one will not find such a transfinite set anywhere except as a name. That is why one must avoid actually taking the transfinite as a thing that contains in itself other infinites. Anything found between zero and one will itself be expressible by a decimal series of integers, which means it finally depends on the nature of the integer itself. The finite but unbounded nature of things means that the universe could stretch back endlessly in time, but it does not appear to, given the Big Bang. It could stretch on endlessly, except that its finitude means it is always menaced by the void. If it avoids the void, it is a miracle. If it does not, nothing comes from nothing, requiring, again, the divine. The issue then is, in part, how we understand the relation between two points on a line that appears to be continuous but is actually made up of discrete points. If the discrete conditions the continuous, then the apparently infinite takes on a new meaning. I will try to return to this when talking about the shape of the whole of things. In this way, the finitude of nature that Fredkin asserts is compatible with the transfinite, insofar as that finite nature is not bounded.

Another way of saying this is that any 'actual infinite,' transfinite, is paradoxically finite in nature. That paradoxical nature is another way of expressing its incompletion and radical self-delimitation. If the universe were truly infinite, it would be incoherent and inconsistent. But the universe everywhere exhibits too much regularity in its patterning to be understood in this fashion. It is also why finite nature is coupled with its being discrete. If nature were continuous, it would be infinitely divisible. But the bit prevents this from being the case. The empty set prevents the infinite from being anything other than the transfinite, that is, a way of marking the self-relationality of the signifier and incompletion. Space might go on forever but cannot be cut up forever. Things are only divisible up to the bit, up to differentiality itself.

Nature does exhibit paradoxical structures, but they are always halted at some point. This has been shown by Patrick Grim and his co-authors in their book *The Philosophical Computer*, where paradoxes such as the liar's paradox are mapped as cellular automata. What one sees here is that those paradoxes produce intricate patterns like ones we see in nature, which shows that they are not incompatible with the discrete and finite nature of existence. Finite nature is then a thesis that follows from the fact that complete randomness seems not to characterize our own experiences and the phenomena we encounter. New objects we encounter, such as quasars or nebulas, do not present totally chance arrangements of matter or a pure lump. This is the case on every scale, such that stars collapsing into a black hole, water molecules in a maelstrom, and electrons circling in their orbits may all have the same arrangement. At each scale, the bit itself might be some new emergent form, such as stars, water molecules, or electrons themselves.

One of the most important lessons computationalism has taught us is that the patterns we see are determined by a set of rules and their iterations. That makes universe seem completely deterministic. But the human mind shows us that at least one system with universal computational ability has arisen that also activates that universality and is able to run new programs. The human mind can switch from multiplying something to adding it. At the same time, even if we have the rules for a computation, it does not mean we know what it will output. This is what Wolfram calls computational irreducibility. One has to run the program. It is not something we can deduce simply from the arrangement of rules themselves. Nobody looking at the letters of one's DNA in a newly fertilized egg would be able to know what that human will look like and grow up into without actually running the program and letting the egg develop. And, of course, then we see that the full code includes the cellular machinery, etc. But at any state of the unfolding of the system, we will see that the rules themselves are in operation. With life, we might find that, if the system consists of many organisms, that the rules have changed subtly due to viral transfer, for instance. These rules are specific instructions for how thing must operate.

For these reasons, computationalism does not deal with laws. Laws are too general. They do not tell us how this particular snowflake takes on its pattern and where it is going. Gravity, the laws of thermodynamics, etc., unless they can themselves be given a computational formulation as instructions, only name phenomenological observations of properties and metaphors for numerical structures (they are many metaphors, for such structures take to be something more than that, like attractors and virtual spaces). Some people often speak of conditions, but conditions for things are too broad and too external. The law of gravity tells you about how every single falling body will fall, but we want to know why this particular body looks the way it does. Laws are superimposed on things. Rules and instructions are those things themselves. A snowflake is the program it is iterating in order take on its pattern. Laws relate to any possible experience, but rules speak to this specific object.

One thing we need to avoid here is splitting the world

into hardware and software prior to the arrival of the living organisms. Each phenomenon, as a finite state machine, exemplifies the running of the rules of a program, but that does not mean there is some other realm in which all these rules exist and that this physical reality is only a reflection or instantiation of this other realm. The reality we know is itself reality. It is hardware/software at once until life. There is not a computational universe existing in another domain where all possibilities are actual and only in this realm of creation some are realized. The universe is finite, and that is because even a computational realm would be incomplete in and of itself. The ones we construct ourselves epistemologically show this. When we try to create axiomatic systems, as Gödel showed, there is always incompletion via the fact some axioms cannot be proved by the system itself.

We should not look for another place to find a place where all is realized. Even if we found the domain of Other, it would operate in an Other way. There is an Other, but it is not of this nature. Fredkin, as we will see, appeals to 'Other,' but, at times, he makes it appear as though that Other is some sort of engine or hardware that enables our universe to exist. We will not accept this aspect of Fredkin's views insofar as it is part of his approach. That rules are there at any step and are being iterated and articulated means that such processes are, in principle, reversible. We can, if we have the rules, always then reproduce the first, second, third, etc., stages. Even though we cannot predict stages that have not arrived, having the rules means we can go back and start from the first step. The rules thus are a way of preventing total information loss. As long as the rules exist, one can reproduce the phenomena.

I have already said computationalism collapses the difference between the model and what it models. That means the patterns we see emerge are intrinsic to the rules even if that pattern is random. This is perhaps the greatest discovery of Wolfram's. His Rule 30 cellular automaton shows that randomness can be generated by rules alone such that randomness is intrinsic to them. Rule 30 does not generate a different pattern each time it is run, but its pattern is random. If randomness comes from rules it is not a matter of systems being perturbed by outside and external influences that are purely contingent and chance driven. That was a view based on an atomism wherein atoms swerve randomly in a void in a blind and purposeless manner. At the same time, Wolfram's notion of computational irreducibility showed that just looking at patterns does not mean we know the rules they are made of. We may simply have to engage in brute experimentation of different rules to find which one generates which specific pattern. We can epistemologically discover the rule, but it means we need to engage in simulation and emulation to do so.

We now study the cosmos by trying to reverse engineer it. This is precisely a design perspective. If one did not think the universe was in some sense intelligently designed, one would not make such efforts to reverse engineer it. Wolfram engages in scientific research by taking a group of programs or permutations on a set of programs and running them all to see what results they will yield. One thereby lets the computation itself show what it does. It is like having automated Petri dishes. In the end, we want to find patterns that reveal to us how things work. In this way, if we find a group of programs that reveal snowflake like patterns, then we have found, at least to some degree, the very programs that such snowflakes are running in nature.

It is I think useful to contrast here Wolfram's discoveries with Charles Babbage's speculations on similar topics. In his "Ninth Bridgewater Treatise," Babbage, the inventor of a precursor of our modern day computers, attempts to illustrate what a programmed system running on its own looks like.[139] In the second chapter, Babbage investigates how laws can change in nature and how such a change

---

[139] Charles Babbage, "Chapter II. Argument in Favour of Design from the Changing of Laws in Natural Events," *The Victorian Web*: http://www.victorianweb.org/science/science_texts/bridgewater/b2.htm [retrieved January 20, 2012].

would indicate that nature itself is programmed. He uses his own difference engine or calculating engine as an example of the playing out of such laws. Babbage's machine was, of course, among the first to mechanize computation itself. Babbage presents a thought experiment where the engine runs a computation and, step after step, seems only to be reiterating the same rule (such as counting the positive integers). After the one hundred millionth step, suddenly, the sequence of the numbers changes. A new rule now appears to be computing the numbers in each step. It appears our own universe is such a program, for we see changes in patterns and programs occur suddenly after a particular step. Our universe is not a fractal one of nested patterns of the same exact type. It does exhibit such features, but, on the whole, there are a variety of programs and laws being run. That means we need to conduct an experiment similar to what occurs in Babbage's thought experiment. With life, we think we know how such a shift is possible; the DNA coding itself is altered or the cellular hardware is impacted. But how is it possible with stars, atomic elements, planets, etc.? Also, life itself is a part of the universe, such that the universe is giving rise to programs, then suddenly altering their programming.

Wolfram explains why we could not predict and know in advance such shifts, but it is not clear that Wolfram's own theory can account for how such shifts occur without simply stating that it is the same rule at work. Perhaps that is the case. Perhaps the same set of rules will suddenly give rise to a sequence that appears to follow different rules but is still running the same program. One has simply reached a particular step in the iteration, per this view, when things shift.

Babbage at first seems to favor the idea that God might be intervening here.[140] However, there is another passage where Babbage seems to side with the idea that it is not a matter of new rules coming into existence, but that the ini-

---

[140] Babbage, "Chapter II. Argument in Favour of Design."

tial set of rules was such that it is still running and giving rise to the phenomena (that is, it is due to God's initial programming):

> The first engine must be susceptible of having embodied in its mechanical structure, that more general law of which all the observed laws were but isolated portions—a law so complicated, that analysis itself, in its present state, can scarcely grasp the whole question. The second engine might be of far simpler contrivance; it must be capable of receiving the laws impressed upon it from without, but is incapable, by its own intrinsic structure, of changing, at definite periods, and in unlimited succession, those laws by which it acts. Which of these two engines would, in the reader's opinion, give the higher proof of skill in the contriver? He cannot for a moment hesitate in pronouncing that that for which, after its original adjustment, no superintendence is required, displays far greater ingenuity than that which demands, at every change in its law, the direct intervention of its contriver.[141]

The original programming included in itself the secondary laws such that, at a certain point, the new set would be turned. This would be analogous to a gene being turned in our genetic code at a certain point. In the end, Babbage sides with God's having designed this program that itself can allow for sudden shifts in how phenomena work. For Babbage, such a God is a better and more exalted designer than one that constantly intervenes in the programming and tinkers with it. We agree.

---

[141] Babbage, "Chapter II."

§16
Darwinian Metaphysics

Before working out how the programmed nature of being functions, it is important to show how Darwinians think the universe works and why their view is flawed. Darwinism cannot exist now without its metaphysical supplement. This is the case, since Darwinism is based on randomness and chance. However, given the sheer improbability of the events it requires to occur occurring on that basis, it must necessarily have recourse to metaphysical theories that ensure that all that is possible will necessarily happen. But by doing so Darwinism deconstructs itself as pure chance and becomes a theory of pure necessity, given that every possibility will arise. Darwinism's necessary recourse to its metaphysical articulation is then its final dissolution.

Since all evidence leads to the conclusion that our universe is itself finite, the fact that improbable events happen means it is designed and programmed. For that reason, one must suggest that this universe is only part of a multiverse. In the multiverse, each possible universe necessarily is born. One then needs no designer or creator, as all exists eternally and infinitely. Each universe instantiates a particular set of laws, such that ours just happens to be the one that looks the way it does. Each universe might appear to be finite, but the multiverse is eternal. This deferral of the problem only works precisely because of the introduction of infinity into the equation. Such infinity eliminates everything Darwinism was supposed to be about in a pure self-contradiction (there is no more blind selection, no more purely random mutation, etc., as that is just how things must be in this actualized possibility), but it staves off the horror of the alternative.

William Dembski may have been the first to detect this point of collapse by way of recourse to metaphysics in the Darwinian edifice. As Dembski notes, depending on chance for events to occur fails, due to the universe itself being too young, despite its overwhelming age, to allow for it to be reasonable to believe such unlikely events happen by pure chance (*NFL* 83). Many Darwinians are themselves aware of this and, on occasion, willing to admit it. There has not been enough time even since the Big Bang to produce all actualities when discussing the precursors of life, and even if one agrees that the universe is "a giant computer" as we put forth, it could not have performed the "number of operations" needed for Darwinian pure randomness to be a reasonable explanation of life (and it is in itself only speculation when it comes to things like the origin of life itself) (*NFL* 84). Dembski argues that it is "illegitimate" to try to save a view based on pure chance by speculating that there are actually more "probabilistic resources" outside the universe we observe and experience in order to make the unlikely appear likely (it actually ruins the entire view as it makes it necessary) (*NFL* 85).

For Dembski, Darwinians needs to find "independent evidence" to show that their conjectures are not outside the realm of probability; otherwise, their view is simply not "plausible" (*NFL* 97). Dembski calls the Darwinian recourse to metaphysics that allows it to speculate that all possibilities are actualized the "inflationary fallacy" and sometimes the "gambler's fallacy" (*NFL* 86). The gambler's fallacy comes from the idea that a person who gets three improbable hands in a row in poker, for example, thus posits that there must be enough "people around the world—heck, around the galaxy . . . playing poker right now to make that run of luck possible!"¹⁴² The fallacy here is that because something improbable happened there must have been the needed number of attempts played out such that it would be inevitable or seem highly probable. For Dembski, the paradigmatic example here is the multiverse theory now popular in cosmological circles. Its main conjecture is that there are multiple other universes (actually, to make Darwinism reasonable, there needs to be an infinite number). Given that there is an infinite multiverse, the fine-tuning for life characterizing our universe no longer is a mystery, as our universe is just one example of a universe, and all examples are actualized (*NFL* 88).

Dembski also categorizes David Lewis's modal realism as an example of this Darwinian view, insofar as Lewis argues any logically possible world is real and existent as much as ours is. There is then an infinity of alternate universes all actual alongside ours. In such universes, the laws of physics are entirely different; the makeup of the universe is entirely different, etc. In such alternative universes, there are alternative versions of David Lewis himself pursuing an infinity of other possible lives. Those other Davids are just as real, but we simply cannot observe them. Dembski notes the main argument supporting such a modal realist view: "According to [Lewis], possible worlds are indispensible for making sense of certain key philosophical problems, notably the analysis of counterfactual conditionals" (*NFL* 89). Lewis then bases his metaphysical edifice on the idea that we need to posit infinite alternative worlds in order to allow that counterfactual statements are true and demonstrable as such. But ultimately, Lewis is only able to produce tautologies like 'I am a human if and only if I am a human in all possible worlds.' But how would I say it is or is not me in the other world if I am not a human? Also, even if we want to know how the United Sates would have been different had the American Civil War been won by the South ('If the South had won, then . . .'), we can never access these

---

¹⁴² Dembski and Witt, *Intelligent Design Uncensored*, 34.

other possible alternatives unless we run simulations on a computer. Such simulations show that if the issue is counterfactuals, then one need not posit actual other alternative worlds more so than ones we can create ourselves. Counterfactuals then simply become the name for how things work in the alternative worlds. But why does saying that things could be different mean that, somewhere, they are? It is here merely a postulate.

Let's return to the multiverse theory (I will later add a new theory to this list when I engage with the work of Quentin Meillassoux, a figure, of course, that Dembski could not have known about at the time he was writing the text we have referred to). Physicist Lee Smolin put forth in the late 1990s an explicitly Darwinian multiverse theory. Smolin contends that any universe emerges out of a black hole such that the black holes in our universe are the starting points of new universes on the other side of the event horizon.[143] However, the universe born on the other side is slightly different than ours in terms of its physical laws and arrangement.[144] For Smolin, the most successful universes are the ones with the most black holes, as they reproduce the most.[145] Thus, from a Darwinian perspective, universes that do not produce black holes will simply vanish and not have offspring. Universes that produce a few black holes will only produce a few offspring. In this way, there is allegedly a natural selection and evolution of universes to make universes that produce more and more black holes. Each universe is unique insofar as the process of reproduction via the black hole changes the basic parameters of the universe. For Smolin, such a process has no time constraints (it occurs over an infinite amount of time). But it is not clear if there is truly natural selection occurring here and why eventually one will not have simply a universe that is al-

---

[143] Lee Smolin, *The Life of the Cosmos* (New York: Oxford University Press, 1999), 93.
[144] Smolin, *The Life of the Cosmos*, 94.
[145] Smolin, *The Life of the Cosmos*, 95.

most all block holes or a black hole immediately upon inception.

Because we cannot detect these alternate universes in any way, we do not know where our universe stands. If this evolution should end in a universe filled with black holes, we might be in the middle of the evolution. Then again, it is not clear what the initial universe would look like other than having to produce at least one black hole (otherwise, unfortunately for Smolin, the process stops after one universe). Despite being a Darwinian, Smolin says that each new alternative universe that is produced with new parameters can only be randomly mutated and yet is not a product of chance, but that is only because he thinks that what rules here is natural selection (and that natural selection is not pure chance).[146] Universes that won't produce black holes simply do not have offspring.

Smolin does not believe there is any overall program or rule or law governing how these universes are produced. It is a matter of pure variation in the parameters of the future universe. This is why the problem of infinite regress is so pointed here for Smolin. Why did the first universe have to be such that it had at least one black hole? If it must by necessity, then that ruins the theory, as it means it is not random. If it is contingent, then it is not clear why it was not possible that the universe produced no new universes but rather ended in a heat death and thus no evolution and life of the cosmos. Smolin here then has to either believe that it was pure chance that the first universe had this quality or design.

Of course, it is not clear—if there are an infinity of universes—how one then calculates the chances of such a universe. If there are a finite number of universes, improbability becomes a problem. It seems that for Smolin it is either necessary that the first universe is designed to give rise to others or simply a matter of chance. However, that means it is possible that no evolution will take place. It

---

[146] Smolin, *The Life of the Cosmos*, 103.

is also impossible to know what is happening on the other side of the black hole without passing through it, but that means not being able to return. Also, Smolin himself says, "most of the universes described by different choices of the parameters appear boring compared with ours," since very few universes will look like ours if the basic parameters of universe and their values are allowed to vary.[147] This makes our universe seem rare, but it also makes Smolin's living cosmos even more unreasonable, as it shows that the chances of the needed universe at the beginning to get the process started are low. If the first universe is simply nothing but hydrogen in equilibrium, it leads to nothing.

This is why Smolin has to try to avoid the problem of such a first universe. Smolin does not want to simply adopt a multiverse model, as he himself argues against the idea that there is a multiverse in which there is "eternal inflation" and that a "vast population of universes . . . continually born with an unchanging distribution of parameters—from an eternal and unchanging vacuum state" makes it so all possibilities are actualized, and thus there is no need to speak of evolution.[148] If we have an eternal vacuum that, out of its empty state, is constantly giving rise to universes, then we will get all possible universes without any need for self-replication and black holes. It means that all possibilities are actualized. Smolin, to have evolution, needs to have only some possibilities actualized, and that means, with life, one needs to have a single origin. Smolin notes himself that the multiverse theory is "both unconfirmable and unfalsifiable" as a theory and thereby "cannot be considered a scientific theory."[149] However, Smolin's model requires that there be a first universe, such that he cannot claim that all

---

[147] Lee Smolin, "Darwinism All the Way Down," in *Intelligent Thought: Science Versus the Intelligent Design Movement* (New York: Vintage, 2006), 157.
[148] Smolin, "Darwinism All the Way Down," 159.
[149] Smolin, "Darwinism All the Way Down," 160.

universes have "ancestors," as at least one cannot.[150]

Smolin agrees that black holes are not permanent and are formed by stars. That means one first needs a universe that will form a star that collapses into a black hole to get another universe. Where does that first universe come from? If it comes from an empty vacuum, where does that come from? If one claims that the vacuum is itself eternal, that claim falsifies itself, since whatever process in the vacuum that gives rise to the universe shows it is changeable over time. If it is changeable over time, there is nothing to prevent it from disappearing. Why did it not disappear before producing the needed universe? Smolin has thus simply reproduced one of the fundamental problems of Darwinism concerning its improbability at another level and thereby simply deferred the problem. Because Smolin refuses the multiverse answer in which an infinity of universes is produced such that all possibilities are actualized, he cannot avoid the same issues that arise with Darwinism itself. There has to be an origin in Smolin just as for biological life, but universes here are formed from black holes. That means one needs a star or something like a black hole already. Smolin is thereby back to positing an eternal vacuum (that is, a false vacuum that randomly, over an infinite amount of time, will produce a universe). That means it is necessary that it produces such a universe. If it produces a universe that will lead to nothing, then life does not start. So it is also necessary that it produces a first universe that can get Smolin's whole process going. But such a vacuum also, in its changing, might change into pure nothing. There is nothing that prevents it. It then could easily give rise to nothing. In other words at some point it is necessary for things to occur. And that necessity points to some reason that allows it and explains it. We usually call that reason God.

Smolin should imagine what would happen if we said there was no first organism or origin of life. We would see

---

[150] Smolin, "Darwinism All the Way Down," 163.

that there cannot be an infinite regress, but must be some first organism. Evolution is meaningless without such a first organism. If life infinitely regresses, then it can never start, since one needs code that itself is not encoded in anything (otherwise one has to reproduce endless codes to ever produce a creature). If there is an infinite regress, then, again, we get all possibilities actualized, just as in the multiverse theory.

An infinite regress also ruins the principle of variation and randomness. Things are not infinitely varied by chance if, by infinite regress, we go through each variation. What Smolin has proven here, if anything, is that the anthropic principle does not hold. This principle says that the universe must be the way it is because we are here. But our givenness could not just be due to a contingent universe that happened to arise, since such a universe is exceedingly improbable. Now, if Smolin had been anti-Darwinian, he could argue that the first universe was designed such that it would give rise to black holes and future universes. Thus, with a design principle in place, the whole motor of the life of the cosmos can be revved up. Natural selection will not work until one has life. That means it cannot work until one gets a first universe and a first one that works. Selection does not work in an eternal vacuum out of which any universe arises. If the vacuum is not eternal, it will then be utterly unclear how it cannot simply become pure nothing.

What we see with Smolin is that to get the process started we need intelligent design, otherwise we have necessity, and with necessity a collapse of Darwinism and its notions of random variation. We posit God to show how the universe is designed. Multiverse theories posit an infinite universe in which all possibilities are actualized in order to avoid God. But in doing so, they also destroy Darwinism. Smolin's attempt to save Darwinism cosmologically did not lead to his theory's adoption by the physics community. That's probably because it has the inherent problems we have highlighted and due to the scientific community being wed to a multiverse model. Notice that in our model and the opposing one chance is non-existent or minimalized. This is why, as we will see, the work of Meillassoux is so interesting and unique, insofar as he is willing to allow pure randomness (although at the expense of being right).

Smolin himself believes both multiverse and intelligent design theories are equally untestable:

> The logic is the same whether that single creator is an eternal primordial vacuum state or God. Theories with a single creator are untestable, because they lack all the detailed improbable structures and correlations that a system ordered by reproduction has.[151]

This lack of verification is only true if we forget that we have long ago entered into the realm of metaphysics itself. It is thereby a metaphysical contest that plays out at this point. It is not arbitrary that Darwinism and its collapse lead to metaphysics. A metaphysical supplement is needed for any theory, especially one that claims to comprehend all things.

Smolin believes that his "Darwinian multiverse is falsifiable since it has lots of structure. But all that structure is contingent and time-bound."[152] But every universe has lots of structure. If the issue is that it is contingent, then also intelligent design theorists argue such a thing. God could have created all possible universes but only created this one. That makes this world in itself contingent. This is in stark contrast with the multiverse theory. It necessarily posits an infinite number of worlds, so that our existence as humans and life's emergence seem not only probable but necessary. The multiverse is itself a metaphysical speculation designed to prevent the inevitable conclusion that a contingent and singular universe must be created by God

---

[151] Smolin, "Darwinism All the Way Down," 166.
[152] Smolin, "Darwinism All the Way Down," 166.

and designed. The multiverse is thus the last line of defense of atheism (and Darwinism is, of course, one of the key names, if not the name, for modern atheism). But as Smolin notes, this theory is not at all testable. No one can detect an infinity of universes. No one can detect that all possibilities are actualized. It is a metaphysical postulate. And thus, given that it is posited by scientists, it functions as a counter-religion. It's the last line of defense for atheism. It's trench warfare here, and atheism's at the Hindenburg line. Reserves will be coming from the east in the form of Meillassoux, but they will be no match for the American doughboys charging ahead for God and country.

Smolin here makes atheism and intelligent design seem more symmetrical than they are. Not only is intelligent design related to a contingent world, but God is, of course, compatible with the idea of all possibilities becoming actual. This could happen in the mind of God. God can also function as the sufficient ground for such realization and name its principle. We are not aware of any mechanism other than divine creation that can account for things like our universe, its programming, and fine-tuning for life. On the other hand, the multiverse view presents itself as scientific, even though, in principle, one cannot observe infinitely many universes. If these are the only two positions, then clearly intelligent design is a better account for how the universe came into being, as we have seen even with Smolin.

Physicists' advocacy of the multiverse theory makes one wonder whatever happened to Occam's razor? Apparently, the last person using it cut himself and bled to death (perhaps he will be found soon). It is also interesting that the multiverse view accepts that the universe itself is finite. It only ever posits an infinity of finite unfolding universes and never argues that our universe itself is infinite such that all possibilities will be realized in it. This is probably so, because we have seen that our universe has an origin. It also has not explored all possibilities. Clearly, when it comes to biology, not all life forms have come into being. Multiverse theory is an implicit acceptance of the fact that our universe is actually fine-tuned for life and that such fine-tuning is improbable. Otherwise, such an inflation of universes would not be needed. Given the contingent nature of our universe's beginning, recourse to God, who intended to create it in this way, is inevitable without a multiverse.

Of course, one can say here that the refusal to accept God encourages scientific creativity and that acceptance of God would halt such investigation. That does not seem reasonable, given that knowing that God created the world would only lead one to investigate it further. If one then came across a phenomenon that truly could not be explained other than by positing multiple universes, then that possibility would arise again. But here it is arising in order to prevent a theological conclusion at all costs. In the retreat to the Hindenburg line, scorched earth tactics are being employed.

Keep in mind that some creationists will challenge what we say here. They will argue that an infinite Creator in his pure gift of being would not simply offer up one universe with a limited number of possibilities realized. The universe is, for them, infinite itself. But the Jewish monotheistic perspective informing this text says that God ceases creation. That is what the Sabbath day means. Not all is created. God rests from creation. Such pantheisms with their specific views of infinity are positing that there is a notion of God compatible even with a multiverse, but it is not one we accept. It is with the multiverse that the methodological atheism that underpins the scientific endeavor and forms its metaphysical supplement manifests itself. Scientists know that they only observe one universe. It is their pure dedication to methodological atheism that necessitates no acceptance of intelligent design no matter the nature of the evidence.

One interesting point here is that the multiverse theories have yet to come up with a mechanism for creating more than one universe other than allowing for infinite time. What that means is that the multiverse theory piles up one mathematical speculation on another that our own universe, in its own construction, resists. It is important also to note that scientists never posit a pure nothingness as the origin of the universe. It is always a false vacuum that somehow eternally persists. But such a vacuum is charged with energy. That means it is related to matter, as energy and matter are ultimately the same thing. Matter itself is not eternal. It has to come from somewhere. The false vacuums we encounter in this universe are always the result of space itself, just as black holes always presuppose a star that collapsed. It is then not clear why the eternal vacuum is not of the same quality.

Nick Bostrom nicely articulates the multiverse view:

> Consider a random phenomenon, for example Hawking radiation. When black holes evaporate, they do so in a random manner such that for any given physical object there is a finite (although, typically, astronomically small) probability that it will be emitted by any given black hole in a given time interval. Such things as boots, computers, or ecosystems have some finite probability of popping out from a black hole. The same holds true, of course, for human bodies, or human brains in particular states. Assuming that mental states supervene on brain states, there is thus a finite probability that a black hole will produce a brain in a state of making any given observation. Some of the observations made by such brains will be illusory, and some will be veridical. For example, some brains produced by black holes will have the illusory of [sic] experience of reading a measurement device that does not exist. . . . It isn't true that we couldn't have observed a universe that wasn't fine-tuned for life. For even "uninhabitable" universes can contain the odd, spontaneously materialized "freak observer," and if they are big enough or if there are sufficiently many such universes, then it is indeed highly likely that

they contain infinitely many freak observers making all possible human observations. It is even logically consistent with all our evidence that we are such freak observers. (*EE* 224–225)

These false vacuums are always seen as consisting of radiation, such as the radiation that emerges when a black hole dissipates (Hawking radiation). However, a black hole is a collapsed star. It may produce something random, but it is itself based on a nonrandom process and presupposes something. This radiation also demonstrates the contingent and non-eternal nature of such a false vacuum. This Hawking radiation is said to be so random such that it could produce at random some object such as a Boltzmann brain. That is, from the radiation here in the vacuum, a finite object could form. Many think this false vacuum is nothing, but atoms are made up of empty space almost completely. However, this empty space is itself a function of space rather than being nothing.

Atheism needs to believe that the void is empty space as false vacuum and that it is eternal. There is no pure nothingness in this world. What is always left is empty space, which is a function of space itself. It is, at most, the empty set, the mark of the void. It is thus something, something with properties and effects like any of the other real stuff that we encounter. This is partly so because space is not a container. It is something real and a relation within and of what is created. Space, as we know it, is not static. It has topological properties that allow it to be twisted, bent, cut, etc. That is why the empty set as empty space can help to form all that is in this world and make up its very textuality ('textus' means 'the woven').

Our reasoning here shows that any ultimate theory of everything is going to start with the empty set or its equivalent, such as a single geometric object (I doubt it will be a vibrating string), and explain how that empty set itself involves the unfolding of it. For instance, the best current theory of everything is Garrett Lisi's in which he tries to show how all of reality is the unfolding of a single 248-sided symmetrical geometrical object (a snowflake of subatomic particles which is itself mathematizable as a Lie group).[153]

Space came into being with the Big Bang. And all is spatial. It is what we never do not encounter. All is spatial and thus part of space. The most basic aspect of all we encounter is space, but almost all of space is empty. But if atoms are mostly empty space as nothing, then what is an atom's nucleus in relation to? Of course, today physicists speak less of a false vacuum and more so of the celebrated Higgs boson and Higgs field. But ontologically the principle is the same. Even the void is allegedly filled with the Higgs field, even if there is no matter and radiation. But that just means the Higgs field is the new name for the false vacuum. It is not pure nothingness. There is a particle here. The Higgs is thus another name for the empty set. And the search for it is actually very explicitly for the empty set, what is included in everything to make it substantial. To make the Higgs particle emerge from the void is to confront the emptiness of the empty set marking all matter. Empty space is thus thought to be charged with something that makes things thing-like—gives them mass. However, the formation of something like a brain or something truly functional is infinitesimal. One needs still infinite time to ensure that something useful could come about, which, of course, works against the fact that the thing itself is dissipating and made of radiation. At best then, one can posit an infinite regress from the multiverse perspective. But in such a regress it is not clear why the universe would not encounter nothingness, given the finite and contingent nature of each universe. Nothing comes from nothing. The very possibility of nothing requires God, the eternal One. The multiverse must be infinite; otherwise, to explain an improbable universe, one has to posit something equally improbable or

---

[153] Garret Lisi, "Garrett Lisi on his Theory of Everything," *TED.com*, February 2008: http://www.ted.com/talks/garrett_lisi_on_his_theory_of_everything.html [retrieved January 20, 2012].

entirely necessary. That is why the multiverse cannot be made of a set of a few alternative worlds.

The Kabbalah, for example, offers, at times, a vision of God creating and destroying alternate worlds before creating this one. But it is always a finite and denumerable number of worlds. Physicists want to produce theorems that will indicate that a multiverse will not require fine-tuning itself to produce a finite number of universes including ours, but the multiverse theory is already an admission that there are such a larger number of possible universes as to make such a model dependent on fine-tuning. These considerations, of course, have caught the eye of the most committed atheistic physicists. Militant atheist physicist Victor Stengers has argued for a biverse theory in addition to allowing for the possibility of a multiverse.[154] Stengers writes the following about the vacuum:

> Vacuum polarization occurs in the presences of other bodies. If it occurs in the absence of any bodies, in a really empty vacuum, it can contribute nothing, since the process conserves energy exactly and it came from a state of zero energy. On the other hand, quantum tunneling can be crudely understood as a quantum effect that results from the Heisenberg uncertainty principle: a temporary upward fluctuation in the particle's energy sends it over the barrier.[155]

Stengers here admits the vacuum presupposes bodies and matter. However, Stengers literally believes that there can be a pure zero state on its own that is not pure nothing. He writes:

> Let's assume it starts out as a sphere of radius equal

---

[154] Victor Stengers, *The Fallacy of Fine-Tuning: Why the Universe is Not Designed For Us* (New York: Prometheus, 2011), 147.
[155] Stengers, *The Fallacy of Fine-Tuning*, 147.

> to the Planck length (the smallest it can be with our operational definition of space). The entropy of the universe at that time is equal to the maximum entropy of a black hole of the same radius.
>
> Thus the universe starts out with maximum entropy or *complete disorder*. It begins with zero information. It has no record of anything that may have gone on before, including the knowledge and intentions of a creator. If a creator existed, he left no record that survived that initial chaos. Once the universe exploded into the inflationary big bang, the entropy in any volume less than the Hubble volume is less than maximum, leaving room for order to form.[156]

Here, Stengers is declaring that the universe begins with zero information such that it is literally in a state of pure nothingness. But nothing can come from nothing. Only God can create something from nothing. That is why God's creation occurs through sublation of the void into its mark. That mark is not zero information. It is the primordial bit. That mark does, in fact, record what precedes it. It records nothingness by including it. The empty set is the inclusion of nothing. The knowledge of the intentions of the creator can only be known via the effects of the creation itself and our engagement with it. The only record the creator needed to leave is the first mark.

Stengers insists that there is an initial chaos. But that is misleading. The universe did not start out with total entropy, but with order. And that is what is amazing about it. It was in low entropy at its initial point. It is thereby not in a state like that of a black hole. Stengers imagines a universe that begins in complete disorder and maximum entropy that then suddenly shifts out of that entropy into a state of order. Even if we were to agree with Stengers that there is chaos at the beginning, it cannot be maximum entropy and

---

[156] Stengers, *The Fallacy of Fine-Tuning*, 113.

a state of zero information, since the very existence of matter and energy itself means there is information.

Stengers thinks, of course, that the universe arose via quantum tunneling. But this can only make sense if one posits a multiverse, since quantum activity cannot take place without there being matter, time, and space as quantum processes cannot occur prior to there being a universe. There is information even in a false vacuum state, as Fredkin argued earlier—all the bits are in the off state. What is noteworthy about the early universe, as Lee Smolin notes, is that all seems to come into being at an instant:

> It is true that if we trace back the history of any particle, we find an initial singularity at which the density of matter becomes infinite. However, what is not true is that all the particles in the universe meet at their first, singular moments. They do not. Instead, they all seem to spring into existence, simultaneously but separately, at the same instant. Just after the first instant of time, the universe already has a finite spatial extent.[157]

The singularity out of which the universe begins is, at most, matter in a state of infinite density and not maximum entropy. Smolin here suggests that all particles spring into existence at the same instant. But that is to say they spring together as a single set at the same instant. The fist mark is a set of bits. From the first instant of the empty set, then we have suddenly a set of bits all coming into being at the same time. We need to see this as two sides of the same coin, for, as I have argued in a previous text, the very name of God, YHVH, is both another name for the empty set and as a set, which is itself a proper name, itself a form of lettering.

Now, of course, people will here say that there are many other four-letter sequences, much less other letter sequenc-

---

[157] Smolin, *The Life of the Cosmos*, 84.

es. Why then YHVH? The point here is that there is only going to be one such divine name for the universe as such, even if others are possible. Even if there were infinitely many possible, only one will occur. All the other possibilities are then merely epistemological projections, as there is only one actuality. Here, Lacan's determination of the subject is illustrative. Every speaking being, for Lacan, enters the symbolic and becomes a speaking being alienated in the signifier by passing through the phallic signifier, but that phallic signifier can be different for every subject. The phallic signifier is itself a series of letters, extracted from language, that are precursors of other signifiers and affect them. It is because the letter plays a role that slips of the tongue are possible. Half of one word is united with half of another. One needs then to pay attention to the letters. However, given that there is only one created world, there is then just the one name of God, despite other possibilities.

The reason we write the empty set YHVH is to emphasize that the primordial bit is here not simply the void state, but already is an inscription of the coding for the universe in compressed form. Now, it is conceivable that YHVH, as expressing this code in its lettering, might be proven wrong, but that would require translating it into a bit string and discovering that bit string is not at the heart of the creation via simulation. The point is that if we ask 'what is the universe computing?' The answer is the Name of God and not simply the empty set as such. That lettering refers to nothing in the world, hence it is empty, but at the same time it is itself a bit string. That bit string itself names the name of God as the fundamental program that the universe is running. But that bit string is itself counted, as any number of others are theoretically possible and can be considered in epistemological reflection. And the contingency of that bit string means, given its finitude, that this universe realizes a specific set of possibilities. It is self-delimiting. It has a specific history.

§17

DARWINISM'S APOTHEOSIS
Quentin Meillassoux's Atheism of Radical Contingency

Quentin Meillassoux offers a radical interpretation of contingency in his text *After Finitude*. Here, in contrast to our view, Meillassoux wants to show metaphysically that all of reality is a hyper-chaos. For us, on the contrary, chaos is itself only truly enacted as pseudo-randomness, as the chaos that is founded on rules. Chaos is like possibility; it is founded on something actual and ordered. We then project disorder on its basis, since almost everything we encounter is ordered. Whereas Meillassoux is saying anything can happen at anytime, a pan-ontic computationalist approach says that all that appears is based on iteration such that even if something appears seemingly out of nowhere, it has a very clear basis in the programming of things. In the unfolding of a program, there is neither a potentiality nor set of possibles that are actualized. It is only the iteration of rules themselves. Each stage of the phenomenon is itself the rules themselves. One cannot foresee what will occur due to computational irreducibility rather than those things merely appearing out of nothing. Even something apparently miraculous would then be due to God's programming rather than some total divine violation of the fabric of the cosmos.

With his emphasis on radical contingency (anything

can happen at any time), Meillassoux is himself really trying to substitute an atheism of chance and/or necessity with an atheism of pure contingency. That is, if Darwinism as metaphysics argued that all is the result of random mutations, such a view collapses, given the truly improbable odds of such random mutations giving rise to what we see. This, in turn, led Darwinism to fall back on a metaphysics of total necessity (the multiverse) that paradoxically nullified its view of chance.

For Meillassoux, such a move by Darwinism was not arbitrary. If one wants to maintain atheism, then it is only by way of hyper-chaos. I think Meillassoux is correct here. As Graham Harman (Meillassoux's chief English language inter-preter) explains, for Meillassoux, if something has any reason, then it can be shown to be necessarily how it is.[158] Even if something is said to occur by chance, one can only determine the odds of something happening (1/6 for a dice roll for instance), and if the universe is following set rules and laws, that thus confines chance occurrences within a larger deterministic world (*QM* 48). For Meillassoux then, chance is just the other side of necessity and dependent on it for its calculation. Meillassoux argues that reality is ultimately ruled by the necessity of contingency itself, which means that anything can happen at any time for any reason. Meillassoux founds this view not on an argument against necessity as such, but by toppling chance. He argues that if the world itself is subject to the Cantorian transfinite, then there is no way to calculate chance and probability, for if there is an infinity of possibilities, then one can no longer say that one thing is more or less likely than another. Meillassoux's main view thus depends on a realist reading of the transfinite such that any and all phenomena can be read as

---

[158] Graham Harman, *Quentin Meillassoux: Philosophy in the Making* (Edinburgh: Edinburgh University Press, 2011), 34. This book also contains selections from unpublished works of Meillassoux. I refer to both Harman and Meillassoux's points in this book; all subsequent citations indicated as *QM*.

being subject to it.

The problem is that the transfinite in this sense does not seem to mark individual phenomena. For instance, if one rolls a die, it seems that there is very clearly a defined set of possible die rolls. All phenomena in this world appear to be finite, definable in finite terms, and marked by the finitude of time. For this reason, if Meillassoux is right, he needs to argue that being as such is informed by the Cantorian transfinite. It is the Cantorian transfinite that makes totality in the sense of making a set of all sets impossible (even if it cannot limit local finite totalities other than rendering them incomplete) (*QM* 48). For us, that means that being is radically incomplete. For Meillassoux, it means, first and foremost, not only that reality is inconsistent, but that it is infinitely and eternally so. But this is where the problems begin.

Meillassoux must contend that there is necessarily "something rather than nothing" (*QM* 30). This means it is necessary that there always be something (there cannot be nothing), but whatever is, is as such contingently what it is (it could be otherwise). The two ideas are inextricably linked here: being always is, and all that is, is contingent. This is necessary because the transfinite only characterizes being as such insofar as it marks it as lacking a totality as such. But that means being must always be, since if it at any time can be ruined by nothing, then it requires something else to bring it into being (nothing comes from nothing). But Meillassoux cannot void the menace of the void precisely because he has rendered everything as contingent. To be contingent means to be possibly otherwise and that includes not being at all. That means everything that is can possibly not be. And that means that all cannot be even if there is no set of all sets. All could not be. The void is thus possible and topples Meillassoux's edifice.

Meillassoux wants an ontological proof, as it were, of the necessity of contingent being, which means a disproof of the necessity of the void/nothingness. This is a classical philosophical view. If the void is, it is void and thereby not.

If the void is not, it is, once again, simply void. Either way, the void is not admissible. But despite this classical philosophical gesture, the void still haunts all ontology. Meillassoux cannot possibly prove the void cannot be, because he cannot rely on the classical Parmenidean philosophemes that excluded the void. He cannot because such philosophemes relied on the necessity of eternal being, but the necessary and eternal is something that Meillassoux undermines, since to be contingent is always to possibly not be. That is as true for Meillassoux as for any theory of contingency. All could not be. The possibility of all beings not being is then one more possibility.

One does not have to show that the void is necessary. One here needs only to show it is possible. To show it is possible will help us to see the necessity of God rather than the void. Notice here the difference with classical metaphysics. There one proves being could not be eternal by presupposing that all things have a beginning. If all things do not have a beginning, if there is an infinite regress, then we would never reach the moment we were in, as an infinity would have to lapse from the beginning until now (the classic view rejects infinity as any thing other than a potentiality). For us, the point is that even in an infinite regress or infinity of infinities one cannot avoid the void and its mark, the empty set, and the implications of such. For Heidegger, to think being without beings was to think nothingness. The 'nothing nothings' as Heidegger puts it. In this way, for Heidegger to consider the void is to prove it. If it can be, it will have been. But for us, that does not show the void is necessary—only possible.

Meillassoux says all he knows is that his mind, and its structure is contingent, that he may die for instance. But that in and itself does not show all is contingent. If I deny that I am nothing, nothing happens. If I deny that being is contingent, it becomes nothing. If I deny that being is, it is not. Nothing more happens. Being does not remain. It cannot remain any more than can Meillassoux if he admits that death is real. Of course, phenomenologists like Levinas would argue that death is impossible precisely because consciousness cannot undergo it. But to agree with Levinas is to agree with a purely idealist view that depends on consciousness being the last arbiter of the nature of being. And Meillassoux's project is in large part about escaping that trap. To agree with Levinas is to say consciousness is some eternal necessity that cannot be evaded because I cannot imagine dying and cannot encounter and experience my own death, but Meillassoux is saying the same thing about being. Being cannot know its own death. Being must be because it cannot know that it is dead. The void is not.

However, this impossibility from the perspective of consciousness or contingency does not rule it out. That is what it means to be a Lacanian Realist. The impossible is the Real. There is something rather than nothing. The void will have been as the void is only accessible to metaphysical reason. This is why metaphysics must rely on the empty set to deal with the void. It must treat the void as something to understand this world. The void is possible, but its possibility does not prove it is undeniable because to deny it or affirm it is to see it. It insists, and the empty set marks that insistence. God also insists, just at a further remove than the void, for God is responsible for it. The void then separates us from God. There is nothing between us.

To assume that the complicated comes first, something, leads one to God or to Meillassoux's hyper-chaos. But it is not clear why something exists in all its complexity: ". . . nothing is necessarily simpler than something. That's Leibniz's answer to the question. 'Why is there something rather than noting? For nothing is simpler and easier than something.'"[159] For Leibniz, only God could answer the question of how the less simple was rather than the simplest of things. For Meillassoux, how does contingent being avoid the void if it is hyper-chaotic? Only an invisible hand could guide things to avoid such a fate. It's the simplest one imaginable. If being is infinite and allegedly eternal, it

---

[159] Chaitin, *Meta Math!*, 59.

would have already passed through infinite time. How can it avoid the void without that being either miraculous in itself or a sign that all is not contingent? Meillassoux has to explain how being has avoided its ruin infinitely many times. Being cannot be necessary—even as the necessity of the contingent—since, any instant, it can disappear.

The world itself is contingent as an act of creation, creation out of nothing. It is that creation out of nothing that proves its contingency. And the nothing itself insists outside of being and other than being. The void will have been in the empty set. If the void is a possibility in itself, then one cannot say that being necessarily is. The void's possibility is a necessary aspect of contingency. God and the void then haunt Meillassoux's view. God insists insofar as His possibility proves his necessity. And the void—insofar as its possibility—is the mark of being's non-eternity. But it must be clear that God and the void are not the same, even if they appear at times so from our view. God self-effaces and thereby allows the nothing to be. And it is the basis of what we all are. Otherwise, nothing comes from nothing. We should thus hear things literally. To say no thing is necessary, as Meillassoux does, is to say that nothing is a necessary possibility. It marks the absolute necessity of everything as non-necessity. God is thus necessary here rather than contingent. There is no true contingency without the necessity of God.

It is absurd to ask if God being necessary means he necessarily created things or could not do otherwise since the very nature of things shows they could have been otherwise. It's absurd also to ask if an apple could be otherwise. It could be an orange, but then it would not be what it is. We ask if an apple could not have been eaten, and that makes sense. We can even ask if an apple could be green rather than red, but that makes it appear as though there is a substance apple underlying changing properties, but the properties themselves are a function of the thing's programming. Contingency relates just to a thing in its modality of existence and not in the modality of its essence or nature. This is why modal categories are intrinsically related to being as such; otherwise we have to speak of substance and accidents.

It is not contingent that God is necessary. It is necessary. And given the void and its possibility, God is unavoidable for there to be being. Given the void, one can accept that reality is marked by the transfinite, but this does not render it inconsistent to the degree Meillassoux argues. It marks it as radically incomplete and makes it so that each being is truly contingent and singular, but it does not render being eternal. Infinity and eternity are not the same thing, even if Meillassoux treats them as if they were. That is strange, given his insistence on the contingency of things. The infinity of things also paradoxically does not close off the existence of an Other, an outside, in the way Meillassoux wants it to (*QM* 92). Meillassoux thinks the Cantorian transfinite excludes the Other and the outside, but even Cantor himself recognized it does not, given his appeal to God as absolute infinite. In this way, Meillassoux is right that our world does not refer to another universe (Meillassoux is not offering a multiverse theory as such) but wrong to think that the Cantorian infinite eliminates the Other and otherness as such (*QM* 192).

Here, Meillassoux does insightfully note that negative theology wanted both to avoid the scandal of saying God exists like any other creature and at the same time avoid the seeming blasphemy of stating that God does not exist (*QM* 236). But this shows us more so that in the struggle between theism and atheism the issues revolve around more than God and involve such critical points as whether being itself is eternal, whether the world is purely inconsistent, etc. Meillassoux also believes that the transfinite renders impossible any "secret principle hidden away" that a demiurge would use, but the transfinite itself is always dependent, not the empty set (*QM* 92). The empty set itself is finite, marks the transfinite as finite, and is marked always by its relationship to the void. It is the empty set that appears ex nihilo. It is the basis of being rather than a hyper-chaos.

Now, for Meillassoux, advocating radical contingency overcomes the problems of an atheism of chance also because it does not require that every possibility be actualized (that is, in not being based on chance it does not yield ultimately to its reverse side—necessity). If all is contingent, then one particular pattern might repeat itself endlessly and then suddenly change for no reason. The world thus, for no reason whatsoever, can operate by one set of laws and then suddenly operate according to another. Pure contingency does not require that things constantly change per Meillassoux. However, this is also why the only way to verify Meillassoux's view is by way of his metaphysical argument based on an interpretation of Cantorianism. Any world of any type operating in any way can match his theory, given that contingency can include repetition and apparent order. It is the most thoroughly non-falsifiable theory imaginable.

It is contingent for Meillassoux that a particular thing exists but not that there exists something. That is necessary. For this reason, Meillassoux must agree with Kant that existence is not a real predicate, but his Cantorian argument works against this idea (QM 34–37). For Cantorianism to work, anything that is conceivable must exist—even if in a domain like a Platonic heaven or in the mind of God—unless one bases things on the empty set and its creation, as we have attempted. That is, Meillassoux cannot have it both ways. He cannot argue that Cantorianism renders being itself infinite and eternal without arguing at the same time that existence is a real predicate. But if he admits to that, he is faced with the ruin of contingency in the sense he puts forth. Kant said existence is not a real predicate such that every time I think about a thing it is just a thought. One can only know it exists outside of the mind via empirical observation. But we only empirically observe the finite. To say the Cantorian transfinite characterizes being as such means that it must exist in and of itself in the world and not simply as a possibility within the mind.

Now, we might say numbers do include existence as a

real predicate, since every time I think one thought, it is one thing. The concept itself exists by its own articulation as an existing thing. But then Meillassoux has to posit something that is thinking all things at once, like Cantor did. And that, again, brings us back to God. A unicorn that I think may or may not exist, but if I think the number 2, then it exists in and through the thought of it. Meillassoux does not want to say all that is possible is actualized, since that ruins the idea of radical contingency, but it is not clear how he can avoid it other than positing a God that is for instance forming the domain to found the Cantorian (*QM* 93). After all, the hyper-Chaos has various divine attributes, such as omnipotence.

Meillassoux believes he is radicalizing a Kantian worldview (what he calls 'correlationism' throughout his work) insofar as correlationism showed that being and thought are not the same (what can be thought is greater than what is), but to call upon Cantorianism is to unite again being and thought and to suggest that anything that can be thought (even if only in being written and posited, as the transfinite cannot be thought in full by a finite mind) marks being as such and renders it inconsistent. Meillassoux then, rather than canceling the identity of being and thought, more so needs to swallow up all of being into that which human thought only pretends to think—the infinite. Reality is not then greater than thought and mind, but itself shown to be marked by it. Whatever is said to be thinkable and constructed in the mind is. Meillassoux is therefore an absolute idealist ('correlationist') and in being so must assume that thought and reality cannot be incommensurable. Meillassoux thus is saying essentially that we as finite humans have thought the absolute and thought it as transfinite. The absolute is then known allegedly by thought to be radically irrational and inconsistent.

What is interesting is that Meillassoux often speaks of things occurring in the world "*ex nihilo*", but he cannot possibly mean that things appear out of pure nothingness, because his philosophy attempts to reject the void as such

(*QM* 176). Meillassoux must argue the world "is capable of everything" including not doing something, but the world we actually experience does not appear to have these properties (*QM* 178). The world's lacking this structure makes accepting Meillassoux's view more and more a matter of faith in his worldview rather than a position one accepts given its explanatory power. This is surprising, mainly since Meillassoux himself characterizes his position as being anti-religious in nature. However, it seems, at most, that Meillassoux's view can have a theological or anti-theological value. Meillassoux argues that life itself inexplicably emerges out of matter in an event that cannot be predicted or explained (*QM* 178). But it is not clear how such a view is more helpful in understanding life than one of special creation. It appears on its face to be merely the inverse.

Given that phenomena we meet with in the world seem to follow basic laws, Meillassoux's view is, on the face of it, not very persuasive. Meillassoux himself then leaves the available options at two when it comes to understanding life—his position or one of design—given that he agrees with intelligent design theorists that a Darwinism based on chance has no "reasonable probability whatsoever" and that the origin of life is "incomprehensible in terms of chance" (*QM* 185). In fact, Meillassoux argues that the laws of physics as we know them are incompatible with life, and life, as such, breaks with the laws of physics (I think he may have in mind here the second law of thermodynamics) (*QM* 186). In other words, in agreeing that life's appearance and development cannot reasonably be based on the aleatory, Meillassoux's meta-physics offers great comfort for intelligent design theorists, since it shows, at least, that the issue is a metaphysical one and one between randomness as pure contingency and divine design.

In fact, Meillassoux sees it not only as "highly unlikely" that consciousness should emerge along with life, but also that matter itself is not an occurrence one can see as necessary or highly likely (*QM* 185). Meillassoux thinks he has exited "the current alternative between chance and finality," but he has really only, at best, exited the alternative between chance and necessity (*QM* 186). Meillassoux is clearly writing before the revolution in thought heralded by Wolfram, such that he can still believe the only way to think an improbability that is not a matter of chance or necessity is via contingency. That is, Meillassoux is blissfully unaware of the manner in which the improbable and the inconsistent, the random and the eventual, can themselves arise out of programming itself.

§18

INFINITE COLLAPSE
The Possible Is Not the Actual

One of the things the preceding analysis of the false vacuum and multiverse theory reveals is the difference between the ideas of eternity and infinity. The vacuum of multiverse theory is always being thought of along the model of a black hole, which is not eternal because it collapses due to its being a product of mass. Eternity names something unchanging and thoroughly timeless such that it precludes the void and nothingness as such. God is the eternal Other of Being. But the transfinite does not preclude the void and its possibility. That is why trying to demonstrate the nature of Being by determining it as transfinite does not exclude its being created and finite in nature. The infinite as transfinite is the infinite made finite. It is itself based on the empty set and its reiteration.

One way people may take this point would be to say that the idea of infinity itself is not infinite, but we should not think of ideas as mental representations. Ideas are marks. The idea of infinity is itself the mark of the infinite. This is why we are not falling prey to the fallacy of composition here. For Cantor, that mark was the Hebrew letter 'aleph.' The aleph itself is a name for the marking of the infinite. That marking is to write $[1, 2, 3, 4 \ldots \omega]$. It is then by way of its inscription that the idea becomes possible. The idea is a mark and a line. It is the inscription of a line marking a boundary. It is the very bounding of the infinite into the mark. It is a mark of something it can only refer to (the void). That the void can only be referred to does not render the mark here nonsensical. It is the transfinite.

Each number is finite and ω marks also itself as limited, as the limit. When we do transfinite mathematics, we are still performing operations on signs and letters. This is not arbitrary, because these marks themselves contain the very logical properties they are said to present. The letters are therefore not truly representations of something. They are not analogies or resemblances; they are the things themselves. The empty set is the set including nothing itself. The transfinite sign is the transfinite itself, even if it refers to a function as well. The transfinite is the infinite made finite, and the fact that it is marked with a sign only embodies that. This is why the transfinite is about the self-referentiality of marks. The mark marks itself and refers to its place, just as the transfinite captures infinity simply by marking an end and writing the lowercase omega. The lowercase omega is the limit number that notes the end of the series of positive integers. Lowercase omega is larger than any other positive integer and thus not finite. Lowercase omega is a sign that says 'this is the mark of that which is larger than any other positive integer.' It is that name.

Each number is finite. Lowercase omega interrupts the repetition of finite numbers. This lowercase omega ends the repetition by marking it as ended and limited. It is thus another name for the second side of the brackets forming the set. And yet beyond the finite, it is still written with a sign that notes its limit. It is bound by the mark itself. It only states 'this is the number greater than all others and not finite.' The transfinite is always written out by a sign—a sign that is only ever a mark on a page or in the mind. Aleph is itself only the cardinality of ω such that it is another way of marking the mark, a way of writing it again as naming ω's equivalence with other infinities.

This is why again the transfinite is finally the empty set itself. That is a formula mystics of all kinds long ago bequeathed to the world. What this formula means it that even if we were to obtain a viewpoint that allows us to look at everything, this everything will reveal itself to be nothing. The infinite is the same as the nothing. To posit infinities of infinites is to return to nothing and to a zero point of information. For what is even a large amount of things in the face of the infinite? That is why when ideas like Cantor's transfinite and Chaitin's Omega are posited, we finally collapsed back to the empty set upon which all was based. An attempt to render the all or the totality returns us to the basis of anything.

Something is always a relation to nothing. A multiverse of everything and every possibility is really just the false vacuum, the empty set. The set of all sets is the empty set. But here we see it is more precisely the empty set, the mark of the nothing, which is united with the infinite in this sense of the transfinite. Mystics spoke of pure nothingness being identified with the absolute infinite. But we reserve those two terms to name that which insists beyond being and not as two terms that characterize being in itself. Instead, the formula 'the infinite is nothing' can only be addressed truly by way of the empty set and the transfinite.

Cantor showed us that we can have two infinite sets—such as the infinite set of evens and infinite set odds—that intersect at no place and yet can be put into one-to-one correspondence. The lack of overlap between the two means the only place they meet is in the empty set. Precisely. The empty set is not pure nothing but rather its mark. Even though the set of evens and set of odds are both transfinite, they are two repetitions of the empty set itself. Two infinite sets meet at the empty set, because the empty set is a subset of all sets. It marks sets as sets. The empty set is thereby what is included in every number and as on the outside at the same time. It is included in the set and yet also allows the set itself to be an element alongside all the things inside the set. The whole or totality then, as set, is but one more element. It is the empty set's iteration that makes possible any sign and any set. But at the same time, it is not simply its place or its function. It can be subtracted from it. The empty set is related to the void. It includes it, but it is not bound to it as if it were bound to its place. It is thereby not determined, but rather indeterminate and radically so. It's incorporating and instantiating space, but that makes possible multiple other signs; for each sign with its name is another set and another inscription of the empty set. In this way, the empty set in its iterations both makes possible and undercuts any fixed meaning or term to repeat the Derridean point. It shows the world to be radically incomplete and marked by the transfinite. The empty set is thereby locally transcendent, even though it is always included in any set.

This transcendence is also what allows for there to be positive terms, because, through iterability, the empty set can function at any point and be newly determined. It is a positive term. The empty set is counted and then becomes 1. That 1 can then function in many other contexts. It is also the oneness or unity of a thing and allows it, like a name, to exist alongside of what it is. However, unity is still as one related to the empty set. That is, it is still relational at its core, related to the void, related to the place of its inscription. The empty set as such ensures the transcendence of what it includes, the nothing. And also, as the name of God refers to the transcendence of the impossible Other, existent sets in being marked as radically incomplete always generate another element outside their totality. If we speak of the set of all animals, we already have the non-animal. That's not arbitrary. It's because the empty set as bit is always a relation to two states: on/off, 0/1. This is why the other state always merges once a determination is made. The empty set should not be thought of as inscription solely in the sense of writing in an empirical sense of marks on a page. A false vacuum is an empty set. We are speaking here of phenomena of all types and not just empirical marks on a flat surface. For this reason, even if one analyzes things from the perspective of infinity and thereby without any time bound, one is still led to self-delimitation and to a finite universe.[160]

People who know machine language will tell you that computer programs self-delimit by indicating in their bit strings how they are to stop, and thus the computer reading the bit string can see where to stop. Another way of noting the transfinite is to note that there is no set of all sets, but that lack of a set of all sets does not touch God. For God, as Cantor himself demonstrated, is the absolute Infinite beyond the transfinite itself. The lack of a set of all sets marks Being, but God, as at the very least Emmanuel Levinas and Jean-Luc Marion taught, is otherwise than Being. However, given their phenomenological orientation, both Marion and Levinas saw this beyond as ultimately a beyond of consciousness, something that we cannot intentionally grasp in principle. It is not a matter of another side of the coin that we flip over to reveal. It is something like the consciousness of the other person that can never be unveiled. For that reason, Levinas founded our relation to God on our relation to the other who we encounter in this world via the face. But that means that it was consciousness itself that was bracketing God. We are arguing that what it is on the side of the subject is also on the side of substance, to make the Hegelianism explicit. Being in and of itself is inconsistent and incomplete—not just mind. God himself brackets himself from being, withdraws Himself, and thereby marks being. It is not a question of the limitations of mind. It is something that marks all things in their very nature. The transfinite is thereby not just a function of language or logic, but being. This is what is called today the "speculative turn" in Continental Philosophy.

The Hegelianism of the turn insofar as it involves

---

[160] My use of this term and the general idea I take from Chaitin even if he thinks only finite programs do this. We are arguing even the infinite does: see Chaitin, *Meta Math!*, 78–81. It is on this book that I am depending for all my claims about Chaitin, unless otherwise specified.

transposing structures—once thought to be exclusive to the inner workings of mind and failing to reach the world—onto the world itself does not mean Hegelianism itself is totally triumphant. For example, the Hegelian dialectic was only ever about a specific set of programs—nested patterns or fractals. The dialectic, whether it is the dialectic of particular and universal, part and whole, subject and object, or any other of the limited shapes it takes was only ever a question of the same pattern repeating itself or repeating itself in a limited number of permutations. Hegel is not the thinker of the letter (even if we can dig up a text where he contrasts the letter and phonetic writing to the hieroglyph) because the letter leads us to Rule 30-like patterns, wherein pure randomness is generated by rules.

Anything can be a signifier and set, as anything can be made a letter. This is what happened with hieroglyphics. Look at Hebrew. Many say the third letter *gimmel* was originally a drawing of a camel (*gamel*), but today it functions as a letter as in any phonetic system. The letter is thus when the semiotic sign is overturned and representation ends. *Gimmel* today does not symbolize a camel but functions in phonemic relation with the J sound (dʒ), as in English. The letter leads us to programs of various types and for specific phenomena, where the dialectic of constantly repeating part-whole relations in the Hegelian sense is not at work. The program, insofar as it is marked by the bit and letter, would look to Hegel like purely mechanical repetition—a very Jewish adherence to the letter of the law rather than the articulations of spirit. In this way, even if Philosophy itself is exhibiting dialectic structure, that does not mean the dialectic rules at all scales and at all levels.

Also, to argue that being itself is incomplete means it cannot count for itself. This is one of the main consequences of the transfinite. It requires the absolute Other, as Cantor so pointedly reminded us even at the end of his life, in poverty, and from the depths of the sanatorium. This is, again, because, even if we adopt the perspective of the transfinite and allow all to be marked by it, we still see it collapse into something finite in itself. The transfinite always collapses back into its mark, which is the empty set, its basis. In other words, in this world, there will be no way to show that all possibilities are actualized. And not all possibilities will be actualized. Let me put the thesis as bluntly as possible: even if we posit an infinity of cases as possible, we only ever get one actual case or a finite number. A multiverse then could only ever be itself finite in character.

We can call this, if we want, the 'Principle of Finitude' as opposed to the 'Principle of Plenitude.' The Principle of Plenitude argued that our world, for instance, exhibits maximum diversity. In the extreme, this plenitude implies all possibilities are actualized. But only ever a finite amount is. Life is the perfect case study of such limited diversity. Life forms do not exhibit all the possible options, and that means that life was planned and programmed. Evolutionary theory supposed that all happens randomly. To make that randomness reasonable, it needed to have all possibles realized, even if it meant positing the multiverse. In this way, even the universe allegedly was a product of chance, although such a view of chance quickly collapsed into a positing of necessity. We then are faced with a world where the amount of diversity has to be to finite in the actual world. Evolutionary theory needed every possibility to be tried to that the odds against the purely random were not astronomical.

Now, Darwinians will argue here that natural selection is what limits things to a finite number of cases. But, as we have seen, natural selection is just a tautological expression of the fact of finitude without explaining it. We say and will say that life does not explore all possibilities because of its specific programming. In that way, it is self-delimitation that is at play in life. There is a code, CSI, from the beginning, and that is why it does not articulate all possibilities. To say that not all possibilities are realized means that being itself is contingent. It is contingent that this world, with its actual structure, came into being. It was not necessary. There is only one necessity, and that is God; because if God is possible, then God is necessary. God only fails to obtain if God is not necessary or if necessity itself is nonsensical. God then names the only possibility that must necessarily obtain outside of mind. God marks this exceptionality.

Many will say that this modal/ontological argument only shows that if God is possible, God is necessary. But God is impossible. That is partly true. God is impossible in this world. That is why God withdraws to create it. But God's being the impossible Other for us here does not mean that the Other does not obtain outside of such a finite but unbounded space. Leibniz also believed that of all the possibilities, not all exist. For Leibniz, God selects from possibilities and chooses the best of all. Even if God can conceive of all possibilities, God only allows certain ones to occur, but that makes it appear as though what unfolds is merely a realization of something already present. That view misses what it is involved in saying: that things are programmed to unfold as they do. God need not realize each possibility, but only one in order to create the world as it is. Programming delimits possibilities.

With what we call the Name of God as the ultimate program of the universe, we have a way of knowing what does, in fact, exist from this name. And it is not all that is possibly conceivable. We thus look at the world and see it as the elaboration of a finite set of rules that is the Name of God. It is not a question of deduction, as Wolfram showed, but it is something that could be, in principle, emulated by re-running the program itself. It is computationally irreducible, and yet it is eminently knowable in its emulation. That shows that everything conceived can exist in fact. And if all is made up of bits, then one will say that God, from the perspective of eternity, sees all at once as bit strings. Even if we posit an infinity of possibilities epistemologically, in being itself and its observable actualization, there only ever is a finite number realized. That is another way to restate the idea that being in and of itself is incomplete. It is not a failure of ours that we are not omniscient, that we cannot see being as full realized in all its imaginable possibilities. It is inherent in being itself, even as infinite to self-delimit. The logic of exception is not just a logic of the linguistic signifier, because being itself is marked by the letter at its very heart. And, for that reason, being is incomplete, insofar as it is always missing one constitutive exception: the impossible Other, God. The logic of exception strikes existence itself at its heart, because God insists on being found missing and missing out.

Many think such paradoxes are limited to language. Language cannot account for itself and give a complete description of itself. This is known as the thesis that there is no meta-language. The incompletion of language itself has been shown by any number of figures over the last 100 years. Kurt Gödel probably most famously demonstrated that there is always at least one statement that cannot be proved to be true in an axiomatic framework. Alan Turing demonstrated this Gödelian incompleteness in relation to computer programs via the 'halting problem.' The halting problem only reveals incompleteness precisely when one does not bound programs in terms of computing time (that is, one sees programs as operating over an infinite or endless amount of time with infinite memory resources). However, there is no computer that would ever run for an infinite time that we know about. It is thereby a thought experiment. Now, if and only if there is no time limit, we do not know in advance if a program will halt or not.

Heisenberg's uncertainty principle has to be seen as part of this family of problems. Heisenberg argues that we can only ever obtain part of the information that we would need to have a complete understanding of any system. We can pick and choose from the information open to access, but, once we make a choice as to some portion of information, another portion becomes opaque to us. There is then a limit in things as to how much can be gathered about them. But what Heisenberg is naming here is the incompletion of things. Things are inherently under-determined in their finitude. They are radically open. It is not that a complete thing we do not have a full idea of is hidden away from us. It is rather that the thing itself is open.

Think here of sets. Take the set of Americans. This set has only ever contained a finite number or people, but the set of American refers to all who have been, will be, and can be Americans. That means there is a place in it marked for an infinite number of people, even if, in fact, there only ever will have been a finite number of Americans. The set is thereby inherently finite for us, but, as a set, it is radically incomplete and open and thus transfinite. It can be put into one-to-one correspondence with the infinite set of positive integers, even if to do so we need to just state that American number 4,000,000,000,000 is followed by American 4,000,000,000,001 as place-holder terms. When we go to determine the contents of the set, we only find a finite number counted. That is, if we choose to look at this set, we cannot get all the information about all Americans.

This same thing is going on with the uncertainty principle. The more I know about the set, a portion is lost to me. If I go to count it now, those who will be American only are noted by placeholders. What if we say that all space aliens are deserving of American citizenship and are Americans? We cannot deny this, because this set is itself incomplete and open. We cannot say that those space aliens are not already included in the set of Americans. Through declaring space aliens are Americans, we force them into the set of Americans. We take the set of space aliens and force it into the set of Americans.

The infinite set of Americans also yields a power set. We cannot know, given the infinity involved, what infinite sets are included as subsets, given that infinite sets can have infinite subsets (as per the positive integers, which have an infinite set of even, odd, etc., numbers). Again, if we go to measure the set of Americans, we are taking it in terms of not knowing yet what power sets/subsets are revealed—part of the information is opaque to us. All of this is based on the extensional nature of the set. This extensionalism is itself ultimately ontologically founded on the empty set. The empty set includes nothing in it. It is just the brackets of the set. That is why it is radically open and incomplete. It can include any element. A set simply is what it contains, and it can contain anything whatsoever, in any order. Anything can be included in it. Any set we would differentiate and name is already marked by the same logic. It is just a repetition of the same and a repetition of the empty set.

There is no defined continuum (per the work of P.J. Cohen) between one transfinite set and its power set. Any infinite set can be forced into it and out of it. That is, one can see it as having been included, just as we saw with space aliens and Americans. Many transfinite sets of things can then be forced to be seen as intervening in between being American, for example, and its proper subset. That is to say, we would say, per common sense, that that there is a subset of Americans such that it includes nothing more than those Americans rearranged (just as we have odd numbers, etc.). But the positive integers in its subset reveals the set of reals, etc., because there is nothing that prevents the elements themselves from being permuted in any number of ways. Numbers can then be simply put one over the other (2/3) to create a new number. So any property here can enter into the extensional set. So if you were to say all Spanish speakers are American, this property was indiscernible and not seen as being part of the set but now is revealed and extracted or forced out. In making that clear, we have blinded ourselves to another portion of the information contained in it.

No observer in the world can know more than a finite amount of information about anything. Observation here is key, because if all that is, is numerical (all is number and mathematizable), then how does one differentiate what is and what is not? The only way is by having recourse to empiricism in the same way Kant did. Existence is always something we know via observations. That all is bits, for instance, means that only the ontological proof of God can give us a priori knowledge. Otherwise, while we can know all is bits, we do not know a priori that bit configuration. Observation tells what there is in the same way a census tells us how many Americans there are, despite the transfinite nature of the set of Americans. We need observation, because we know things are finite in actuality (anything we observe will be finite), even if all is marked by the transfinite and thus incomplete and open.

We now say openness means unbounded, just as the universe always is observed as finite but could be unbounded. That is, if one takes off in a space ship, one can keep going on indefinitely (if one had the proper fuel resources). This does not mean one cannot go in the reverse direction. We could say all true Americans are English speakers. We now have attempted to delimit the set of Americans. We thus try to keep the set finite. And that finitization can be enforced; at any time the set of Americas is observed to be finite and as having a finite number of members. But, at the same time, due to the set's radical incompletion coupled with its inconsistency, one can isolate another property that was not clearly part of the set. It was indiscernible in the set of Americans before, and it can be selected out of the transfinite set. This is a supremely political operation. I am clearly following Alain Badiou here, although it is not clear Badiou is explicitly formulating things in precisely these terms.

We can say any set is infinite insofar as it is a set, that it is radically open and incomplete. Observation is then a perception of it, but that perception is only ever of a finite portion of it, because only ever a finite portion exists in actuality. Observation is finite. We then have uncertainty as to what is not being accounted for in our fine observation, but we should not confuse a thing with our perception of it. A phenomenon's being radically open is not a function of our perception of it, and neither is its finitude. Both things are a function of the very being of the thing. Perception and observation tell us about what exists, in fact, and not about being.

When speaking of the being of things, we can speak about infinities of infinities. But, as Kant noted, we observe the existence of things as such. What is actual is only ever finite, and that is due to the self-delimitation inherent in things, precisely because, in their being, they are marked by the transfinite. The transfinite paradoxically reveals radical finitude. A potato is itself a set, but we only ever observe a portion of it due to its being incomplete. At the same time, that potato can be summed as a finite thing, as a mathematical formula. It could probably be generated from a single cell, if we had the right code. It is thus compressible into a single cell—if not a single strand of DNA. There is thus a finite bit string expressing it and making up its being. That bit string is open insofar as its computation has to unfold. Those finite sets of rules unfold. Even if the unfolding appears random, it is still a finite set of rules unfurling. In the case of the potato, there seems to be a clear and non-random pattern at work. It is thus incomplete only insofar as it is still working out its program. Despite being incomplete, we can have a complete description of it in its coding. It is incomplete always at different levels that can be marked.

This is why Heisenberg said things are a matter of choice. If we choose to measure one thing, others become opaque. Many have wanted to see this uncertainty principle as showing that what we observe as actual in the universe is structured by our observation because we are doing the observing of it, and we are included ourselves in the universe. In this way as it is said, the universe is "observing itself."[161] However, that self-observation is, again, Hegelian. We need to see this incompletion and uncertainty as part of the very fabric of being and not dependent on us or our observation. Our observation reveals it to us, but it would be there even if we did not observe it. It is not consciousness that is the fundamental missing piece of the universe, as someone like Slavoj Žižek contends, but God himself that marks the universe as lacking. We are then situated inside that framework itself and reveal it to ourselves.

Gödel's undecidable sentence is always generated by

---

[161] Barrow and Tipler, *The Anthropic Cosmological Principle*, 4.

any framework that, at first blush, appears to be complete. There is always an exception. This exceptionality occurs precisely because the letter and differentiality are at the heart of things. If we define something as being the case, there will be something that is not the case by contrast—any mark is related to its place and to the void. It is differentiality itself, as embodied in the letter and the signifier, that makes it so there must always be an exception. The exception defines the rule. The signifier is not significant because it is arbitrary, but because of its negative differentiality. Ferdinand de Saussure's insight was that a language is made up of a network of pure difference without any positive terms. A signifier has its value only in relation to all the other signifiers. The letter, on the other hand, the phoneme, is only ever related to itself and the void, to itself and another letter. The letter is not a message, but is meaningless in itself. That is why the bit is always the relation 0/1. 0 only means off, in contrast to on. It does not matter that a certain voltage associated with 0 is on a continuum with other measures. At the same time, the letter is meaningless in and of itself. If one just writes out a string of zeros and ones, no one will have any idea what it means. The bit string is a meaningless carrier of a possible meaning by way of its transformation. In this way, nothing has its own inherent meaning; all is arbitrarily connected to a meaning because it is a pure difference.

What then of positive terms? They are the reverse side of the system. It is not really that the signifier is related to the signified, as Lacan showed us, but that signifiers are related to other signifiers in which there is a meaning effect. The reverse side of each is the signifier or letter as purely positive term, as identity in and of itself, as signified. But that is something that is part of a different structure, the imaginary, for example, for Lacan. Such remarks are, to some degree, clichés of the last 50 years of theoretical reflection. What is new is that these properties are no longer to be thought as pertaining simply to language or unconscious thought, but to being itself. They mark a snowflake as much as a dream. Second, this relationship to reality brings in dimensions that were dismissed until recently.

Think here of the traditional post-Structuralist clichés about paper money, value, and gold. The Saussurean view led to the view that money only has a purely arbitrary value that is fixed by exchange and convention. There is nothing inherently valuable about paper or even gold. It is only ever a matter of what values it takes on in the system itself. In this way, if one ever advocated the gold standard as a way of halting inflation, one would be laughed out of the room as not acknowledging the revealed truths of Structuralism.

Think here of a counterfeiter who can produce paper money that is indistinguishable from the kind the government prints. If every value is just a matter of what one receives for it, then one will offer things in exchange for this money. But if such a counterfeiter floods the system with this money, then prices will rise, and value will be ruined. Value is ruined here precisely because the goods available are finite. One cannot divide them up infinitely. If one could, they would not rise, but rather sink to nothing. Counterfeiters can, of course, keep printing more and more money. However, the more money entering the system, the more the prices will go up. The printer will never be able to keep up, as eventually the very price of making the counterfeit money will itself rise. Counterfeiting thus ruins, in this model, the value of money precisely by its constant repetition. One will eventually lose the money one put into counterfeiting in such a scheme (*RU* 66-67).

Gold and paper money are exchanged on markets where their value is determined because they do not have any value in and of themselves. But there is a distinct difference between paper and gold. Paper, insofar as it is marked by signs, can be printed seemingly endlessly, but gold resists such endless reproduction much more in its finitude. The inflation of signs was taken as having no effect on their values. No matter how many times I say the word 'gold,' it still holds the same value. The same is not the case with money or gold, because even if we can print paper money indefinitely or for a very long time (entropy would prevent it from being printed endlessly, given the need for printing presses, etc., a point I will return to), it is always chasing a finite number of goods. The scarcity of goods was never thought by this framework.

The rarity of gold also plays a role. The reason alchemists searched for a way to transform lead into gold was to overcome this problem. Today, we could, if we wanted, transform lead into gold. That is because we have discovered the atomic structure of all things and their adherence to the mathematical. Post-Structuralism was never interested in such questions. It would never deign to consider why lead could not be transformed into gold and what the implications of being able to do so are. It was focused on texts and the signs repeated in them in their purely arbitrary quality. It is the convergence of a system where the sign is repeated indefinitely in relation to finite systems that causes inflation and the ruin of value. In this way, putting money on the gold standard is to put paper currency in relation to another good that is finite and thereby related to another system in order to weigh it down.

We can also say that even if we allow the sign to be repeated infinitely, it will also lose its value. Why? Precisely due to the differential nature of the signifier. It is important to differentiate the signifier from the letter. The signifier is itself a function of the letter. It is when 0101010 is taken as a set. The signifier therefore captures the element of the set itself as mark. But all signifiers are differentially opposed to each there. The signifier and the letter are therefore almost names for the same thing. However, the signifier makes sense because, as Lacan said, it represents a subject for another signifier. The letter does not represent at all. For instance, in DNA, a sequence of letters is not enough unless they form signifiers, genes, that can be meaningful and function in the right way. A string of bases as letters is meaningless without also something to decode them and translate them into specific genes, words. As Hegel liked to point out, when we write down that 'A is A,' we have to repeat A, thus producing a new one that is itself different. In this way, there is always difference in repetition. The inflation of the sign also affects its own value. For this reason, even in its inflation, it is producing its difference and an exception.

This exception can be an internal exclusion or radically external. For instance, Gödel was focused on sentences that made sense within a language or axiomatic system but at the same time did not belong. Take the liar's paradox for example. 'I am lying' is a sentence that makes sense within the framework of sentences typically subjected to tests of truth and falsity, but at the same time does not belong, since if it is true, it is false, and if it is false, it is true. This Gödelian problem is not a problem for finite things when a rule limits them. As Dembski argues, we can say that, "there are only so many distinguishable word combinations that we can utter and only so many distinguishable sound combinations that can strike our eardrums" (*ID* 218). In speech, it is not the case that we can speak of a word being endless in length. It would then never reach us and be heard. Words spoken have to be some finite length, which means that we can hear them. There is then not a transfinite set of words, and that means the set of all words is easily computable. Any finite thing is computable per recursion theory, including "everything a finite being does" (*ID* 219). For that reason, "computers can as well be programmed to compute Gödel sentences for computational systems external to themselves" (*ID* 219). The issue is not seeing Goedelian issues for computation by way of a reference to infinity in a finite system, but seeing them arise internally:

> The problem then is not to find Gödelian sentences for computational systems external to oneself. The problem is for an agent to examine itself as a computational system and therewith produce one's own Gödel sentence. If human beings are noncomputational, then there won't be any Gödel sentence to be found. If on the other hand, human beings are

computational, then by Gödel's theorem, we won't be able to find our own Gödel sentences. (*ID* 219)

From within a system, we cannot find the Gödel sentence and thus account for it. But from an outside perspective, it can be found. The universe itself is finite such that something from the outside can compute it.

This is the same as the Turing halting problem. Computer programs can stop, halt, and issue some sort of result of their computation. On the other hand, it is possible for computers to get caught in endless loops (hence in bad sci-fi movies the computer says 'That does not compute'). This reference to computers is very apropos here. Patrick Grim and his co-authors showed us already, over a decade ago, that logic and even logical paradoxes can be mapped by cellular automata.[162] This groundbreaking book (that was given far too little attention) showed that logical propositions and their mapping led to patterns like fractals. That is, logical arguments can themselves be translated into rules for cellular automata. This reveals that something like the liar's paradox produced a nested pattern, a fractal. This shows that if one has a computational ontology like the one we are attempting to articulate here, that something like the liar's paradox is part of the very structuration of being. It is part of it and only one particular program. It is only a program of one type. For instance, the Half-Sayer sentence ('This sentence is as true as half its estimated value') reveals a fractal pattern wherein one can see where the pattern gravitates around points and where it moves away from others. What this suggests is that there are programs for entities that have this pattern in the world and are computing it. There are thus entities in the world computing the Half-Sayer sentence and the liar's paradox. In other words, the Church-Turing thesis that anything that can be com-

---

[162] Patrick Grim, Gary Mar, and Paul St. Denis, *The Philosophical Computer: Exploratory Essays in Philosophical Computer Modeling* (Cambridge: MIT Books, 1998).

puted can be computed by a digital computer is here given ontological weight rather than just logical significance. The program is itself articulated using the same language. We then see that these paradoxes are included in computational reality and part of finite nature. In fact, they are directly part of it. Being itself is beset by paradox, and various phenomena illustrate it by their computation and patterning.

If all things can be translated into the language of cellular automata, then we see that there is a universal language, even if that langue is nothing more than the relation of cells, of bits. Wolfram showed us that randomness can be produced by a finite set of rules. But if we have a purely random program, it can be completely non-computable and thus not algorithmic in nature. Randomly selected programs might simply give us something useless. But it won't give us something outside of rules themselves. Almost all computations that occur are bounded in time for their unfolding such that we will know if the they halt or loop eventually. Turing's halting problem asks us to look at all possible programs and to do so without putting bounds on time. If we do, we can never know with certainty in advance if a randomly selected program will halt or not. We do not know. We cannot know. It is unsolvable.

Let's go back to the liar's paradox version of these issues. 'I am lying' is a Gödel sentence. If it is false, it is true. If it is true, it is false. It is undecidable if it is true or false because it is both true and false at the same time, neither true nor false, either true or false (things are said to be one or the other), and all at the same time. What makes this possible is differentiality itself. The bit shows this very well in its permutation. The bit is 0/1 (either 0 or 1) and 01 (both zero and one, especially with the qubit). What then is neither 0 nor 1? It is the radically transcendent, the absolute Other. God is thus the name for the neither/nor and always haunts the radically undecidable and incomplete nature of things. God, of course, thus radically transcends the world. This shows that the finitude of the world always makes reference to the Other. But when we talk about Gödel sentences, we are talking about a sentence (that is, a thing), something that is part of the world. The sentence of the liar's paradox is a completely finite sentence. It is a sentence that in its structure, grammar, number of words, etc., is not uniquely different from any other sentence we can construct in English. However, this sentence is different because of its undecidability. What makes this possible is again the relation 0/1 itself.

The sentence 'I am lying' always hides the qualifier 'it is true that I am lying.' The truth is itself always presupposed by lying and the false. This is like saying that there is an infinite set of true things and all things are taken to be true, but in doing that, we immediately hit the liar's paradox. There is always at least one thing that is neither true nor false.

Let's return to the multiverse. One would say that out of this infinity of possibilities only one is our universe. It is just one set among an infinity of sets. If each finite universe is the playing out of a set of rules, as each is finite, then our universe is but one program of many possible programs. We should not think of all these possible programs as abstract concepts. It is precisely that each is a program—a finite bit string. We then, if we are followers of Leibniz, say that God chose one of these programs, our universe, because it was the best of all possible programs. But we have been trying to show that only one program can be selected or a finite number. Some may want to say that the only program that can be selected is the one which will give rise to observers such as us, because only such observers can delimit the program by observing it from within. To say there is only one possible universe is to say then that it is only one finite set of rules that will give rise to us. The universe then has to be of the type that gives rise to observation that, obviously, itself detects what actually exists. Existence is simply detecting what is in actuality. Out of all the possibilities that are, the one observed is the one that exists. We cannot observe any other possibility or actuality; therefore our universe is the only one, as it is the only one to be shown observing itself. Many different universes thus do not exist. Only one exists, the one observing itself to exist. The number of possible universes that really exist are only the ones that are observed.

Some here will say that there are other universes in which there are other people making the same claim. We obviously cannot know that, so it will be said that it cannot be ruled out. For this reason, we will have to show that any alternative universes can only be simulations of a single finite universe and thus that any and all observable universes or universes with observers are computationally equivalent. Due to that, even if there are other universes with self-aware observers, they are themselves built on the basis of a universe that, at its point of departure, was finite in nature. And in that way, we will show that there is only one possible universe, despite all the possible universes of the multiverse.

Jürgen Schmidhuber, in a couple of brief and succinct but extremely dense essays, has posed these questions in a somewhat new way. In an essay entitled "A Computer Scientist's View of Life, the Universe, and Everything," Schmidhuber asks whether our universe can be computed using a "very compact algorithm" and argues that, indeed, there is a "comparatively short algorithm that simply encodes probable next sets by a few bits" as our universe is "greatly compressible."[163] Schmidhuber argues that the program computing our universe must be compact, as otherwise our universe would be very random—as the longer an algorithm is, the more randomness is possible as a result of it.[164]

Schmidhuber posits a "Great Programmer" for our universe, and, for instance, explains Heisenberg's uncertainty

---

[163] Jürgen Schmidhuber, "A Computer Scientist's View of Life, the Universe, and Everything," in Christian Freksa, Matthias Jantzen, and Rüdiger Valk, eds., *Foundations of Computer Science: Potential–Theory–Cognition* (Berlin: Springer-Verlag, 1997), 203.
[164] Schmidhuber, "A Computer Scientist's View," 203.

principle by suggesting this "Great programmer" constantly "dumps" the information content of our universe at a frozen state and then restarts things from that state with information missing.[165] Schmidhuber also argues that our universe is finite, since otherwise our universe would be infinite and purely random. But as our universe is not so random, it must be finite and only know pseudo-randomness that results from the iteration of rules. Finally, Schmidhuber asks whether there is a multiverse or only our one universe running its compact program. Schmidhuber argues it is "much cheaper in terms of information requirements" to compute all possible universes than just one "particular, arbitrarily chosen" universe.[166] But here we have to disagree with the Great Programmer listing and running all possible universes, as it is precisely the nature of divine creation to collapse into a singular name rather than all possible names.

Schmidhuber believes that would be inefficient, since an individual universe is "incompressible" (even if in finite form), whereas trying to compute all possible ones does not require an incompressible program.[167] But if the program is compressible, it is not clear how it cannot be finite. If it is finite, it would itself be a first compact program, just like our own universe. While Schmidhuber thinks more is less, we think less is more. Most universes will not be compressible and will not yield the regularity and beauty we see. This means, again, that running all possible programs just to find the few that will yield a universe like ours seems wasteful rather than efficient. Most universes will be irregular and incompressible, since one can list any endless number of bits strings for universes that will have these features. Even if the bit string is finite, it can be still so long as to lead to universes that have features radically different than ours.

---

[165] Schmidhuber, "A Computer Scientist's View," 203.
[166] Schmidhuber, "A Computer Scientist's View," 203.
[167] Schmidhuber, "A Computer Scientist's View," 204.

Also, given that there is an uncountable infinity of real numbers, the number of compressible reals, for instance, are infinitesimal compared to the set of all non-algebraic reals. This would be an example of how even the computable itself is a fraction of the incomputable. Thus, running all possible universes—if it includes the incomputable—would again be wasteful. If it is not incompressible, then it would be an infinite one that produces things at random or simply, as infinite, produces all things. One would then not be speaking about a program run by the Great Programmer but simply the contents of the Great Programmer's mind. At the same time, if there is a simple program that computes all worlds, and it is infinite, then we are again back to a situation like our own world. It would simply be that our world will be the one in which all the other possible universes will be realized.

Further, Schmidhuber posits an infinite regress of programmers: "Several of the Great Programmer's universes will feature another Great Programmer who programs another Big Computer to run all possible universes."[168] But this infinite regress occurs because Schmidhuber clearly has not considered that any programmer of this nature would have to be infinite in nature precisely to avoid such a regress and enable the very first universe to be programmed. However, Schmidhuber is right that our universe shows so much regularity that all the evidence indicates that it is compressible into a compact program, because nothing conceivably prevents it from having been much more random, much less regular, and still becoming so. This last point will require us to posit that not only will our universe not end in heat death or pure randomness but will result in the Omega Point itself. As Schmidhuber notes, the "coding theorem" states that "guessing any of the programs computing some string and the probability of guessing the shortest are essentially equal."[169] What this point shows us is that

---

[168] Schmidhuber, "A Computer Scientist's View," 205.
[169] Schmidhuber, "A Computer Scientist's View," 205.

our search for finding the very program running our universe will itself collapse the moment we are able to find any program that appears to be on the right track. This is also why any incompressible noise in our universe must only ever be seen as pseudo-randomness. If our universe were truly the product of noise or a fluctuation in a vast sea of noise, then reality would not be compressible. Thus, any new information that arises due to noise would have to be the product of rules. Only with Wolfram was this needed dimension of reality empirically demonstrated.

At this point, let's go back to our discussion of transfinite sets of finite numbers. Common sense says that the set of positive integers is smaller than the set of rational numbers and probably a subset of the rationals. The set of rational numbers—in common sense terms—is smaller than the set of reals and probably a subset of it. Common sense thinks this because it thinks the larger always contains the smaller. If we speak of each set as infinite, given the power set axiom of taking subsets, starting with the positive integers, then the rationals would be a subset of the positive integers, in which they are given new relations (thereby producing a set larger in its cardinality). The common sense view also runs into a problem called the Continuum Hypothesis in set theory. It was thought that one could prove a continuum, where, from positive integers to rational numbers to reals, for example, we have a comprehensible continuum of smaller to larger cardinality and thus a continuity of numbers, like we have with finite numbers on a number line. However, things go awry when we keep in mind that all such sets are transfinite. What happens is that we can put the real numbers in a one to-one relation with all the positive integers. That means the reals are not the same cardinality as the positive integers. This lack of one-to-one correspondence is shown through 'diagonalization.' In this way, for instance, what is contained in the number line when it is seen as being infinitely divisible is a larger infinity than if we take the number line as continuous.

There are then infinitely more real numbers, for example, than positive integers.

What Paul Cohen showed is that it is always undecidable whether a transfinite set is of larger or smaller cardinality than one of its transfinite subsets and that one cannot know if there are no infinities in between them. That is, one might think the set of reals is the next transfinite set of higher cardinality than positive integers, but one cannot prove that. One can also not disprove the Continuum Hypothesis. One cannot know if there are but a finite number of transfinite sets intervening. The real numbers nicely demonstrate how that is. Real numbers like pi have an infinite list of numbers after their decimal points and occur in a random and non-repetitive manner. That means within the subset of positive integers we reach a point where we have infinite numbers, themselves being part of a subset. In demonstrating his view, Cohen used a technique called forcing, wherein one examines transfinite sets, such as the positive integers. One then looks at it in terms of a bigger subset of larger cardinality contained in it. In such a new transfinite set, there are many subsets.

The example of integers and reals works well here. The reals are larger than the set of integers. There is therefore no continuity between one transfinite and another. It is not a simple progression of one transfinite set of one cardinality to another one when we start looking at power sets. This seems strange, on the face of it, as it would seem that all these sets should be able to be put into one-to-one correspondence as transfinites, but that is the paradox at the heart of infinity that Cantor discovered. The power set of transfinites are both the same and different than the power set of finite sets. The power sets of infinites can be combined themselves in infinite ways. The lesser contains the greater. This was already true of finite sets. A set with elements A, B, and C has more than three sets, as these three elements can be permuted into more than three subsets. Between the number of elements in the sets and the number of subsets produced and counted in the power set, we can delimit that number from 3 to another finite number. But in extending this logic to transfinite sets, we get sets with larger cardinality, where we cannot delimit things. We cannot say that the power set contains simply a transfinite number of subsets of the same cardinality as the original set or is simply set out in some order. We cannot then say what the distance is between the original set and its power set and show it is a continuum. There might be infinite sets of infinite cardinality between the two. That means anything is inside a transfinite set, given it always leads to and contains its power set.

The infinity of infinities contained there is indiscernible. A difference that does not make a difference is no difference. It is only when what is contained is forced out that it is a difference. Given that any set can be taken as the same as the set of positive integers (that is, in set theory all sets are ultimately transfinite), it is radically one and incomplete. The greater is always paradoxically contained in the smaller. In other words, we have tried to show this is due to the very nature of the empty set and the way it is involved in each set. We can, as we did with Americans and space aliens above, always force out another transfinite set from within another one. We can always get another name out of a set with one name. That is because terms like 'Americans' are universal terms and only names. It is not also a lettering that is a program or code for something. It is an essence, an *eidos*. It is an extensional set that can contain any other name. For that reason, given that as a proper name it is a way of marking only its status as set, any name can be added to it and any name extracted from it. Of course, names can be nouns, proper nouns, attributes (e.g., the patriotic one), etc.

The failure of the Continuum Hypothesis is that it allows such universal terms that exist as nothing but names to be struck by the transfinite in such a way as any name can be extracted from them. However, not all things are nothing but names. The Name of God is a name, but also, in its lettering, it is the coding for the program for running creation itself. Universal terms do not have that status, because they are like pure nouns or names. In another discourse, we would call them concepts, but I think the nature of the nominalism is clear here. Nominalism is always about the name. Classically, it is said that reality is made up of individuals and that there are no universals, forms, or essences. Only the mind posits universals, in order to notice similarities between individuals. Species really exist as sets. The form of squirrel-ness is a set where one has collected individuals and not a question of what all things we call squirrels have in common. Nominalism is about the arbitrariness of calling cats cats and dogs dogs. Names are just snapshots of how thing are at the present. There is no humanity, as humanity is only a collection of individuals.

In contrast to this classical nominalism, we have attempted to show how the name itself, as embodiment of the empty set, has a fundamental ontological weight, and that the individuality of things is related to the letter and the permutation of letters. Our constitutive inability to prove the Continuum Hypothesis also reminds us that all things in set theory are themselves based on the empty set. It should not be surprising that we can extract any name and force it out of a transfinite set. One can do so because all members of all sets are based on the base-2 (0/1) already contained in the empty set) and the base-10 (which is itself an elaboration of the empty set or base-2). It was Leopold Kronecker who said "God created the integers; all else is the work of man."[170] Chaitin himself quotes Kronecker and, afterwards, makes a startling statement: "If you prefer, Ω isn't a real number at all, it's a fact about certain diophantine [sic] equations; it has to do only with whole numbers, with positive integers!"[171] If Plato put above his Academy "Let no one ignorant of geometry enter here," then I would put above the new academy of digital philosophy Kronecker's philosophy, to remind us to avoid the pitfalls of the

---

[170] Chaitin, *Meta Math!*, 136.
[171] Chaitin, *Meta Math!*, 136.

atheism of the infinite. When we say God created all integers, we mean in some ways less than Kronecker and to say God created 0/1, and all the rest is finite computation.

Kronecker's statement here should also remind us of Wolfram. A finite set of simple rules produces maximal complexity and allows for universal computation. The human mind is special, but that is because it actually does multiple computations rather than reiterating the same finite set over and over again. The human mind thereby is special, since it exploits its computational power. However, even an amoeba already is as complex, since complexity arises from simple rules. It is Darwinism and its allies that posit the infinite as primary over 0/1 and the integers. It should surprise no one that if set theory is itself the most fundamental of all ontological statements, it demonstrates how within the transfinite might lurk more than just an ordered cardinality. Of course, we also have to note that we cannot disprove the Continuum Hypothesis. That means it may in fact hold.

Many, such as Badiou himself, want to see Cohen's work as showing how everything renderable inconsists by way of the insistence at any time of the infinities of infinities that haunt all sets, all things, and all beings. This view overlooks how we can construct limited intensional sets, that we only ever observe finite state machines and sets, etc. That is, at most, we can see how a universal term itself cannot as such exclude anything. Not being able to exclude anything does not mean that, in fact, the set does not exclude. Badiou then can, at most, show us a dialectic of the state and its overturning via an inherent excess. We always exist within the regime of the state. The overturning of the state is only a passing phenomenon. There is always a state and always finitude, because any transfinite is always built up out the finite, upon the empty set. Even if we have a set of all real numbers, those reals themselves are the products of functions and relations between integers. The finite haunts the transfinite. Even if the number 2 is a product of 1 and 1, the number 2 has new properties (it is an even number, for instance). We still have the new arising as an emergence of the finite and its permutation and conjugation. This extends to the rationals, reals, etc. The transfinite emerges from its finite base, but it is not independent of it. Badiou, in order to put forth his view, has to speak as though it is. This is his way of trying to cancel the divine Other. However, there is an Other that is not built on the basis of the finite, and that Other insists and marks the finite itself as created.

Recall multiverse theory. It said essentially that all arises on the basis of the false vacuum, the empty set, but we now see that means that it does not arise out of the infinite itself but is always struck and constrained by the finite. Badiou wants to believe that numbers emerge out of the infinities of infinities, which are unpresentable. However, the absolute infinite is the eternal Other that has withdrawn from the world. That is what marked the world as finite. It is not that the numbers 3 and 4 emerge out of infinities of infinities, but on the basis of the empty set. That empty set emerges out of the void itself through creation out of nothing. Chaitin notes this view is Leibnizian (although it is not clear that Leibniz had a deep enough understanding of computation to work out the details):

> It is the mystic elegance of the binary system that made Leibniz exclaim: *Omnibus ex nihil ducendis sufficit unum.* (One suffices to derive all out of nothing.) [In German: "Einer hat alles aus nichts gemacht." Word for word: "One has all from nothing made."] Says Laplace:
>
>> Leibniz saw in his binary arithmetic the image of Creation ... He imagined that Unity represented God, and Zero the void; that the Supreme Being drew all beings from the void, just as unity and zero express all numbers in his system of numeration....

> Leibniz's vision of creating the world from O's and 1's refuses to go away.[172]

All only comes from nothing thanks to God. On this Leibnizian point, we agree. But unity for us is not represented by God. God is beyond all unity insofar as unity describes created beings. Leibniz's view here is, of course, profoundly influenced by the Kabbalah that he read and studied (perhaps also the *I Ching*). But even if Leibniz had this insight, without a fully computational view of reality as such, it will not work. And when Leibniz actually worked out a metaphysics in detail, he was still viewing things in terms of subject-predicate relations and implications rather than computation.

The stakes here are clear. One position is an inversion of the other. They say it is the other way around, that infinity founds the 1 or the 2. But we say the transfinite is conditioned by the finite. The finite conditions the transfinite. It is connected to it at its inception. And all of being itself is a play of the transfinite, the empty set, etc., because nature is finite. The unconditional, the Other, is otherwise than being. The Other removed himself from being to allow for there to be nothing. We see then, even if we allow things to vary over an unbounded time and to be marked by the infinity, that can only mean being is marked as finite and giving rise to the finite. The finite in its finitude also cannot help but refer to the Other (and we will return to this when examining Fredkin's idea of 'Other'). Cohen's forcing is here of interest (and again I am working off of what Badiou has already signaled with his work) as it shows we can always differentiate a number of sets out of a transfinite set.

We cannot prove the Continuum Hypothesis as true, but we also cannot disprove it. It is undecidable as to whether it holds or not. How does that show us that all possibilities are not actualized and only a self-delimited finite

---

[172] Chaitin, *Meta Math!*, 61.

universe is ever found? It shows us this because, in our forcing out the other set, we only ever can find and observe a finite number. It was only ever on the basis of a finite set in its openness that such indiscernibles were extracted. The name of the set was marked by the empty set, but that did not mean it had an actual infinity of members. It had only a finite amount. We thereby only ever have a finite set of names.

That transfinite set can lead us to various discoveries, but we must begin on the basis of a finite name. The first name is the empty set, the name of God. We always start with Name $(0) = [\ldots]$. It is only thus that we can have Name $(\alpha + 1) =$ a well-defined subset of the power set of (Name $(\alpha) \times P$). Everything depends on simple elements that themselves cannot be named, but are finite in number. One of the things we see here is that Badiou was showing us the path toward transposing the logic of the signifier onto being itself with his assertion all is math, all is sets, but sets, numbers, and elements are not enough, finally, as one also needs bits, algorithms, computation, rules, bit strings, etc., in order to comprehend all phenomena. What we see here is that even if we take things to be transfinite and defined, they still lead to the production of something new, but something only ever finite in nature. Immeasurability leads to novelty, but at the same time to names which are incomplete and unbound, still finite in their status as names.

While we can always find in any set—even if transfinite—any name, it always depends on the fist name for that to be possible. The first name is a relation to the unnamable and nameless One. This is like Turing's attempt to prove that any computational language, any software language, must be finite and consist of finite bit strings. It must have a defined alphabet. The same is true in natural languages like English. In English, we do not have words that are 100 letters long, much less infinite words. Each word is finite and even more delimited than 100 characters. There is always an upper bound on the size of any word. If the words would not have an upper bound in this sense, then it would take increasingly longer and longer to read or hear that word. It would never be scanned, and thus the program would never run. If words could be an infinite number of characters long, then there would be no way to differentiate words without diagonalization, but that may take infinitely long itself. Thus, to have a world that exists as ours does, we need to have a finite alphabet and a finite world.

If the multiverse were truly part of existence and infinite, then such finite sets would only be infinitesimally small fractions of what is possible. It would be so small that the self-delimitation into a finite number of such worlds would itself be a miraculous act that would only be explicable by reference to the divine. Thus, nothing requires that there be anything, but nothing can show it does not take place. In fact, everything indicates it does. This world itself is incomplete and thereby develops, but it is always a dialectic between the necessary finitude of the world and the infinity marking it as incomplete. We always will be in a world that has restricted the names to a bound. There will only be names of, for instance, so many characters in the Twitterverse so many people today occupy. One must delimit the names; once we do so other names will not be nameable and will disappear. However, because all the names are marked by the transfinite, those names do exist at another level and can be called in being. They may not make any sense within the given alphabet, but they can occur. There is a way to list them. It is something the letters themselves make possible.

Let's say we have a given alphabet that restricts us to names of no more than 30 characters. We can permute each name with 30 characters and arrive at any number of new names of more than 30 characters. A name will not necessarily refer to anything we encounter in the world. It will thus not be distinguishable as such from the empty set. It will then have, essentially, the properties of the empty set. This is because, at a key level, the empty set is the indiscernible set. It is real and yet only nameable in relation to the nameless. It can name any property and be part of it. It can be added to any situation and to any set. It has a generic extension insofar as anything can be included in it, but the empty set by itself does not include everything.

What attempts to include everything is the transfinite. The empty set then always needs a second name to expand itself. That second name is the aleph. The aleph has a little bit of everything in it. It has all the numbers inside it, for instance. It has each discernible and numerable positive integer, for example. The empty set has truly no property that distinguishes it. It is indiscernible in and of itself, while the transfinite set includes all and thus marks itself as all-inclusive. The empty set and the transfinite are thus two names for the same thing. It is the name of that which is indiscernible and yet enables determination, since it cannot be found in this world and yet insists in all of the numbers run through until the end. Thus, no number can determine the transfinite, just as no property can determine the empty set. Each is synonymous and yet embodies the very act of naming in and of itself. They both are the representatives of the whole range of possible numbers and sets but, at the same time, not anything in and of themselves.

Because the empty set and transfinite are two sides of the same coin, we can thus say what exists in a universe is itself a matter or observation of a finite number of things. We observe and collect into sets what is observed to be in fact, but the amount is always finite. The transfinite has collapsed into the finite. That might seem random, but it is observation that picks things out and places them in the set and lists them. The empty set is itself and its subset at the same time. That is another way of showing how it is included in every set and situation.

Now, we have highlighted incompletion and how the transfinite marks that. But from Gödel, we also learned that not only is there an exceptional something that is not included in a closed totality, but also we learned that that all things can be thought as exceptions. This is also what Lacan was showing via his graphs of sexuation. A Gödel sentence was part of the system and made sense as a sentence, but, at the same time, there is no decidable way to engage with it. There are many things going on with Lacan's graphs of sexuation. Levi Bryant has argued that his "onticology" is an expression of the feminine side of the graph.[173] What this means is that Bryant argues that all entities, all beings, are singularities, exceptions. It means that there is no universal term or rule that comprehends why all these entities are collected together. This is because Lacan's graph is based on saying that there are two ways (and only two ways) to collect things together: intensional sets and extensional sets. The male side shows an intensional set at work. All things having a certain property are grouped on this side which leads to their being at least one exception—that thing which has the opposite property. On the female side, we have an extensional set, where all things are grouped together simply because they happened to have been grouped in that set. There is then no consistency or rule for why they are together. They are simply put together under the rubric 'Woman,' but the universal 'womanhood' does not exist precisely since it is not a matter of an intensional set. All things listed under 'woman' are simply part of an assemblage. This means there are exceptions.

However, notice that on each side of the graphs, there are two rules. The second rule on the feminine side reads: "There is not an x that is not subject to the phallic signifier."[174] This means there is not any being that is not subject to the rule of the signifier. All are the same. In other words, all beings are equal and equally finite. For speaking beings, it means that for women, there is no woman who is not caught up in the workings of the signifier and speech. There is no outside.

---

[173] Levi Bryant, *The Democracy of Objects*, §6.1.
[174] Jacques Lacan, *On Feminine Sexuality, the Limits of Love, and Knowledge, 1972-1973* (Encore: The Seminar of Jacques Lacan, Book XX), ed. Jacques-Alain Miller, trans. Bruce Fink (New York: W.W. Norton, 1999), 74.

The formulas Lacan uses here are each a *double* negation of the corresponding one. That means that if male side is A, then the female side is not not-A. In other words, at one level the two sides are perfectly equivalent. What Lacan is teaching us here is that speaking beings are all the same insofar as they are speaking beings. They are all subject to the signifier. It is on the basis of the signifier (the mark of negation, subjection to the phallic signifier, etc.) that makes it possible in the first place to group things into two types of collections. In this way, a true ontology of the letter, a Lacanian Realism (as, for Lacan, letters are of the Real and not the Symbolic) means treating all beings as subject to the letter, the empty set. For Lacan, reality is always something seen through the framework of fantasy, which is the conjunction of the symbolic, real, and imaginary. However, mathematization can touch the real itself (in addition to perceptual reality) because it is about its literalization, and that means that being includes both the male and female sides and necessarily so.

What Lacan's graph shows is that even if one lived in Amazonia or Herland, the graph would still be operational insofar as one is a speaking being. There need not be any empirical men at all. The male side says that 'All x are such that x is subject to the signifier,' but that does not say that any such x actually exists. The only thing the male side says exists is the exception, the one who is not subject to the signifier. Even in Amazonia, then, there would be consciousness of the exceptional one of this kind, even if there was not a single living and breathing male to be found.

Bryant wants there to be no singular exception. For that to be true, one has to argue intensional sets are impossible and/or non-existent. However, that seems rather hard to do. From the perspective of the subject, the signifier alone allows for the constitution of intensional sets. Insofar as being itself is subject to the letter, intensional sets can also take place. For a theologian, one needs truly for there to be only one intensional set and the most universal. It is preferable then that the only intensional set be that for any being, said being is subject to the letter. That generates a single exception. A theologian wants such a single exception demonstrable in this way—by way of how all beings are equivalent and equal. If there is only one intensional set, it is enough to set up a logic of exception on the other side of the logic of inconsistency, the feminine side of singularities.

This ontology of exception is true of a Lacanian realism of the letter, since it is not about detailing attributes that all things of a type have in common. We are not interested primarily in listing the particular attributes all snowflakes have in common. All snowflakes can be singularities with their own unique programming. The issue is that they have that programming and that any being has such programming insofar as it is a being. Beings are thereby not comprehended truly by their reflecting some universal term but insofar as they are involved in a specific lettering. What would be more devastating for a computationalist metaphysics would be if all things are singularities in the sense that there is no program that itself can be seen to give rise to irreducibly complex programs with their own singular bit strings. To avoid such a problem, we need need to recall why there are two sides of the letter. It is both empty set and program, intensional and extensional, etc.

It does not matter here if intensional sets are only a species of extensional ones. It is enough for each to be possible and constructible, for them to each be constitutive of existence as such, even if one only has one example of each. Ultimately—just as for Lacan—two sexes, two collections, are themselves based on the signifier. Insofar as we speak of beings as a whole and not just speaking beings, the letter is what makes possible the division between the two sides of ontology: incompletion and the logic of exception via the universal name, and inconsistency and singularities by way of the programmed lettering. In many ways, what Lacan has revealed to us is that, between the one as exceptional and the many as singularities, there is always two-ness, whether that is two sexes or the world in its relation to the Other.

Let us return to the ontology of the letter. Here, all beings are subject to the letter, just as speaking beings are subject to the signifier. That means that being itself is Janus-faced, just as speaking beings are in their sexuation. On the one hand, each being is a singularity. Originally, created being was a point. Multiplicity arose only by inclusion and iteration. This point is the ineffable and incommunicable name, YHVH. It is so unpronounceable that it is only pronounced as another word ('hashem,' for instance). It is made up solely of vowels. It is therefore missed when one says 'Jehovah.' In English it would be something like 'EAIA.' It is, for instance, a singular program as a singular and irreducible complex bit string. That means there is no being that is not such a program, made up of bits. On the other hand, there is always an exception, the Other, who is otherwise and outside of being by necessity. While every being is unique in terms of its actual bit string, for instance, each being is equivalent, insofar as all those bits strings are contained in a set, the brackets of the empty set. This is an intensional claim though which, given the nominalism we sketched earlier, it is about the name alone, the universal term and its implications.

The intensional set collapses into the extensional insofar as one can always force out of it anything, but that does not mean one does not have intensional sets as such. In fact, one seems to have nothing but finite sets, finite nature, and finite state machines in our world. Keep in mind here that, from the perspective of being, the Other is impossible, for the Other is not subject to the letter and could not be. If it is true that there is Other, it is false. If it is false, it is true. The Real Other, then, insists from outside of being.

The female side of the graph does exemplify the idea that there is no universal term (no universal universal). That means there is no way a finite discourse can account for itself. It is not closed off and cannot speak of its origin. The origin is always presupposed. One is always inside the letter and signifier. The signifier itself makes possible Lacan's graphs, because it is the name as pure differential term. The name can then be a property or a proper noun. Woman is a proper name, which is why any speaking being can be grouped under woman. All are different, but the group of men is always limited. It is limited by the name as attribute, of having something, of being marked in some way.

What Lacan himself misses here is that the name is also as a set, a bit string, a code and a program, which, in its iteration, gives rise to a particular phenomenon. Bryant only focuses on the inconsistency made possible by extensional sets and the signifier to the exclusion of the necessary other face of this Janus-faced structure. If there is an intensional set that speaks in universal terms and provides closure, it generates also the extensional and inconsistency. But, on the other hand, the inconsistent itself proves the rule that nothing escapes the universal term and finitude (recall the existential statement on the feminine side). Language is incomplete and also made up of singular terms. Each word is a differential relation to all others and, yet, one particular set of letters. If we try to restrict language to a set of rules, it can always be struck with inconsistency to show that a word is missing and forced out of the rule. What that means for beings is that, at any time, a new being can emerge. We do not just have, for example, the first ten positive integers; there are many numbers that can be named and computed. The positive integers will never be a complete set. At the same time, any new number will itself involve the base-10.

§19
Parallel Processing

I have used throughout cellular automata as a model for understanding how all phenomena are computational by nature. Many will probably have already thought that this model is lacking insofar as it only shows one particular program at work—whereas if each thing is itself programming, then a model that involves the parallel processing of multiple programs would be more appropriate for attempting to think through what is going on with living things and with being in general. Von Neumann, of course helped advance the revolution in computation by developing serial processing. Such serial processing involved the sequential running of instructions, one instruction at a time, in an ordered fashion. Parallel processing, by contrast, involves instructions for various programs being executed simultaneously.

Kauffman has already attempted to understand biological systems using the model of parallel processing. He writes:

> The network, insofar as it is like a computer program at all, is like a *parallel-processing network*. . . . In such networks, it is necessary to consider the simultaneous activity of all genes at each moment as well as the temporal progression of their activity patterns. Such progressions constitute the integrated

> behaviors of the parallel-processing genomic regulatory system. And, as we shall soon find, it makes very precise sense to conceive of and analyze the expected self-organized behaviors of such parallel-processing networks. Doing so, however, requires that we develop insight into some of the main construction features of the networks.[175]

What Kauffman has us imagine here is that each segment of the genetic code that codes for a gene might be running at the same time. We then can see the phenomena that develop out of the simultaneous running of programs as emergent phenomena, just as we saw emergent phenomena in cellular automata. However, each program is running here at the same time itself and would be like cellular automata, except that they now, in their results, interact, possibly. Life is thus an internal process where the genetic code in its subroutines executes different sets of instructions simultaneously, rather than sequentially.

One of the fascinating things about computer code is that it is always enacting instructions. When we read computer code and study it in classes, we are reducing it to a code that is a subset of spoken and written language. However, computer code, as it is in itself, always involves action. When we enact spoken language, we can just describe something or comment on something, but computer code is always executing, operating, and carrying out. It is not attempting to represent anything. It is not reciting itself to convey a message but rather in order to produce a result and link to other rules.

At the same time, outside of life there are necessarily other programs running, such as the weather. For Kauffman, such a model of parallel processing aids him in his desire to see life as arising out of blind and purposeless random processes:

---

[175] Kauffman, *The Origins of Order*, 442.

> Here . . . ask what orderly behavior emerges nevertheless. Note that such behavior is occurring in a *parallel-processing network*. All elements compute their next activities at the same moment. If we find order in random networks, then random parallel networks with random logic have order despite an apparent cacophony of structure and logic.[176]

It is not clear why parallel processing exhibits randomness. Programs run their instructions in a non-random fashion. The logic of their execution is not a matter of pure chance. Also, in a genetic code, not all elements compute at the same time. Some may, but some may simply be dormant and need to be turned on by others. It is also not clear that the genetic code is itself the same as a blind toss of a four-sided coin. Kauffman is right: there are emergent phenomena, but they can emerge from seemingly, purely deterministic programs like cellular automata. What we see in life is serial processing in addition to parallel. If there is parallel-processing at work, then that means that something like the environment itself might control development, insofar as activities outside of the genetic code have an influence.

There are, of course, other processes going on in a cell itself, as a cell does not just consist of DNA. Many experiments have, in fact, shown that one cannot simply insert DNA of one species into a nucleated egg cell from a different one and expect that cell to develop into the creature of the type associated with the extracted DNA. This is because there are all sorts of other machinery running other codes in the cell in parallel. The programs run at the same time or one may lead the other to activate in a distributed network. The DNA in a nucleus needs to communicate, for instance, with the DNA in the mitochondria. Both may be running their programs simultaneously such that, if the two are not matched well, processes cannot execute. The cell will not

---

[176] Kauffman, *The Origins of Order*, 192.

grow and will not produce energy if the coding is not correct, and that shows parallel processing itself at work fairly forcefully.

Many take such phenomena as evidence that genetic programming alone does not control how a fertilized egg, for instance, develops. However, it shows more so that more than just the nucleus, with its DNA, is running a program. When an egg has its DNA coding switched out in the nucleus, the egg develops in a way it would have anyway, probably due to that coding being presented in other parts of the egg. The egg still dies, because it does not have the right coding to produce the right proteins and other materials to cause functioning. Parallel processing is thus one of the barriers of cloning. One needs the right type of cell to clone (to clone sheep: a sheep cell, for instance), since each cell is an assemblage of areas that run their own specific programs that are unique to a particular type of cell. Even if the cell's hardware here is important, that does not mean that genetic programming is not controlling development. It just means we cannot think of the programming as not being run simultaneously in many different places at the same time.

Many point out that many animals have the same basic DNA and yet have different cell types, but this is due to the hardware in the cell having different programming and running differing programming at the same time. Creatures as different as worms and mammals have similar programming, but obviously look differently. These considerations show us that a sequencing of the code for a particular person or type must involve all the hardware/software of the cell itself. The key is fertilized egg cells, and cells of these types have different programming disturbed throughout. All of these different programs and subroutines must run at the same time and be coordinated to allow for development. One should not forget the amount of cascading change that can take place, because a change in one element will be limited by the fact that it is only one program of many running at the same time.

Of course, each human being has trillions of cells that all contain the same genetic code, but have also differentiated into different types of cells where different instructions are at work. Life is an assemblage of many different algorithmic processes that lead to emergent phenomena. Parallel processing is wider than the cell. Natural selection, even though at best a marginal phenomenon, would be seen as one algorithm inside Gaia, which would contain a very large (but not infinite) number of organisms simultaneously active. Natural selection as a program actually reduces complexity. It chooses only one type of thing out of the many that might be available. The criteria can change over time, but that already presupposes that the situation has changed. What remains reproduces itself and thereby begins to differentiate itself again due to the elaborations of the code itself. Natural selection thereby does not enable proliferation as much as reduce it. Natural selection is a way of also showing that not all that is possible becomes actual. Some things survive, but natural selection more so leads to the iteration of the same, since it only will select differently if the criteria changes, given some specific change in the environment. In this way, natural selection, insofar as it plays any significant role, is actually opposed to evolution. Evolution is occurring via the iteration of the code. Natural selection is then anti-evolutionary. That should be a shocking thesis. It is hindering rather than facilitating the development of life. The code has to find ways around what is called natural selection.

Think about a dog breeder. If a dog breeder wants small dogs, he keeps breeding smaller dogs together. He eliminates from the selection pool big dogs. This leads to only one type of thing, a breed. A selector takes out one thing and repeats with little to no change. Evolution works at the level of code that is contained at any event, even in the thing selected. The code is there, even with its dormant sequences. Natural selection, if anything, slows down evolution. However, natural selection also has to vary randomly to truly fit a Darwinian perceptive. In fact, we need to allow that natural selection is reducing complexity to explain what happens in between evolution leaps rather than the leaps themselves. Given the actual evolutionary record, changes have not come slowly and gradually. Again that means that natural selection is a name for what is slowing down evolution rather than for what is driving it. This is obvious since natural selection is just the tautology that whatever survives, survives. Selection is thus just a name to state that some things keep surviving. The record of life forms show that, for long periods of time, the same thing keeps surviving.

If random change was really at work, then natural selection would have to be random and the creatures would have to be randomly changing on a scale that leads to a different record of life forms. Also, the optimal solution from the perspective of Darwinism, when it speaks of natural selection, is that organisms will produce as many offspring as possible, but viruses do that already, so they have already achieved maximal evolution from a Darwinian perspective. These viruses do change, but not because they are being selected for as much as due to the code itself, its interaction with the environment, its flexibility, etc. Also if natural selection is an algorithm in Gaia, then, following Wolfram, we can say that its seeming randomness itself will be the function of rules, of a subroutine that plays out all the time. This is one of the most fascinating results of Wolfram's research. He has shown us that the more we increase the rules of a program, we do not necessarily produce more complexity. Maximal complexity can be produced by a few very simple rules. Thus, those who believe that things being governed by rules would yield uncreative order have been proven wrong. Chance is not needed to produce complexity. For that reason, almost all computation is equivalently complex. It also means that scale is irrelevant, as amoebas and humans both exhibit a similar complexity.

We do not have to speak of feedback loops operating as much as different programs running in parallel to each other. The perspective of Gaia itself shows us that all such parallel processes are subroutines of one code. A feedback in one program is probably, more so, a nested pattern program. Such massive parallel computing at the same time undermines any hierarchy as such, since no one program seems to be dominant. Natural selection would be just one algorithm at work. Insofar as we can look at things from the perspective of Gaia itself, we can see all these programs as part of the same set. That means that independently running programs are subroutines of larger program just as much as independent programs. We then have code within code in a mereology of bits, sets, and letters.

The interesting question is how individual programs are themselves segmented into subsets that make them distinct and individual. If life itself produces one overall system, Gaia—in which all living things function and work in tandem, engaging thereby in what looks like various feedback loops wherein the execution one program can effect another—then not only is Gaia itself developing using a similar computational model as a cell, but also it becomes more difficult to see a cell as an isolated, individual thing. Empirically, what separates a cell form the rest of the world is a membrane. We speculated earlier that the membrane may have merged with a replicated molecule in an act of symbiogenetic integration. The same is true of the origin of life itself. DNA code cannot operate without proteins, but DNA makes proteins. That means something distinct from DNA was needed from the beginning. Life presupposes the two. But if all is Gaia, then the sectioning of things into independent codes is somewhat arbitrary. All living things are subroutines of an overall program.

Gaia itself arises out of the microbial world by creating the materials that become our atmosphere, for example. We have an oxygen rich atmosphere thanks to early life, rather than life emerging first in such an atmosphere. Life also helps to influence the temperature on Earth. It influences the nature and contents of the oceans. The biosphere is like a cell except on a much larger scale and with a lot more moving parts. This program has ensured that, for instance, the amount of oxygen in the atmosphere has been about the same. It is the simultaneous running of all programs—rather than some feedback mechanism that works through force and causality between independent things—that accounts for how this occurs.

We then see that at each level there is a code and computation. There is code at the level of DNA, but Gaia is itself a computational system. Its coding is the set of all its subroutines. Order is found in the system insofar as it is made up of a set with many subsets. It is one, gigantic bit string, wherein there are clearly markers for different subsets. But this bit string is itself compressible to the very first cell, if not to the first DNA or RNA sequence with which life begins; for all of Gaia emerged from that cell and/or sequence. The rules are running simultaneously, even if, at times, there may be serial processing both within a subset and between subsets.

The rules operating at a global level are not necessarily the same as those operating at the local level. We should resist seeing life as simply fractal. Programs may have a nested structure in their results, but there are many possible such structures. Programs also can have other structures at work. Gaia on a global level might be a system more like a flame than a living thing. The subdivision of the subsets itself can be seen as a form of invagination. In an embryo, the original volume of the cell is constantly divided, such that one has a ball of cells, but the ball is the same as the original cell. We can than see the system as being like a cake that is sliced by its very functioning, but still one cake. No organism exists without countless programs running their algorithms all at the same time and thus being orchestrated in a symphony that is part of one scheme.

Of course, many will say that it is wrong to think of this like a cake that is cut up into pieces. That is fine, because the code itself is already a differentiated segment itself in any number of ways. When we try to understand parallel processing, we need to see how, from one large set of rules, there are many individual rules of different types at work at the same time. It is not a fractal model, where the same rule is running at all different levels. One can have fractal phenomena involved, but not necessarily and not necessary the same fractal. With a fractal model, we can zoom into and out of the phenomena at various scales and see the same pattern repeated. For a fractal, every part is like the whole and a microcosm of that whole. This is reflected endlessly, going up and down. Life and the universe do not appear to have such a structure. A tree does, for example, but it does not appear that even a fish does. In a tree, the tree grows using the same repeated pattern. From the bottom of the tree to its outermost branches, the tree is constantly splitting in the same way as it grows outwards. The new segments then repeat the same splitting and growth pattern.

Such fractal patterns are said to have irreducible complexity, but it is actually reducible to simple rules. That is true, but it does not mean we are within a microcosmos that is a mirrored reflection of the macrocosmos for all things. Not all things are self-similar. In fact, it may be that trees and plants are unique in this regard. Fractals thereby do not contradict the idea that the universe is regular and ordered. In fact, it makes things appear even more regular and orderly than they actually are. There is an order even in the seeming unruliness of the world, and that order is just as simple as fractals. This is because a fractal ultimately is a program, a set of rules that reiterate like any other program. We can write down the program for plants or clouds. This goes for code too. Code is not just a repetition of the same sequence over and over again. It has a more pseudorandom appearance than that.

A fractal means the same program is being run at every level and scale. However, look at the human body itself; it is made of trillions of singe cells each with its own very long set of rules inside of it. The human body is nothing like a fractal. It is not even like a human cell. In fact, even subsections of the human body, like the kidney or the eye, do not resemble it. The human body involves many different programs repeating themselves and forms that merge algorithms in a computational reality. At the same time, these algorithms operating simultaneously are interacting with each other. So even if we take Gaia or the universe as a whole to be unknown to us in terms of its programming, that does not mean there is not one perhaps long and perhaps very intricate program that comprehends it. The universal program for the universe must at some point be compressible, if only due to the regularity we see in the world.

Fractals might help us explain how clouds take their shapes, but they are not thereby at work in all phenomena. Although any individual algorithm might produce nested patterns, many others lead to random patterns. However, parallel processing does not exclude such processes themselves being subroutines of one overall program. It might be a long program. It might be one more involved than any we have yet encountered, but we should not see this large number of programs running at the same time as not being able to be part of one single set. A set can always have subsets, which, in turn, have subsets, etc., all the way down to the coding itself and its bits. In this regard, life on a global scale is not different from any other phenomena, such as a flame or a sun. We will return to the question of the set governing the entire universe and the program it is running.

§20
Entropy

With this model of parallel processing, we can approach what would be the most important parallel process (and it's not natural selection)—entropy. If there is parallel processing, then entropy is just one of those parallel processes. Given the universality of entropy, the main question about entropy is whether it is a specific program built into all programs, a function of all possible unfolding of programs, or an external program that runs in parallel to all programs and affects them. Entropy, of course, names the idea that the universe always increases in disorder, as per the second law of thermo-dynamics.

Many believe entropy explains why time unfolds in an irreversible manner. Many, at the same time, do not explain what makes entropy itself possible. They take it as a brute given, as an effect witnessed in all systems. That is, there are multiple explanations of entropy and exemplifications of it, but not necessarily a fundamental theory explaining what it is and how it came to be built into the fabric of the cosmos. Entropy allegedly names the tendency for all things to move to the most random state when there is no force or energy preventing such a move towards chaos. This view, in a way, presupposes that all things of all types on all scales are independent entities—each moving in its own trajectory and on its own path. Because things are moving in their own way, unities and order tends to be fleeting. However, this view takes all things as only being externally related. It therefore has to see ordered patterns as the result of chance itself or the result of some outside force. However, the order we see in the world is itself too prevalent. Things, except perhaps at the micro-level, are not constantly flying apart. And even when they do, they are always replaced. Our skin sheds cells and constantly replaces them. I do not see how that is due to externally related independent cells. There is systematicity here, and that systematicity means a program is at work.

Entropy says if one releases a gas into a box it will disperse in the box until the gas molecules are in a perfectly random state. Ice is water in a highly ordered state. Ice tends to melt into liquid water where the molecules of water are in a disordered state relative to ice. If one drops some ink into a glass of water, the ink will diffuse out randomly through the glass. However, entropy is not reversible, such that the gas, if it was in an ordered state before diffusing, will not (the probability is infinitesimal—it is not impossible) rearrange back into the previously ordered state. Entropy thus relates to information and probability insofar as there are exceedingly more possible states for things to be in randomly than for them to be in an order state. That is a brute fact of all phenomena. It is then a wonder that we have all the order we do. It attests to the programming involved, since, if atoms, for instance, simply moved about always randomly, the chances that we would have as much order in the universe as we do would be infinitesimal.

Things are tending to a disorder state, and yet unorganized configurations are not almost unheard of. There are almost infinitely (it is still a finite number, as all phenomena are finite state machines) more ways to be disordered than not. Many see random mutation in the genetic codes (the celebrated mechanism of Darwinism) as itself an example of entropy. Sagan and Schneider say that,

> if the world is a cellular automaton spawned by the mind of God, it is one in which the behaviors governed by the second law have been given a peculiar primacy. From an idealistic informational viewpoint, the second law may (like probability theory) be a name of, even a metaphor for, our ignorance; but from the point of view of observation, the behaviors governed by the second law apply not only to computers but to a vast array of real and imaginable systems that naturally "figure out" how to come to equilibrium . . . .[177]

What should be highlighted, besides the idea that even in the divine program entropy is somehow built in, is that we do witness things resist entropy all the time. Every living thing is a negentropic system. Life then is perhaps special in decreasing entropy and reducing randomness. Living systems take in energy from the outside and organize it. All of life on earth is dependent, ultimately, on the finite but vast supply of energy provided by the sun.

Things we witness in the world are not in a state of total entropy and chaos. Rather, we see how constantly phenomena defy—often for very long periods of time—entropic forces. Organisms are open systems that trade energy and information with the things outside of them. They are thereby not fully closed off from the world. Organisms are not alone this way. Flames take in oxygen from the surrounding environment to fuel themselves. It is, in fact, probably the case that one cannot find any system that is truly closed off from all others. Being closed off means only that, temporarily, the system is not receiving input. Isolated systems, like chemicals in a sealed test tube, are only temporarily and relatively closed off.

The openness of systems means, in part, that entropy is itself increasing, insofar as heat is given off. Systems create

---

[177] Sagan and Schneider, *Into the Cool*, 31.

waste products. However, the openness of systems does not mean that entropy is not necessarily internal. Often, internal mechanisms are mistaken for entropy as such. For instance, life codes for processes that lead to the termination of the organism. It is thus genetics itself that disallows a particular entity from reaching a specific age, rather than any external process or program built into the universe as such. Think here of the infamous 'telomeres.' Most human aging and lifespan issues are seen as connected to them. Telomeres form the ends of chromosomes and prevent the chromosomes from disintegrating or the chromosomes from interacting with each other and thereby becoming damaged. Every time a cell divides, chromosomes shorten a little. Telomeres prevent the chromosomes from unraveling and disintegrating during such division. Young people have longer telomeres than older people. This means that someone born with longer telomeres will simply live longer.

One could say that entropy itself is destroying the telomeres, but entropy does not control the length of the telomere. It may also be programmed into a cell how many times it is allowed to divide before undergoing senescence. In this way, entropy, again, is not responsible for break down, but rather the coding itself. There may also be specific subroutines in the genetic code that lead to the buildup of more waste and affect the material integrity of various other forms of life. If one removed those specific subroutines, then the creature would live longer, despite entropy constantly being at work. The issue was the programming of the subroutines themselves rather than entropy.

Of course, if entropy is encoded in everything and has specific programming, then, if one could find its programming and remove it, it would be ended. Interestingly enough, if there is a program that instructs a cell to stop dividing, it appears that these instructions can themselves be turned on and influenced by the environment; insofar as stress on the cell and on the organism may lead the cell to execute this information from the code, leading to a series of effects. In this way, the program that itself indicates how many times a cell is allowed to divide might currently be dormant. If one turns it off, then cells will be able to divide endlessly. However, even if entropy is part of internal programming, it may be a sequence so vital or so integrated that it cannot be removed.

Heat is the most fundamental kind of entropy, as heat is energy in a purely random state and thereby of little use to any other system. But if entropy is itself a function of rules, of programming, then, like Wolfram's Rule 30, chaos is a function and species of rules themselves and inherent in a particular set of them. Entropy produces heat due to the first law of thermodynamics, of course; energy as such is never created or destroyed but only ever converted into another form. Entropy does not decrease unless energy is brought in, but, at the same time, that energy is itself given off in heat.

Recall that cellular automata are, in principle, reversible. If one knows the rules, one can then return to the fist state of the system, the first iteration of the rules. Cellular automata thus can be programmed to reverse themselves and return to their initial states and begin again. At the same time, cellular automata may show that the number of patterns they can produce decreases over time, which quickly reveals how the automata are themselves compressible into a few simple rules. That means that a system has a limited number of patterns possible and, over time, reveals that. In this way, what would appear at first like a random pattern reveals itself to be well-ordered.

It is important to remember that at the Big Bang nothing but pure energy is posited by physics, such that one can only say that later on things emerged with mass as this primordial energy became stars and galaxies. Einstein's famous equation already showed that energy is a form of matter and vice versa. For this reason, many have wanted to say energy is the basic substance of all things, but energy itself, insofar as it is another name for matter, has mass and thus can itself be seen as discrete. Energy itself is found mostly as heat, and work thereby is itself a process that needs to be explained rather than an entity one should reify. Energy is the name for what does work and allows for work to be performed. It is said that the energy from the Big Bang has been expanding and diffusing ever since, but, at the same time, as it does so is being reduced more and more to heat and radiation, to purely random form, such that, in the end, the universe will itself die in a heat death and be reduced to nothing more than radiation. The energy from the Big Bang then is a purely condensed form that has been unraveling ever since. The question here is whether it has become more chaotic or actually taken on more and more detail. But if all is the unraveling from this point, then, each time an event occurs, it is actually the latest update of a process that has been happening for a very long time. Even if the universe then allows energy to be converted from one form into another and converts the overall amount, it is still due to entropy leading, on this view, to less and less organized forms of energy. This in itself also points to the finite nature of the universe.

We can always try to confirm the finite nature of the universe by noting how the night sky is not filled completely with stars or how the cosmic microwave background radiation does not have all possible wavelengths expressed. The finitude of the universe means it is a closed system cut off from any outside source that would imbue it with more energy to prevent heat death. The proposition of heat death has, of course, been taken as proof that the Nietzschean notion of the 'Eternal Return of the Same' is not physically possible. To recall Nietzsche's argument: if matter is finite, and time infinite, then eventually the same material configurations will appear over and over again. The Eternal Return of the Same is then a problem haunting any theory of finite nature—such as pan-ontic computationalism—since while space might be finite, it may be unbounded; and while nature is discrete, that does not exclude it goes on indefinitely.

Of course the eternal return might have the positive effect of resurrecting the dead back to life. However, given entropy, the chances of such resurrection appear to be zero or near zero due to the infinite other possibilities in such a universe. With entropy, the chance of things returning to a previous state is as likely as broken teacup suddenly reforming. But if there is infinite time, then even such infinitesimal possibilities become likely. What this view is asserting is that all the order we see around us, from galaxies to stars to planets to people, are all just isolated islands of order in a vast sea of randomness and heat and radiation. What is interesting is that this view then agrees that the universe was itself in a highly ordered state at the beginning and has only decreased in order and increased in randomness over time.

With all that being said, the eternal return of the same was never an inevitability, even given finite matter and infinite time. Take numbers as an example. All numbers can be seen as based on the base-2 or base-10. The counting and permutation of such numbers leads to infinites in which there is no return of the same. 2 is already different than 1, and 3 from 2. One can go on this way infinitely. One even reaches numbers that are themselves infinite, such as reals like pi. Cantorianism, therefore, in and of itself, was a death blow to Nietzscheism. The problem here is that while Nietzsche was one year older than Cantor, he received more attention than Cantor (too much, in fact), the greatest theologian of that generation. Cantor shows us that even from a finite number of terms and even from the empty set alone, one can have an infinity of combinations that all do not simply restate the first. There is difference even in repetition. Recurrence is undone. It is not impossible, but it is not necessary, even given the conditions Nietzsche described.

Given the infinity of combinations and infinities of infinites, the possibility of Eternal Return tends towards zero as much as does even a single recurrence. A Nietzschean view presupposes that reality is a closed system. However, the paradoxes we have already tried to engage with and articulated under names like Cantor, Gödel, Turing, etc., show us that reality itself is not closed insofar as it is incomplete. This means reality is perhaps only open to the future. It also means for us that, insofar as God is not a positive entity in the world (not one amongst created beings), God is only found in the deadlock and impasses (this would be a theological translation of Žižek's attempt to render the Lacanian Real qua impossible) found by way of the paradoxes a finite world finds itself in. It also means it is not closed off.

Entropy often, as previously mentioned, merely renames processes and gives us only the illusion that we have explained them. Entropy names something real, it appears, but that does not mean, as a name, it offers an explanation. Entropy is actually a name, most interestingly, for, again, why not all possibilities are actualized. Not all potentialities that one can imagine will be realized, and entropy is the name of that fact. Entropy thereby eliminates potentiality and reduces it to nil. People believe that if something happens, it had to be pre-figured in some way. Entropy shows us that not all truly was potential. This is, in part, as we have contended, due to the programming involved. Entropy, again, in this way, may itself be more so related to programming, to a program that self-delimits potentiality and possibility and ensures only the finite actuality.

Here, by finite actuality, we mean nothing more extraordinary than a leaf on a tree that stops growing at some point. If that leaf is computing and actualizing a program, then we need to know why it stops growing at the point it does. It seems that its self-delimitation is already coded in it such that it indicates to what extent it should grow. We would not say there that possibility itself is infinite in nature. For those who believe there is a pool of endless infinities of potentiality, entropy shows that window is constantly closed off and proves illusory. Reality is not full of endless possibilities. It is full of actualities. Most believe entropy is an inevitable part of the universe and would only be overcome entirely if the laws of the universe themselves were to change, such as may happen if the universe starts contracting and going backwards. However, this view also makes it a mystery as to why the universe should have started in such a low entropy state at all and from whence it came.

If entropy is part of the fabric of the universe and part of its programming, then we should be less surprised when things defy it due to their own programming. Both are thus programs. If entropy is an eternal parallel process, then it is constantly attempting to shuffle and randomize processes that, in the running of their programs, work against this. Entropy would then be inevitable, but, as information theory has shown, it has a rule and formula. What we see in the unfolding of programs such as cellular automata is entropy defied. This may mean that in programming itself, it is possible for a Maxwell's Demon effect to arise. Thus, while entropy might be a program, it might also be the face of what, within programs, arose as an effect of them just as we have a Maxwell's demon effect as well. The iteration of rules rules out disorder and chaos. As a result of rules themselves, some type of Maxwell demon could be seen as part and parcel of rule iteration in programs. That many systems are in non-equilibrium states and far from maximum entropy, especially in replicating systems, may show us how programming itself is both responsible for entropy as well as its very opposite.

When things are attracted together to form an ordered system, whether by way of tension or energy, entropy itself is defied, and Maxwell's demon seems to be at work. Entropy, of course, works on programs and the bit strings that any program of any type can be compiled into. We see order at the macro level, for the most part. It is not possible to create energy from nothing, such that entropy that functions on energy must itself be part and parcel of energy and also created with it. Even though we see order at the macro level, for the most part, at the micro level we see random states with no seeming evidence of a pattern to them:

> At the heart of Boltzmann's thesis is this realization: Practically all the microstates for a complex system are 'random' microstates. They are microstates with no evident pattern. Atomic positions and velocities are so evenly distributed that large-scale properties such as temperature and pressure are uniform through the system. (*RU* 67)

When we look at the motion of these microstates, we see that these microstates, these atomic motions, themselves can be conceptualized, following Boltzmann, as having random motion. We can then say that, while with microstates there is randomness, this randomness affects things at all further scales. What Boltzmann's insight about how to treat entropy in terms of the laws of motion itself shows is that entropy is most probably a random program running at the level of the microstates and all microstates, such that it affects all other scales and phenomena. What this means is that entropy is a program. It is probably a Rule 30 program itself that works out always at the quantum level or simply any level beyond a particular micro level.

Boltzmann, of course, is partly famous for thinking that our universe itself was created through a random fluctuation within a high entropy field of energy and radiation (*RU* 100). That means that it was only by chance that entropy was violated, given the infinite time that this vacuum state was allowed to persist. However, we have already addressed such a theory via our critique of the idea of a multiverse. Just as energy cannot be created out of nothing by natural processes, even a minimum entropy state is still something. It is not pure nothingness. Seth Lloyd offers a similar model as Boltzmann, except for directly using information theory. Lloyd argues the universe contains "random bits whose origins can be traced back to quantum fluctuations in the wake of the Big Bang."[178] For Lloyd, these random bits "serve as seeds of future detail ranging from the position of galaxies to the locations of mutations in DNA."[179] It is not clear why the Big Bang would give rise to random bits. Lloyd simply says that there are random quantum fluctuations that act like coin flips and generate an asymmetry of bits as a result. But we would then expect to see a universe with very little order result. Entropy measures information and thereby is related to bits insofar as the Shannon way of defining randomness is the same as the logarithmic function that Boltzmann discovered defines entropy. This shows that entropy is a part of information and informationally formed.

Energy, in its transformations into different forms, can, of course, be rendered as a processing of information and transpositions of information. Informational systems themselves are taking energy in and outputting heat, just as any other system. Nonetheless, entropy still, from this perspective, only describes how information is randomized, how bits would be randomized, rather than explain why that occurs. If all information is running some sort of computational algorithm and program, then is entropy just some unavoidable emergent effect of any and all programs as such? That does not seem true insofar as if one runs a cellular automata endlessly, it does not lead to more and more disorder in the patterns. We have suggested that entropy itself is a program being run at the micro-level of all things, perhaps at the quantum level; it is therefore not a dimension of information but a specific program interwoven into all things, insofar as it is woven into a microstate and the random motion of these microstates. Lloyd takes it as *the* fundamental program rather than a subroutine of a larger program. That is why the cellular automata we run for experimental purposes do not exhibit entropy, they do not

---

[178] Seth Lloyd, *Programming the Universe: A Quantum Computer Scientist Takes on the Universe* (New York: Vintage, 2007), 59.
[179] Lloyd, *Programming the Universe*, 59.

have these microstates—only the CPU, for instance, on which they are run does. We then see that, besides specific subroutines that build up waste or cause damage, genetic coding does not have the code for entropy, unless one of these subroutines is the same sort of Rule 30 program as we are saying is constantly being run at the level of microstates.

Information is randomized, since, at one level of the scales, a program is running that affects a scrambling of the code. That means that if we only have, for instance, in the genetic code, programs that run and cause damage or break down; that entropy is part of a family of such programs. It just happens to be the one running at the level of microstates and computing their motions. Given that entropy is primarily a program running at this level, it is not surprising that genetic mutation has only marginal effects. DNA replicates trillions of times, but the information remains basically, more or less, the same, despite such a large amount of replications. This is partly because other computational programs are running at the same time to prevent widespread error. There must be error-correcting codes here, as well. If entropy is but one program in such parallel processing, then it can be relatively neutralized.

Lloyd seems to think that random, quantum fluctuations are possible for everything we see, including the size and shape of galaxies. Per this view, the microstates are quantum, ultimately, and randomized. It is not clear where this random quantum state came from. Lloyd seems to think it is purely random, but we are arguing that, as Wolfram has shown, randomness is itself a function of rules. Lloyd argues that, at the Big Bang, the universe did a staggering number of operations on the bits present, given the primordial energy present at that time.[180] The degree of energy available at this time was amazing. However, energy does not emerge from nothing naturally. Lloyd imagines that, after an exceedingly short span of time, the initial bits

---

[180] Lloyd, *Programming the Universe*, 46.

were created; this initial energy inflated into a very large amount of information.[181] We then see, essentially—from a small amount of information that was the compressed form of the universe as such—information inflates at a staggering pace. Lloyd speaks as if all of this was random. The universe being in a low entropy state with a few bits of information that exhibits the universe in its compressed state should give us pause. Those bits are its essential programming. One should not look at what is happening here as random. The random fluctuations rather should be seen as themselves a program that is part of this development and woven into it—a program at the quantum level. If such quantum fluctuations are random, they will lead to deflation and disorder and not the order of the universe with its spiral galaxies and nebulae. Energy is not here simply being jostled around. It is unfolding per the program it is.

The massive energy itself here allowed for countless iterations of the program first articulated here in a timeframe our concept of a second cannot even describe. It was the energy itself that was the programming that enabled such accelerated iterations. It is wrong to say there is no order here. The mere fact that energy was in its pure form means it was not just heat and radiation. If it was just heat and radiation, then one could speak here of no order and maximum entropy. Rather, we are talking about a low entropy state. One then has a situation wherein the compressed state of the universe is itself in need of only a few bits to be described. As the universe expands from this initial inflation, it diffuses this energy, and thus its iteration of rules slows down, too. The computational time becomes something like what we know. However, the program built into that compressed state contained the Rule 30 program for entropy itself to work always at the level of microstates. Quantum and/or atomic particles are, on this view, shuffled around in a random way that affects everything. The amount of information and bits needed to describe this

---

[181] Lloyd, *Programming the Universe*, 45–47.

program is probably small, despite this random effect.

It should, again, give us pause that a long and complicated program is not needed here to explain things. Lloyd calls this inflation of information from the initial compressed program the 'Bit Bang.' Here, there is such a compression that, to speak of substance, is misguided, which is why it is best to speak of a name, an empty set. This was the first and only creation out of nothing of the first material and involved the concentration of all in all. It is space itself as a first spacing. From this space, with only the dimension of a name, all else follows. The primordial bit is where matter as we know it comes from. The Bit Bang itself is the consequence of the fact that the universe began at a point of total compression, a singularity, a point. Some would say that this rapid iteration at the Bit Bang cannot be explained using bits alone, such that one would have to say energy is another face of matter, and matter and mind are irreducible to information, to number. That may be true. Notwithstanding, it is an irreducibility that is not independent of information. It is an irreducibility that only arises due to all being informational in nature.

Information does not, in itself, have mass or charge, but there is not mass or charge or extension without it. One should not overestimate what is not informational—it is only ever a function of the information, for information is itself indifferent to matter. This is a dimension that Claude Shannon exposed, since Shannon showed how to render information as bits in such a way that this information makes sense without needing to represent something, refer to something, be true or false, etc. Information here is then translatable between different systems.

The singular, concentrated point referred to by Lloyd is the first creation, the Name of God. Given that the universe starts with a small amount of bits in its compressed state, we can see how the first law of thermodynamics plays out here. The overall amount of information here is the same in the same sense as all numbers are themselves products of the base-2 or base-10. In that sense, the total quantity of information does not increase or decrease. It can only be scrambled. Except we now see that its scrambling is only part of the programming, whereas other segments of the code are involved in the building of structures. We need more bits to describe the universe once it expands outwards for billions of years, creating more and more space. Nonetheless, that information itself is only a constant elaboration and iteration of the initial compressed program. The large scale structuring of the universe then is itself a function of the program found at the beginning of the universe when it was initially created in its state of raw energy out of nothing.

Energy cannot be created out of nothing by natural processes. Neither can information. This information itself is the creation of God, who withdraws from the world to make this point at which his name would be left as a mark. The compressed form of the universe is itself a bit string and also simply a set that contains that bit string. This bit string is the first moment of creation. Lloyd wants to explain the origin of this bit string via "the laws of quantum mechanics."[182] For all that, it is not clear where quantum processes can come from, unless one posits some sort of pre-existing vacuum. However, we have already dispensed with this idea via our critique of multiverse theory.

Because we disagree with Lloyd about the origin of the first bit string, we also disagree with how it led to what filled up the universe as a result, such as atomic elements, planets, stars, and galaxies. Lloyd thinks this is only a result of random processes. But there is still too much order in these phenomena for them to be the result of random and chance events. A galaxy, given the way the stars are arranged in it, is not in some disorder state. Randomness itself leads to disorder as seen with entropy. Galaxies are not random clusters but have hierarchies and circle around an axis. What is then responsible for the particular arrangement of things is the initial coding of the universe.

---

[182] Lloyd, *Programming the Universe*, 48.

Wolfram himself believes he has already shown how quantum processes can be shown to emerge from the simple programs by which he is trying to experimentally simulate the universe.

Instead of saying that the universe consists, at its origins in the Bit Bang, of a random bit string, one should say instead that that string is itself irreducibly complex. This bit string proclaims creation and determines its behavior. We can see here that nature does not destroy bits, but it includes them as part of its original programming, a program that runs at microstates and quantum level that scrambles information and thereby degrades phenomena. This pseudo-random motion then leads to atoms themselves at the next scales to jostle around. Here we have a "bit flow" such that the more iterations of a program one has, the more "bit transformations in a short time," the more heat produced as a result.[183] Heat is then the function of the running of programs.

Lloyd describes bit transformation in this way: "After the swap, the bit reads 0; it has been restored to 0, or erased. The second bit reads 0 or 1; it has a bit's worth of entropy—the same entropy as the first bit had before the swap."[184] Thus, one can permute bits, flip them, iterate them, etc., but information remains the same, insofar as it is still a matter of bits. Of course, if one adds bits to the programming, one has added information, in a sense. For this reason, as we saw with Dembski, the notion of the conservation of information must be limited, insofar as, in the one sense, information itself is just iterations of 0/1, but, in another sense, the longer a bit string, especially if it is irreducibly complex, the more information is involved. Thus entropy is, in our view, caused by an internal set of rules that is part of the original programming of the universe itself. Of course, things can break down and not be related to this microstate program that is constantly running. Two

---

[183] Lloyd, *Programming the Universe*, 71–76.
[184] Lloyd, *Programming the Universe*, 78.

or more sets of things can interact and thus alter each other, such as when a small organism is affected by the weather system.

Entropy itself is about information being scrambled, in the sense that the code of a thing is itself being broken down by the random program that at the micro-level is constantly undermining its running. As with all programs, there are still rules being iterated: the rules of the universe itself, not in the sense of a law, but a very specific program. The universe thus has given its programming an entropic subroutine that relates to all programs and information.

§21
Divine Name Verification
Chaitin's Omega and the Compressibility of Being

All programs can be ultimately compiled into zeros and ones. It is not surprising then that it was Leibniz who can be said to be the first one to discover how to write numbers in binary form. Today, we can, of course, write any letter we want in binary form, much less any number. Letters are thereby, in this way, turned into binary digits. In Hebrew, this was already the case. Leibniz wanted a 'universal characteristic,' wherein any possible language could be transcribed. 0/1 is the closest we can get to that universal lettering system. It may be fair to say that no one after Shannon, Turing, and von Neumann has truly examined what a bit-string is, how it functions, and what its nature is more than one of today's living geniuses, the inventor of Algorithmic Information Theory, Gregory Chaitin.

Chaitin has, in many ways, translated the paradoxes of incompleteness—such as Gödel's incompleteness theorem and the liar's paradox—into the field of computation directly. In this way, Chaitin has shown that there are non-computable numbers and that that is another sign that the universe is incomplete, does not activate all possibilities, etc. Chaitin's work on irreducible complexity and non-computable reals deserves particular attention for us, since, if the divine name itself is the compressed form of being as such, then Chaitin himself is the most prominent thinker of compression and the non-compressible. Chaitin has, according to his claims, exposed with his notion of the Omega number (Ω) an infinite real that is both non-computable and non-constructible.

The infinity of Ω is then more radical than the infinity one sees exhibited in the number pi (also a real number) and the Cantorian transfinite. Although pi cannot be expressed by a finite sequence, since it is an infinite number, pi is still itself computable and constructible, since it is compressible, even in its infinite complexity, to the relation between the circumference and diameter of a circle. The numbers, therefore, of a pi sequence, while seemingly random, are actually the result of a very clear rule. Chaitin speaks of how prime numbers appear in an apparently random way throughout the sequence of positive integers, and yet we can determine them.[185] Prime numbers themselves show irreducible complexity, given that they can only be factored by themselves and the number one. Their being seemingly randomly distributed throughout the number line is, perhaps, true, but they can be computed, as we saw with the cicada. While even today's computers have only been able to compute pi to a relatively small number of decimal places, every additional decimal place is added per a clearly defined rule. In this way, one would learn what is, for instance, at the millionth decimal place, but, at the same time, the basic program and rule iterated would be the same. The pi computation then determines an infinity of decimal places, the infinity of pi contains an "infinity of information," but, at the same time, it is always compressible to the same program, despite its randomness (*RU* 230).

Randomness means that there is no reason why one number or bit is in its place rather than another being in that place. Randomness means there is no reason for the bit or number that comes after the previous one and no indication it would be next in line. Everything is contingent here

---

[185] Chaitin, *Meta Math!*, 14.

and without reason. All is unpredictable. Notice the difference with Wolfram. Wolfram is not saying that all is unpredictable, but it is simply not knowable in advance. There is a reason why one thing follows another, and it is due to the iteration of rules. Things do emerge, since one has to run the program to see how the rules will play out. Here, emergent phenomena appear as a glider does in a cellular automaton, but it is from rules rather than a purely arbitrary occurrence. The infinity of, for example, positive integers is the same. There is a very simple rule for generating such numbers, even if each number has its own interesting properties. It is also not a random sequence. If one speaks about the infinity of odd numbers, one knows no number in that sequence is going to end with a two.

But with Ω, one cannot make such claims. It is entirely opaque until one would begin delimiting particular decimal places, and, even then, one would have infinity to go. Chaitin's Ω has no compressible program made up of simple rules. There is no shorter program for it. It is not compressible, and that means the number has as many bits as would describe it in the program itself. The program that would compute it is as infinite and as complexly as Ω itself. That is to say, an Ω number is a both a number and program bit string that is the same length and the same complexity. It is an infinite sequence of numbers and bits in random order that is not, in any way, reducible to a finite set of rules as, for instance, pi is. Ω thus has infinitely many digits, such that one cannot determine where they are if one is given even part of the bit string making up an Ω program. It would take an infinite amount of time to compute Ω, and one would have to do it one step at a time. Ω thus names pure, infinite randomness and complexity. Even if one had, for instance, a million bits of an Ω number figured out, one would still have an infinity of bits to determine, and those bits would be in perfectly random order. Ω bit strings are thus indistinguishable from flipping a coin.

We can never know, then, the Ω number, but Chaitin argues we can know such numbers do exist and must exist.

Ω poses a problem even for God's own omniscience, given that other infinite numbers as constructible are reducible to a knowable rule. Here one needs an infinity of time to construct the number. Of course, God, as timeless and eternal, would possibly grasp an infinity at once, such that even a random infinite would to be to God no different than the base-10 itself. Here, we can also wonder why anyone should even agree with Chaitin that Ω numbers exist. They cannot exist in a finite universe.

Chaitin believes that most real numbers are Ω numbers, such that numbers like pi are part of a negligible, almost non-existent set of real numbers—ones that are computable. Cantor's argument that one always presupposes any number as preexisting in a predefined domain may not work with Ω, since the number itself cannot be produced. If the number cannot itself be produced or even written in the same way as, say, a number with a million digits can, then it is not clear why its existence must be presupposed. Ω itself may be nothing more than the program to flip a coin an infinite number of times. In fact, even in the infinity of Ω, we can sill always know that 0/1 will happen ½ of the time. Thus, in its lawlessness, it is no more lawless than flipping a coin. Every time one did so, one would come up with a new Ω.

Ω is not compressible in any sense and infinitely so. Its randomness means it has no organizational pattern running throughout. Even if one did, by chance, find some pattern in it, there would still be infinitely more of it randomly to work out, thus rendering that local compression irrelevant. Of course, those advocating a multiverse have to advocate that if all of being is computation, then it is computing an Ω number. They would then have to argue that our universe is but a localized sequence of this infinite sequence. Our universe, then, might seem regular and structured, but within the context of a random and infinite bit string, it is but a blip that does not prevent its non-compression. If being can be characterized by an Ω computation, then the Name of God exists truly as something unknowable and ineffable. It exists as an infinite name—not a delimited, empty set that is also finite lettering. It also means, as per Meillassoux, that being itself is infinite and eternal and totally random. If all of being is infinite and computing an Ω computation, then it will never end, and anything is possible. Things that happen truly do not happen for any reason, and all is random. The universe has a program, but it is infinite, and there is no way we can conceptually compress it into something shorter than that infinity.

While I am not sure that Chaitin believes Ω characterizes all of being as Meillassoux does (Meillassoux never refers to Chaitin, even though Meillassoux's interpreter and translator Ray Brassier does, as we shall see), Chaitin does believe that Ω characterizes numbers and mathematical reasoning as such. Chaitin believes that Ω shows that mathematics ultimately has no proper structure and no ordered reason for the way it is. It is not ultimately reducible, for instance, to the base-2 or the base-10 and its permutations. It is, for Chaitin, the other way around, just as for the multiverse theory. The base-2 and base-10 and all other numbers appear randomly out of the infinite background of Ω. Just as for Meillassoux, anything that appears does so for no reason and without cause. There is total chaos that is purely random, even if it has local instances of structure, and out of this chaotic fount that is being comes the eminently compressible and finite world that we just happen to exist in, just as the mathematics that we engage in as children (and even later) is but a random blip in the sea of Ω.

Interestingly, the only specific Ω that Chaitin has claimed to determine is the probability of the Turing Halting problem. Chaitin claims the probability of the Turing problem is itself an Ω number. That is, it is an infinite real number between 0 and 1 that cannot be fully known. If it were a program, it would itself never halt. It contains an infinity of bits. In claiming an Ω number characterizes the probability of the halting problem, Chaitin is saying that Ω, despite its infinite randomness, can be defined and referred to as a particular number. This particular real number is, of course, called, appropriately, 'Chaitin's constant.' Recall that the halting problem is the problem of knowing in advance if a program will stop and produce a result or go on forever, whether in a loop or simply by endlessly computing. Turing's famous result was that one cannot know in advance if any program will itself halt or not. There is no program that can determinately compute for such information. As Brassier notes, this was stunning, given that a Turing machine illustrates universal com-putation

> that could not be computed by finite means in order to show how even a 'universal computing machine' capable of duplicating the operations of any possible computer could not compute in advance whether or not a given program would carry out its task within a finite length of time or carry on indefinitely.[186]

In other words, we see that even the universality of the computer yields to the logic of exception. There is always at least one program that cannot be articulated and that is the program that would indicate if all can or cannot be computed in advance. If one did have such a program that could tell one in advance if programs could halt, one would not be able to check the program doing the checking; but then one needs a program for that program, etc. Of course, with programs of finite length, one can simply run the program and see if, in fact, it does halt or not. One may not know in advance; it would be computationally irreducible then, in Wolfram's terms, but it is not impossible to know. It is because of infinity, of allowing programs to run over infinite time, that Turing was able to produce the problem he did.

---

[186] Ray Brassier, "Nihil Unbound: Remarks on Subtractive Ontology," in *Think Again: Alain Badiou and the Future of Philosophy*, ed. Peter Hallward (New York: Continuum, 2004), 50–58, 55.

Chaitin's constant is about taking all of the infinite programs and randomly picking one. The constant tells one the probability that one has picked a program that halts. Following Brassier then, we can say that Chaitin's constant is itself simply a reformulation of Turing's halting problem paradox in algorithmic form.[187] That is, there is a fundamental identity between Chaitin's constant and paradoxes of incompletion. Chaitin's constant details the incomputable, but it also gives a numerical expression to what such paradoxes say. Incomputable numbers here mean nothing more than that there is not a finite set of rules for generating the number. Chaitin's constant is thus another name for incompletion itself. One could say that if the liar's paradox were to be given mathematical expression, it would be, as a number, like the Chaitin constant. Just as the liar's paradox is a restatement in common language of Gödel's paradox, the incompletion seen in the liar's paradox is as incompressible as an Ω number yet different from Chaitin's constant. They would be as equivalent as Gödel's notion of incompletion and the liar's paradox. This may show that incompletion haunts every and any inscription and writing.

More importantly, it shows us that incompletion is not just connected to undecidability, but that it is connected to inconsistency in the sense of infinite randomness and complexity. Inconsistency is thus not simply another name for how thing are collected into an extensional set, but also for how things are connected to the randomness of such a collecting as such. Insofar as incompletion characterizes being, it means that the finitude of the world is connected to infinite complexity, even if finite is another name for its relationship to inconsistency. They are two sides of the same coin and, somehow, two names of the same thing. We can then agree and answer 'yes' to Brassier's rhetorical question:

---

[187] Brassier, "Nihil Unbound," 56.

> Isn't there a case then for maintaining that Ω indexes the 'not-all-ness' (*pas-tout*), the constitutive incompleteness whereby the Real punctures the consistency of the symbolic order, at least as much as the excess of the void does for Badiou?[188]

Except for us, it is not a matter simply of the symbolic order, but of being itself. It is the Real here as impossible—the impossible otherness of God in God's self-effacement—since it is something otherwise than being that ruptures the order of creation and renders it incomplete and fractured. That does not mean there is simply randomness as such, for finite bit strings, even if irreducibly complex, can be generated by rules. Their irreducibility is not then incompatible with rules and their iterations. This is another way of saying that contingency and creation are not incompatible with finitude and an ultimately compressible program for all of created being. Despite Ω, we do not find a world in which things randomly occur. All appears regular and patterned rather than the result of coin flips. There is undecidability and excess, but not in the sense of purely aleatory events that occur, and that is because the reverse side of Ω is, again and always, the empty set. On the other side of inconsistency, there is the incompletion characterizing an incomplete and open universe with intensional sets and finite state machines.

The world itself is not random, by all appearances, which means that inconsistency and incompletion are themselves not incompatible with the divine Name of God, with a world that is itself the articulation of a particular finite program. Given its random infinity and non-compression, Ω is strictly esoteric, unknowable, and impenetrable. Only an infinite mathematics would be able to truly comprehend it, and not any finite program that we can construct or any set of mathematical axioms we could

---

[188] Brassier, "Nihil Unbound," 57.

list. Of course, all the programs we work with, no matter how long, are ultimately finite. Most are compressible to smaller programs. There is then a finite sense of non-compression. A finite program is non-compressible if it cannot be seen as the iteration of a smaller program or defined using fewer bits. Science itself likes to find reducible programs that will show how many other phenomena arise. When we say that our universe is intelligible, we mean that it is not random and has order and structure, but that it is compressible.

Ω, on the other hand, is the secret number that cannot be written and cannot be known. If Ω, as infinite, occurs without reason and as pure randomness, then, by relation, we can see finite incompressible bit strings as themselves existing without reason and perhaps on the very basis of Ω. Given the randomness and infinity of Ω, we cannot predict what the next bit would be, even if we had already written down a million of its bit places. That means the next bit will appear as randomly as tossing a coin. There is no prediction, then. Ω renders predictability null. Ω is thus a purely mystical (some will say mythical) number that is ineffable. It can be posited, but not truly known. Ω would then seem to be a very good candidate for the Name of God—perhaps even a better one than YHVH. Ω contains much more interest as a candidate than YHVH, it would seem, since it involves total ineffability, total mystery, etc. Perhaps, we could say that Ω expresses the name of God in its infinite dimension while YHVH does so in its finite dimension. The problem is that if Ω characterizes the universe and being as such, then being has no purpose, no sense, and no structure. All is random existing things. It thereby seems to preclude God himself.

Chaitin, using mathematics and his own human cognitive powers, speaks of Ω, but even Chaitin cannot know what Ω is as such. If Ω is the name of God, it means that God left us with an arbitrary world. One we should not, in principle, have any hope of understanding. Any local principles we could delineate would themselves just be one random result in an endless chain of results. Of course, given the infinite randomness of Ω and its inscrutability, one can only point to it. One has taken, on faith alone, that it does exist. If it is, it just is in its infinity. After all, one can never know one has named it or that one is inside of it (if it is the program all of being is computing). Given its infinity, it is not clear why it would not contain all possible information, all possible numbers, and all of mathematics, for example. Nonetheless, it is a wisdom we cannot access, because we cannot ever know its full, infinite computation and thereby cannot know what parts of it are to mean. No one can delimit and define Ω, so no one can say if it does exist.

Ω would thereby be interpreted by Meillassoux (if he were ever to engage with it) as not the Name of God, but what substitutes for God himself. Ω would then be God and not the name of God as we understand the term. Ω is a way of stating, again, the absolute infinite, it would seem, an infinite so infinite in its meaning that it is beyond the transfinite and definable and constituted infinite itself. This is why Ω does not pertain to our world, it is Other than our world.

Ω is proposed on this reading as the creator. We can then say that Ω is a Name of God, but only in the sense that it names God in his absolute infinity without relating that to God's actual creation of this world. This world is finite, such that if Ω expressed how this world works, it would be random and structureless. Given the pattern and order we see in this world, Ω cannot be the Name of God as we have defined it. Ω names God as absolutely infinite. Whereas aleph and lowercase omega named the transfinite for Cantor, Cantor reserved the term 'absolute infinite' for God. Ω is another name for this absolute infinity. It is an infinity treated as such as to be so infinite it cannot be comprehended and known. It is beyond any constructible infinite and beyond any computable set of rules. It therefore could not name anything that occurs in being, as such, and only what insists beyond and outside of Being. This is why finite and irreducibly complex bit strings on the background of Ω

appear to appear for no reason. They are created. If something happens for no reason, it comes from nothing as such. There is no true preexisting cause.

Omega itself as a number, as infinite bit string, cannot rule out the void. It is based on nothing, on the void, insofar as it is based on an iteration of bits, even if infinite and random in length. Thus, the empty set is itself from nothing; the nothing is before the empty set, and is irreducibly complex as a bit string, whether we write it as 0 or 01. In other words, the bit string 0 is irreducibly complex and thereby appears for no reason. It is created form nothing. Even an infinite bit string that is irreducibly complex made of 0 and 1 is still something created out of nothing. Brassier discuses the relation between irreducibility and what we discover in the world in this way: "There are non-reducible, improbable mathematical truths everywhere, quasi-empirical 'facts' that are gratuitously or randomly true and that can only be integrated by being converted into supplementary axioms."[189] Brassier believes Chaitin shows this by showing that in an Ω bit string one still cannot say in advance what irreducible bit strings, even if finite, would belong to that set. However, it appears that we can say that, as infinite, an Ω bit string would have to, at least, include any bit string. In other words, if we take all the subsets of Ω, they would contain, by force of Ω's own infinity, all possible numbers and finite, irreducible bit strings. That is why Ω is not God and only the name of God, concerning God's absolute infinity. The world we have is not an embodiment of God in this absolute infinity. It is a creation of that absolute infinity.

Zero itself is not compressible, because it cannot be described in fewer bits than the thing itself. It is therefore, in Chaitin's terms, a random number. Randomness has been identified with the incompressible. Many other numbers are therefore also irreducibly complex, insofar as their bit strings cannot be further compressed. They thus are, for

---

[189] Brassier, "Nihil Unbound," 57.

no reason, on this reading. But if that were true, then things would suddenly pop into existence. We know that there are random bit strings expressing integers, and those bits strings are irreducible, and yet all positive integers are themselves produced by iterations of the empty set. This means that there is a finitude adhering to all numbers and things, despite Ω, and that we cannot rule out that Ω is nothing more than the idea of randomly iterating 0/1 over infinity (merely a program that states to infinitely flip a coin). Chaitin himself has put forth that, even if we can say that any irreducibly complex bit string is for no reason, we can only grasp a finite number of such bit strings by way of any finite program. In other words, in any n-bit bit string and program, one can only discuss and show an irreducibly complex bit string of no more than n bits. This seems wrong insofar as, with 0 alone and its iteration, we can be lead to bit strings that are irreducibly complex and much more than 1 bit. That is to say, Chaitin, like multiverse theory, is arguing that Ω exists and precedes any finite entity. For us, it is actually the reverse. This is why one needs to first examine Ω by way of the program stating to flip a coin infinitely many times or to express every possible point on a number line or relation between points on a curved surface.

Even if Ω itself presupposes the primordial bit 0/1, Ω is a name of God, but it is not a name more profound or important than YHVH. God has many names, and these names, other than YHVH, refer to God's attributes. Ω is thus an attribute, as we have stated. It is God as absolute infinite, as absolute creator. Ω does not exist beyond this naming. Ω refers to that which is, in itself, beyond Being. Ω, as a name, is itself bound by the finite, like any other name. Ω is then, in this world, only a name of what cannot be known. Ω does not exist in this world. Ω only insists from outside of being, and that is because Ω names God as infinite creator. I believe this is the conclusion Cantor would come to. There is no Ω in this world, just as there is no set of all sets. Certainly, one can refer to this idea and attempt to define it. However, the very idea proves itself unable to be rendered in this world.

God is often identified, especially by pantheists, with the set of all sets. Rather than approach God in this manner, Cantor, of course, approached God as the absolute infinite beyond any transfinite cardinality. Ω is the ultimate transfinite. It is the transfinite of complete disorder and chaos, the transfinite as perfect entropy. Now, some will say that there are an infinite number of Ω numbers insofar as an uncountable infinity of reals can be Ω. True enough, on the face of it. However, keep in mind that, in a sense, this was already known by way of number lines, once real numbers were known. Between zero and one, there is an infinity of infinities of real numbers. The same is true of all spaces between any positive integers on a number line. Such a view presupposes that one can divide a number line infinitely. Beyond this not being possible in physical reality (given that one would need to somehow get past the Planck length, need an infinitely shrinking knife, etc.), this viewpoint simply repeats Zeon's paradoxes. Reality is discrete, but it is also continuous. That continuity means that we have to, at some point, show how the discrete lead to continuous. Otherwise, those arguing that the continuous is primary will win the day and point to such infinities as abstractions.

All of these infinite reals are themselves random, infinite bit strings. They are therefore made of the finite, which explains the self-delimitation into finite numbers, a finite world, and finite mathematics and why there will only ever be one Ω ever discovered. Any other Ω derived by future mathematicians, such as Chaitin's constant, will be soon revealed to be the same exact number and indistinguishable from Chaitin's constant. That is, even if Chaitin's constant must be, for instance, a number between 0 and 1 as the probability of a computer program halting, if one had the infinite bit strings of each Ω, many would say one could differentiate them through diagonalization. If one uses base-10 numbers instead, the diagonalization seems as obvious as it does for differentiating even and odd transfinite sets. However, all the Ω numbers have the same cardinality, and that is why, at one level, they are equivalent. They cannot have a different cardinality than the set of positive integers. Diagonalization, of course, cannot be completed by us. We could never do an infinite diagonalization between the omega numbers. It is only by noting the lowercase omega that we could stop numbering, and by writing the aleph that we could note the equivalence between lowercase omegas. In this way, Chaitin's Ω is no different than Cantor's aleph, insofar as it is a written number. It is rather the randomness that is unique here. We cannot come to the non-computable real. It will never compute. That is why we are left with the symbol Ω, just as we are left with the lowercase omega and the aleph for Cantor. Also, because it relates to the halting problem, it then shows us the failure of diagonalization to be truly done by us, until its end reflects on the nature of finite numbers and finite programs. We cannot know in advance if a program will halt, even though it is finite. Finite, irreducible bit strings appear as if for no reason. Chaitin is thereby in agreement with Wolfram's notion of computational irreducibility. One cannot know what will happen until the thing plays out. One cannot know in advance where things are going.

That one cannot complete diagonalization means one has to count numbers themselves to see where they will lead. One must write them. Inscribing them is irreducible. One has to put in an effort to get any number, even if one does so on the basis of other numbers. To know how to compile a specific program into zeros and ones, one needs to specify it as such and list all the bits. All information is irreducible—not just mathematical information—even when it is finite. Nonetheless, this irreducibility of information does not preclude that there are programs that produce results.

Any specific set of zeros and ones is a structured set of integers and can itself express an integer in binary form. We know, at the same time, that one has rules for the generation of any and all integers. For this reason, at the same time as accepting what Chaitin has said, we can say that n bits can yield for us much more than n bits of information. Or we need to say that all information itself is compressible to the primordial bit itself, just as all integers can be generated by iterations of 0. There is no structure in 0, for example, just as there is no structure in any other finite, irreducibly complex bit string. They do not have any structure. However, that does not mean they are not produced and made possible by a structure.

There is no pattern at the level of the bit string in its irreducible complexity as a thing. Irreducible bit strings are things, in themselves, without structure. Notwithstanding, even those things in themselves are made up of bit strings and can give way to a rule that yields them. We can comprehend such finite bit strings, even if we cannot comprehend Ω numbers with their structureless, infinite strings. Knowing where any particular bit is, even in an infinite bit string of this type, is a matter of chance. We can only know what it is listed out. Deductive reasoning does not get us anywhere here, despite these things being part of mathematics. At some point, certain things have to be accepted as they are. That is why, despite all the numerology throughout human history, it was not until Peano that one truly understood how all numbers are generated by 0 itself. The numbers were things in themselves that appeared for no reason. Several theories had to be tried, until, finally, the code was cracked. This is also why the insight that all can be mathematized—that anything can be expressed in mathematical terms and as a mathematical structure—is so important for metaphysics and theologies, even if it is not important to the scientist. It shows that anything in its thing-ness is such due to this quality. It is a finite bit string as such—and probably irreducibly complex.

While Chaitin often speaks as though he is the true heir of Leibniz, he actually is striking a blow at Leibniz and the principle of sufficient reason. He wants us to see the irreducibly complex as appearing for no reason, as just being there. However, as we saw, irreducible complexity is not itself incompatible with there being simple rules for generating it. These are two sides of the same coin. From the one side, things are singularities, and on the other side they are a function of iteration. In this way, as Paul Davies argues, Chaitin's theory leads to the need for empirically discovering mathematical truths rather than deducing them.[190] Incompletion and randomness in mathematics mean that we discover things through brute repetition, iteration, discovery, observation, etc. If we cannot know things in advance, that is not because the answers will be random and inconsistent as such, but due to the need to see how things are actually computed.

The properties of numbers on this view are empirical. This is why we say they are created rather than being eternal. This is precisely what the positive integers always reflected back at us. The number seven has properties which lead to all sorts of numerological attributions of perfection (it is prime and yet the sum of 3 and 4, which are the end part of the sequence 1234, which adds up to 10, and therefore, unlike 5, is perfect, as 5 is only 3 plus 2) and, at the same time, is a brute fact. The principle of sufficient reason is therefore not truly overthrown here, because there is no Ω in our world. To say that our knowledge is limited is not interesting. What is interesting is to find the limits of being and existence themselves. To find the origins and limits of being is what is at stake truly, and not what limited human cognition can know. Integers then, for instance, insofar as they can be articulated as irreducibly complex bit strings, appear for no reason. At the time, like any other integer, they are part of a clear and definable sequence. This is also why creationism seemed to be the only possible answer for explaining living organisms. Each living organism is an irreducible bit string, for instance, in its DNA sequence. It therefore appears, for no reason, as created.

---

[190] Paul Davies, *The Mind of God: The Scientific Basis for a Rational World* (New York: Simon and Schuster, 1993), 133.

Since chance itself cannot reasonably account for such complexity, one needed to posit God. We are suggesting that God is always in the picture as creator, precisely because, in addition to this irreducible complexity, there is the Name of God, the compressible program that the universe is running. Life itself, as we suggested, in its entirety is compressible into the first cell out of which all of Gaia arose. In this way, even if one can epistemologically posits an infinity of irreducible, finite bit strings, this does not exclude that there is a program for generating them. That seems illogical, given their irreducibility, which is why informational irreducibility must be seen as not simply expressing or relating to Ω, but also to Wolfram's notion of computational irreducibility. In other words, we have irreducibility in the sense of not knowing in advance how a program will unfold and that the results of that program itself might be so complex as to not be compressible, despite arising out of other things.

Ω names an incomputable real. We should take that literally. It names God as incomputably real beyond being. Creation, in its dynamic computation, is thereby always fueled by that self-withdrawn real. It automates and structures creation while also allowing it to count and produce the contingent. It will be precisely errant, while, at the same time, being a product of rules. God's self-withdrawal strikes being with the void and, in doing so, maintains God at an unreachable distance and enables the nameless one, whose very name comprehends the world itself. By naming the void in being, one comes as close to the truth as one can. Just by naming Ω, we do so, as well. God is thus that which must be acknowledge and cannot just be a name, as with Ω, since if God is possible, God is necessary. God is unthinkable and yet makes all being possible and intelligible by leaving behind his name in His act of self-bracketing. The unthinkable as the inscrutable is therefore the source of delimitation itself. God self-delimits himself in order to enable the finite, which itself is an elaboration upon the void, the primordial bit, 0/1.

0/1 is itself not compressible, such that we see here how the finite and infinite cross each other through this idea of irreducible complexity. Notice that, per Chaitin's theory, something that cannot be compressed must be taken as random. For Chaitin, Ω is an example of perfect randomness that is unpredictable and inconsistent. We say that inconsistence is part of divine insistence itself. It is another name for the pure excess of creation from the void. What is on the other side of the void itself is inscrutable and in the excess of the creation. It renders creation itself incomplete and leads to the undecidable and the open. We are always caught between the absolute infinitude of the Other and the finitude of the computational universe. There is an abyss between the two. We will have to ask if we should simply shrug our shoulders and say that the abyss is unreachable or if being is headed in another direction, the Omega Point. That is an omega that may in itself be a name for how Chaitin's omega itself can be real and part of this world—no longer unknowable, but now actualized in some sense. Nonetheless, we are on this side of that Omega Point, for now.

For Chaitin, as far as Ω is concerned, any real number does not have a finite representation, like pi. For us, Ω is just another name for the program that randomly flips a coin endlessly. The symbol is a finite presentation of the real number itself. Every time it runs, Ω appears. If we ran it infinitely, we would reach all the possible Ω numbers. This is why Fredkin says that real numbers and the transfinite can exist in Digital Philosophy, despite its notion of finite nature.[191] In our world, then, we can agree with Dembski, who says that, "Noncomputable functions are an abstraction. To be non-computable, functions have to operate on infinite sets" (*ID* 220). The only way in which there are infinite sets, for us, is in terms of their radical openness

---

[191] Fredkin, "A Physicist's Model of Computation," *Digital Philosophy* [weblog]: http://www.digitalphilosophy.org [retrieved January 20, 2012].

and not in terms of their having an actual infinite number of members. That is why, when we actually compute, we use integers and numbers and thus work on finite sets and run finite programs with finite bit strings. It is not here just a matter of abstraction, as we are arguing that such infinite sets are themselves a function of the finite. They are a function of 0/1. They therefore exist as names, and can name even that which only insists.

The Name of God is thus an irreducibly complex but finite bit string. Our world is not an infinite omega. There is thus, at least at first, only one universe. There is no multiverse. The void itself strikes it down. Our world exhibits reducibility and compression according to all our observations. Observation itself is coupled with such reducibility. Observation will not happen in Omega. Irreducible complexity, in its finite form, does refer to brute facts, but that is only one side of the Janus face. They hold as irreducibly complex and appear in their glory as things in themselves. Nevertheless, that does not mean they are not also part of the world, at the same time.

It is interesting at this point to bring the Anthropic Principle into play; for if the multiverse or being itself is somehow characterized by Ω, then the type of universe we have is infinitesimally possible. It is then wondrous and miraculous that we actually exist in it. Life would be incompatible with other possible universes. One can imagine given this sort of infinity—one with totally random occurrences at all times, such things as people suddenly floating away. One can imagine a universe with just a single, living, Boltzmann brain. That we happen to live in a universe so well-ordered that leads to life is then truly inexplicable from an Ω perspective. The appeal of Ω is that it seems to exclude beginnings and ends and, in its infinity, renders being eternal. Since the only way to make and construct the omega numbers is to list them bit by bit, they will never end. If it never ends, it may never have begun. If reality is infinite and one is within such a computation, it would presumably not have a beginning either. This is why its dependence on being counted out must be seen from the perspective of the bits themselves. The empty set, 0, always presupposes the void it includes (it's a set containing nothing). It involves, necessarily, a relation to absence and negation in its very structure. It is always related to its place. And that relation to nothing is what requires anything built out of if it to be ultimately finite—even Ω.

While Chaitin wants to see Ω in its infinite irreducibility and complexity as showing, like Gödel did, that a total theory of mathematics and existence is not possible, that view looks at things from the perspective of axioms rather than from the perspective of the very material that axioms can themselves ever regulate. For Chaitin, the infinity of bits in Ω are irreducible brute facts that one cannot deduce from any principle, but that does not mean that, as stated, written, or produced, such facts do not themselves depend on a minimum materiality—the minimal materiality of the empty set. We account for what appears for no reason with numbers, sets, and computation itself.

These points are similar to the points we are trying to make with evolution. Evolution itself might lead to irreducibly complex organisms, but it is on the basis of a program, not on the basis of pure chance. In this way, there is a something simpler than an infinite and random bit string itself, and that will always be the bit itself. Mathematics, as an axiomatic theory, might have infinite complexity in the sense of being incomplete, but one only needs a finite theory of everything to engage the finite complexity of being that we see around us. The plenitude of an Ω world does not actualize itself. Our world will not capture the excess of Ω, but it only needs to have the sources for noting that and for noting the tools for which any possible mathematical fact could be written. It does not need all numbers. It does not need even the base-10, only the base-2.

It is the same with language. If one allowed for words to be infinite in length, then the English language would have an infinity of words. No one would ever read them. No one would ever hear them spoken. They would sound like pure noise. And that pure noise is the very voice of God, the one 'seen' at Sinai. As is well known, at Sinai, the Jewish people saw the voice of God. That means they saw the voice as text. That voice was too terrible to be taken in, and so they only recognized it as the voice of God (they only heard the first two commandments—"This is God, and there is no other"), and left to Moses the job of making sense out of the pure sonic boom. That is also why it is said that they saw the voice. We see the voice when we see letters. One cannot hear an infinity, but one can recognize an infinity just by seeing a finite number of letters. Those letters can then be permuted. For this reason, in our theology, the only way Ω can actually take place is as the words of a sacred text.

In Judaism, that text is called Torah. Torah is then Ω. Of course, the Torah we have is made up of a finite number of letters. Each letter is itself a number. In this way, the Torah is itself a listing of numbers. There would be several ways to write those numbers, given the combinations one makes. It also can be seen as a number between 0 and 1. The holy *Zohar* asks a simple and famous question near its beginning that even one first learning Kabbalah is taught. Why does the Torah, if it's the book of books, not start with the first letter of the alphabet (aleph), but instead start with the second (bet)? The reason given is that the shape of this second letter is such that it seals off what came before. The second letter then cuts off the one, the first letter, and renders a point—a point beyond which nothing can be said. At the same time, the Torah is a finite number of letters. It is a finite set of integers. But that means it is only part of an infinite bit sequence, the voice of God that was seen. That bit sequence is perfectly random from the perspective of numbers. Even though the letters combine into words that make sense, if one listed the numbers, I do not know of any simple and finite set of rules that would generate such a sequence.

This is why the Kabbalah often speaks of the Torah itself when all its letters are taken together as the Name of God. It is the Name of God as Ω, as a reference to pure noise and creativity, of infinities of infinities out of which emerges the finite. We only have part of this Ω sequence. Perhaps, more parts of it will be revealed, but that would only be done letter by letter. In this way, we are saying that, paradoxically, the universe is less complex and more reducible than the Torah itself. Torah is only the finite parts we can detect of an infinite random sequence. We have been, for a long time, engaged in the attempt to do nothing other than try to decode and delineate the sequence that has been given. We want to understand it, and the amazing thing is that, despite its being an Omega, we can. It is a message that makes sense. However, a random and chaotic sequence should be undecodable and completely opaque.

There are, of course, more real numbers than texts that can be written in any language. If Torah is Ω, then it would lead one to think that there are many Torahs. Notwithstanding, for the text to be truly the Torah, it needs to have those letters combine into words and sentences that are intelligible. That is the Torah we have—the one that begins "In the beginning . . . ," rather than being a nonsense string of letters. Here, the Hebrew language is unique when compared to languages like English. Each letter is itself a number and a way of inscribing them. Omega is mainly unknowable and has no structure, so the Torah itself looks the way it does as digits—as one random number after another—since it's a finite part of that Ω sequence. Even in that structureless infinity, in the finite part, we have the miracle that the words make sense. That would be true of close to zero of such Ω texts.

For Chaitin, Ω, as infinite without structure, meant that mathematical truths have no pattern, and we are never going to have a final, axiomatic system for comprehending all mathematical truths. The same is true of Torah. We will never be done with it. It is eternal. Even if we know the fist million letters, there would be a next one. One we cannot know. One that would appear in the same way as one would toss a 22-sided coin. We cannot know what the next letter will be or when it will be revealed, and yet there is the

Torah, just as there is Ω alongside pi as infinite reals. If the Torah is the word of God, given God's status as absolute infinite, the Torah could only be an infinite sequence. If it were an infinite sequence, like the positive integers, it would be supremely reducible. It is an infinity of the Ω type that allows for the Torah itself to be both a mystery and achieve full complexity. The Torah as Ω is then infinitely complex and irreducible, and that means it is true for no reason. The Torah could only be handed down by God, from the voice of God. It could only be spoken to us out of the fire, as God did at Sinai. It is only something created. That means we would never know, just by looking at it, why it is the way it is. It is pure creation. It arose out of nothing. There is no sufficient reason for it in this world. This Torah is true for no reason other than its having been given. It is like a pure accident. There is no proof for it other than the revelation itself. It must be revealed. There must be an event in which God spoke to make it known. Otherwise, it would not be knowable without searching endlessly for it. The Torah is therefore revealing to us the light of wisdom and also showing to us what we cannot know and what the limits of our knowledge are. There is no upper bound on Ω, just as there is no upper bound on divine wisdom. Divine wisdom, for us, looks like Ω. Omega is the closest we can get to it. For the eternal Other, the lack of an upper bound means simply that it is only from the perspective of the timeless that its wisdom is fully revealed.

Ω is taken by some to be proof that there is no set of all and thereby nothing outside this world, which is itself infinite. They would be right if they were looking for axiomatics, but not if they are looking for the divine code that masters our world and not if one is looking for the manifestation of divine wisdom in our world. Ω is a name of God and does not preclude the Name of God. Ω is the name of God's wisdom, of his absolute creativity, and of his transcendence. The Torah itself is not the code of the universe, unless one takes it as a finite set of simple rules. There are, of course, times when the Kabbalah speaks in this manner—that God looked into the Torah before creating the world to know how to create the world. But I do not think the finite set of rules coding our world is quite so long. Rather, Ω names God in himself as pure creation.

The universe demonstrates reducibility in its regularity and order. This regularity means that repeated patterns do not truly add new info to the universe, as all is reducible and compressible. Only the Torah is a mystery that cannot be obtained through rational means and the type of computation we see at work in natural phenomena. Most incomputable reals will never be specified or even given names. Torah is one of the few. For Chaitin, no system could be constructed that could survey all possible incomputable reals. That means, even if there is an infinite number of Torah's, we will never know them.

The universe cannot be Ω, primarily due to its regularity. Only by positing a multiverse would Ω obtain. However, the multiverse is struck down by its dependence on the false vacuum, the empty set, and its failure to be eternal. Once we have compressed part of our world, we have shown it is not Ω, since the only way to overcome that compression is to say that, from the perspective of infinity, it is but a drop in the bucket. There is a still an infinity of complexity. We say that infinite complexity is scalar and is built up from the finite as its permutation and its articulation. It is built on taking the discrete nature of the world as itself infinite when that discrete nature is a demonstration of the world's finitude. We thus side with Wolfram over Chaitin. If Wolfram is right, Ω is just another example of computational irreducibility. One can see Wolfram and Chaitin, perhaps the two most important metaphysicians currently living, as two sides of the same coin. Wolfram names the compression of the world, in its finitude, to an ultimate program, while Chaitin points to the way in which the world is always open, due to its incompletion, and made up of irreducible complexities.

Of course, many will here argue that Chaitin swallows up Wolfram. They will say that if being includes Ω and Ω

numbers, then it is, in itself, Ω. That would mean our world should not look like it does. This is why, perhaps, the ultimate proof of our view will only come at the end, at the Omega point. If the world ends in heat death, then it would prove that Ω was always there as part of things, that the beautiful flower blooming that we see as we look around our universe was only a blip in a sea of noise. To stave off Ω, one then needs to argue for the inevitability of the Omega point, and perhaps we are already at that point—for Ω would, in and of itself, preclude such an end. It would do so, since the Omega point means there is, in some sense, an infinity of finite complexity and that the world itself is not purely random and disordered. The stakes are then high. One needs to demonstrate the Omega point in order to avoid Ω itself from swallowing up the world. To say that the world is Ω is to say that it comes from and returns to pure entropy. Thus, its returning to pure entropy would show it was just a fluctuation of an infinite background of noise.

We have already argued that pure entropy will not give rise to our world, but we will also need to argue it is not its endpoint. Our universe is a collection of the compressible and the result of compression with such a small probability of being that only an actual infinity would make it seem possible. But if that infinity is itself noise, then it is clear where it comes from and why it persists. Only with the Omega point does the world make sense. An Ω world is one in which there is no design and where the laws of nature suddenly change for no reason at any time. Time will abruptly run in reverse. Everything could happen and would happen. In this way, an Omega point universe would be nicely suited to the special creation of life. It would not rule out God suddenly creating the human, for example. The human could simple occur for no reason.

In our world, not everything does happen, due to the self-delimitation related to the incompletion of the transfinite release upon our own world. The only things that must be are God and numbers for us. With the name of God, history itself is unavoidable. God is not His Name. God is unique in being exceptional, and there is no unity in this world like this exceptional one, who is unique and indestructible. Everything has a history and has to happen one step at a time. In an Omega world, history becomes senseless. The Name of God, as we render it, is, in part, nothing more than to say that the world is intelligible and makes sense. The world has sense, as the universe is not an Ω computation. It is computing a finite set of rules. It is not random and not a result of chaos. That Name of God is irreducibly complex, but it is finite and only ever n bits long.

At the Omega point, we will know not Ω, not a pure randomness and disorder, not heat death and pure radiation. We will know eternity and the infinite in another sense. If things in the world or the Omega point appear random, that would only ever be the randomness of pi, which is generated by a program n bits long. This is all opaque to us now, as we are on the other side of the point at which the Omega point is revealed. The Name of God insists on a Wolframian solution to being. Wolfram showed, with his Rule 30 discovery, that things can be both random and compressible at the same time, random and inherently rule-based at the same time. To say our world is computing the Name of God is to say it exhibits finite perfection despite incompletion showing its imperfection. A perfect number is, of course, a number in which all its factors, when added up, yield that number (1, 2, 3 divide into 6, and 1 plus 2 plus 3 equals 6). The world's relation to the void enables the same relation. Six is, of course, not the only number of this type. There is one that is 35 digits long. Those digits look perfectly random when listed. Nonetheless, it is a number as perfect as six. The universe, too, may look like this number, but it is compressible.

The finite, first part of Ω would have to be incompressible; otherwise we would know we are not in the midst of Ω. An Omega universe still would allow life's tape to replay. That is because even if Omega cannot be computed, it is still a computation as such. It is a real number, differentiable from the other reals. We than have contingencies, but always the same contingencies over and over again if we were able to replay or recount the Omega sequence. It therefore looks purposeless, but at the same time cannot be altered. Stephen J. Gould said we would not see the same thing happen if we ran the tape of life over again due to contingency. Here we have the most random description of the universe possible and see that that would not be the case.

Evolution and any competing theory will one day be tested by computer simulation or emulation. That is ultimately the only way to test these things. It may not be possible to replay the entirety of life, but it will be possible to replay at least significant parts of it. If one sees the same things occurring over and over, no matter how one realistically allows for random variation, then I will be proven right. If one receives different results each time a true simulation is run, Gould will have been proven right. I am not very worried about being proven wrong. That means even if the things we witness from an Omega universe were random, they would still always follow the same random sequence.

The Name of God is an elegant program. The Name of God is the truth of the universe. It is its mystery and its revealed face. But to know it, we would have to simulate the universe itself. That is a sense of inscrutability different than Chaitin's Omega; if the universe were describable by Omega, the ultimate secret of the universe would be, in the end, completely and totally inscrutable as such. Davies himself says that Omega is a "magic number" in the ancient Greek sense and a Kabbalistic number, such that when we speak of Omega, we have entered the field of "mystical revelation," given Omega's inscrutability.[192] One needs mystical revelation, because the number can only be partly determined, due to its infinity. Davies also interestingly

---

[192] Davies, *The Mind of God*, 134.

says that,

> even if we were to be given Omega by divine transmission, we would not recognize it for what it was, because, being a random number, it would not commend itself to anything special in any respect.[193]

Due to the impenetrable nature of Omega and the fact that there are infinitely many incomputable reals, we can easily say that any sequence of bits we would randomly generate through flipping them is the opening sequence of some Omega.

One does not need to know all possible elegant programs to know the Name of God. There may be, in principle, infinitely many such elegant programs. We only need to find the one matching our world. Being is a universal computer, so it can compute any reality, but it does not—at least not yet. And that is also proof of the Name of God. This is the most exalted name there is, for it's the name for the nameless at its core and thereby at the heart of every other name. It is woven within them. Rashi himself said that life comes from the earth, and that all is already concealed in its becoming actual of what was previously. The emergence of new things is then the unraveling of what was hidden in what already was. In that way, everything was created already in the first creation, since one only had to bring it forth. The Talmud calls the temple the "foundation stone" (*Yoma* 53b), meaning it was the first part of the earth created by God. We then see here how there is planet formation theory based on concretion around a first particle. All others that are named are named by it and in relation to it.

Others might call the Name of God simply the equation for everything that is in the universe. This equation would then be everywhere we look. It is expressible mathematical-

---

[193] Davies, *The Mind of God*, 134.

ly, because all is mathematizable. Numbers are built into nature. Gravity, for instance, affects things by curving them, but such a parabolic shape is expressed using a simple equation. All things are, at bottom, nothing more than information and structured sets of integers adhering to simple rules. At bottom is the bit, which means math itself. This is why speaking of the Name of God requires, at the very least, a commitment to a realism concerning integers. The Kabbalah taught us long ago that the four-letter name of God is the true path of divine revelation and of the meaning of all that is. This name irrigates the tree of the base-10, the ten sefirot:

> It is you who brought forth ten emanations we call them the ten sefirot to direct the worlds that are hidden, not revealed and worlds that are revealed. Through them you conceal yourself from human beings, but it is you who connects them and unites them and because you are within them anyone who seeks to separate one from another of these ten sefirot is regarded as if he had caused a separation within you. It is the four-letter name which is the path of spiritual emanation. This name irrigates the tree of the Sefirot with its arms and branches, like water that irrigates a tree that then grows through that irrigation. O master of the universe, You are the cause of all causes and reason of all reason who irrigates the tree through that spring. That spring it is the spring like the soul to the body, in that it gives life to the body. Regarding the sefirot each one has its name which is specific and with those names are identified the angels but you do not have a name that is specific for your essence saturates all names. It is you who gives perfection to them all. When you

> withdraw from what remains of all their names are like a body without a soul.[194]

Often, people speak of things like energy, force, and charge as if they were just 'things,' but, at bottom, such things are numbers themselves. In this way, it is not enough to speak of finding an equation for being unless one commits oneself to the corresponding metaphysics.

---

[194] *Machzor for Rosh Hashanah*, ed. Rabbi Menachem Davis (New York: Artscroll, 2003), 215–217.

§22

THE KABBALAH OF BIOLOGY
The Programming of Life

Let us say something more about evolution before turning to the Omega point. Chaitin himself, of course, recently has attempted to apply his own Omega theory to evolution.[195] Chaitin however is still working within a purely Darwinian framework. That is surprising, given that in *Meta Math!* Chaitin notes the theory of Margulis, for instance, and "problems with Darwinian gradualism."[196] Chaitin himself notes that changes in genetic coding can have large effects, but says that "trading useful subroutines (this is called horizontal or lateral DNA transfer)" works best for doing so."[197] Chaitin thus is clearly aware of the problems with Darwinism. And yet, in his essay "Life as Evolving Software," does not speak about exchanging subroutines, for example. Instead, Chaitin believes that the complexity of life is like mathematical complexity. For this reason, he thinks the Busy Beaver function can simulate evolution. A Busy Beaver function is, of course, one in which the function always attempts to compute the largest possible num-

---

[195] I refer here to his essay "Life as Evolving Software," in *A Computable Universe: Understanding and Exploring Nature as Computation*, ed. Hector Zenil (Singapore: World Scientific Publishing, 2012), 277–302.
[196] Chaitin, *Meta Math!*, 182.
[197] Chaitin, *Meta Math!*, 182.

ber, given a particular computational framework. When the framework shifts, the Busy Beaver begins again to search for the largest number. Because math includes endless numbers, the Busy Beaver function cannot stop. Chaitin is thus trying to show that the randomness and incompletion he found in mathematics will lead to unending evolution.

However, it is not clear that life is constantly trying to solve the same problem over and over again. Biology also does not have infinite complexity. It is finite and has only finite complexity. For Chaitin, math has infinite complexity because it includes the Omega numbers, but life is always about finite coded sequences and finite bit strings. While one can permute numbers indefinitely, it is not clear that biology has this limitless quality. Also, biology does not realize all possibilities. There may be no final truth in mathematics; but with organisms, if one has incomputability, the organism would be stuck in a loop or never be able to pass on its genetic code. Biological evolution then would have to deal with finite state machines and finite complexity. One would need to show from that how life forms constantly change and are altered.

If one makes biology into mathematics, the game is too easily won here. This is why Chaitin would have been better off trying to simulate lateral gene transfer and symbiogenesis rather than Cantorianism. Chaitin is an expert in programming languages. He would then have possibly found a way to uncover the finite set of rules that evolution is working with. Instead, the genetic code is treated as though it were computing numbers as a Busy Beaver function does. But no empirical evidence really supports that. Life also may not endlessly evolve. There may be a finite number of possible forms that at some point will be circled through. Chaitin adopts the Busy Beaver function because he thinks that if we treat evolution finitely, we have to treat it as a closed system. However, the finite nature of the genetic code does not make it complete. That is because we need to see incompleteness as a function of being itself. In the case of the genetic code, it means more DNA letters can always be added to it. Any genetic code is an incomplete set.

The genetic code is not a Busy Beaver trying always to find the biggest number. In fact, the human genetic code has less base pairs than smaller organisms. Evolution is not about producing larger things. Sometimes—on an island, for instance—things shrink. Chaitin sees the Busy Beaver function always finding the most efficient way to compute the biggest number, given the mathematical point of departure, but because one can have infinities of infinities, the function will never offer a final answer. The Busy Beaver program never halts, because ultimately it is trying to calculate infinity. The genetic code is not. Even if it keeps permuting letters, that does not mean one has a better entity. Again, humans have less genetic information and smaller bit strings than other organisms.

Chaitin also, in his model, relies heavily on random change. In this way, the deck is stacked, but not in a way that simulates life. The Busy Beaver is constantly trying to compute infinity, and, at the same time, it has its bits being flipped randomly. Not surprisingly, despite the bit flipping (simulated random mutation), Chaitin's function never ceases and never goes astray. It is not clear why, if Chaitin, is aware of the work of Margulis, for instance, he restricts himself only to random algorithmic mutations. In a book entitled *Proving Darwin* I received from him some time after this manuscript had been written that elaborates on the essay we are here discussing, Chaitin does refer to the work of Sandin in a sentence and says viruses could be the source of algorithmic mutation, but that viruses can introduce large scale change does not mean it must be random in nature.[198]

Now, Chaitin uses the Busy Beaver function to overcome any limits. Because the busy beaver is predesigned to always mathematically look for a specified thing, one does

---

[198] Gregory Chaitin, *Proving Darwin: Making Biology Mathematical* (New York: Pantheon, 2012), 68.

not have to try out every possible mutation and every possible bit configuration. In this way, as well, the goal of the system is built in. It is always to get to the biggest number. If one has calculated the biggest number, one can then double it or square it or add it to itself. Chaitin is thus designing a way for evolution not to have to go through every possibility and actualize it, but, at the same time, in self-delimiting evolution, Chaitin prefixes the goal and stacks the deck.

What would have been interesting is if Chaitin had tried to find a way to simulate life's development without doing a Busy Beaver computation. Chaitin, in his book, states that the role of the Busy Beaver computation is to weed out mutations that do not work.[199] The genetic code would indicate in itself where to stop, as it does when it grows a leaf, for instance. Chaitin then could have shown why the genetic code functions the way it does. The genetic code, as a program, after all, has to indicate how to stop growing a leaf. It is not something that is externally imposed. It has to be coded in the compiled 0/1 of the genes. Also, if one truly allows random mutation to take place, then one will try to flip many bits at once. It is not clear this happens in nature. The Busy Beaver thus constantly eliminates the very randomness Chaitin allows in his system. Because there is a defined goal, there is a selector. But if Chaitin wants a Darwinian view, natural selection must be a random selector. It's not going to choose the best thing in the sense of the most efficient or the most capable of doing an activity. The Busy Beaver program here is always selecting a specific type of program at each stage. Chaitin himself admits, in his book version of this vision, that his use of the Busy Beaver as an oracle enables his system to include "'divine inspiration' that enables our mathematician organisms to evolve, to improve themselves, to become substantially smarter."[200] In other words, we have, again, intelligent design mixed in.

---

[199] Chaitin, *Proving Darwin*, 46.
[200] Chaitin, *Proving Darwin*, 89.

And, as Chaitin notes (again in his book), having an oracle function here is a way to enable the computations involved to compute something it would not otherwise by adding, in essence, intelligence.[201] After all, oracles are something intelligent programmers add onto software in order to filter and prevent errors. To think that oracles like a Busy Beaver would arise on their own is a bridge too far.

Of course, here also for Chaitin there are no time limits. In nature's finitude, there is always a time limit. At most, Chaitin here has shown that if one sets up a function with a preset way of doing things and preset goal and then adds variation, one will have a system that grows endlessly and does so better than pure chance. Chaitin's model is therefore too stuck in Darwinism. It ends up proving, like other simulations, ironically, the value of intelligent design versus Darwinism. Perhaps, at some future point, Chaitin will take more seriously the notion of the genetic code as software exchanging subroutines, for instance, and will produce a new model for us. If he does so, my argument here is, of course, that he will be led to the conclusions we have been laying out here. What this means is that the path not taken by Chaitin is to look at the genome as a programming language rather than the history of life as a Busy Beaver.

All programming languages can be compiled into finite bit strings. One can, for instance, as Wolfram has shown, reproduce snowflakes using algorithms alone. Very few challenge him on this and yet challenge the idea that life itself is also programmed. They challenge it because life can change in its programming, seemingly, whereas a snowflake cannot. The genetic code and life are computing their future states from their present states, like anything else. We need to understand how the genome is programmed to understand life's development. But the computation itself might need to involve the genome plus cellular machinery and the environment. It will certainly, if we want to know why any particular organism looks the way it does pheno-

---

[201] Chaitin, *Proving Darwin*, 46.

typically. Simply saying all is contingent is to say we do not know, but also to make a claim about how the world works that is at odds with what how it works in all other cases. This means, to truly see how evolution is programmed, we need to see how, given the initial sequence, that sequence changes over time, just as a series of sequences. That means following it from the first RNA sequence or first cell to the human being. In doing so, we need to see, following Margulis and Sandin, how bit strings merge and segments of them are transferred.

With Margulis, one bit string might be incorporated into another as a full subset. With Sandin, isolated sections will be integrated. What this shows us is that any bit string already has to be seen as divided into subsets. We also have to think sexual reproduction, where a new organism is not only the merger of two halves of bit strings, but also the re-sequencing with a minimum number of errors of those bit strings in the process. This is a mixing of programs (*NKS* 386). Such mixing is needed because the code itself, without such interaction, will not try out all possible programs. If all of life is compressible into the first cell, then even the viruses and bacteria adding new coding are part of the overall system of life. In this way, what appears as random mutation, code insertion, etc., is all part of an overall computation unfolding.

These changes in the programming have an important effect on the details of what the program produces. It is not natural selection driving things, but life computing its initial compressed state and elaborating it into Gaia. What these processes show is that there is not going to be a fixed mutation rate. Rather, one might have to sequence the genomes of entire organisms, trace histories, and then, based on that, determine how one bit string came to be another (unless one is able to simulate the very sequence's unfolding). That would involve only looking at genomes' software, separated from any hardware or environment. But that would be okay, insofar as the issue is not knowing why creatures look a certain way, but only how the software has taken on its permutations. It would be like taking the different versions of Windows OS and asking how one gets transformed into the other and if there is some rule or set of rules for it. That would not tell you about the hardware used to run it and how it changed. It would not say what the 'desktop' looks like, but it can, in and of itself, express something about the coding. We are thus searching through the great book of life by listing all its letters and their permutations. However, we may see that the genome, in this way, is only part of the story, since it does not tell us, without being sequenced with cellular machinery, etc., what life is. It would be the evolution of the genome alone, but that in itself can tell us many things. In doing so, one will then look for the rules and operations that enabled it to occur. And from that research, the inherent laws of evolution will begin to manifest. But it will only be by doing the new kind of science advocated by Wolfram, without doing the laborious work of looking through the archeological remains of life.

What evolution itself is computing will here become clearer and clearer. This is a monumental process. We cannot know—in advance or from looking at the history of life in terms of, for instance, fossils or the menagerie of forms—what the computational operations are. Like with any computation, one goes from one state of bits to another. To understand evolution, we need then to know how, in fact, such genomes look as bits and lay them out to understand the algorithm at work. To do so is also not to ask about the origin of life, the origin of the software involved. That means viruses themselves have to be understood as not only inserting code from other species into our genome or code from the virus themselves, but also remodulating and sequencing our DNA. Unless one is to take all these events and transformations as purely contingent, one will need to do new scientific work.

Now, this is not to say that scientists have not already done some of this work. However, they have done so only under the influence of Darwinism. They have not thereby fully understood that they are engaging in an archeology of software and not simply tracing chance changes. Today, this work is almost wholly focused on comparing differences and chalking them up to random mutations. Ultimately, one will need to engage in brute program emulation and repeat until one finds the right algorithm empirically, as a Wolframian approach would suggest. It is only ultimately by such a simulation that one can show that random mutation, for instance, is only a marginal phenomenon in the development of life. One runs the emulation.

If we need to start with the first replicated RNA strand, then there will be a tremendous number of possible programs to try. In this first sequence, we may find more of the future sequenced than we might now like to think. For instance, Spetner discusses how, from Talmudic and Midrashic sources, the RaDaL (Rabbi David Luria) put forth an evolutionary theory to show that animals necessarily change and evolve, but that there are 365 basic species that were first created and out of which they grew (*NBC* 212). All the species we see today are permutations and elaborations on these earlier forms. Each is then a microevolutionary development of these 365 basic forms. What might be true is that we can find 365 such basic templates as subsets or irreducible bits strings for these future species types in the first sequence itself.

What is important is that we remember that the "symbol strings" involved in the development of life itself are also informed by a "grammar;" such a grammar can specify how these symbolic sequences are to be coded for length, for how they can be combined, for how they can undergo inversion and substitutions, etc.[202] One has to see these transformations as being like the transformations bit strings undergo in Turing machines, where the grammar consists of a finite set of rules to specify the way in which these grammars work. These grammars are not random, even if they are immanent to the bit strings themselves. If

---

[202] Kauffman, *Origins of Order*, 382–383.

they were truly random, then the entirety of life would not be part and parcel of the same living language. It would mean that, when looking at a human versus a tree, we would see two codes as different as Chinese and English.

These grammars are important, because the elements of the code have no determinate and inherent meaning. If the grammars here were random, as Kauffman contends, then we should not see the same genes at work in very diverse creatures.[203] Lateral gene transfer also would not be possible. A grammar is inherent in the living language, but it is not random; otherwise creatures would develop in haphazard ways. To speak here of grammar is like speaking of algorithms, insofar as they specify how one string can be transformed into another. Like a computer program, the genetic grammar makes clear that there have to be constant ground rules about what sentences can, for instance, function as genes and what cannot. Grammars do enable these Turing machines to take an input and translate it into an output. Rather than random grammars, what we see is the combination of pre-existing words into sentences and sentences of longer lengths, just as we do in our own spoken languages.

If all things are here made up of bits at their most basic level, then how do we specify individuals? And how are there types? All is made up of letters, but—just as one can take a word and switch one letter to change the sense yet retain the same message and effect—so one sees that two things are identical in one sense, despite this sort of difference. We also see that new individuals emerge on this basis. The signifier emerges on the basis of the letter and also despite it, given the letter's meaninglessness in itself. Two children of the same parents might only be different by 30 letters out of billions. They are still two individuals, if only due to those 30 letters. Two books that differ by 30 letters are probably going to be classified as being of the same type. Some things seem identical, like two hydrogen atoms.

---

[203] Kauffman, *Origins of Order*, 388.

However, identity really only means substitution. Two things are identical and of the same type if one can substitute for the other functionally and meaningfully without noticeable loss. Even hydrogen atoms are individuals.

As Manuel de Landa likes to point out, every atom is born in a star and formed by nucleosynthesis, one at a time, and has its own history. De Landa wants to trace the history of each atom rather than seek its meaning, its status as a bit or element. Substitution is the key to knowing two hydrogen atoms are of the same type. Any two can work with oxygen to make water. In fact, two hydrogen atoms might appear the same, except for being isotopes. There is always difference and differentiation. This differentiation itself is a product of the letter. The letter is always already different from itself, as it is split between itself and its place of inscription, its inscription and its absence. This is why individuals are always collections and sets. However, the sequencing can, at the very least, indicate what many of the subroutines are, where they come from, what function they perform, etc.

Of course, Margulis and Sandin still speak as though everything is contingent. Only by actually looking at the computation involved in life's development will one be able to agree with that. People believe life is different than other computational phenomena because the code is changed. However, code changing over time can be a computation in the same way that a planet moving from one state to another is a computation. Genetic codes are of course extremely complex, insofar as the entire sequence is made up subsets. One cannot here, of course, also forget that the environment can also alter the code. At the same time, Margulis has shown us how changes in hardware can be passed on—in particular, changes in the cell's hardware. That means it will not be enough to see the code and its subsets at work, but one must also see the code as interacting with other codes—the nucleus with the mitochondria, for instance. For that reason, it may not be possible to examine life without compiling the cell with all its machinery.

If the universe itself can be the unfolding of a single program, it is not clear why life cannot be, as well. The only way to do this will be for biologists to become computer scientists and make use of the resources found in that field. For instance, one will begin having to see various genetic phenomena as subroutines, literally, and to understand their functioning by looking at how subroutines work in computer languages. Physics and philosophy are themselves forced to become digital in the wake of the computational revolution now unfolding. Life is then but one special case where hardware/software split, but all phenomena are themselves computational and thus need to be understood with reference to programming.

Let's first look at what is called an oracle. An oracle, in computer programming, is a tool for deciding if something is correct or false. The oracle checks outputs and then tests them in relation to preset criteria. In other words, oracles are a form of artificial selection. Natural selection simply names the idea that some things reproduce and others do not. If one wants, then, one can see an oracle at work that makes that decision. Oracles test things to see if they have failed or not. One can say thus that Gaia as a whole, for instance, has an oracle function in it that determines what will pass and what will fail based on the output, the genetic sequence. It is as though each individual organism is asking the oracle if it is one to pass on and how many will it pass on. And the oracle answers. The oracle could be pre-programmed to change how it answers and determines the values over time.

The oracle here is not random, but rather has a preset type that cannot and will not pass the test. For instance, a sterile organism will fail the oracle. The oracle is, in theory, that which determines what genetic sequences are meaningful and which ones are not. The oracle itself we are speaking of here is part of Gaia itself. There might be an oracle at the level of the cell, for instance, but it would have a much more limited function, such as simply testing things in order to know to instruct another mechanism to come into play.

Let's also look at the subroutine. This notion is very aptly named, as it names a subset of some larger set that codes for specific procedure or set of instructions. At that same time, a subroutine, as a subset, can be extracted and could fit into another program, if needed. Subroutines thereby can simply function like a computer within a computer. That is why they both can serve as models for understanding genes, but also the integrated and inherited machinery of the cell. One simply needs to make the cell the overall set. Subroutines are themselves activated and can be called into action and instructed by other elements of the code. What this means is that we need to look at the genetic code as being an assemblage of subsets that have specific computational abilities. It may then be possible to categorize them as one does, for instance, different cellular automata programs.

Also, one needs, in the code, a way to instruct it when to end. Computer programming already instructs us as to how that is done. One has a section of code that does that by, for instance, indicating each function must turn off. We need to be more shocked than we are that a butterfly's genome contains all the needed information to produce both a butterfly and a caterpillar, including the chrysalis that produces the former. A butterfly would therefore form a very good example of how to understand evolution in capsule, not simply in the sense of seeing how a code has new information added to it via lateral transfer and symbiogenesis, but in terms of how the code itself, even without such additions, produces transformations.

Part of the key here is seeing the code itself as treelike in structure, insofar as it is subsets within subsets. One still has one overall set, whether that be the cell or the finite living language of all. The set theory used here is always finite when it comes to life. One will have chains, but the chains come to end, even if they are hierarchically organized. And if a butterfly genome contains information for producing many different states, what is amazing is that the code has a latent code in it. Each genome contains information not being used, whether to build up things or to enable future developments. When the right instruction comes, this code can be activated. That is why viruses are like software patches being sent out by the code. Random mutation here is not at work, insofar as it is the execution of code already present that leads to structural change.

The concept of convergence already led us to believe certain things are inevitable, but if we begin to see how all life is inherent in the first cell, then all of life is a single organism. This means we must not just see specific genetic sequences as having subsets within subsets, but all of life as being a subset within subsets. Even an individual human is then a subroutine. The Darwinian view held that such subroutines are formed with no problem, as if it was the same as putting together any 12 letters to form a word. Just as not every twelve-letter sequence makes sense in English, so not just any sequence will lead to a subroutine.

It is always a question of finite sets when it comes to the living code of life, as well as when it comes to computer software. That is, the transfinite intrudes only in terms of the radical openness of the set to take in new info from a virus, for instance, and extensionality, insofar as the specific set is whatever is contained in it. If all is subsets within subsets, then there is some sort of hierarchy involved here. It is also an ordered hierarchy. Humans are made of cells, but cells are not made up of humans. As we saw with the empty set, there is some simple relation, at bottom, that is iterated throughout to form the hierarchical complexity. That does not mean each level shows more complexity, but that each rank is built upon the previous and that each level is iterated from the previous one. It also does not mean that at each level we have all possible permutations of the previous level realized. Life does not consist, for instance, of all possible ways of combining cells together. That is because there is program delimiting what will arise.

Insofar as we talk about sets within sets, any possible set

must be taken as being a concrete individual. A subset can be just as complex as a larger set. A subroutine can itself be a universal computer, but it will still be included in a larger set. It is a matter of inclusion rather than complexity here. When we look at life as being a series of sets within sets, we are not looking at it differently than we need to look at existence as such. Nonetheless, this view has particular implications. One implication is for evolution itself. Evolution itself is probably more so an arrangement of pre-existing subsets within the original self-replicating sequence, for the most part, than truly about the creation of genetic information. First, we see that there are various levels and scales of being. Any particular focus on an aspect of being is thus a matter of resolution. By resolution, we mean scalability. It is important here, though, not to think all things are fractals such that we will see the same pattern repeated necessarily at each level. It is more like a map, where we see at one level the continents and at another level the layout of cities. At each level, we only have one and the same object, insofar as we have iterations of the one Name. To look at a particular human cell is already to lose the human body. We are not speaking here of looking at the human body as being the same height as a human cell. If one zooms in on a map, one may know one is looking at a map of a particular state. Like with a high-speed camera and its ability to focus, one sees more and more structure come into shape the more one resolves the image. But we can also zoom out. What looks at first to be an independent set with subsets, such as a cell, in zooming out shows itself to be one of trillions in a human body, etc. The zoom in can only ever take us to the bit itself. The zoom out is unbounded, only in the same way as the universe is itself finite, but unbounded.

Because the universe is incomplete, we will not be able to stand outside of it. That means when we want to say what the whole set is we need to look at what it is in compressed form and look again to the letter, just as we did when looking for what it is at its lowest scale. We see then that there is a mystical identity between the largest and the smallest here, just as there is a mystical identity between the empty set and the transfinite. This is what holism means here. It means that all is connected by way of the Name of God, by a set of letters, but also that the finitude of the created world is such that what connects all things is also the smallest and largest expression of them. The God's eye view here is to see things as bit strings and to see all as related to one bit string. When we look at the fist bit string, though, it is, in itself, meaningless. It is just a string of letters, like YHVH. It has, at this point, almost zero information. Almost nothing can be learned of it before its iteration, before the Bit Bang. It is inscrutable in and of itself.

Think here of what is called the Holographic Universe theory. This theory proposes, if I understand it, that the universe is bounded like a sphere, and on that sphere are encoded two-dimensional bits. The information then, so encoded, is projected holographically as the reality we are and exist within. Here, we need to ask what God sees. God sees then, first and foremost, the information itself, the bits. If we look from the outside in we, first and foremost, see the grid of information that is encoding the universe. If one wants, one can focus also on the hologram that constitutes an image of the world. On the inside, we are blind to this coding, as we are to the hologram itself. We are in the image that is projected from the surface. One of the founders of this theory, Leonard Susskind, has detailed in a book his debate with Stephen Hawking over the nature of black holes and if information is lost when something disappears into such a black hole.[204] What Susskind tries to show is that information is never completely lost and erased. Information may get incredibly scrambled up to the point where we have no idea how to re-constitute it, but even black holes do not eliminate information completely. In this way, in principle, one can always produce what hap-

---

[204] Leonard Susskind, *The Black Hole War: My Battle with Stephen Hawking To Make the World Safe for Quantum Mechanics* (New York: Back Bay Books, 2009).

pened and reproduce the things, since, for us, they are made up of information. The information of the thing that falls into the black hole is encoded on the surface of the black hole in bits.

It is then no wonder that Susskind was the founder of Holographic theory, as here we have the same idea, in principle. One of the important aspects of this theory is that it founds the three-dimensional world on the basis of two dimensions. This is also necessary for a digital philosophy of the discrete. The discrete itself is two-dimensional in essence. God is thus not the set of all sets in the sense of a container. God's Name is only the set of all sets in the sense of being the compressed form of all (rather than including) everything as an intensional set containing all other intensional sets. To say there is no set of all sets is not to eliminate the Other, but to say the world is not whole. And it is through the letter that keeps subsisting as letter and by way of its relationality that this non-whole is marked and marked as open.

All we have of God in this world is God's Name. This is how we address and encounter God—through his Name and the effects of His creation. That does not mean we can only speak about the act of addressing itself as an act without reference. It means what is addressed is precisely what the name requires as its impossible reference—the nameless. At the same time, in addressing God, we are addressing the letters that the world itself is made up of and that are computing it. This is the metaphysical point, in terms of one of its most important practical implications. However, given that everything is a set within sets, the only bound is the Name of God itself.

We need to also look at how things are computed at various selected contexts. Resolution thus involves evolution and involution. Involution is when a set appears cut off from everything else. We see the set in its relative independence, as a system unto itself. Here, we are taking it as a bit string operating on its own. Take our favored example of a flame. One can abstract from all else and just look at a flame and the program it uses to compute its persistence. The flame is but one thing transforming into another. That can mean it has its bits flipped or that it switches them around. A new rule is created or activated. The caterpillar becomes the butterfly, if we capture things over enough time. At one level, we have one genome, one set of rules. At another, we have new rules coming into play. At the same time, if we look at two parents uniting and producing a child, then we have two genomes becoming one. And what of symbiogenesis, where two things are combined without losing their relative independence and thereby not simply mixing their programs together? Here, we have convolution of part and whole.

Let us name two other concepts here. Revolution, following Badiou, is when we force out of a transfinite set a name that was previously indiscernible in it up to that point. Solution is when we sequence things to see how what a set contains is not some random grouping but a particular set of values. Given that here there are different levels and scales, we should not expect Gaia to be computing the same exact rule or algorithm at every level of life's development. At the level of chemicals, that predates Gaia as such, there is one type of computational programs and set of rules at stake. One letter here is stitched to another, one more letter is added, a series of letters is doubled, and in all cases one needs to find the rule involved. When we speak of the world of viruses and bacteria, another set of rules might be dominant. The cell itself causes a major shift on how life operates, but sexual production does as well. There are different stages that emerge out of each other, just as life itself emerged from matter. These are all elaborations on the first compressed code that we could not have deduced but see in its articulation.

We do an injustice to the power of life itself when we reduce everything to the one note song of 'natural selection.' Recall how 'natural selection' was reduced to a tautological explanation for life, but it was also applied to all possible behaviors and activities. It thus became a simple teleological explanation, where the final goal of all things is just passing on their genes. If we ask why humans developed philosophy, do we truly believe we can explain it in terms of the selfish gene? Nothing could be seen in terms of this academic Darwinism as itself a product of the code's articulation or a by-product of other functions. Everything had to be seen as oriented to one final and tautological goal. Thus, almost nothing was explained, because everything was drowned in the acid bath of Darwinian teleology. However, Darwinism, allegedly, was supposed to remove all teleology and rely on blind processes. The explanation of things by the same final cause in all circumstances makes the explanation itself perfectly vacuous. If everything is done to pass on genes, then nothing in particular is explained. The difference between such a vapid way of seeing phenomena versus the way we are putting forth—that argues that such phenomena can be explained via their relationships to the elaboration of a computational code—are clear.

I also want to clarify, again, the difference between an intelligent design theory like that of Dembski's and what we are proposing beyond what was stated in relation to Wolfram during our critique of CSI. When Dembski turns to elaborate his own theological model and to lay out his own metaphysical view, he models it on the idea of the 'word made flesh' rather than on a permutation of letters. This is because Dembski articulates his positive worldview on the basis of Gnosticism and Christianity rather than, as we do, on the basis of Kabbalah and Neo-Pythagoreanism. Dembski argues that, "the word in Christ was made flesh," meaning the "divine logos" that creates all things is actualized by God speaking this divine logos (*ID* 225). Dembski thinks that God's act of speaking "imposes a self-limitation on the divine logos," but we need to see God's speech as the permutation of the letters themselves (*ID* 225). That is, the genetic code, in its transformations, is how God speaks and, in speaking, creates. There is not an already existent and articulated divine logos but that the logos is itself built up out of the primordial bit. Dembski thus sees God speaking specific, divine words that are like pure possibilities subsequently incarnated. The model of already formed possibilities existing in some Platonic realm that are then made flesh is the wrong model. As Bergson taught, such possibilities are a retroactive psychological projection, where we externalize what we can ourselves permute on the basis of the actual and make that ontologically prior. It is backwards and upside down to see possibility as primary.

It is not a matter of failing to work through all the pre-existing possibilities already there, but rather of creation involving a specific program, YHVH, that then elaborates itself. Dembski believes God's divine speech is like a speaker of the English language who never speaks all the words of English, but we need to see English itself as a code built out of simple binaries (*ID*). Self-limitation cannot be thought without seeing it as involved with programming. It is not that God does not exhaust infinite possibilities, but that the transfinite itself is founded on the empty set. We thus can comprehend the divine logos, in large part because we will be able to emulate or simulate it. The world is not ultimate, because it is not complete and because it does not achieve every possibility.

Dembski also relies on a phenomenological model for looking at the world: "I look at a blade of grass, and it speaks to me. In the light of the sun, it tells me that it is green" (*ID* 232). Such a view looks at things only as parts and wholes. A blade of grass is a whole and a unity, a thing, which emerges and is grasped by consciousness. To engage with it truly as part of the logos is to find the program for that blade of grass, to understand it as an iteration of a simple set of rules over and over again—a set of bits, perhaps irreducibly complex, but still a set. By using a phenomenological model in this way to engage with the divinity of creation, Dembski treats information in a semiotic sense, as signs representing something for someone, us. However, information is, in itself, fundamentally meaningless. Shannon information is not semiotic in this sense, as it is syntactic information, differentiality, and not a reference to a thing. Even semiotic signs are themselves dependent on such syntactic information.

Dembski is right that "creation is a gift," but it is given via the letter (*ID* 234). It is a token. This does not rule out that prophecy itself interprets the will of God and thereby deals with signs. As we saw with the Sinai event, the revelation there was an overwhelming voice that, in its infinite nature, dispensed to the prophet a sea of letters rather than pictures and images.

§23

OTHER, OMEGA POINT, AND THE GARDEN OF EDEN

The question of the relationship between God and the world and the revelation of God in the world cannot be avoided if we both posit nature as finite and recognize the dynamic flux involved in life (its computation) that leads to evolution. Life is part of the universe, and the universe itself is evolving. The finite nature of things itself necessitates a reference to what Fredkin calls 'Other.' Fredkin asks: "What can we know about the *Other* place?"[205] If to speak of the Other is, for Fredkin, to ask about the cause of finite nature—the purpose of the world—if our finite world is itself a subset of some larger world, and if Other is "the place where the computer is, the one that runs" the processes making up our universe, then one needs to ask if one can know anything about Other.[206] Fredkin makes it clear that he thinks Other is not part of the universe (Other "is in an *other* place") and that it forms the actual computer that runs all "of the informational processes" of which we are made, including "space and time and matter and energy."[207]

---

[205] Edward Fredkin, "A New Cosmogony: On the Origins of the Universe," *Digital Philosophy* [weblog]: http://www.digitalphilosophy.org [retrieved January 20, 2012].
[206] Fredkin, "A New Cosmogony."
[207] Fredkin, "A New Cosmogony."

Fredkin thus sees this world as a function of Other, but it is not clear we can know anything about Other.

For Fredkin, Other helps to explain why "the rules" of our existence are the way they are.[208] Theories that do not make reference to Other can only explain "what might have precipitated the Big Bang" by reference to "some kind of magic."[209] Fredkin thus takes Other very literally. It is another type of existence, of which our world is a subset. Thus, we can ask about "how many spatial dimensions" Other has, know that Other does not obey the laws of thermodynamics, determine the minimal portion of Other that is needed to create our world, and assume Other is "vastly larger than our Universe."[210] Other must be, at the very least, of a nature to operate our Universe, and therefore we can know more about Other as we learn about our own world, even if we cannot know why Other is "running our Universe" on it.[211]

Fredkin is aware that many will say that questions about our world have been deferred by his concept of Other and asks: "Has the puzzle as to the origin of our Universe simply been put off to *Other*?"[212] Fredkin answers that Other may be eternal and operate outside the laws of thermodynamics, such that questions about beginnings do not make sense there.[213] Here, Fredkin reifies the Other, I think. The fact that our universe is finite does not necessarily mean it is enclosed within something larger than it. If our world is marked by the transfinite, then there is no set of all sets, such that we should not look to Other as solving the problem of how our world fits into a totality. In this way, our finite and incomplete world does make reference to Otherness, but it is not an Otherness that will be just another

---

[208] Fredkin, "A New Cosmogony."
[209] Fredkin, "A New Cosmogony."
[210] Fredkin, "A New Cosmogony."
[211] Fredkin, "A New Cosmogony."
[212] Fredkin, "A New Cosmogony."
[213] Fredkin, "A New Cosmogony."

place, even one characterized by radically different laws or rules. This is because Fredkin assumes that our world being computational means it must be run on a computer. Our world computes as hardware/ software in one (at least until the origins of life). In this way, we can understand the computational nature of finite state machines immanently. Fredkin's metaphysical rendering of the question of Other is thus too pantheistic.

Many believe that infinity necessitates that God be all inclusive of all possibilities. However, that is a pre-Cantorian notion of infinity. It is also pre-Wolframian, insofar as we see that all possible worlds are computationally equivalent. In this way, to say something exists in all possible worlds does not offer any more information than to say it is computed or could or will be computed in this one. Many think pantheism is necessary to preserve God's omniscience, since God, as all things, then merely has self-knowledge when knowing all possible mathematics. However, God's omniscience is better preserved by not making God dependent on there being a set of all sets or requiring a set of all sets for divine knowledge to be possible. It is better that God only need be able to see the implications of the empty set in its iteration.

If God included all, it would mean that God, as computable, would have to contain a copy of God within God himself. That leads either to an infinite regress or to a finite element that God himself is made up of. God is not made up of the empty set or a finite element in the way the transfinite is. That is what makes God radically transcendent and absolute. Knowledge of something is to know it as bit string. God is not a bit string. Only his holy name possibly is. We therefore here orientate cognition around the bit rather than around totalities or unities.

One of things the Cantorian notion of the transfinite does is fully ruin any recourse to this type of pantheism, where all is part of some eternal and infinite Other. This is why Fredkin has to say that Other is not "a universe just like ours, but larger" and "in another [kind of] place."[214] The otherness of the Other is thus inscrutable as such. That means we also should not assume that it is a computer running our world rather than a function of our world. Our world is an immanent computer that must, as finite yet unbounded, make reference to Otherness. Because Fredkin should not just use the notion of Other to defer ultimate questions about our world (as then all the same problems will arise); the very fact of Other, in its otherness, is that it must be radically different than anything found here. This is why, as far as Other is concerned, we must only speak about Other as the eternal, necessary, and impossible. Other is always God.

God is not a positive entity in this world. God is not in this world. God can only be approached negatively. God is called 'hamakom' in Judaism, often meaning 'the place.' We should not take this literally to mean some all encompassing space of which we are but a part or projection. Rather than seeing our world as inside of some larger computer called Other, we need to deal with the computational nature of our world immanently. Transcendence and the transcendent are thus found by way of the inherent limitations of that immanence. The universe cannot account for and explain itself, but that does not mean there does, in fact, exist something outside of it other than the Real Other, God. We should then drop discussion of Other via a spatial metaphor and relate it to as Otherness.

Fredkin, by force of reason, speaks of Other as eternal (not obeying the laws of thermodynamics), but that means we need to, by force, posit an Other that is absolute and self-explanatory. Fredkin's discussion here should remind us of the holographic theory we spoke of earlier. There, reality itself is seen as a three-dimensional holographic projection of a two-dimensional code. Nonetheless, one still, even then, needs to ask how the information was inscribed on the holographic film at the edge of material existence

---

[214] Fredkin, "A New Cosmogony."

and how such materiality itself came into being. Black holes, of course, do not take place in space, such that many think this holographic film is inscribed on the event horizon of a black hole. This returns us to questions concerning false vacuums and the impermanent nature of these things. Fredkin himself is positing the fantasy of us exiting our world here to enter a space called Other, even though he denies all the spatial metaphors involved.

Recall here Wolfram on computational equivalence. What this principle shows is that nature itself is already fully computationally complex in itself. For this reason, we should not hope that in Fredkin's Other we will find something more computationally complex. Other can only refer to radical otherness. We should also not see Other as a multiverse, since computational equivalence means that all universes will be capable of the same computational intricacy. Thus, all universes, even if we can epistemologically posit them, will end up being identical to the universe we already know. All words are thus equivalent, which is why we should focus on this world in its finitude and not on others. Rather than focusing on other worlds, we need to focus on this world and its relationship to otherness.

For this reason, rather than asking if Other is as some larger container, we should ask about when our world will become Other—if that is possible. The person who has, of course, done the most work on this topic is Frank Tipler, with his Omega Point theory. In an essay entitled "Omega Point as Escathon" Tipler first laid out his theory. Of course this theory was also hinted at in Tipler's book with John Barrow, *The Anthropic Cosmological Principle.* In that text, the Omega Point is defined as the point "at which life will have gained control of all matter and forces."[215] In this way, the Omega Point names both the ultimate point of evolution for all of life and for existence as such. We need here only talk about our own universe, since, following Wolfram, given the computational equivalence of all possi-

---

[215] Barrow and Tipler, *The Anthropic Cosmological Principle*, ix.

ble universes and worlds, when we ask about the ultimate nature of the universe, we will see it leads us to ask about what any such equivalent universe would be capable of, given its full computational complexity.

Of course, Tipler's Omega Point theory is an outgrowth of the work of Teilhard de Chardin. Chardin is famous for conceiving all of existence as evolving from matter to life to mind, until we reach human consciousness, which self-reflectively engages with itself. Thought is thus an endpoint of evolution for Chardin, such that "man discovers that *he is* nothing *else than evolution become conscious of itself.*"[216] Tipler's Omega Point theory tries to take things one step further by asking, with reference to the actual material workings of the universe, how the universe will become conscious of itself as itself and not just within human consciousness. The universe, at this point, becomes an intelligent universe in the same way that, with humanity, life became conscious.

For Tipler, the Omega Point is reached when "life has completely engulfed the entire universe" such that it incorporates all materiality into itself and takes control of it.[217] How this happens is more so a matter for physicists. The key is that, whether this process happens by sending out nano-probes (such nanotechnology would interact at the atomic level and control things and thus directly take control of the computational possibilities at that level) that adhere to all atoms or by some other method, the Omega Point names that moment when all matter is alive and computational in the same way as living organisms, but guided by intelligence (whether that be humans or some

---

[216] Pierre Teilhard de Chardin, *The Phenomenon of Man* (New York: Harper, 2008), 221.
[217] Frank Tipler, "The Omega Point as Eschaton: Answers to Pannenberg's Questions to Scientists," in *Beginning with the End: God, Science, and Wolfhart Pannenberg*, eds. Carol Rausch Albright and Joel Haugen (Chicago: Open Court, 1997), 156–194, 168.

post-human entity such as robots).²¹⁸ If life does become robotic, presumably, the evolution of life will speed up, since robots can make copies of themselves and self-engineer at all times.

The computational equivalence of all universes collapses at the Omega Point, since here all universal histories can be programmed and run. The universe itself can take on new shape. One of the things that would need to be done would be to change the universe into one headed towards a Big Crunch rather than a heat death (insofar as that is not already the case). The universe would then make use of the collapse into a singularity as an unending fuel source to defeat any entropic problems. The measurements we have now of our universe seem to show that it will not lead to the Big Crunch, which is why the Omega Point would have to involve the universe's forced collapse back to its singular point, the same point it existed in at creation. It is only then that the universe can become immortal, insofar as it can live off and in this singularity.

This is also why, ultimately, the Omega Point must also result in a condensed computer that itself emulates the universe and all it can do, as the universe as we know it would be condensing back down to a singularity. The universe would then be able to emulate any planet or bring into being any material entity. Such a universe would avoid Nietzsche's eternal return of the same, insofar as its computational ability means it has access to the transfinite as such. In this way, it could compute new numbers that have not yet been counted in the same way as it could arrange matter in unheard of ways. For Tipler, the Omega Point is best thought of as a point at which one exists in a gigantic computer (here, that computer is, again, literally existence itself). Once we reach the Omega Point, then experience becomes eternal, in which "all past, present, and future events occur at once."²¹⁹

---

²¹⁸ Tipler, "The Omega Point as Eschaton."
²¹⁹ Tipler, "The Omega Point as Eschaton,"165.

It is important to remember that here we have a finite state machine existing for an unending amount of time and processing an unending amount of information. This is why the Cantorian transfinite is important, as it shows how such an unbounded computation is possible. The Omega Point involving a condensation down to a singularity is important, since information processing will be limited by the laws of thermodynamics, otherwise. In the condensation to the singularity, then there must be a topological twisting of space to enable endless storage and inscription of information. The inscription itself requires energy—and an endless amount. That can only be found at the singularity. Such singularity has infinite density itself. The singularity, in itself, is an asymptotic point diverging to the infinite. Such an asymptotic divergence allows, as Tipler explains,

> for an infinite amount of information processing in between now and the final singularity, even though there is only a *finite* amount of proper time between now and the end of time in a closed universe.[220]

That the universe is finite here is a decisive condition of its being able to become infinite. A finite universe only endures for a defined amount of time, but, because it collapses into the infinite singularity, it can include "infinite subjective time" of a person existing only as a simulation in the Omega computer.[221] The finite nature of the universe and of humans as finite state machines is thus not incompatible with an infinite Omega Point. Given that the Omega Point only occurs with the collapse to the singularity, we see time here reversing backwards and the rolling back of everything that occurred since the Big Bang. But in doing so, existence is enabling its powers of computation to become infinite in themselves. In this way, life engulfing the

---

[220] Tipler, "The Omega Point as Eschaton," 166.
[221] Tipler, "The Omega Point as Eschaton," 166.

universe may only be needed in order to initiate the collapse rather than needing to guide the collapse into the singularity itself and to erect a powerful and condensed supercomputer running off the singularity.

In the collapse, all of space and time becomes one at the Omega Point, such that "all the different instants of universal history are collapsed into the Omega Point."[222] It is then not a set of all sets, but the infinite point at which sets keep permuting into their power sets, infinitely. In this way, all of life touches all things, the whole of universal history exists at a point: "*the Omega Point 'experiences' the whole of universal history 'all at once'!*"[223] Eternity occurs here and now.

Now, Tipler thinks that we should identify the Omega Point with God. In this way, we would say that the Omega Point is the point at which our finite world becomes the Other. But this is because Tipler sees Omega Point as being itself a totality. It still would not be a totality, given that there can be no such set of all sets. In this way, Omega Point would not be a person. Even at the Omega Point, God would insist as absolute infinite and eternal Other. All the information processing going on at the Omega Point can generate self-aware beings like us, but that does not mean it will be God, incarnate. The very conditions that make possible such endless evolution prohibit seeing God as the collective here. The Omega Point is when our world becomes other, but it does not become God Himself.

Tipler believes that God evolves, but what we are witnessing with the Omega Point is not the God who withdraws to allow for the creation of the universe returning as creation achieves its final state. This is true because even at the last state it must involve endless evolution. Pantheism fails here too. Tipler notes that Schelling argued that God is all things, such that the destiny of all is the destiny of God

---

[222] Tipler, "The Omega Point as Eschaton," 168.
[223] Tipler, "The Omega Point as Eschaton," 168.

himself.[224] Rather than God making himself part of becoming, we say that God is always radically Other to us, even at the Omega Point. We know God through his name and effects, and not as something that becomes, as the universe does. The universe's becoming fully self-aware and computational does not make it God. Schelling puts forth his view, because, as a Christian, he must argue that God can be made flesh. God, for Christians, engages in human suffering and life. Even at the Omega Point, for us, God is not the set of all sets or 'all in all,' but remains supremely Other. God's self-effacement is not a prelude to a God who will have been fully actualized in and as the world itself. Creation has purpose, but it cannot be to return to God in this manner. We thus see what is first and last here is the singularity, the point of infinite density, rather than God.

God, in the most eminent sense, is always Other, the impossible Other. Omega Point is supremely possible. It is the summation of the possible rather than the impossible. God is unique and exceptional, such that even transfinite cannot conceal that. Tipler notes for Schelling there is "Deus implicitus" that becomes "Deus explicitus," but God cannot not be Other, for us.[225] God is then the only one, the only exception to Omega. God is what he is, even beyond Omega, because God's withdrawal not only makes possible the first singularity, but also the last. It is closer to what would be called the Messianic Age and the resurrection of the dead, but neither of those events include God divesting Himself of his supreme otherness.

The Omega Point is thus the world to come. Such resurrected selves are possible precisely because what we are as selves is not the actual atoms that make up our bodies at this moment. The self is a pattern and program that is thus, in principle, independent of any atomic composition we are made up of at any particular time. The self can thus be seen as a computational reality. The Omega Point then names

---

[224] Barrow and Tipler, *The Anthropic Cosmological Principle*, 156.
[225] Barrow and Tipler, *The Anthropic Cosmological Principle*, 157.

the point at which our universe becomes a universal computer that is not simply running one universal program. It names the point at which the universe can run any program of any possible type. It is therefore a gigantic computer in the fullest sense of the word. It is as though the most functional computer we can imagine ourselves building is the material universe itself as it collapses back down to a singularity.

The existence of consciousness in such a process is understandable to us, as emulated persons who exist in a world as real to them as our world is to us (that is, insofar as we are not already at the Omega Point without realizing it). Such conscious minds would not even necessarily know that they are in such an emulation in the same way as, when we are asleep and dreaming, we cannot know the difference between the waking and dreaming state. As Descartes taught us long ago, we cannot know with certainty if we ourselves are asleep or awake. A dream is but a simulation. We experience ourselves simulated every night when we go to sleep. Our brains do not know the difference. All that is important is that we observe it and, in the dream, observe ourselves. Simulated versions of us would observe themselves.

We then do not know and cannot know if we are already at the Omega Point. We would not be able to access the computer running our simulation. This is also true, since our own reality itself clearly is computational. This means that we are already structured sets of numbers being computed, just as a simulated person inside a computer would be. Tipler "invoke[s] the Identity of Indiscernibles" and identifies "the universe and all of its perfect simulations."[226] If all that is are sets of numbers, sequences of bits, then, if those sequences are identical, the things are identical. The person in the computer simulation who has the same format and pattern as me is the same as me. This is also, again, the principle of computational equivalence at

---

[226] Tipler, "The Omega Point as Eschaton," 181.

work. If one can compute the world per se, then that world is identical to ours. But, also, if all worlds are computationally equivalent, then they all converge at the Omega Point. Any possible universe of the same complexity could emulate and simulate our universe, just as we could theirs.

Given that all things are structured sets of integers, a simulation is just the same computation carried out in the same way:

> In computer science, a simulation is a program, which is fundamentally a map from the set of integers into itself. That is, the instructions in the program tell the computer how to go from the present state, presented by a set of integers, to the subsequent state, also presented by a sequence of integers.[227]

Because our reality is fundamentally computational, a simulation of it is precisely simulating the program our world is running and computating it. As long as one has the right program for transforming bit strings along with the initial bit strings themselves that will be transformed, then such simulations can occur on any computer or computational entity powerful enough. Our entire universe is expressible as a finite set of rules. And that means it can be simulated and emulated. Existence, as computational, is the transformation of one set of bits into another, but, in a universal computer such as the Omega Point universe, one would be able to engage in endless mappings of that type and thus all possible computations. Such structured sets of integers exist, since, as we saw, numbers are involved with existence, which is a real predicate of them.

A discrete universe is one that can always be emulated, even by a universal computer of smaller size. If it can be simulated, that means it can also be changed. Its basic pro-

---

[227] Tipler, "The Omega Point as Eschaton," 182.

gram could be altered. A simulated universe need not be identical to ours. In the simulated world, we could have bodies of a different nature. Our bodies are, of course, also computational and made up of the same material as anything else. As simulations, they can become more computationally capable. For instance, such a simulated body might be able to re-grow an arm that has been amputated.

Since all of reality is computational, all things are already thoughts and forms inside forms. But with new programming, such virtual machines will become capable of new possibilities. Our minds will also be different. Tipler notes:

> The human brain can store only about 10^{15} bits (this corresponds to roughly a thousand subjective years of life), and once this memory space is exhausted we can grow no more. Thus it is not clear that the underlying resurrected life is properly regarded as 'eternal'.[228]

This means that our memories will not be human-like at the Omega Point, as we will have expanded minds connected directly into a larger storage capacity and computational capacity. We will thus become more so parts of the universal mind than we are now.

Some say that if the Omega Point is possible, it always already will have been. Before entering into this question, let us approach it obliquely by probing what it means for the universe itself to be simulated within a computer or at the Omega Point. This means there are possibly many simulations. In other words, if one universe can be simulated, there could be simulations within simulations. A computer could emulate not only our universe, but another one on a computer in that universe, etc. This is possible for the reason the first emulation was itself possible—the mapping of

---

[228] Tipler, "The Omega Point as Eschaton," 187.

the structured sets of integers that is the universe. If one has the bit string that makes it up, one can simply run that bit string. Is there an infinite regress here? Is our universe being run by another universe, etc.? First, this is no more possible than, as we noted at the beginning, for the code for a living organism to be infinite or be encoded by something further down infinitely. If that was the case, the program would never be able to engage in the simulation, since it would have to copy an infinity of things to get the computation started.

Interestingly enough, to my knowledge, the most profound philosophical engagement with this issue took place in a sci-fi novel—Greg Egan's *Permutation City* from 1994.[229] In this novel, Egan refers to what is called a 'Garden-of-Eden' cellular automaton. (*PC* 165). A Garden-of-Eden pattern is one that suddenly appears within a cellular automaton before even one iteration of the program occurs: "No other pattern of cells can give rise to it. If you want a Garden-of-Eden configuration, you have to start with it—you have to put it in by hand as the system's first state" (*PC* 165). It is not something that arises then out of many rules having been repeated: "it's every bit as *consistent* as a physical universe. There's no jumble of *ad hoc* high-level laws; one set of rules applies to every cell" (*PC* 165). It appears at once as if from nowhere at all (hence the name).

In Egan's novel, which is about an entire civilization, called 'Elysium,' of conscious people that actually resides on a computer chip, a character, Paul Durham, tries to prove to himself that, even if he is a simulation, he can continue to exist, even if the simulation shuts down, by referring to a Garden-of-Eden pattern:

So if I set up a cellular automaton in a Garden-of-Eden configuration, run it though a few trillion

---

[229] Greg Egan, *Permutation City* (London: Millennium, 2003). All subsequent citations included as *PC*.

clock ticks, then shut it down . . . the pattern will continue to find itself in the dust—separate from this version of me, separate from this world, but still flowing unambiguously from the initial state. A state which can't be explained by the rules of the automaton. A state which *must* have been constructed in another world—exactly as I remember it. (*PC* 165)

Durham here refers to his 'dust hypothesis.' This hypothesis essentially states that if existence is infinite, it will always find a way to reassemble even a simulation that has been ended (*PC* 121). In this way, Durham believes the universe is not essentially random (*PC* 122). "Everything was consistent. Everything was explicable" (*PC* 160). If it were, that would make it very improbable that a universe like Durham's would just arise. In this way, creating the simulated universe shows that the universe is structured. We are, of course, arguing that the dust hypothesis is wrong and needs to be replaced by a creator hypothesis, since only a creator can explain the initial Garden-of-Eden configuration needed for things to occur.

For Durham both the universe and the simulation are infinite in complexity: "The dust theory implied a countless number of alternative worlds: billions of different possible histories spelled out from the same primordial alphabet soup" (*PC* 160). Part of the idea here is that if the character is a simulation in a computer, the character is a simulation of a person who exists outside the computer chip (or at least thinks he is). Egan's gamble is thus that such an emulated copy would be able to know him/herself as a copy, but also continue to exist even if it is ended, as long as it exists in an infinitely expanding program: ". . . if a Copy *could* assemble itself from dust scattered across the universe . . . then why should it ever come to an *inconsistent* end? Why should not the pattern keep on finding itself?" (*PC* 160). Of course, given Durham's dust theory, the construction of Elysium by Maria, a programmer hired by Durham, using 'Autoverse' technology is "superfluous," as his simulated world would assemble itself in the dust and occur in any event (*PC* 181). However, Durham is wrong here. One always needs a first construction, even if one discovers, at some point, a Möbius strip-like topological loop explaining it.

The simulated world Durham wants to create would be as complex as our universe (*PC* 96). Given the infinity involved, one cannot truly say what is a copy and what the original: "The patterns had merged seamlessly; there could be no way of saying that one history was true and the other false" (*PC* 161). Anything simulated is just as real as what it would allegedly be a copy of. Given infinity, one has incoherence. One cannot say which came first. Any two or more identical patterns become indiscernible. Each is a copy of the other identical pattern. For this reason, Durham takes comfort that even if he is terminated, another Durham somewhere will build the Garden-of-Eden and allow for the eternal existence of the Durham pattern (*PC* 161). The 'Paul Durham' we deal with in the novel thinks he is but the 23rd incarnation of Paul Durham (*PC* 163). In a purely circular form of reasoning, Durham argues that if he "can track [his] past to a Garden-of-Eden configuration, that will be conclusive proof that [he] *did* seed the whole universe in a previous incarnation" (*PC* 165). But, given that Durham, in any incarnation, is not self-made, we say there needs to be a Garden-of-Eden configuration divinely instituted.

Something Gordon McCabe has argued is here very relevant. McCabe, in an article entitled "Universe Creation on a Computer," argues that if complexity is about the amount of information a system can encode, then a finite system will only seem to have a fine number of states possible.[230] Such a computer will only ever have a limited

---

[230] Gordon McCabe, "Universe Creation on a Computer," *PhilSci Archive*, University of Pittsburgh: http://philsci-archive.pitt.edu/18 91/1/Universe CreationComputer.pdf [retrieved October 1, 2012].

amount of space. Such a limited computer cannot simulate a universe of similar complexity or a great one, since one would not have the amount of memory and informational space to encode it. Thus, a universe run on a finite state machine can only ever simulate a less complex and more finite universe. Each level of implementation of universes would thus necessarily need to be less complex than the original computer on which things run. For this reason, as Fredkin showed, Other has to be eternal and infinitely greater than our own universe, ultimately, but also our universe would need to achieve infinity to truly be able to emulate a universe as complex as the one we now know.

In Egan's novel, if a simulated copy dies, it wakes up as the real person outside the computer chip. The person outside the computer chip then remembers who they were and what they did as a simulation inside the computer chip, but, as with any memory, it could be false, a dream, etc. In this way, Egan leaves things ambiguous at a certain level. In any event, Egan believes that a Garden-of-Eden pattern is only possible in a simulation. It is not possible thus in the 'real world' outside the computer chip, allegedly. This is because Egan thinks "there *can be no explanation*, no sensible prior history; the Autoverse doesn't provide one. No Big Bang: General Relativity does not apply, their space-time is flat, their universe isn't expanding" (*PC* 237). I think Egan is wrong here. Our universe, I have been arguing, is itself such a Garden-of-Eden configuration, and we necessarily point to a Big Bang. The Elysium world must be expanding by its very nature. The lack of explanation is really an indication of the divine instantiation of the Garden-of-Eden. However, Egan seems to agree with Tipler, of course, that anything computable, anything renderable as structured sets of integers, can be emulated on a computer, including consciousness, the universe, etc. But Egan is here making a fairly bold assumption that infinity is already at work for a Garden-of-Eden configuration to be possible. He is right that we can easily configure a computer that, with one press of a button, spits out the entire Bible. This possibility itself shows that no computer can be the most efficient or elegant one possible, because one can always purposely design a computer that does one task more efficiently than any other program or computer. This means there is no one best of all possible worlds. We must always see that our world is computationally equivalent to all others, ultimately.

Many think the 'God algorithm' is one that computes things in the most efficient way possible. Such an algorithm thus can solve problems using the least number of steps. But no matter how efficient a program is, one can always construct a very simple one that, with one step, produces an entire thing. One can produce a program that, in one step, puts out the solution to a complicated math problem and only that problem. The Garden-of-Eden pattern and Omega Point are not then the best of all possible worlds in the sense of doing all things in the most efficient way possible. Our world is not the world that does all things using the least possible steps or performs activities most efficiently. God algorithms supposedly use the least amount of information storage and time, but one can, for any particular issue, always construct a particular program just for that issue. For this reason, the real God pattern is the one that produces the entire pattern of a thing in the first step. This is what happened at the Big Bang. Another computer, even if it is very efficient, would not be able to do so by random means or otherwise.

Durham is trying to build such a computer in 'Permutation City' by making use of all the computing power of the computer chip in order to build a Garden-of-Eden pattern (he hires Maria DeLuca, an expert in 'Autoverse' programming, to engineer it). But in this way, what Durham is really doing is trying to show that the Omega Point is possible. The Garden-of-Eden pattern that Durham wants to construct will be an infinitely iterable and complex cellular automaton pattern that evolves endlessly. Such a cellular automaton is like the 'Spacefiller' one that Conway discovered in his 'Game of Life.'[231] Such a pattern constantly creates new space by creating new squares and fills up all the possible space of the game:

> Maria could almost see it: a vast lattice of computers, a seed of order in a sea of random noise, extending itself from moment to moment by sheer force of internal logic, 'accreting' the necessary building blocks from the chaos of non-space-time by the very act of *defining* space and time. (*PC* 167)

In this way, such a pattern does not have to show a repetition of patterns, for instance, as Wolfram now teaches us, but can actually create more space as it endlessly expands without bound. The Spacefiller is thus an instantiation of something with a finite set of rules that is perfectly unbounded. For Durham, such a world will go on despite entropy, as it is like a "crystal" rather than a "balloon" stretching out, and entropy is created by stretching space, as "everything becomes more spread out, more disordered" (*PC* 186).

Durham is interested here in the Garden of Eden, ultimately, to show that if his world can possibly produce a Garden-of-Eden pattern, then Durham can exist and persist, even if the computer chip on which he resides is destroyed. That is, what Durham wants to prove is that he can go to heaven and that his world can be resurrected. This means Durham wants to show that the Omega Point would include him. This is true, even though, in the novel, problems arise precisely when the residents of Elysium try to figure out the rules of their world (*PC* 271). In Egan's novel, the residents of Elysium might change the rules, but Maria points out that doing so is "like claiming that a VR environment could alter the real-world laws of physics in order

---

[231] "Permutation City," *Wikipedia*: http://en.wikipedia.org/wiki/Permutation_City [retrieved January 20, 2012].

to guarantee its own internal consistency" (*PC* 271). Maria is actually wrong, and the claim she makes seem absurd is right. Since Elysium is just as much a real world as our universe with its rules, learning the programming rules could lead to taking over the computational power. That is, in Egan's novel, problems occur when people start uncovering the rules leading to a need to restart the simulation, but precisely because there is "no rigid hierarchy of reality and simulation any more," people inside the simulation can affect changes in the world (*PC* 282–283). At the same time, Egan is trying to show that, even using a finite computer chip or other processor, one can produce an indefinitely existing simulation, since a pattern that constantly fills space and never ceases to attempt to fill space is possible.

The Garden of Eden is thus just like the Omega Point. It allows for an infinite number of iterations without any eternal return of the same. In the computer chip world of Permutation City, Durham convinces people to upload themselves (he has several billionaires investing in his project) into the Garden-of-Eden computer that he has built. (Apparently, in our world—in a real-life movie—the role of Durham will be played by Ray Kurzweil, once he has the necessary computational power and tools.) If the computer works, then Durham will prove retroactively that all the times he experienced himself as dying and waking up with memories of the past were themselves actual experiences, rather than false memories or dreams. He wants to prove they are actual experiences and thus wants to prove, at the same time, that the Durham who exists in the computer chip is precisely a simulation of a Durham that exists outside of it. In this way, the Garden-of-Eden pattern is only possible on the basis of a finite and limited universe—the one outside of the computer chip. We can therefore say the Omega Point is only possible on the basis of a finite nature and finite cosmos—the very one Fredkin outlined for us.

The radical conclusion of these considerations, for us, is that the infinite reality of Omega or the Garden of Eden is necessarily based on a first, finite world. It is not the case that we are lost in an infinite regress, as one finite computer can simulate and emulate another. We do end up at an irreducible level, just as, in our world, we ended up at the bit/empty set. An infinite computer is necessarily built upon a finite one. One then does not explain a finite state machine by referring to another finite state machine but to a finite bit string, and even an infinite computation would itself be founded in the end on such a finite bit string. Even an infinite world cannot count for itself and must, like a Garden-of-Eden pattern, appear out of nowhere as created. Durham believes that "if his condition was eternal and irreversible, it hardly mattered what the God who'd made it so was named," but we have tried to prove that knowing what that the name of that God is does matter, even if the eternal and irreversible depend on God to be created (*PC* 246).

Such an infinite pattern (the Garden-of-Eden) is itself incomplete as infinite from one angle and thus not a sufficient reason for itself and its own existence. There is not then an endless hierarchy of computers emulating each other. This point is probably brought home most forcefully by the fact that a Garden-of-Eden configuration must be designed intelligently and instantiates its pattern from the beginning. Our world is such a pattern. It was born in the Big Bang itself. It thus had the full pattern compressed and condensed at the very instant of creation. The Omega Point itself will bring it about a second time via intelligent design by mind in this world. The first move is thus the last move. The initial configuration is just as complex as the last one. And all such worlds that have this arraignment are computationally equivalent. This is again why we should not speak of the best of all possible words, but of all worlds being equivalent and a Garden-of-Eden pattern. All such Garden-of-Eden patterns that produce worlds are the same, and their initial configuration is their final one.

Let us now return to the idea that we are already at the Omega Point. We are not. We are this side of it. The universe itself is a Möbius strip. We are traveling on it to return to the first point. We, as observers, are needed to create the universe into being because we are needed to bring about the Omega Point. This is what Hoyle called backward looped causation.[232] Our world is actually created from the future, for Hoyle. All the information brought about in the future in a backward-looped causation brings about its own creation. The universe therefore will have been. Its future state brings about its past one. As Paul Davies put it, if what we call today the physical world (the world comprehended by physics) is really computational, then "the universe would be its own simulation."[233] This is what it means for Hoyle to say that we live in an intelligent universe, as, in the future, intelligence will construct our universe.[234]

Hoyle here was anticipating the Omega Point theory. Our universe is the result of intelligent design. It is simply unreasonable to think that our universe resulted from unintelligent and blind processes, as has been noted many times. There is thereby a loop in the shape of a Möbius strip that stretches from the future to the past. Recall that a Möbius strip is itself always formed when a strip of paper, for instance, is cut and then twisted. The strip is thereby formed by torsion and an incision. The self-withdrawal of God, for us, is that cut and the unraveling of the program of the universe that enacts the torsion. It is not a matter merely of cause and effect. Time here has to be thought spatially and topologically. When we reach the end, we return to the beginning. This itself can be thought computationally, insofar as the initial state is a compressed bit string containing the very program that will lead back to the singularity itself. However, we should not here think that the universe is creating itself in this sense or that it permits itself to exist and is thus self-sufficient. It is precisely because it needs itself to be instantiated with one stroke as a Garden-of-Eden pattern that shows it must be created by

---

[232] Hoyle, *The Intelligent Universe*, 246–248.
[233] Davies, *The Mind of God*, 123.
[234] Hoyle, *The Intelligent Universe*, 214.

something beyond it.

This looped causation is also only possible for a universe that has a finite set of rules. If it has an infinite set, it will never loop. The future thus reaches back into the past, for Hoyle, in order to constitute itself. The inextricable bond between past and future means the universe always will have been. We are on this side of the Omega Point. It always will have been for us. And we will only know it has arrived when the messiah comes and announces it and the resurrection of the dead. Hoyle thinks that this shows that "everything exists," if, in fact, "at the courtesy of everything else," but that is both unknowable and also not yet true for us.[235]

We are on this side of the Omega Point, but the Omega Point, insofar as it is intelligently designed, may not allow all things to arise. Anything could happen, but that does not mean anything will be programmed to do so. Let us here try to connect the Omega Point to Chaitin's notion of Omega. Such Omega numbers were infinite, insofar as the decimal places could go on endlessly and randomly. Even at the Omega Point, if such a computation was tried, it would appear the same way—as a random world in which things happen suddenly and for no reason. Chaitin's Omega also shows us why the world must also be thought of as a loop and topological space, since the problem of real numbers becomes much less pressing when one thinks of numbers as the relations of points on a line. However, that presupposes we can connect conceptually a computational reality with its geometrical expression. Here, the Holographic principle shows promise, since it shows the world contains finite information, that information grows as the two-dimensional film expands its surface area, and that it is not to be thought three dimensionally as a volume or space except, insofar as it is projected by the surface expansion itself. We then might see a Garden-of-Eden pattern is itself expanding the surface of the holographic film. It could then be

---

[235] Hoyle, *The Intelligent Universe*, 248.

computed endlessly, in the same way that one could set up a computer today to attempt to endlessly compute pi.

Let us also compare our vision of the final state of things with one that is currently popular in Continental Philosophy. Ray Brassier, in his book *Nihil Unbound,* draws on a quote from Jean-François Lyotard wherein Lyotard says we are already dead and nothing due to the inevitable future heat death the universe will undergo.[236] Because Brassier is certain the world will end in pure radiation and disorder, we should see that "nothing will have happened," because nothing in the end makes any difference as it is all erased and destroyed.[237] That means we have to see ourselves as already dead and obliterated. We are only destined for oblivion. We must accept that even though the sun, for instance, will die in approximately 5 billion years, that we have to see ourselves as *"dead already."*[238]

First of all, Brassier's claim here is purely dependent on empirical measurements. If tomorrow the measurements are found to be mistaken, such that we are headed for a Big Crunch, then Brassier's theory becomes much less pressing. Second, this theory assumes it understands what entropy is. But we have argued entropy itself is a form of pseudo-randomness built into the universe. It is thus part of the very programming of the universe itself. Next, if the Cantorian transfinite marks our world, and all is computational, then another future is very much possible. Most interestingly, we can easily invert this Lyotardian argument to disprove it. If heat death is right, then we should be already dead, but we are not, which means if something is already the case, it is that we are inside the Omega Point itself.

We are obviously placing our philosophical bets on red rather than Brassier's black. In fact, it is itself inevitable, insofar as backwards causation can only explain how we are

---

[236] Ray Brassier, *Nihil Unbound: Enlightenment and Extinction* (London: Palgrave Macmillan, 2010), 223–224.

[237] Brassier, *Nihil Unbound*, 205.

[238] Brassier, *Nihil Unbound*, 223.

here in the first place. So, in the end, we must look to the great numinous finality that is the Omega Point to understand our future. However, that will call for a fuller theory of space and time, as well as of looped causality. It will also call for an Angelology to understand exactly what type of minds we will have in the end.

Bibliography

Babbage, Charles. "Chapter II. Argument in Favour of Design from the Changing of Laws in Natural Events." *Victorian Web*: http://www.victorianweb.org/science/science_texts/ bridge water/b2.htm [retrieved January 20, 2012].

Barrow, John, and Frank Tipler. 1988. *The Anthropic Cosmological Principle*. New York: Oxford University Press.

Behe, Michael. 2006. *Darwin's Black Box: The Biochemical Challenge to Evolution*. New York: Free Press.

Behe, Michael. 2008. *The Edge of Evolution: The Search for the Limits of Darwinism*. New York: Free Press.

Brassier, Ray. 2004. "Nihil Unbound: Remarks on Subtractive Ontology." In *Think Again: Alain Badiou and the Future of Philosophy*, ed. Peter Hallward, 50–58. New York: Continuum.

Brassier, Ray. 2010. *Nihil Unbound: Enlightenment and Extinction*. London: Palgrave Macmillan.

Bray, Dennis. 2011. *Wetware: A Computer in Every Living Cell*. New Haven: Yale University Press.

Brockman, John, ed. 2006. *Intelligent Thought: Science versus the Intelligent Design Movement*. New York: Vintage Books

Bryant, Levi. 2011. *The Democracy of Objects*. Ann Arbor: Open Humanities Press.

Chaitin, Gregory. 2006. *Meta Math!: The Quest for Omega*. New York: Vintage.

Chaitin, Gregory. 2012. "Life as Evolving Software." In *A Computable Universe: Understanding and Exploring Nature as*

Computation, ed. Hector Zenil, 277–302. Singapore: World Scientific Publishing.

Chaitin, Gregory. 2012. *Proving Darwin: Making Biology Mathematical.* New York: Pantheon.

Chardin, Pierre Teilhard de. 2008. *The Phenomenon of Man.* New York: Harper.

Clune, Jeff, Kenneth O. Stanley, Robert T. Pennock, and Charles Ofria. 2011. "On the Performance of Indirect Encoding Across the Continuum of Regularity." *IEE Transactions on Evolutionary Computation* June 15: 346–367.

Clune, Jeff, Charles Ofria, and Robert T. Pennock. 2007. "Investigating the Emergence of Phenotype Plasticity in Evolving Digital Organisms." In F. Almeida e Costa, *Advances in Artificial Life*, eds. Luis Mateus Rocha, Ernesto Costa, Inman Harvey, and Antonio Coutinho, 74–83. Berlin: Springer.

Davies, Paul. 1993. *The Mind of God: The Scientific Basis for a Rational World.* New York: Simon and Schuster.

Davis, Menachem, ed. 2003. *Machzor for Rosh Hashanah.* New York: Artscroll.

Dembski, William. 1999. *Intelligent Design: The Bridge Between Science and Theology.* Nottingham: InterVarsity Press.

Dembski, William. 2007. *No Free Lunch.* New York: Rowman and Littlefield.

Dembski, William, and Jonathan Witt. 2010. *Intelligent Design Uncensored: An Easy-to-Understand Guide to the Controversy.* Nottingham: InterVarsity Press.

Dennett, Daniel. 2006. "The Hoax of Intelligent Design and How It Was Perpetrated." In *Intelligent Thought*, ed. Brockman, 33–49.

Denton, Michael. 1986. *Evolution: A Theory in Crisis.* New York: Adler & Adler.

Dewey, John. 1998. *The Essential Dewey.* Bloomington: Indiana University Press.

Egan, Greg. 2003. *Permutation City.* London: Millennium.

Fodor, Jerry, and Massimo Piatelli-Palmarini. 2011. *What Darwin Got Wrong.* New York: Picador.

Fredkin, Edward. 1992. "Finite Nature." Web: http://64.78.31.152/wp-content/uploads/2012/08/finite_nature.pdf [retrieved January 20, 2012].

Fredkin, Edward. 2012. "Digital Mechanics." Web: http://64.78.31.152/wp-content/uploads/2012/08/digital_mechanics_book.pdf [retrieved January 20, 2012].

Fredkin, Edward. 2012. "A Physicist's Model of Computation." Web: http://64.78.31.152/wp-content/uploads/2012/08/PhysicistModelofComputation.pdf [retrieved January 20, 2012].

Fredkin, Edward. 2012. "A New Cosmogony." Web: http://64.78.31.152/wp-content/uploads/2012/08/new_cosmogony.pdf [retrieved January 20, 2012].

Fredkin, Edward. 2012. "Introduction to Digital Philosophy." Web: http://64.78.31.152/wp-content/uploads/2012/08/intro-to-DP.pdf [retrieved January 20, 2012].

Goodwin, Brian. 1994. *How the Leopard Changed Its Spots: The Evolution of Complexity*. Princeton: Princeton University Press.

Grabowski, Laura M., David M. Bryson, Fred C. Dyer, Charles Ofria, and Robert T. Pennock. 2010. "Early Evolution of Memory Usage in Digital Organisms." In *Proceedings of the Artificial Life XII: Proceedings of the Twelfth International Conference on the Synthesis and Simulation of Living Systems*, eds. Harold Fellerman et al., 225-231. Cambridge, MA: MIT Press.

Grim, Patrick, Gary Mar, and Paul St. Denis. 1998. *The Philosophical Computer: Exploratory Essays in Philosophical Computer Modeling*. Cambridge: MIT Books.

Harman, Graham. 2011. *Quentin Meillassoux: Philosophy in the Making*. Edinburgh: Edinburgh University Press.

Harman, Graham. 2011. "Realism without Materialism." *Substance* 40.2: 52–72.

Hoyle, Fred. 1988. *The Intelligent Universe*. New York: Holt, Rinehart, and Wilson.

Jablonka, Eva, and Mary Lamb. 2006. *Evolution In Four Dimensions: Genetic, Epigenetic, Behavioral, and Symbolic Variation in the History of Life*. Cambridge: MIT Books.

Johnson, Donald E. 2010. *Programming of Life*. Sylacauga: Big Mac Publishers.

Kauffman, Stuart. 1993. *The Origins of Order: Self-Organization and Selection in Evolution*. New York: Oxford University Press.

Kauffman, Stuart. 1996. *At Home in the Universe: The Search for the Laws of Self-Organization and Complexity*. New York: Oxford University Press.

Kurzweil, Ray. 2005 *The Singularity is Near*. New York: Viking.

Lacan, Jacques. 1999. *On Feminine Sexuality, the Limits of Love, and Knowledge, 1972-1973* (Encore: The Seminar of Jacques

Lacan, Book XX), ed. Jacques-Alain Miller, trans. Bruce Fink (New York: W.W. Norton.

Lenski, Richard E., Charles Ofria, Robert T. Pennock, and Christopher Adami. 2003. "The Evolutionary Origin of Complex Features." *Nature* 43 (May): 139–144.

Lewontin, Richard. 2002. *The Triple Helix: Gene, Organism, and Environment*. Cambridge: Harvard University Press.

Lisi, Garret. 2008. "Garrett Lisi on his Theory of Everything." *TED.com*: http://www.ted.com/talks/garrett_lisi_on_his_theory_of_everything.html [retrieved January 20, 2012].

Lloyd, Seth. 2006. "How Smart is the Universe." In *Intelligent Thought*, ed. Brockman, 179–191.

Lloyd, Seth. 2007. *Programming the Universe: A Quantum Computer Scientist Takes on the Universe*. New York: Vintage.

Margulis, Lynn, and Dorion Sagan. 1986. *Microcosmos: Four Billion Years of Microbial Evolution*. New York: Touchstone.

Margulis, Lynn, and Dorion Sagan. 2003. *Acquiring Genomes: A Theory of the Origins of Species*. New York: Basic Books.

McCabe, Gordon. "Universe Creation on a Computer." *PhilSci Archive*, University of Pittsburgh: http://philsci-archive.pitt.edu/1891/1/UniverseCreationComputer.pdf [retrieved October 1, 2012].

Meyer, Stephen. 2010. *Signature in the Cell*. New York: Harper One.

McGhee, George. 2008. "Convergent Evolution: A Periodic Table of Life?" In *The Deep Structure of Biology*, ed. Simon Conway Morris, 1–31. West Conshohocken: Templeton Foundation Press.

Morris, Simon Conway. 2003. *Life's Solution: Inevitable Humans in a Lonely Universe*. New York: Cambridge University Press.

Perakh, Mark. 2006. "There is a Free Lunch After All: William Dembski's Wrong Answers to Irrelevant Questions." In *Why Intelligent Design Fails*, eds. Matt Young and Taner Edis, 153–171. New Brunswick: Rutgers University Press.

Poundstone, William. 1985. *The Recursive Universe: Cosmic Complexity and the Limits of Scientific Knowledge*. New York: Contemporary.

Protevi, John. 2013. *Life, War, Earth: Deleuze and the Sciences*. Minneapolis: University of Minnesota Press.

Rana, Fazale. 2008. *The Cell's Design: How Chemistry Reveals the Creator's Design*. Grand Rapids: Baker Books.

Ross, Hugh. 2009. *More Than a Theory: Revealing a Testable Model for Creation.* Grand Rapids: Baker Books.

Schmidhuber, Jürgen. 1997. "A Computer Scientist's View of Life, the Universe, and Everything." In *Foundations of Computer Science: Potential—Theory—Cognition*, eds. Christian Freksa, Matthias Jantzen, and Rüdiger Valk, 201-208. New York: Springer.

Schneider, Eric D., and Dorion Sagan. 2005. *Into the Cool: Energy Flow, Thermodynamics, and Life.* Chicago: University of Chicago Press.

Smolin, Lee. 1999. *The Life of the Cosmos.* New York: Oxford University Press.

Smolin, Lee. 2006. "Darwinism All the Way Down." In *Intelligent Thought*, ed. Brockman, 153-168.

Spetner, Lee. 1998. *Not By Chance: Shattering the Modern Theory of Evolution.* New York: Judaica.

Stengers, Victor. 2007. "Physics, Cosmology, and the New Creationism." In *Scientists Confront Creationism: Intelligent Design and Beyond*, eds. Andrew J. Petto and Laurie R. Godfrey, 131-149. New York: W.W. Norton.

Stengers, Victor. 2011. *The Fallacy of Fine-Tuning: Why the Universe is not Designed For Us.* New York: Prometheus.

Susskind, Leonard. 2009. *The Black Hole War: My Battle with Stephen Hawing To Make the World Safe for Quantum Mechanics.* New York: Back Bay Books.

Tipler, Frank. 1997. "The Omega Point as Eschaton: Answers to Pannenberg's Questions to Scientists." In *Beginning with the End: God, Science, and Wolfhart Pannenberg*, eds. Carol Rausch Albright and Joel Haugen, 156-194. Chicago: Open Court.

Wells, Jonathan. 2002. *Icons of Evolution: Science or Myth?* Washington, DC: Regenery.

Wolfram, Stephen. 2002. *A New Kind of Science.* Champaign: Wolfram Media.

Wright, Robert. 2001. *Non-Zero: The Logic of Human Destiny.* New York: Vintage.

www.ingramcontent.com/pod-product-compliance
Lightning Source LLC
Chambersburg PA
CBHW061926220426
43662CB00012B/1814